THE REALM OF ENDS

OR

PLURALISM AND THEISM

All tended to mankind,
And man produced, all has its end thus far:
But in completed man begins anew
A tendency to God. BROWNING.

Aber die erkannten thatsächlichen Verhältnisse können allein unsere
Gedanken nach diesem Mittelpunkte der Welt wenigstens convergiren
machen. LOTZE.

THE REALM OF ENDS

OR

PLURALISM AND THEISM

THE GIFFORD LECTURES
DELIVERED IN THE UNIVERSITY OF St ANDREWS
IN THE YEARS 1907–10

BY

JAMES WARD,

SC.D. (CAMB.), HON. LL.D. (EDIN.), HON. D.SC. (OXON.),
FELLOW OF THE BRITISH ACADEMY
OF THE NEW YORK ACADEMY OF SCIENCES
OF THE DANISH ROYAL SOCIETY
CORRESPONDENT OF THE FRENCH INSTITUTE
AND
PROFESSOR OF MENTAL PHILOSOPHY, CAMBRIDGE

THIRD EDITION

Cambridge :
at the University Press
1920

CAMBRIDGE UNIVERSITY PRESS
C. F. CLAY, Manager
LONDON : Fetter Lane, E.C. 4

LONDON : STEVENS AND SONS, Ltd., 119 and 120 Chancery Lane, W.C. 2
NEW YORK : G. P. PUTNAM'S SONS
BOMBAY, CALCUTTA, MADRAS : MACMILLAN AND CO., Ltd.
TORONTO : J. M. DENT AND SONS, Ltd.
TOKYO : THE MARUZEN-KABUSHIKI-KAISHA

First Edition 1911
Second Edition 1912
Third Edition 1920

PREFACE

THESE lectures are intended to serve as a sequel to the course delivered in the University of Aberdeen some ten years previously. If at that time I had foreseen that I should presently be favoured with the opportunity to lecture on the *Realm of Ends or Pluralism and Theism* I might well have entitled the earlier lectures the *Realm of Nature or Naturalism and Spiritualism*. There my endeavour was to establish the priority of the idealistic, or—as it seems clearer to say—the spiritualistic standpoint; and here I have tried to ascertain what we can know, or reasonably believe, concerning the constitution of the world, *interpreted throughout and strictly in terms of Mind*.

At the outset, this world immediately confronts us not as one Mind, nor even as the manifestation of one, but as an objective whole in which we discern many minds in mutual interaction. It is from this pluralistic standpoint that our experience has in fact developed, and it is here that we acquire the ideas that eventually lead us beyond it. For pluralism, though empirically warranted, we find defective and unsatisfactory : but the theism to which it points is only an ideal—an ideal however that, as both theoretically and practically rational, may claim our faith though it transcend our knowledge. Such is a meagre outline of the present lectures. The summary contained in the last of them may take the place of further prefatory detail.

The two lectures on Hegel (*Lectures VII and VIII*) are, it must be confessed, largely a digression. It was my intention to treat of Kant's philosophy in like manner—in both cases in order to substantiate the contention that anyhow, avowedly or not, pluralism is the starting point of speculation. But on second thoughts I felt that perhaps I had already done too much.

In *Lectures XIX, XX* I have embodied portions of a paper, entitled *Faith and Science*, read before the Synthetic Society in 1902. This has already appeared in a volume of that Society's papers privately reprinted by the Rt Hon. A. J. Balfour in 1909.

The preparation and delivery of these lectures were frequently interrupted by an illness that began soon after my appointment and continued till its close. I desire to take this occasion to thank the Senatus of the University of St Andrews for their extreme patience and forbearance then and since; and I cannot but rejoice that now at last these lectures, all defective though they be, are through this indulgence out of my hands.

I have still to express my obligations to generous friends: first, and especially, to Professor J. S. Mackenzie of Cardiff both for his long and careful criticisms and for the arduous work which he kindly undertook of reading through all the proofs; again to Professor G. F. Stout of St Andrews for many valuable and astute comments; and finally to my colleague, Professor W. R. Sorley, not only for his literary help but for his continuous encouragement throughout my labours.

JAMES WARD.

TRINITY COLLEGE, CAMBRIDGE.
September, 1911.

P. S. A second edition of this book being called for within a year, it has only been possible for me to correct sundry misprints, which various friends have kindly pointed out, and to add at the end of the volume some Replies to Criticisms.

J. W.

July, 1912.

PREFACE TO THE THIRD EDITION

AT a very awkward time for me the publishers have called for a new edition. I have, however, amended the text in more than a hundred places and have added several pages of further *Replies to Criticisms*. I must ask leave to call attention not merely to these, but also to the earlier replies as likely to be helpful at any rate to serious students. I would refer especially to those dealing with the important comments of my esteemed colleague, Professor Pringle-Pattison. By way of elucidating my own views I have ventured to examine certain views of his.

Perhaps I may also call attention to p. 451 and note.

J. W.

August, 1919.

CONTENTS

PART I.: PLURALISM.

LECTURE I. INTRODUCTORY.

LECTURE II. THE ONE AND THE MANY.

LECTURE III. PLURALISM.

Contents

xi

PART II.: THEISM.

LECTURE XI. THE IDEA OF CREATION.

LECTURE XII. THE COSMOLOGY OF THEISM.

Lecture XVI. The Problem of Evil and Optimism.

Lecture XVII. Moral Evil and Moral Order.

Lecture XVIII. Theories of a Future Life.

Contents

PART I.

PLURALISM.

LECTURE I.

INTRODUCTORY.

Mr Bradley concludes his metaphysical essay entitled *Appearance and Reality* with the admission that science is a poor thing if measured by the wealth of the real universe : he finds that "in the end Reality is inscrutable," and is confirmed in "the irresistible impression that all is beyond us." Everyone must acknowledge this to be a more honest conclusion than the pretended demonstrations of many philosophers. Nobody now-a-days—save here and there a man of science off his beat, like Haeckel for example—has the hardihood to rush into print with a final explanation of the Universe. Still without perpetrating this folly can we not attempt to advance, to get more insight than at present we have? Surely this is possible, for though ignorance be inevitable, no specific errors are necessary.

But we must have some method : in particular we must be clear where we start from. It is a favourite phrase now widely current that the universe has many *aspects*, and such a conception has the merit of making us vividly realise a source of error too often overlooked in the past—I mean confusion of standpoints. Precise orientation of these various aspects of the world is one of the first duties of philosophy, and the ascertainment of the supreme and ultimate standpoint is perhaps its chief concern. Now of these various aspects the two most sharply contrasted are those which lead us to speak of the world of mechanism and the world of morals, the subject-matter of the natural sciences on the one hand, and that of the moral sciences including history on the other. The one Kant was wont to call the Realm of Nature, the other the Realm of Ends; assigning to the former as its characteristic mark the notion of 'empirical necessity,' to the latter that of 'practical freedom.'

It would be superfluous to spend time in picturing out this contrast in detail[1]: we have only to think of comparing some classical work of science—say Newton's *Principia*—with one of history—as, for example, his contemporary Clarendon's *Great Rebellion*—to realise impressively the complete diversity of the two realms. Regarding the scientific ideal of Nature as a rounded whole, we may safely say that the world of science and the world of history have little or nothing in common : their terminology, their categories, their problems are wholly different; and so too are the philosophical questions to which they severally and immediately give rise. The one never reaches the individual and concrete, the other never leaves them ; for the one spontaneity and initiative are impossible, for the other

---

[1] Cf. my article : 'Mechanism and Morals,' *Hibbert Jl*, Vol. iv. 1905, pp. 79 ff.

Yet both *realms* an but *aspects of world*.
1) the 'naturalistic' aspect 2) the 'spiritualistic' aspect.

inertia and rigorous concatenation; to the one the
notions of end and value are fruitless, nay meaningless,
for the other they are of paramount importance.   And
yet the two cannot be separated, for Nature not only
provides the scenery and properties of history but the
actors themselves seem to have sprung from its soil, to
owe their position largely to its cooperation, and to
come into touch with each other solely through its
means.   After all, these so-called realms are but
'aspects' of one world; and it is precisely this fact
that makes their seeming contrariety and incompatibility a problem for philosophy : where and how are
we to find the final unification or mediation of the two?
It will be one step towards a solution if we can determine which aspect is the more fundamental.   It hardly
needs to be said that since the dawn of speculation the
claims of both aspects have had, as indeed they still
have, their advocates.   Those who assign the priority
to Nature we call Naturalists : those who contend for
the priority of free agents we may call Spiritualists.
In a previous course of Gifford Lectures[1], which I had
the honour to deliver in Aberdeen ten years ago, I endeavoured to show the superiority of the spiritualistic
position.   The main lines of the argument can be very
briefly indicated and I trust it will seem to you fitting
that I should recapitulate them by way of introduction
to the further inquiry into the nature of the spiritualistic
realm and to the discussion of some of its problems,
which I propose in the present course to attempt.

Reviewing the progress of the natural sciences
since the times of Galileo and Descartes we may note

[1] *Naturalism and Agnosticism*, 3rd ed., 1906.

? *exact meaning of mechanical explanation?*

2 marks
of physical science

① preliminaries of mechanical explanation.

i.e. a law of mathematics or mechanics

two characteristics. First, in so far as the qualitative variety and the complexity of concrete things are considered, we find several distinct sciences each with its own special concepts and methods, though all are more or less inductive and experimental. But all qualities and complexities whatever that natural objects present, and all the changes that they undergo, appear to involve quantitative constants and configurations admitting of more or less precise determination and measurement. As soon indeed as the movements of sensible bodies were found to admit of exact description by the science of mechanics the hypothesis at once presented itself that, as Newton expressed it, "the other phenomena of nature might be deduced from mechanical principles." And, as we all know, the hypothesis has been amply justified, though not indeed absolutely verified in every detail; mechanical explanation has therefore long been accepted as the *ne plus ultra* of what a scientific explanation can be. So much is this the case indeed that even the intractable problem of life is still generally regarded as only an outstanding difficulty and not as a veritable exception to the universality of mechanical laws.

We come now to the second characteristic. For long this mechanical theory was held to furnish us with the knowledge of the empirical reality which our sensible experience was supposed only obscurely to symbolise: it bore, in fact, the name of Natural Philosophy. But as its purely formal character became more apparent, and mathematical equations enabled it to dispense with the real categories of substance and cause, physicists themselves were the first to perceive and to proclaim that this mechanical theory was after all but an abstract and ideal scheme—a pure science, which can only be actually 'applied,' as we say, with the help of the calculus of probabilities. And what diversity and irregularity the seeming simplicity and uniformity of large numbers may cover human statistics sufficiently show. In place then of the concrete world of sense symbolising this abstract scheme, it has now become clear that it is the abstract scheme itself which symbolises the concrete world from which it set out. It also indeed reveals something of the law and order that there prevail ; but what the concrete world really is and what is the source of the law and order that it manifests are questions still wholly on our hands. But to call such descriptive scheme pure or rational science is to emphasize its source in mind ; and when this intelligible scheme of our devising, with which the scientific inquirer greets Nature, is confirmed by Nature's response, are we not justified in concluding that Nature is intelligent or that there is intelligence behind it ?

When however the physical realists—those I mean who regard the mechanical theory not as an abstract summary of Nature's routine but as presenting fully-orbed reality—when these realists are called upon to explain the relation of this mechanism to mind they become involved in hopeless inconsistencies. The mechanism is by definition an absolutely closed system, determinate in all its movements down to the minutest detail. Not merely does it brook no interference, but interference is strictly speaking inconceivable : the semblance of such could only mean the presence of

'Naturalism' calls the contents of the world as "phenomenal" and those of consciousness as "epi-phenomenal".

further mechanism hitherto concealed. Mind then is to be interpreted as an impotent and shadowy concomitant of brain, which is itself but a part of this mechanism inextricably linked in with the rest: we are conscious to be sure, but only conscious automata. This would seem to be the one possible conclusion from the naturalistic premises, if any conclusion were possible at all. But it also becomes a complete refutation of them the moment we raise an obvious question which Naturalism, owing to its absorption in the material aspect, has entirely overlooked : the question, I mean, How from the standpoint of consciousness is any knowledge of this independent mechanical system to be accounted for ? Or, what comes to the same thing, how from the naturalistic standpoint can it be known that consciousness is concomitant with certain mechanical motions? Agreeably to its contention for the priority of its own standpoint, Naturalism terms the contents of its world phenomenal, and those of consciousness merely epiphenomenal. But now the tangible, visible, sonorous world, the world of external perception—from which the naturalist starts and to which in all his observations and experiments he appeals to verify the applicability of his theory—this world belongs entirely to the epiphenomenal series. So too does every concept in his theory as such ; so that his appeal to experience to validate it is but an admission of its connexion with the perceptual, the so-called epiphenomenal. In short, awaken the naturalist from his mathematical ecstasy and the 'epi' at once drops away from our phenomena, while his phenomena—since he regards them as independent existences—turn out not to be phenomena

at all.   On the other hand, if we leave him where
we found him, oblivious of the essential implications of
experience, and contemplating *per impossibile* a closed
system of mass-points in motion, then assuredly the
notion that these have dependent, epiphenomenal, concomitants or 'collateral products' will never dawn upon
him, or even admit of statement without contradiction.
But a workable interpretation of experience compels
us not only to reject this distinction of material
phenomena and mental epiphenomena, but to reject
also the tacit assumption that our percepts are merely
subjective modifications.   This whole distinction of
phenomenon and epiphenomenon is but the old story
of the Cartesian dualism over again.   But after puzzling
the world for nearly three centuries, it seems—at least
as a philosophical tenet—in a fair way to disappear.
Make two mutually exclusive halves out of the one
concrete world : in the one you will find only your
own so-called subjective states and have to become a
solipsist ; in the other the organisms you would find
there you could call only automata at the best.

   This brings us to another inconsistency in which
Naturalism is involved ; for, even if conscious, the
automata as part of the continuous mechanism are, as
already said, powerless to withstand or to control it :
consciousness is only comparable to a shadow that
incidentally in some mysterious way accompanies their
working.   To be sure we *seem* active, ever striving for
ends, and the historical world would become meaningless if we were not.   We do not infer this activity : it
is *prima facie* an ultimate and constitutive fact of our
daily experience and of its historical development.

None the less we are asked to believe that it is false, because otherwise the mechanical theory cannot be upheld. Granting then for the moment that our sense of activity is illusory, we have at least in turn the right to ask how the illusion can have arisen. Pure mechanical science recognises neither activity nor passivity, but only mass that is inert and motions that are reversible. But inertia is a negative term and becomes meaningless if we have no experience of activity. Such activity, however, as the historical world implies could not be found in the physical world unless that showed signs of being intelligently directed : but then such evidence could only be appreciated by beings who were themselves active. Moreover that evidence would be fatal to the mechanical theory itself—for a mechanism admitting of direction could not be a closed system—and so with the fall of the theory would fall also the objections to our common-sense conviction that were based upon it.

All this however is negative argument; but positive arguments are not wanting. For instance, we say that 'knowledge is power,' and so 'to be forewarned is to be forearmed.' In proof we can point to instances innumerable in which the very knowledge of what in 'the natural course of things' will inevitably happen is the sure means of falsifying such a forecast. To take the very simplest illustration: lifeless masses do not get out of one another's way as masses under living guidance almost invariably do. Were it otherwise, the actual course of things would be vastly more calculable but would cease altogether to be intelligible. Solely because, though inviolable, what we significantly call the 'laws' of Nature can yet be turned to account, do they deserve the name of laws ; and what limits our power is not their inflexibility but our own ignorance. Or again, compare living organisms and their pro- cesses, on the one hand, with inanimate objects and the changes that they undergo, on the other. We note at once an ever-increasing complexity as we rise in the scale of life, from the *amoeba* say to ourselves ; and also in our artificial products as we rise in the scale of civilisation, say from the African kraal to the European city. The steady downward trend, the katabolic, levelling tendencies attributed to unchecked mechanism we find not merely suspended but reversed wherever there is life and mind. The notions of form, adaptation and control here force themselves upon our notice in contrast to matter and its blind, purposeless collisions. Undeterred by this amazing contrast, however, those who uphold the theory that Nature is really a closed mechanism must, and do, refuse to draw any line : living and lifeless, artificial and natural, are distinctions of no account from the point of view of the mechanical whole : life and mind are the concomitants of certain of its workings but the determinants of none. Still the prevision just now referred to and this sharp con- trast are there, and have to be accounted for *somehow* : to allow that they exactly tally with the presence of life and mind and advance continuously as these advance is but to state the problem, not to solve it. To be content with this is as veritable a specimen of what Germans call 'beer philosophy' as the profound remark that great rivers run through populous towns.

In the first place a series of coincidences so vast

cannot be casual and disconnected; and yet if the mechanism on the one side is a closed system, the living experience on the other cannot be even its 'collateral product,' as we have already seen. The hopeless *impasse* of dualism again confronts our naturalist, and he is fain to appeal to metaphysics; but the appeal he trusts is harmless, since he only asks for an *Unknowable* Reality to unite his mechanical phenomena with the psychical epiphenomena that run parallel with them. It is needless to enlarge on the absurdity of such metaphysics: that has been effectively exposed more than once already[1]. It is enough to note that all this agnostic monism comes to is the admission that there *is* a connexion and the confession—perhaps I should rather say, the contention—that this connexion is inexplicable. But what precisely is this connexion as a fact, and why is it inexplicable? We must turn to experience for an answer. There we find not indeed a dualism of material phenomena and mental phenomena, but a duality of object presented and subject affected, of subject striving and object attained: an interaction that is only inexplicable because for every finite experience it is ultimate—is its basal fact.

With this fact of the duality in unity of experience before us we are at the historical standpoint, the standpoint of the concrete and individual. Tracing the gradual development of experience we can see how the distinction between the real and the phenomenal arose, how with the advance of intersubjective intercourse and the growth of language the so-called trans-subjective objects, objects that, so to say, were common property,

[1] Cf. Bradley, *Appearance and Reality*, pp. 127 ff.

ceased to be regarded as property—or relative to experiencing subjects—at all, while the objects of immediate experience were regarded as the *peculium* of the individual and so as not objects at all : in other words, we can see how the psychology of dualism came to shut itself *in* and the physics of dualism to shut itself *out*, by sundering the one world of experience into two halves, an internal and an external, both abstractions and so both devoid of reality.   In particular such epistemological reflexion at once discloses the abstract character of the entire mechanical scheme, to which I have already referred.

Again, the light which experience on its practical side throws on the whole process and progress of knowledge is of fundamental importance.   We are not simply cognitive beings : moreover, knowledge does not evolve itself, as it were by some purely immanent process, while we merely look on.   Even if it may be so unfolded when acquired, its acquisition is only secured piecemeal, by arduous effort, and many misadventures.   All this implies motives, implies ends to be attained : we seek knowledge primarily because it proves an aid to more and fuller life.   Apart from this its quest would be unintelligible : this brings it within the scope of the realm of ends.   Finally, if we consider the main structure of knowledge, we find that its fundamental principles of unity, causality and regularity are derived from this standpoint : in other words, the main structure of our concept of Nature is entirely anthropomorphic.   The unity of Nature is the ideal counterpart of the actual unity of each individual experience, where synthesis ever precedes analysis, and things are only distinguished relatively to each other so long as they are apperceived together by the one subject. The category of causality we owe to the interaction of active subjects with their environment and especially with each other, and we attribute it analogically to what we then call the interaction of natural agents. Then as to the regularity of Nature or the universal, reign of law, this never has been, and never can be, empirically established, nor does its denial involve any contradiction : that is to say, it is neither demonstrable nor axiomatic.   It is a postulate that has its root in our primitive credulity. Were this *anticipatio mentis* never confirmed, knowledge would be impossible ; but confirmed as it is continually in our earliest experience we thus advance to an *interpretatio naturae* as an orderly and intelligible system, a cosmos that evinces directly or indirectly the all-pervading presence of mind.

To sum up in words that I have lately used elsewhere :—" We are active beings and somehow control the movements of the bodies we are said to animate. No facts are more immediately certain than these, and there is nothing in our actual experience that conflicts with them.   From these facts we advance to the abstract concepts on the strength of which Naturalism, by a grievous misapprehension of its own standpoint, attempts to question them.   Stationed at the very outskirts of the knowable and intent only on the quantitative aspects of things—like those fabulous beings of geometrical romance, the inhabitants of Flatland—it finds impassable barriers which have no existence in the fuller dimensions of concrete experience.   But we, orientating from this more central

We accept the `Spiritualistic` standpoint.

position, may retort upon Naturalism with the words of Goethe,

> Das Unzulängliche *unattainable inadequate*
> Hier wird's Ereigniss: *happening*.
> Das Unbeschreibliche
> Hier wird's gethan.

Having satisfied ourselves, then, that mechanism is not the secret of the universe; that, if it is to have any meaning, it must subserve some end; and finding generally that increased knowledge of Nature's laws means increased control of Nature's processes, we accept the facts of experience in which subject and object interact, rather than the conclusions of dualism, that mind and matter are for us two alien worlds and all knowledge of Nature an inexplicable mystery[1]"— we accept the spiritualistic standpoint and its Realm of Ends as the more fundamental.

I have called this position spiritualistic monism to distinguish it from materialistic monism, which we may disregard as obsolete, and from neutral or agnostic monism, which we may fairly treat as an inept and ineffectual attempt to get round the deadlock of dualism. But if this position be indeed the more fundamental, it ought to be possible, it may be urged, to see directly from this standpoint how the appearance of mechanism arises, or at least to make some progress towards accounting for it in terms of life and mind. Unquestionably it ought: and in fact, as we shall presently see, attempts have been specially numerous of late to meet this demand in a more or less scientific

[1] *Philosophical Orientation and Scientific Standpoints*, Berkeley, California, 1904.

fashion. Meanwhile we may remind those who demand of us an explanation of the appearance of mechanism, that, if the term be strictly taken, there need for spiritualism be no such appearance at all. The more completely we can interpret the world as a realm of ends the more completely the tables are turned upon naturalism. As this contends, in the words of Huxley, " for the gradual banishment from all regions of human thought of what we call spirit and spontaneity[1]," so that, for the gradual banishment of what we call inert stuff and directionless energy.

To see how the case stands let us recall the contrast between science and history just now referred to. The first effect of this contrast was the extragavant commonplace that history as unscientific had no interest for the philosopher. The final result may be the other extreme, that science as general and abstract has no interest for the philosopher; since he is concerned only with reality, and that is concrete and individual out and out. At any rate the thought of the last century made a very decided advance in this direction : in the course of it what were formerly called the descriptive or natural history sciences culminated in the philosophy of evolution, while abstract physics is lapsing, as we have seen, from its old supremacy as the mechanical philosophy to the rank of a merely descriptive scheme[2]. As compared with the nineteenth century the eighteenth—though it produced great historians— was a century devoid of historic sense. Its speculations

---

[1] *Collected Essays*, Eversley edn, Vol. i. p. 154.
[2] Cf. Boltzmann, quoted in *Naturalism and Agnosticism*, Vol. i. p. 166, 4th edn, p. 162.

concerning the origin of society, of language, of religion, show this. And, as the most recent historian
of scientific thought has pointed out, the work of
Laplace shows this too. Both his *Mécanique céleste*,
"dealing with the general laws of motion and of
lifeless masses," and his *Théorie de la Probabilité*,
"dealing with the arithmetical properties of large
numbers of units, leave out of consideration that
hidden and mysterious phenomenon [fact] to which
alone is attached...all that commands interest in the
created world—the existence of individuality[1]." And
yet it was in the latter of these works that Laplace,
brushing aside freewill as a palpable illusion, proclaimed the implicit omniscience of the mechanical
theory in a passage that I took for the text of my
former lectures[2]. In like manner the belief in fixed
and immutable species prevented Laplace's great contemporary, Cuvier, from appreciating the genetic
view of nature, where the supreme importance of
the individual first appears as—to quote an expression
of Hegel's—'involving the species and genus in
itself,' where variation and heredity become the central
problems of biology and where the classifications of
system-makers cease to be of value save as a preliminary clue. I have mentioned Hegel, and—whatever may be thought of other sides of his philosophy
—its value in this connexion can hardly be over-

---

[1] J. T. Merz, *A History of European Thought in the Nineteenth
Century*, Vol. I. 1896, p. 124.
[2] It was reserved for Clerk Maxwell to point out clearly the
inevitable limitation of the Laplacean data. Cf. his *Life* by Campbell
and Garnett as quoted by Merz, *op. cit.* Vol. II. 1902, p. 559.

estimated. "If the historical literature of our time," said Zeller, "no longer contents itself with eruditely unravelling or critically sifting traditions, piecing together and pragmatically elucidating particular facts, but seeks first and foremost to understand the fundamental continuity of events, to comprehend broadly the development-of history and the spiritual principles that control it, this advance is due not least to the influences that Hegel's *Philosophy of History* has exercised[1]." Now for Hegel human history meant struggle for rational freedom, as for Darwin natural history meant struggle for existence: both are teleological concepts, both imply individual agents and unique events, for both the physical world is provisionally a means to ends. The historical method, then, we may say, is altogether the product of the nineteenth century and there we find it claiming "to have invaded and transformed all departments of thought." "A belief in this method," said Sidgwick in the course of a polemic against it, "is the most widely and strongly entertained philosophical conviction at the present day[2]."

Even the negative side of this transformation, the waning of scientific realism, is largely due to the growing conviction of the central importance of the concrete and historical. It is not merely the truth that laws imply agents, nor again the truth that scientific laws are only abstract formulae—what here becomes apparent is that scientific generalisations are an economic device necessitated by our limitations.

[1] *Geschichte der deutschen Philosophie*, p. 824.
[2] 'The Historical Method,' *Mind*, 1886, p. 203.

But it is to Ernest Mach, a physicist who has turned philosopher, that we owe the most impressive presentation of this truth. "In reality," he says, "the law always contains less than the fact itself, because it does not reproduce the fact as a whole, but only that aspect of it which is important to us, the rest being either intentionally or from necessity omitted[1]." If we were capable of that intellectual intuition of which some philosophers have dreamt, there would be no enforced omissions, no intractable residuum, no sundering of 'that' and 'what' in our knowledge; history would not be left outside science, but rather science be taken up into history. We should not start with the abstract and general, unable to reach the concrete and individual, but being fully acquainted with every individual we should be relieved of the incommensurability of fact and law. Omniscience of this sort would surely bring us nearer to reality than the omniscience of Laplace's imaginary spirit with its completed world-formula. Order there would needs must be in any world, or it would not be a world at all. But

---

[1] Mach, 'The Economical Nature of Physics,' *Popular Scientific Lectures*, p. 193. This necessary limitation of discursive thought has led by two distinct but more or less complementary attitudes towards concrete reality. Elated by the power and precision that generalisation secures, science was encouraged to hope that by extending its network of general relations it would at length completely encompass the individual, while yet at the same time tempted to despise the particular as mere 'stuff' of no account save as it was formed by participation in general ideas. It was mainly the former tendency that led to the philosophic indifference to mere history and experience as unscientific that characterizes Descartes, Bacon and Hobbes for example. The latter tendency shows itself in Schopenhauer's singularly inconsistent contention that history is a mere hurly-burly (*Wirrwarr*), only the accidental form of the appearance of the idea.

It may be possible, setting out from mind, to account for mechanism: but it is not possible, setting out from mechanism, to account for mind.

in a realm of ends the order and meaning would be primarily the outcome of the purposes of the active beings composing it: only to discursive intellects such as ours could this order emanating from individual agents appear as a warp and woof of external law shaping some primordial stuff. As naturalism claims to approximate to a complete formulation of this phenomenal order, so spiritualism may claim to approximate to an interpretation of the underlying reality; but it will have this advantage, that while it may be possible, setting out from mind, to account for mechanism it is impossible, setting out from mechanism, to account for mind.

Such an approximation to a spiritualistic interpretation we actually have in the history of the living world. Here we are ever in the presence of individual things, from which science indeed sets out, but to which it can never return, individuals marked down by dates and places and actually designated or admitting of designation by proper names[1], individuals who have no 'doubles,' whose like all in all we never shall meet again. The events with which we have here to deal are the unique acts and deeds that have their origin in individual centres of experience, not events that seem to occur uniformly as resultants of universal and unvarying law. Further, it is not the intrinsic nature of objects but their value for the particular individual that immediately determines each one's attitude towards them; and as the individuals vary so do their interests and pursuits. But *quidquid petitur petitur sub specie boni*: the idea of the good,

---

[1] To which therefore no concept is adequate.

as Plato long ago taught, is here the supreme category[1]. If however there were as many goods as there are individuals and all were disparate and independent, this would not help us much. But the individuals of history are none of them isolated, for though no two be altogether alike no two are altogether different. So community and co-operation become actual goods, struggle a possible evil calling for readjustment, and the harmonious realisation of individual ends the ideal consummation, the "one far off divine event to which the whole creation moves."

Meanwhile the course of history shows us the gradual building-up of society and civilisation and therewith the attainment at each advance of ends that were inconceivable at an earlier stage. But these ever-widening social groups and ends of ever-increasing scope are still in every case individual and concrete. The subordinate individuals or the particular aims which the wider embrace are still to be regarded as members or constituents of an articulate whole and not as instances of a general class, in which the content diminishes as the extent increases[2]; for in these historical wholes, we must again insist, there is never complete homogeneity of parts. On the contrary, the higher, over-individual ends, as they are sometimes called,— politics, industry, science, literature, art—imply a differentiation among men that in spite of its significance would defy classification. The more organized the community the more diverse the individuals it includes, and the more man appears

[1] *Rep.* VI. 505 A.
[2] Cf. Rickert, *Die Grenzen der naturwissenschaftlichen Begriffs-bildung*, 1902, p. 394.

as the historical animal. At the same time the realisation of these ends invests him, so to say, with a new
environment, a metamorphosis of nature, an artificial,
humanly created, medium, which throws the immediate
environment of the naked and resourceless troglodyte
more and more into the background. *Entre l'homme
et la Nature*, said Comte, *il faut l'humanité.*

Still, it will be objected, beyond humanity and
history, beyond, if you will, the whole realm of sentient
life, Nature is there all the while, and there as no
mere background but as the basis of the whole, the
fundamental plasma which can only be shaped because
it is itself determinate and orderly. Granting this we
may yet urge that there is nothing in Nature, when
we try to envisage it as a whole, that is incompatible
with a spiritualistic interpretation. In the historical
world we place determinate agents first, and the order
and development which we observe we trace to their
action and interaction. It has never been shown that
we need, nor made clear that we can, interpret Nature
otherwise.

One problem of supreme importance to such an
interpretation does however arise, and this problem
the objection we are considering directly suggests.
We have only to an insignificant extent shaped
Nature, we have not made it; we are not even
settlers from a foreign clime but aborigines seemingly
sprung from the soil. But the principle of continuity is supposed to turn the edge of this objection, and to this principle pampsychism appeals,
though it does not rest on that alone. "Nature never
makes leaps," said Leibniz. Every organism has its
peculiar environment, the simpler the one is the simpler

the other will be. Recent knowledge has shown the range of life to extend far into the region of what was once regarded as the inanimate, purely physical world, and it has further shown the lowest known organisms to be highly complex and extremely varied. But there is nothing to suggest that we have reached the limits of life : all we can say is that our senses and the artificial aids and methods of research at present available do not enable us to discriminate between yet simpler forms of life and *their* environment; not that these do not exist. There is then, it is contended, no warrant for the assumption of a completely inanimate environment at all : we ought rather with Spinoza to conclude that " all individual things are animated, albeit in diverse degrees[1]." We ought so to conclude too, because—continuity apart—what can neither do nor suffer, what is nothing for itself, is truly nothing at all; for—again as Spinoza maintained—every individual thing, so far as in it lies, endeavours to persist in its own being[2]. On this, the pampsychist view, Nature thus resolves into a plurality of conative individuals; and the range and complexity of the correspondence between a given individual and its environment marks the stage to which it has advanced in its interaction with the rest. But to cite Spinoza is to give point to the difficulty that has still to be met.

Will a plurality of interacting subjects account for itself and for the unity which interaction implies? This is the question which in the following lectures we shall have carefully to discuss. Suppose we decide this question in the negative, that will not affect the

[1] *Ethics*, II. 13, Schol.
[2] *Ethics*, III. 6.

main issue as between spiritualism and naturalism: for such ground of the world of living and acting things would—if we should be led to assume it—surely be itself living and acting. In any case then we have a realm of ends, the only question is:—what is its constitution, how is its harmony secured; is it, so to say, a more or less orderly democracy, is it a limited monarchy, or is it possibly an absolute one?

This is none other than the old and formidable problem of the One and the Many; and this, it has been said, will be *the* philosophical problem of the twentieth century. Certainly there are few questions more to the fore at the present time. It is fitting then that with this we should begin. But with such a problem much depends on the side from which we begin and the method that we adopt. The great idealistic systems of the nineteenth century began with the One as absolute and adopted what may be generally described as a speculative or *a priori* method. Of the greatest of these systems, that of Hegel, even its most sympathetic critics have allowed that, however perfect its ideal may be in itself, its attainment is, and must ever remain, humanly impossible. And this verdict, I do not think it audacious to say, is easy to justify: it simply amounts to protesting that we can never transcend ourselves. The first requisite of philosophy is organic coherence: it cannot, so to say, have two independent growing points, and so long as experience is the one there can be no finality about philosophy. As experience advances its meaning will unfold itself to reflexion more and more: so further progress makes further regress possible and what is last in the order of experience brings us nearer to what is first in the order of time or of knowledge. On experience as it develops, ideals of the pure reason may rise to perish never, which were certainly not discernible at first ; and though present now, their full meaning is still unrealised. The superlative, the absolute, the infinite are limiting notions, and for aught we know are notions only : ideals of the reason they may be, but then reason itself is an ideal. There seems no end to the process of rationalising experience, but—as I said at the outset— at least there may be progress, and our confidence, that, as Hegel maintained, the real is rational and the rational real may deepen as we proceed. But we must start where we are and continue as we have begun, letting knowledge grow from more to more. To say this is to imply that those idealists who have attempted to begin with the Absolute have not really done so. That they have not has been amply proved by their critics and admitted by their apologists. But at any rate in the flights of pure thought up to the Absolute the atmosphere of empirical fact by which it is sustained is too diffused to be detected, and when that summit is reached the particular, the many, of actual experience tend to disappear or to be explained away. Thus their "alleged independence"—in which we empirically believe—Mr Bradley declares "is no fact, but a theoretical construction; and so far as it has a meaning, that meaning contradicts itself, and issues in chaos.... The plurality then sinks to become merely an integral aspect in a single substantial unity, and the reals [the many] have vanished[1]." Nevertheless the inevitable reaction, which the impossibility of philosophical finality involves, has already set in: indeed Mr Bradley

[1] *Appearance and Reality*, 2nd edn, p. 143.

prophesied as much : " Monadism," he says, "on the whole will increase and will add to the difficulties which already exist[1]." Whether the second half of his forecast will turn out to be as true as the first remains to be seen. At any rate the plurality of the realm of ends is what is most patent to us at the outset : if the difficulties of Pluralism point the way to Singularism[2] they will at least serve to make the character of the One clearer than any ' cheap and easy monism ' evolved at a dialectical show—such as Mr Bradley in a famous passage has himself described[3]—can ever do. It will be well too as regards method to let the spirit of the time lead us ; turning aside from what has been described as " Naturalism's desert on the one hand and the barren summit of the Absolute on the other," to follow the historical method as far as possible in tracing the gradual evolution of ideas, but trusting to speculative methods only in the endeavour to divine the most satisfactory solution of the problems to which they gave rise.

In the next lecture then we must try to ascertain the genesis of the ideas which lead to the problem of the One and the Many, and then we may proceed to examine the solution which those who are called Pluralists or Personal Idealists uphold.

[1] *Op. cit.* p. 118, *fin.*
[2] This term, first used by Külpe as the correlative of Pluralism (*Einleitung in die Philosophie*, § 14), may not be happy; but it is after all better than Henism ; and it is not misleading as Monism according to present usage, i.e. with a qualitative as well as a quanti- tative sense, certainly is. Wolf, who invented the term, used it, as I have done, only in the qualitative sense as applicable either to materialism or to spiritualism.
[3] *Principles of Logic*, p. 533.

Pantheism = "a polite atheism"
Schopenhauer -

LECTURE II.

THE ONE AND THE MANY.

It is very commonly assumed that idealism or spiritualism is synonymous with theism, or at least inseparable from it. It is true that idealists are rarely atheists, but it would be dogmatism to assert offhand that they cannot be. Still less can we say that if not monotheists, they must be pan*theists*, in the sense of denying the reality of the world altogether as Spinoza is commonly credited with doing, and so was called by Hegel not atheist but acosmist. *Pan*theism in the sense of identifying the world with God is but 'a polite atheism,' as Schopenhauer has said, but such a pantheism is not compatible with idealism. So "from a world of spirits to a Supreme Spirit is a *possible* step," is all I ventured to say in my former lectures at Aberdeen[1]; for it is not straightway evident that it is a necessary one. Many of those called pluralists or personal idealists deny the necessity, and some even question the possibility of any such step.—We cannot, of course, admit a multiplicity without any unity. A One of some sort is obviously implied in talking of a world at all; but may not the Many account for their own unity instead of requiring a One, an individual of

[1] *Naturalism and Agnosticism*, earlier edns, I. p. 202; 4th edn, p. 494.

another order, to account for them? May not the
unity of the world be analogous to that of a society, so
presupposing the individuals associated? Or must we
assume beyond and above the Many and their unity an
Absolute One, of which they are somehow the appearance? This is the problem of the One and the Many
to which we have now to turn. As an essential preliminary to any attempt to deal with it we have agreed
first of all to ascertain, if we can, how the ideas of the
One and the Many arise in the course of advancing
experience and thought.

The correlation or duality involved in all experience,
that namely of an individual subject and its objective
environment, is often described as a duality of Ego and
Non-Ego, of Self and Not-Self. But it is important
to note, on the one hand, that this objective Not-Self
is not presented as another self, but simply as an
'Other.' Also it is equally important to note, on the
other hand, that this objective 'Other' has always for experience a certain continuity or unity, which—though it
differentiates more and more as experience develops—
never completely disintegrates into a disconnected
manifold or mere plurality. Again the relation of the
subject to this objective continuum is always one of
more or less dependence. But the subject, as we have
already seen, is not wholly inert : it is always active and
selective to some extent ; otherwise, indeed, it could
never be aware of its dependence. As experience
extends and the objective differentiates, the subject too
advances in initiative and acquires new powers; but
never, so to say, overtops and outstrips the Non-Ego. On
the contrary, increasing knowledge though it secures in-

creasing power also deepens this sense of dependence. Primitive man attempts to subjugate or circumvent Nature by magic, but science has long since taught us that our ends of self-preservation and physical better-ment are only to be attained by such adaptation and adjustment as Nature allows.

But the advance of Science, it is said, does not merely deepen this sense of our ultimate dependence on Nature, it also tends increasingly to emphasize Nature's complete independence of us. We talk of our life as a struggle, but at least Nature does not deign to struggle with us. We talk of shaping and selecting; but the further our knowledge of this in-terminable Other confronting us extends, the more inevitable to many seems the conclusion that in truth it is we who are shaped and selected by Nature. Such in brief is *die geläuterte Naturbetrachtung des denkenden Naturmenschen*, as Haeckel calls it; and the only Absolute One, in which Naturalism believes, is the result. And what ultimately is this Absolute which Haeckel's clarified vision discerns? It is per-manent substance; more definitely, it is the kinetic world-ether, whose mass and energy are eternally con-served, and whence the Many result as atomic souls by an inexplicable condensation or concentration. This world-ether is the only 'creative divinity' that Haeckel allows. And Herbert Spencer comes very near to this when, in the recent revision of his *First Principles*, he suggests that "the only supposition having consistency is that that in which consciousness inheres is the all-pervading ether[1]." We have then here that form of so-called *pan*theism—in which all the stress is on the

[1] *First Principles*, 1900, p. 201.

'*pan*'—the pantheism that maintains—as Schopenhauer put it—"that the world is there in virtue of its
own internal energy and through itself"—a world in
which consciousness, according to him, is a secondary
and unfortunate episode.

But this polite atheism, as I have already said, we
cannot accept. Though but a reed, to use Pascal's
words, man is a thinking reed, and cannot be merged
in or emerge from such a world, however vast it be.
Man only knows the world as it faces him and he inter-
acts with it, and he knows it only so far as he finds it
intelligible. And finding it intelligible he can only conclude that it is not after all an alien Other but has its
ground and meaning either in another Self or Supreme
One or in a community of many selves. This much we
are taking as already clear. Let us turn then to consider
the idea of the Many, which in fact we reach first and
which leads to a concept of the Absolute still older
than that of objective substance.

The individual subject soon learns to distinguish
certain objective differentiations or bodies, in form and
behaviour resembling that particular differentiation
which is present in all its own experience as the
body or organism that it is said to animate. These
other bodies it regards as each one animated by a self,
and it often finds that it is itself so regarded by them.
But such other selves only tell on the individual's
experience, because their bodies form parts of the one
objective whole that is so far common to them all, and
through which all their intercourse and interaction are
mediated. That is to say, only the bodies and their
movements are presented as objects, the indwelling
selves (or souls) and their experiences are not thus

presented. To mark this difference we may adopt Clifford's term and call these other selves and their experience 'ejects.' In the infancy of the human race this ejective analogy ran riot: primitive philosophy, if we may credit the untutored savage with such a luxury, found life and mind everywhere. But it was still life or mind set in the matrix of a common environment, possessing always a definite embodiment and location therein and manifesting itself solely by this means. We can imagine other selves transcending ourselves indefinitely, as we can imagine them indefinitely lower than ourselves, in what we call the scale of being. But if we hold to the continuity which a scale of being implies, we must imagine them all—higher and lower alike—as subjects in correlation with objects and not as in themselves absolute or complete. As Hegel's unfortunate colleague, Beneke, was fond of maintaining in opposition to him:—"The human mind is incapable of devising or excogitating anything absolutely; on the contrary it must derive either from external or from internal experience the essential elements of all that it imagines or thinks[1]."

On the lines then of that experience which brings us into communication with our fellow-creatures, the experience that underlies the animism, mythology, and polytheism of primitive culture, we can at best only imagine an experient who is *primus inter pares*, at any rate so far as the duality of subject and object is concerned: we cannot reach on these lines the thought of an Absolute One. Even the living and true God, who is the object of worship in monotheistic religions, cannot be identified with the Absolute, for worship im-

[1] *System der Metaphysik*, 1840, p. 496.

plies mutual distinction and mutual interest. Moreover
the history of religion shows clearly that the idea of a
supreme and only God has been developed through
polytheism, and has so far an anthropomorphic basis.
For "pure monotheism," as Dr Caird has said, "God
was merely one subject among other subjects; and
though lifted high above them, the source of all their
life, was yet related to them as an external and independent will[1]." But the point on which we have to
insist is rather that to be a subject at all, in any sense
that we can understand—so long that is as the term
subject carries any meaning for us—is to be confronted
by an Other as object. A supreme subject then taken
alone, no less than the objective World so taken, is
but a one-sided abstraction and cannot be veritably an
absolute reality.

Certainly, it will be said, the true, the absolute
Absolute is not exclusively subjective, still less exclusively objective: it is the unity of both.—Mythology
had its cosmogony and even its theogony, but in rising
towards the idea of a Supreme Spirit, speculative
monotheism, at all events, has tended to conceive both
God and the World *sub specie aeternitatis*. The entire
objective world and the many finite subjects which
interact with it or within it, in all their totality and in
all their distinctness, are, it is said, to be conceived as
eternally present to God as His own creative intuition
and self-manifestation. The world *is* for God too, but
not as for us, merely as given fact, but entirely as
thought or deed. This sublime ideal is again a limit
towards which our thought can only approximate; and
the history of thought shows not only how gradually

[1] *The Evolution of Religion*, 1893, Vol. II. p. 72.

the advance towards it has been made: it shows also that difficulties emerge as this ideal is more distinctly conceived.

But let us note the steps. All finite beings, we have found, are in part passive and only in part active; but they appear as increasingly active the higher in the scale of being they stand : God as the Supreme is then to be regarded as purely active and wholly free from external constraint. Whereas *we* can only shape and arrange so far as the elements and forces of nature permit, for God there is no nature; no need for mechanism to transform 'chaos without form and void' into a cosmos teeming with purpose and life: for him there is only his own creation. But this idea of creation, creation 'out of nothing,' is hard to seize. Not only does the Mosaic account—with its void and formless earth, its primeval darkness and the spirit of Elohim brooding over the waters—fail to reach it; but the philosophic specu-lations of Plato and Aristotle failed to reach it too. Both recognise a *materia prima* as a sort of half-real, indeterminate, potential stuff—wholly receptive and yet more or less recalcitrant—to which form and life are imparted, but which itself was never made. All this suggests a generative process, nature but not creation; indeed Plato, in the *Timaeus* at all events, compares this primary matter, as Aristotle called it, to a nurse or receptacle of all generation[1]. Such ideas point to a dualism not to an absolute Unity: God and Nature are distinct. And, in fact, both Plato and Aristotle in different ways explicitly separate Nature as the sensible

---

[1] Cf. *Timaeus*, 49 ff.

world from an intelligible world which is the direct
object of the divine thought and contemplation.
Between the two worlds they fail to establish any
satisfactory connexion[1]; but if we leave the sensible
world out of account, we have in the Platonic world of
ideas and in the divine νόησις νοήσεως of Aristotle
a unity of subjective and objective which we may fairly
call the Absolute, since it is perfect and complete in
itself.   Of this the sensible world is a superfluous and
imperfect—nay an impossible—replica, that can neither
really be nor be really known.

And if we are to be in earnest with the notion of
creation out of nothing does it not equally eliminate
any idea of generation or of reproduction, does it not
suggest that sort of eternal 'static perfection' which
such processes as producing, impressing, or in-forming,
exclude?   A subject who is *actus purus*, clear therefore of all the limitations pertaining to space and time,
who apprehends not by sense and comprehends not
by discursive thinking, what object can he have which
is not himself?   Must we not say then that he does
not *make* even out of nothing, for what is made cannot
be its Maker? and yet if the Maker is absolute, what
else can it be?   He acts, but his acts are immanent
not transeunt: he becomes his own Other only that
he may be conscious of himself, and so we call him
causa sui, and interpret this as meaning an absolute
self-consciousness.   Such at any rate has been the
usual outcome of philosophic monotheism: it tends to
end in acosmism.   Aristotle's position, for example, is
summed up by Dr Caird as "the pure self-conscious-

[1] Cf. Caird, *The Evolution of Theology in the Greek Philosophers*,
1904, Vol. II. pp. 238 ff.

ness of God, in which subject and object and the activity that relates them to each other—νοῦς, νοητόν and νόησις—are perfectly unified and which, therefore, is complete in itself without reference to any other object,"—but such absolute self-consciousness "cannot logically be conceived as going beyond itself to create the finite world of movement and change[1]." The same dualism between God and the world reappears in the philosophy of Plotinus—a philosophy in some respects an amalgam of the Platonic and the Aristotelian—the same inability, that is to say, to show, as Dr Caird puts it, "how God, who is absolutely complete in himself, can yet be the source of existences which are external to him and not included in the process of his own life[2]." In the philosophy of Spinoza, to which, as already said, the name acosmism was first applied, this difficulty is specially apparent. His many expositors have failed to show any conceivable connexion between what he called *natura naturata* and God, in whom all the modes and distinctions of the former disappear, and whose existence, as Spinoza himself has said, is "*toto genere* different from theirs."

In fact, observing that 'creation out of nothing' has another side—*ex nihilo nihil fit*—we might not unfairly say that this is the side which the acosmic tendency of Absolutism inevitably emphasizes. The world of finite existences created out of nothing is nothing; that is to say, it is *Schein* not *Sein*, appearance not reality, as the Eleatics first proclaimed :

---

[1] *Op. cit.* II. p. 241.
[2] *Op. cit.* II. p. 257.

it is the Mâyâ of Brahmanism, the inexplicable illusion enveloping the One, that

> ...like a dome of many-coloured glass
> Stains the white radiance of eternity.

But the conclusion that reality cannot be Many led naturally to a yet further development of the idea of the Absolute.   The Absolute in the end was conceived not so much as the unity *of* subject and object but rather as a unity that transcends both.   Such an Absolutism we find, for example, in the One of Plotinus, the Substance of Spinoza and the *Neutrum* of Schelling.   And I fear we must allow that those who would add Hegel's Absolute Idea to the list are probably right, unless indeed we are willing to admit that it is—as he himself as good as says—not the Absolute but only its shadow.   But there is still a step.   After all, we and all our speculation belong to the world of so-called 'spurious existence'; and as to the One, so transcendently different from all that we know—none of our concepts are applicable to it.   It is *Nicht* in contrast to *Icht*, as Eckhart quaintly says. We ascend to it, as the 'negative theology' of the Scholastic mysticism taught, by dropping one after another every determinate predicate, so that we end by saying with Proclus that the One or God is above substance and life and intelligence, and cannot even be called One except figuratively; or with Basilides that it is rather to be called absolute non-existence, or again with the author of the *Theologia germanica* that it must be called Nothing, by which is meant that it is nothing of all that created things can conceive, know, think or name[1]. No doubt the mystics did not intend by this rejection of all positive determinations to imply that there was no God or that God was nothing: rather, as Höffding puts it :—" In the mystical concept of God, as well as in the Buddhist concept of Nirvana, it is precisely the inexhaustible positivity which bursts through every conceptual form and turns every determination into an impossibility." It was in this sense that Fichte said that "every so-called concept of God is necessarily that of an idol[2]." Thus not merely graven images are disallowed, but in the end all determinate thoughts, of this super-essential, super-rational, super-personal, nay, super-absolute unity[3] that is neither subject nor object and in which all difference begins and ends.

But there is yet a possible concept of the One to be noticed which experience directly suggests—that of the world-soul, the eject to which the world belongs as its organism. But for the present this notion only interests us in that it formed a sort of *tertium quid* or mediating principle by which Plato and his Neo-platonic followers attempted to connect the permanent and intelligible world with the sensible world of the finite many that ever change and pass. And the attempt is obviously futile, for from the point of view of the Absolute there is no sensible world with which to connect itself—were such connexion in itself possible.

---

[1] Cf. art. 'Mysticism' by Prof. Pringle-Pattison in *Ency. Brit.*; Mansel, *The Gnostic Heresies*, 1874, p. 146; Höffding, *Philosophy of Religion*, 1910, § 21, and note 37.

[2] *Werke*, v. p. 267.

[3] So Nicholas of Cusa. Cf. Caird, *Evolution of Religion*, II. pp. 73 f.

The world-soul is really one term in an emanation to which the very fulness of the Absolute somehow gives rise, but which as little concerns it, as the chance reflexion of its beams affects the effulgence of the sun itself. This ingenious analogy of emanation suggested by the solar radiation, though common in ancient thought, is most fully elaborated by Plotinus. As it is the precise converse of the modern doctrine of evolution, this process might be conveniently called devolution; for as that is a progress from the lower to the higher this is a decline from the higher to the lower. With every remove there is not only less perfection but seemingly also more plurality, more diffusion. The *νοῦς*, which proceeds immediately from the One, is already beset with the duality that even intuition implies; the world-soul, which follows next, is necessarily pluralised into particular souls; each of these in turn is resolved into higher and lower faculties by its relation to the body which it shapes and informs, while this body again is infinitely divisible. Beyond all is matter as mere indeterminate emptiness, darkness and evil, the utter contrary in all respects of the absolute fulness, light and perfection of the One. In a word plurality and separation with their broken lights are the marks of imperfection and unreality: our very birth, i.e. the assumption of a body, is in part a sin, in part a punishment; and the only remedy for this evil lies in a mystic reunion with, and absorption in, the One.

We have thus passed in review several ideals of a supreme Unity which speculation, regardless of experience, has elaborated—an Absolute Object, an Absolute Subject, an Absolute Self-consciousness, and various attempts to transcend such duality as consciousness implies. The first two we reject not as being *one* but as being one-sided : since subject and object are essentially correlative, neither alone can be absolute. Still even these ideals point the moral that our whole review suggests—*Nulla vestigia retrorsum.* An absolute reached by way of abstraction is the lion's den, where all plurality disappears. In whatever sense you say absolute in that sense you cannot say many. If there were an absolute substance or an absolute subject there could not be many substances or subjects, unless these terms were equivocally used ; as substance for example was by Descartes, and subject by Fichte. And if absolute means perfect and complete, why should—nay, how can—what is in itself absolute become splintered up into infinite modes that are neither perfect nor complete ? We can imagine them as mutually determining each other, but for it they are but 'invulnerable nothings' with which it has no concern. This is the difficulty that has been specially emphasized by critics of Spinoza. It recurs in a more concrete form, but then as illustrating the one-sidedness of an absolute object, in the naïve procedure of such thinkers as Spencer or Haeckel when they jump from a homogeneous plenum or uniform all-pervading ether to the discrete atoms into which it somehow has to be, and yet nohow can be, resolved— unless some directing agency or prime mover be forthcoming from without. Similarly the Absolute Ego of Fichte can only be got under way with the help of an unintelligible *Anstoss* (or impact) determining it to posit its non-Ego.

We come then to the ideal of an absolute experience as the unity, it might seem, of Absolute Subject and Absolute Object, an Absolute that is no longer one-sided and without distinctions. But again there can be only one such consciousness, and it must be transparently clear, a light, so to say, in which is no darkness at all. In our experience the contemplation of what we sometimes call the eternal truths of reason and again the intuitive certainty of our consciousness of self come nearest to this ideal. We find accordingly that ancient speculation laid more stress on the former, as in Aristotle's νόησις νοήσεως ; and modern on the latter, as in Hegel's *sich selbst denkende Idee* : though both aspects are always present. Outside such an Absolute there can be nothing at all, and within it nothing that is imperfect, mutable or obscure. The more clearly we realise this ideal the more inevitably three conclusions force themselves upon us : (1) Here there is nothing wanting : this intelligible world is perfect and complete in itself, (2) from this transcendent standpoint the existence of the finite Many—the sensible world—seems impossible, and (3), granting its existence, the connexion between the two worlds is inexplicable—inexplicable at least apart from assumptions incompatible with the character of such an ideal. The way upward to this by abstraction and idealisation is comparatively easy—though such methods cannot pretend to yield real knowledge ; but the way back has in fact only been possible by means of myths and metaphors, which are not even logically consistent. Not-being or the non-existent is always endowed with some sort of potentiality or receptivity, which

...the One Spirit's plastic stress
Sweeps through......
Torturing the unwilling dross, that checks its flight,
To its own likeness, as each mass may bear.

We talk of creation out of nothing. But if the qualification 'out of nothing' has any meaning at all it implies a transeunt activity on the part of the Creator and a certain lack of reality on the part of the creature—a lack of reality which sinks back to complete unreality when the creature is compared with the Creator, as Meister Eckhart, for example, maintained. But on the other hand what possible meaning can we assign to transeunt activity on the part of the Absolute? If then we emphasize the notion of creation simply and regard the creative activity as purely immanent, then as with Spinoza *causa* is the same as *ratio*; what is said to be created is the intelligible world, where, *sub specie aeternitatis*, all things follow from the 'nature' of God "in the same way as from the nature of the triangle it follows from eternity and for eternity that its three interior angles are equal to two right angles[1]."

I have referred to the method by which such ideals of the Absolute are reached as a method of abstraction and as, therefore, necessarily defective. It will be well, if possible, to make this clearer. What we may call the three unities of experience, the unity of the subject, the unity of the object, and the unity of both in self-consciousness, are hardly to be questioned. Now the objective side of experience, to begin with that, is always[2] a complex or differentiated whole : the more

---

[1] *Ethics*, I. xvii. n.   [2] Save at its ideal limit. Cf. p. 195.

primitive the experience the fewer, the simpler, and the vaguer the differentiations ; but an objective continuum wholly devoid of diversity would yield no experience. Yet such a homogeneous whole is just what we reach by abstracting first from all the qualitative differences of particular bodies, and then from their particularity or discreteness : in place of an ordered cosmos there then remains only a continuous plenum, as in the Cartesian concept of matter or the modern concept of a primordial ether. Mistaking abstraction for simplification, we call that absolute which is really only above all relations because it is completely indeterminate. As we have already seen, the cosmos or concrete whole cannot be called absolute, if we regard it as what is experienced, that is as objective; but this abstract resolution of it into an ἄπειρον escapes such one-sidedness, only because this cannot be objective. Turning to the ideal of an Absolute Subject, we find that this again is reached by an abstract procedure, though a different one. Generalisation up to an ideal limit is out of the question here ; instead of that we have one phase of the empirical subject selected and made absolute. Ignoring the receptive side of experience altogether we try to conceive a pure activity. In Fichte's phraseology, *Gegenstand* implies *Widerstand*, object implies opposite : a subject then for whom there can be no opposition is one for whom there can be no object, no other. It again escapes the charge of one-sidedness only because such an Absolute, though called by Fichte an Ego, is no subject in any sense that we can understand, as Fichte was careful to maintain. Finally, the ideal of an

Absolute experience is reached by abstraction, whether we regard its contents as the intelligible world of eternal ideas or as the *identity* of subject and object in self-consciousness. The Platonic system of archetypal ideas or eternal patterns is after all for our experience not independent of the many nor prior to them, but is simply a system of abstractions resulting from such comparisons, generalisations, and analogies, as the sensible world itself suggests to us. A consciousness again which is self-consciousness and nothing more, which is solely and completely a 'self-revelation,' whose whole content is self—self explicated in self and through self and for self, such a consciousness is from the point of view of experience an abstraction. A part of such experience as we can understand is taken for the whole; for we are never conscious of self save as we are conscious of not-self. The two factors are analytically distinct but not actually separable : so far then self-consciousness alone seems to be an abstraction. If we nevertheless elect to regard this ideal as the sole and ultimate reality there seems no place left for finite experients and the sensible world, as I have already urged. And not merely so, but the impulse to pass beyond multiplicity to unity, to which we have so far yielded, carries us on to a final simplicity beyond all explication, where mysticism hails 'Naught as every-thing and everything as Naught.' If on the other hand, keeping to experience, we admit the abstract character of this ideal, then we have the problem of the unity of the many still on our hands.

But what sort of unity can we reach if we refrain from all attempts absolutely to transcend the Many ?

A mere totality or aggregate is obviously no true unity, even though we could know—which is, in fact, impossible—that it was absolutely a totality. Some community or reciprocity there must be : the question is how little will suffice.   It seems clear that either each must be connected with all in at least one way or that all must be so connected with some one.   There must be either a universal principle directly relating all or a supreme, though not absolute, individual, to whom all are related.   The latter will imply the former, so far as through their common relation to the Supreme One all would be related—though it were only indirectly— to each other.   But the converse will not hold ; that is to say, the direct relation of all to each other will not necessarily imply a Supreme One.   Of such a fundamental and universal relation we have an instance according to the atomic theory in universal gravitation. But of course in a realm of ends the universal relation can only be analogous to this in the one aspect of being universal : the two cannot be identified—though they may be related.   Empirical evidence of such a universal relation there can hardly be : we are left then to assume it and to frame some more or less hazardous hypothesis as to its nature.   I say nothing for the present of any difficulty besetting the idea of an absolute plurality of any sort, a plurality of beings only relatively dependent and therefore relatively independent—independent, that is, so far as their bare existence is concerned.   This, on our present supposition, has to be taken as a fact. The idea of a Supreme One as *primus inter pares* again can hardly admit of empirical verification : the very supposition seems to involve an empirically unattainable limit. If we nevertheless make believe that in 'pure thought' this limit is attained and ask how we are to represent the relation of all to this Supreme One, the old ideal Absolute again looms upon us and threatens to absorb the Many altogether. We may recoil from this and say : There might have been an Absolute, provided there had been no Many, but holding to the reality of these we can regard God as supreme, but not as absolute : then we seem to save the Many, but we have only a 'finite God,' or rather the idea of one.

Thus we seem shut up to what looks like a choice of evils. Without an Absolute One it seems hopeless to attempt to account for, and hazardous to attempt to unify, the Many ; and with such an Absolute it seems as hopeless to attempt to retain what independence and freedom the Many appear *prima facie* to possess. And this seemingly inevitable perplexity shows itself throughout the history of religion in a constant alternation between first claiming and then abdicating a distinct position for Man over against God. Think, for example, of the counter doctrines of Augustine and Pelagius and the controversies to which both in ancient and modern times they gave rise. Or again take the vast literature of religious mysticism, from which one instance may suffice :—Eckhart who said: Couldst thou annihilate thyself for a moment thou wouldst possess all that God is in himself, also said, " I am as necessary to God as God is necessary to me." In this connexion I am glad of an opportunity of quoting Mr Bradley, from whose main position I am forced to dissent. " Religion," he says, " prefers to put forth statements which it feels are untenable, and to correct

them at once by counter-statements, which it finds are
no better. It is then driven forwards and back between
both, like a dog which seeks to follow two masters....
We may say that in religion God tends always to pass
beyond himself. He is necessarily led to end in the
Absolute, which for religion is not God. God, whether
a 'person' or not, is, on the one hand, a finite being
and an object to man. On the other hand, the consummation, sought by the religious consciousness, is
the perfect unity of these terms [the Absolute and
God]. And, if so, nothing would in the end fall
outside God. But to take God as the ceaseless oscil-
lation and changing movement of the process, is out of
the question. On the other side the harmony of all
these discords demands...the alteration of their finite
character. The unity implies a complete suppression
of the relation, as such ; but, with that suppression,
religion and the good have altogether, as such, disappeared. If you identify the Absolute with God, that
is not the God of religion. If again you separate them,
God becomes a finite factor in the Whole. And the
effort of religion is to put an end to, and break down,
this relation—a relation which, none the less, it essentially presupposes. Hence, short of the Absolute, God
cannot rest, and, having reached that goal, he is lost
and religion with him[1]."

In the history of philosophy again we find the same
perplexing alternation between asserting and denying
a position for the Many incompatible with the absoluteness of the One : we find this not only in the form of
a reaction from absolutism to pluralism in successive

[1] *Appearance and Reality*, pp. 446 f.

thinkers but what is more remarkable we find it—and
find it invariably—within systems of philosophy that
are avowedly philosophies of the Absolute.   And yet
in truth it is not remarkable, for it could not really be
otherwise.   *Ex vi termini*, there can be no reality
distinct from the Absolute.   But if *X*, *Y* and *Z assert*
this absolute Reality they must thereby distinguish
themselves from it, and even distinguish themselves
the more the more distinctly they seek to realise their
own inclusion within it.   To deny their own individual
reality at such a time is out of the question further,
because only through this have they any notion of
reality at all.   But at other times they easily forget it ;
as the naturalist, for example, forgets the subjective
implications of experience when engrossed in its objects.
Nay, they even assume, once the summit of their
speculation is attained, that their necessary starting-
point, the distinct reality of the Many, is transcended
and annulled.   But the feat of kicking down the ladder
by which you have climbed is logically possible only
when the conclusion reached is at once a necessary
consequence of the premises and also in itself absurd.
No doubt there is always the semblance of a purely
a priori procedure in most philosophies of the Absolute :
the entire construction claims to be the work of pure
thought, true independently of all finite experience.
But Descartes' *Cogito ergo sum*, the proposition round
which, as Hegel said, the whole of modern philosophy
revolves[1], is in this connexion past all question.   And
hitherto all attempts, starting from the Absolute to
respect the Many as this proposition demands, have

----

[1] *Encyclopaedia*, § 64.

proved unavailing. The reality of the Many is either flatly contradicted as by the Eleatics ; or it remains inexplicable as with Spinoza or Hegel. Thus Spinoza, who begins with an absolutely infinite, that is inde-terminate, Substance, ends with a conative Many mu-tually determining each other. Again with Hegel, the Absolute seems at one time to be a perfect Self with no hint of aught beside or beyond its own completed self-consciousness, and at another not to be a self at all, but only the absolutely spiritual,—art, religion and philosophy—the over-individual ends, as they are sometimes called, which become realised in subjective spirits : not self-conscious Spirit but simply the im-personal Spirit in all spirits.

Thus, as it has been said, " both philosophy and religion bear ample testimony to the almost insuperable difficulty of finding room in the universe for God *and* man. When speculation busies itself with the relation of these two, each in turn tends to swallow up the other. The pendulum of human thought swings con-tinually between the two extremes of Individualism [or Pluralism] leading to Atheism, and Universalism [or Absolutism], leading to Pantheism or Acosmism[1]."

This reaction is most pronounced when, as has continually happened, the defects of an absolutist philosophy have given rise to an avowed pluralism or even naturalism. Such after Hegel's death was conspicu-ously the case in the speculation of the Hegelian left, as Strauss called it. So Feuerbach describes his seces-sion from the Hegelian school by saying " God was my

[1] Pringle-Pattison, *Hegelianism and Personality*, 1st edn, p. 153 *fin.*

first thought, reason my second, man my third and last."
For him afterwards however Man is the beginning,
the middle and the end of religion: theology is thus
at bottom anthropology: through social intercourse man
attains to self-consciousness, to reason and morality, and
the divine is but the idealisation of the best and highest.
Hegel's positions then are to be inverted: we must
say not that the Absolute is self-consciousness, but that
self-consciousness is the Absolute; not that God is
love but that love is God, and so forth.—The rigorous
pluralism of Herbart again is to be regarded as in
large measure a rebound from the absolutism of his
teacher Fichte. Still more markedly was the Monadology of Herbart's forerunner, Leibniz, a recoil from
the pantheism or acosmism of Spinoza. Spinoza's one
substance, essentially indeterminate—every determination being for him a negation—is incompatible with
even the imagination of finite things severally striving
for self-conservation and mutually determining each
other; incompatible with the drama of man's bondage
and eventual freedom, for example, which is the main
theme of Spinoza's Ethics. Leibniz then takes his
notion of conation in thorough earnest and defines
"substance as an individual agent." "Were it not for
the monads," he allowed, "Spinoza would be right."
The mediaeval controversies about universals and the
principle of individuation are at bottom instances of
the same reaction, and finally the ancient atomism of
Leucippus and Democritus was a revolt against the
Eleatic singularism.

Obviously the perennial renewal of this conflict is
a sign that pluralism has equally failed to reach a

satisfactory solution of the problem of the One and the
Many. We must allow, as Adamson has said, that no
philosophy has ever managed to reconcile these two
notions of an infinite power and of an infinite variety
of limited individualised expressions of that power[1].
But at all events as regards method the teaching of
history seems clear : the solution is not to be obtained
by passing over the Many at the outset trusting to
deduce them afterwards from an absolute One that is
reached *a priori*. This method has proved itself
illusory : the seeming attainment of the One has
meant the disappearance of the Many. Against
pluralism it can only be urged that it fails or has so far
failed to account for the unity that it in fact involves—
the unity of individual experience as enlarged by inter-
subjective intercourse. But at all events it is, I trust,
clear that we cannot begin by ignoring pluralism
altogether.

[1] *The Development of Modern Philosophy*, 1903, I. p. 107.

LECTURE III.

The most striking characteristic of the nineteenth century, so far as philosophical speculation is concerned, was, as we have already noted, the predominance of what we may call Absolutism or Singularism as presented by such different thinkers as Fichte, Schelling, Hegel, Schopenhauer, and others less distinguished. In the lull which followed upon the common collapse of these various forms of Absolutism the rapid advance of scientific knowledge brought Naturalism or Physical Realism for a time to the fore. But the insufficiency of this physical realism to bear the strain put upon it is at length becoming apparent ; and so the necessity of interpreting nature in terms of mind is again widely recognised. But the recoil from Absolutism still persists ; and accordingly the twentieth century opens with the attempt to work out the idealistic interpretation not in the old way as essentially a devolution of the One, but rather—as far as possible—to represent it as an evolution of the Many. In England, in America, in France, even in Germany—once the stronghold of Absolutism—systems of pluralism, more or less pronounced, are rife. It is hardly practicable and would certainly be tedious to examine them separately and in detail. We shall get a better insight into the new movement if we try to secure distinct ideas of its main

w.   4

standpoint and its salient features, even though in so doing we have to play the dangerous part of eclectics and attempt to frame a composite synopsis of the *tout ensemble*, a sort of Galtonian portrait or generic image of the group.

The pluralistic standpoint in the main is that historical standpoint which we have already contrasted with the naturalistic. But the ordinary historian is content to recognise Nature as indispensable, so far at least as it is the scene and provides the properties of the drama. But this contrast pluralism claims altogether to transcend. To the distinction of person and thing, of nature and history, it allows only a relative value.— Still we shall best realise the position of pluralism by first attending exclusively to the interaction of living agents in the world commonly recognised as historical ; and then, as far as we can and as well as we can, attempting to apply the concepts we derive from this to the interpretation of the world commonly regarded as physical, the phenomena of which science has succeeded in abstractly formulating in terms of matter and motion. Of these concepts perhaps the most characteristic is that of behaviour or conduct. Behaviour is a term appropriate only to what is individual and unique, and is not a mere instance of law and uniformity. No one would ordinarily speak of the *behaviour* of falling bodies ; for, in merely gravitating, bodies display no special character. But we might speak of a ship or a balloon as behaving well or ill : such things have a certain individuality and so receive a proper name. *Per contra* the term individuality always implies behaviour. Indeed whenever it is worth while to give a proper name it is possible also to assign a definite character. Thus Goldsmith talks of "the lazy Scheldt" and the "wandering Po." Now Pluralism assumes that the whole world is made up of individuals, each distinguished by its characteristic behaviour ; but of course it does not find its real individuals in the rough and ready way of popular impersonation : it would not regard a mountain or a river as a person.

Behaviour or conduct again implies some objective or external situation as the *occasion* for every manifestation of activity, but never as its sole and complete *determinant*. There is always some subjective spontaneity or initiative, but there is never any absolute or unconditional activity. Thus, in spite of the etymological identity of atom and individual, pluralism has nothing in common with atomism beyond the bare fact that both recognise a many ; for the atom is credited with no spontaneity and is completely determined from without. Atom and individual or monad are then contraries and cannot be identified or really combined. The so-called interaction of atoms will not account for the contingency displayed in the world ; but what we know as the conduct or behaviour of cognitive and conative individuals may, it is contended, explain both the contingency and the uniformity that we find there. But, before we proceed to consider at more length this attempt of pluralistic spiritualism thus to interpret the world, it will be well first to inquire what we are to understand by an individual or one of the many, and what by the unity that even their plurality implies.

Of course we cannot start at the beginning, for that

that an atom of oxygen can unite with 2 of hydrogen

is not where we are. How far towards a hypothetical beginning the principle of continuity will reasonably carry us is just one of the questions we have to decide. But we must start, where alone reflexion on experience can arise, at the level of self-consciousness. We have already seen that singularistic spiritualism or absolutism really commenced its speculative flight from this level, and pluralism is in no better position. In self-conscious-ness we attain to the explicit knowledge of that duality of self and not-self, of subject and object, without which experience ceases to have any meaning for us. The self of which we are conscious, then, furnishes us with our first paradigm of what we are to understand by the individuals of our plurality. It is assumed that there exists an indefinite variety of selves, some indefinitely higher, some indefinitely lower than ourselves. But even the highest, if there be a highest, will, it is assumed, be only *primus inter pares*, one among the many, and not an Absolute really including them all. Even the lowest also will possess whatever be the irreducible *minimum* essential to being in any sense a subject or self at all.

Such *minimum* implies behaviour directed towards self-conservation or self-realisation. An individual no doubt is often defined as something that cannot be divided without being destroyed, as a clock for instance. But such things are not true individuals or selves: a clock has no interest in, or impulse towards, its own conservation.— Self-conservation alone however, strictly taken and re-garded as everywhere realised, would result in nothing better than a static world, in which there would be no new events and no history. Such a state as final would correspond to the complete rest and quiescence with which, according to Spencer's law of equilibration, the drama of evolution must close. As an initial state it would correspond to Leibniz's pre-established harmony contemplated from without, if that were possible: there would be no interaction between individual and individual. But the actual world, as our own experience teaches us, is full of cross-purposes; and therefore self-conservation in general calls for effort and perseverance.

Though self-conservation implies the *minimum* to be striven for, self-development or realisation is still the aim of many, and was perhaps at the beginning the aim of all; for the beginning would obviously not be a stationary state. Any advantage gained, though merely the result of good fortune, would not be passively surrendered: its loss would be a painful contraction. Thus a new standard of the self to be conserved would be reached. Plainly then, when we talk of self-conservation the main stress is not to be laid on the bare conservation of some metaphysically simple entity, such as the soul of the old rational psychologists. What is meant is rather the maintenance of the most advantageous position attained by the actual self in relation to the world as a whole. This implies that each one is in touch with all the rest collectively and with some more specially. As I have expressed it elsewhere, there is for every subject one *totum objectivum*, which, save in the limiting case, which would answer to an inconceivable beginning of experience, will be more or less differentiated.

By way of summary it may suffice to say that the well-known *Monadology* of Leibniz may be taken as the type, to which all modern attempts to construct a pluralistic philosophy more or less conform[1]. But the theology on which Leibniz from the outset strove to found his Monadology, is, in the first instance at all events, set aside ; and in particular his famous doctrine of pre-established harmony is rejected altogether. The positions retained are (1) that every monad 'perceives'[2] the others, collectively, at least; (2) that every monad is appetitive, seeking pleasurable situations, or at least shunning painful ones. In other words, for every monad the totality of the remaining monads constitutes its objective world, in which continuously changing situations result through the persistent endeavours of each to conserve or improve its position. Each, so far as in it lies, is to be conceived as 'proving all things and holding fast that which is good.' Finally, every system of thoroughgoing pluralism accepts the Leibnizian principle of continuity, at least to the extent of maintaining that there is no infinite gap, no complete diversity between, one monad and another, a principle against which the Leibnizian theology itself offends. We may now proceed to consider the pluralistic schemes as exhibited in the world we ordinarily call 'historical.'

Let us imagine a great multitude of human beings, varying in tastes and endowments as widely as human beings are known to do, and let us suppose this multitude suddenly to find themselves, as Adam and Eve did, in an ample Paradise enriched sufficiently with diverse natural resources to make the attainment of a high civilisation possible. At the outset each

---

[1] Cf. his *Nouveaux Essais*, IV. § 21, and the excellent summary in Höffding's *History of Philosophy*.

[2] In the Leibnizian sense, that is to say.

must needs fend for himself, selecting the vocation and habitat best adapted to his liking and capacity which chance or his superior competitors left open to him; though liable to be afterwards ousted by others less favoured in their first lot, but more capable of turning their experience to good account. "On all hands adventure and misadventure," so at the outset we might sum up the whole: the chapter of accidents would seem to be the first chapter of this history, and Fortune with her rudder or wheel the only power to be clearly discerned. In other words, to a reflective spectator at this stage nothing would be more impressive than the contrast between the stability of their natural surroundings on the one hand and the instability of this striving multitude on the other. But gradually this contrast would become less striking. The fittest would tend to rise in the struggle and partly to exploit and control, partly to educate the rest. Custom and imitation would more and more determine the behaviour of the less gifted majority, while the inventions and discoveries of the gifted few would tend in the end to improve the condition of all. Cooperation and division of labour would compass results impossible to individual enterprise, and would at the same time entail a more intimate dependence of each one on his fellows. —The ever accumulating traditions and products of the past would afford a steadily improving vantage ground of wisdom and wealth for each succeeding age, and a corresponding security against the vicissitudes of earlier times. In short, in place of an incoherent multitude, all seemingly acting at random, we should have a social and economic organization, every member of which had his appropriate place and function, while the ever increasing coincidence of private ends and public ends would tend continually to enhance the unity of the whole.

Turning to the biological world, and regarding the several species of living forms as so many plastic individuals, we should find at an early stage a similar contrast between the continuity and stability of the physical environment and the mutual isolation and ceaseless variation of an indefinite multitude of more or less elementary organisms. And again we should find this contrast gradually diminish as, *pari passu* with the advance of certain forms of life to a higher level of development, what are known as bionomic adaptations came more and more into play.—The primary forms of life apparently are the so-called prototrophic bacteria, lowly organisms which have the power of working up non-living into living materials. But these have no such direct relation to, or concern with, other living beings as all the higher forms of life have and have to an increasing extent the higher in the scale they stand. It would be tedious to attempt to describe, for example, the wide range of such dependence even in the case of *un*civilised man : the bare enumeration of the many plants and animals indispensable to man in the present state of civilisation would be practically impossible. And all these plants and animals, it must be remembered, depend in turn and in manifold ways on others. Half 'the romance of natural history' lies in such bionomic facts[1]. Think of the many curious adjustments between special plants and special insects on which the very existence of both depends, the plant preparing food for such insects as are fitted to pollinate

[1] Cf. Hesse and Doflein, *Tierbau und Tierleben*, 1914, II. pp. 261 ff.

its flowers.   Or again take the wonderful instances of
mimicry by which animals make shift to evade their
enemies or delude their prey ; or the complicated
division of labour prevailing among certain colonies of
ants and bees ; or, finally, those intimate partnerships
between distinct species to which the name of *symbiosis*
has been given, where in numerous cases the association
is so intimate that the very life of both participants
depends upon it.   Readers of the *Origin of Species*
will recall how Darwin illustrates the wide range of this
correlation of organisms from the connexion of cats
and red clover through the intervention first of mice and
then of bees.   The humble-bees fertilise the clover but
"the number of humble-bees in any district depends
in great measure on the number of field-mice, which
destroy their combs and nests," but again "the number
of mice is largely dependent, as every one knows, on
the number of cats" : and thus the cats by keeping
down the mice promote the increase of the clover.
Similar illustrations might be multiplied indefinitely.
Perhaps the most impressive of all is the great length
of what are called 'nutritive chains'; under which
head we may include the reciprocity that is maintained
between plants and animals.   Plants alone are able to
assimilate inorganic matter : hence in a physiological
sense it is true that 'all flesh is grass,' for the food of
all animals either consists of vegetables or is ultimately
derived from them.   On the other hand plants decompose the carbon dioxide which animals exhale, and thus
restore to the atmosphere the oxygen which animals
need to breathe.   "Some of the fresh-water fishes in
a pond," one naturalist points out, "depend upon the

supply of small crustaceans (copepods, etc.), and these
again [depend] on much minuter organisms (infusorians,
diatoms, etc.), and these again, to some extent, on
the bacteria which cause the putrefaction of the dead
organic matter." Another " has shown that even on the
high seas bacteria are present, playing their usual part
of 'middlemen between death and life' by transforming
dead organic matter into inorganic substances which
can be used again by plants[1]." We may then fairly
allow that there is a close parallel between the development apparent in the economic aspects of human
history and that apparent in the bionomic aspects of
natural history. As in the former so in the latter
we find a multitude of comparatively isolated and
independent units gradually advancing, by the survival
of the fittest among innumerable random variations,
towards the realisation of 'a vast and complex web
of life,' whose myriad fibres are all intertwined, though
every one is unique.

If now, from the external correlations of organisms
to each other, we pass to the internal correlations
within each organism, or from bionomics to what might
possibly be called physionomics, we note again the
same progress from relatively independent parts, barely
conjoined and hardly differentiated, to highly specialised
organs intimately associated together in a single living
whole. 'Loose colonies' of single-celled organisms
are supposed to bridge the gulf between separate unicellular, and individual multi-cellular, organisms; the
transition beginning with diminished competition and increased co-operation among the relatively unspecialised

[1] J. Arthur Thomson, *The Science of Life*, p. 193.

cells of each colony[1]. But the specialisation of function
and consequent individuality to be found at first is very
slight.   The common hydra may be halved with im-
punity so that each segment will restore its missing
half, but we cannot in this fashion make two bees or
two frogs out of a single mature one.   Or again the
hydra may be turned inside out and, unless forcibly
prevented from resuming its natural shape, will eventually right itself and once more become normal.   Obviously no such liberties could be taken with an animal
in which more definite sense-organs, limbs, and viscera
had been developed.   As in bionomics then so in
physionomics : every advance entails greater restriction
and specialisation of function, but also greater perfection
—a more intimate mutual dependence and a closer
consensus of members in a more complicated whole.

Though the facts of bionomics and physionomics
are most readily described as they are presented, that
is to say in objective terms, they are, we may hold, only
to be intelligibly interpreted like the facts of economics
and social interaction ; as implying, that is to say,
percipient and conative subjects behaving as severally
or jointly intent on self-conservation or on betterment.
It is easy throughout to recognise more or less striking
evidence of experiences discriminated, retained, and
turned to account.   But now the problem has to be
faced of interpreting the inanimate world in like fashion.
There we can discern, *prima facie* at all events, no
signs of active striving or selective preference or
progressive organization : there we find no unique

---

[1] Cf. Geddes and Thomson, *The Evolution of Sex*, pp. 57, 88 ff.,
310 ff.

individuals, no competing purposes to be adjusted, no tentative efforts to be followed at length by success. First and last, everywhere and always, there seems to be only fixity and uniformity. This is a serious crux for the pluralist, let us see how he may deal with it.

First it is to be noted that in the historical world the progress and development of some societies, species and individuals halt at a certain point, so that a stationary state is reached in which custom, instinct and habit are supreme. Among societies we find savage peoples still as backward as the primeval men of the stone age, and we find others as advanced as the Chinese, who nevertheless have remained stationary for thousands of years. Again some existing forms of life,—such as the Nautilus or the Lamp-shell—so-called 'persistent types,' have remained practically unaltered almost from the beginning of the geological record, while others—as the horse or the dog, for example—have progressed remarkably within a period that is by comparison recent. And as there are some individuals who are restless, enterprising and inventive to the end of their days, so there are others who early become supine and contented, the slaves of custom and hidebound with habits, individuals whose chief concern is to avoid disturbance and let well alone. The simpler their standard of well-being and the less differentiated their environment the more monotonous their behaviour will be and the more inert they will appear.

Now it is to be noted that the environment, resolved into its ultimate constituents, is by the pluralist assumed to be, as Leibniz taught, substantially the same, for all percipients, consisting, in fact, of the percipients themselves. But the degree and the extent to which clear and distinct perception is reached and retained, in other words the differentiation of the environment for a particular monad, will be proportionate to the organization which it possesses and controls. It is thus not unreasonable to suppose that the gradation found within the known world of life extends indefinitely below it. If then certain of the simplest forms of life that we can detect have persisted throughout the gradual evolution of higher and higher forms; and not merely so but if, further, the existence of such higher forms depends on that of lower, may we not fairly suppose that beyond our ken there are still simpler and more primitive forms capable of existing independently of the lowest that we know, and yet at the same time essential, and therefore prior, to the existence of these? Such an assumption is akin to the bold hypothesis so confidently advanced by Leibniz in a well-known passage of his *Monadology*. "Each portion of matter," he says, "may be conceived as a garden full of plants and as a pond full of fish. But each branch of the plant, each member of the animal, each drop of its juices is also some such garden or pond. And, although the earth and the air separating the plants of the garden or the water separating the fish of the pond, be neither plant nor fish, nevertheless they also contain plants and fish but [these] for the most part too minute to be perceptible by us[1]."

On the important point just mentioned, Leibniz however does not insist. Though the elements, earth, air and water are *essential* to the plants and the plants

[1] *Monadology*, §§ 67, 68.

to the animals, the converse does not hold. Apart from parasitic and symbiotic forms, low-grade organisms do not require the presence of more developed organisms within their environment; and even if these are present, they do not bulk as differentiations of the environment for them, as they do for others higher in the scale. But at every stage the correlation of percipient and environment will still be found ; every order of plants or fish will have their appropriate garden or pond, which over against them is by comparison passive, whilst they over against it are by comparison active. It is this activity, this more or less spontaneous behaviour, that according to Leibniz determines the character of every monad. From the physical standpoint it seems frequently possible to isolate special forms of matter, so that they remain chemically unaltered for an indefinite time. According to Leibniz's view what is done is only on a par with what the biologist might do by isolating a number of *Protista* in a globe of water. Let all the water evaporate and the life of its inhabitants is suspended and perhaps extinguished. That some analogous change would not befall the said substances if all the rest of the universe should disappear, I take it no physicist would venture to say. The pampsychist, holding fast to the principle of continuity, maintains—I again repeat—that at all events there are no things wholly inert, devoid of all internal springs of action, and only mechanically related to each other. In a world of such things motion, that is to say change, would be impossible save through the intervention of a transcendent cause or prime mover. This difficulty, which the physicist allows, is, it is contended, only to be escaped by regarding matter in more or less Leibnizian fashion, as but the manifestation of the interaction of perceptive and appetitive monads or entelechies. The attractions and repulsions of which the physicist speaks only metaphorically are, so the pampsychist maintains, to be taken literally, that is as implying impulses initiated and determined by feeling. Empedocles speculating in the fifth century B.C. is to be hailed as 'the Newton of organic nature,' for his principles of love and hate, Nature's *Wahlverwandtschaften*, or 'elective affinities,' have made the whole world kin[1].

Now, if we are prepared to admit that this pampsychist or monadistic theory is *in itself* at least perfectly conceivable and consistent, of a piece with and analogous to what we know and understand best, then it is contended in the next place that the facts which seem *prima facie* to make against it can be readily and reasonably explained. First of all we can all think of numberless instances in which what is sensibly simple and homogeneous is really extremely complex and heterogeneous. In fact we may fairly say that there is perhaps no case in which—either directly by closer inspection or indirectly by inference—we do not find some difference between objects that seem to be

---

[1] Haeckel, *Die Welträthsel*, 1900, pp. 259, 454. Cf. Renouvier, *Le Personnalisme*, 1903, p. 500. Also Zöllner, *Die Natur der Kometen*, 3te Aufl. pp. 113 ff. "All the work performed by natural beings," says Zöllner, "is determined by feelings of pleasure and pain, and that too in such a manner that the motions within a closed field of phenomena are related as they would be if they were carrying out the unconscious purpose of reducing the painful feelings to a minimum" (p. 119).— A view adopted by biologists, such as Nägeli, and probably Reinke and Driesch, and by philosophers such as Paulsen and Wundt.

qualitatively and quantitatively the same.　There seems then to be ample warrant *a posteriori* for the principle advanced on *a priori* grounds by Nicholas of Cusa and afterwards endorsed by Leibniz.　"There is nothing in the universe," said the former, "that does not enjoy a certain singularity, which is to be found in no other thing[1]."　In his correspondence with Samuel Clarke Leibniz wrote :—"There are no two indiscernible individuals.　A clever gentleman of my acquaintance, talking with me in the presence of Madame the Electress [of Hanover], thought that he could easily find two leaves entirely alike.　The Electress challenged him to do so, and he went up and down a long time seeking in vain.　[Even] two drops of water or of milk looked at through a microscope will be found to be diverse.　This is an argument against atoms, which not less than a vacuum are repugnant to the principles of true metaphysics[2]."

But the modern pluralists do not usually follow out the principle of continuity as rigorously as Leibniz did. They hold with him that "there are never two beings which are perfectly alike and in which it is not possible to find an internal difference[3]."　But they do not usually maintain and indeed from their purely empirical standpoint they could not maintain that there is an actual infinity of monads.　In particular they are in no way bound to assume that there are real beings corresponding to any concepts the physicist may find

---

[1] On Nicolaus Cusanus as a precursor of Leibniz see Latta, *Leibniz, The Monadology, etc.*, 1898, p. *222 n.* and the references there given.

[2] "Quatrième Écrit à Clarke," *Opera*, Erdmann's edition, p. 755.

[3] *Monadology*, § 9.

it convenient to frame regarding the ultimate constituents of matter. Otherwise indeed, should the theory
that matter is but a modification of the ether become
established, that, it might be argued, would put an end
to pluralism altogether, ether being real and not phenomenal. Pluralism in fact, as we have already seen,
has no status at all save as a form of idealism or
spiritualism : for it matter can only be phenomenal, it
cannot be real. The tendency of science is to diminish
the seeming variety of the world and ultimately to
eliminate it. Qualities in the end are to be resolved
into diverse arrangements of prime atoms, corpuscles,
or electrons, differing in nothing but their positions
and motions. For pluralism, on the other hand,
quality, even haecceity—to use an old scholastic phrase
—is vital. If there are real beings answering to the
physicist's concept of ultimate atoms then indeed, if
personal pluralism is to stand (I use the word 'personal'
in the widest possible extent), this atomic pluralism can
only be the outside appearance of so many active
beings, each of which is something for itself. But all
that the pluralist does is to appeal broadly to the
principle of continuity and that, said Leibniz, "destroys
atoms." In the real world we can nowhere find that
exact similarity which the mathematician can readily
conceive ; and the contention is that it nowhere exists.
Appearances suggest it, it may be. But that leads us
to a second point.

There are statistical facts in plenty to show that,
where large numbers are concerned, the conduct even
of human beings presents aggregate results that are
tolerably constant, in spite of the variety of the motives

determining the individual agents and the absence of any concerted action among them. Now many of the constants of science are of the nature of statistical averages, and involve—as science interprets them—numbers enormously in excess of those of social statistics, while at the same time the individuals concerned must be indefinitely simpler. Starting from the statistics available in economics, the most scientific branch of sociology, and supposing that instead of trade returns from a score or two of countries we had returns from one or two thousand, the inhabitants of each being increased a myriad-fold and being also severally vastly more the creatures of habit than men now are, we can imagine such statistics would approximate still more closely to those of the physicist. The physicist, like the statist, is always dealing with aggregates, but unlike the statist he finds the constituent individuals to be beyond his ken. The statist is aware that individual variations underlie his aggregates, but they do not interest him : the physicist is ignorant of those underlying his, and assumes that they do not exist[1]. Accordingly he rests content with abstract and general concepts that turn out in the end to be simply quantitative. But it is impossible to deduce quality from quantity or exhaustively to present concrete experience by means of any scheme of mathematical co-ordinates.

Briefly then the pluralist at this juncture insists upon three points :—(1) In the case of living agents the appearance of constancy and regularity is compatible

---

[1] On the features common to Nature and History, cf. *Les Lois de l'Imitation*, by the late G. Tarde, 3me edn, 1900, ch. 1.

with individual variation and innovation : (2) the fixity
and regularity, which the physicist ascertains, avowedly
pertain only to matter as devoid of individuality—to
the *materia secunda*, which Leibniz referred to as mere
aggregation ; (3) some adequate ground for this appearance there must be. It is reasonable to assume, the
pluralist then concludes, that this ground is analogous to
that which we know to underlie the law and order of
the historical world. Regarding this last point we ought
to notice, in passing, that a two-fold interpretation is
possible, the pluralist's is one possibility, the theist
may prefer another. The mutual relation and the
possible conciliation of these two views is a problem
that still lies before us. Just now it is only important
to observe that 'the theistic hypothesis' affords *prima
facie* a more satisfactory explanation of Nature's laws
—which, Laplace notwithstanding, are not self-explanatory—than pluralism at first sight seems to do.
For we should expect the acts of a Supreme Being to
show a more exact uniformity than the conjoint results
of the actions of myriads of lowly monads severally
and half unconsciously striving after mutual adjustment. We here come upon an aspect of pluralism,
which—though referred to in the foregoing exposition
—it will be well to consider in more detail and apart.

Purposive action, it is commonly held, presupposes
an established order, a reign of law, presupposes in fact
that exact uniformity which naturalism formulates in
mechanical terms. This is the physical basis which is
supposed to furnish teleology with its indispensable
πoῦ στῶ. But pluralism attempts to get behind all
this. No doubt a man deliberating how to compass

some definite end, on which he has decided, may think
out a chain of practical syllogisms in the way long ago
described by Aristotle; beginning with the last term
in the causal series he works backwards till he reaches
the first, some act that is which he is in a position
immediately to perform[1]. But the practical syllogism,
'acting on principle' as we say, is an ideal; we do
not always act—above all, we do not begin acting—in
this fashion. The earliest activity is apparently altogether impulsive, determined not by desire for future
satisfaction but by aversion to a present ill. The stimulus
of pain, as a veritable goad, leads to random efforts
for relief. And relief, if it comes at all, may come in
either of two ways. The situation may itself change
for the better, or at length a fitting attitude or movement may be hit upon. In the former case the result
might be attributed to pure chance: if the situation
should recur the sufferer will be practically as ignorant
and as helpless as before. But in reality all changes
in the environment will be the result of conative impulses somewhere; and from such of these as succeed,
the agents, if we credit them with any retentiveness,
learn something. A successful adjustment concurring
with the release from pain will be specially impressive.
In this way the evil and the remedy will be so far
associated that on each repetition of the former the
many tentative movements will become less, and the
one effective movement more, pronounced, till at length
it becomes an immediate, habitual, and eventually even
a mechanical response.

But this gradual development of purposive activity

---

[1] *Nicomachean Ethics*, iii. iii.

is mere psychological detail, upon which it is not necessary to enlarge here. True, it will be said, but all such development presupposes 'the orderliness of things,' and pluralism, we understand, undertakes to explain how this orderliness has itself been developed. Order is heaven's first law, we say, but pluralism essays to get back of all this and to start from chaos, where we can count on no repetitions and therefore on no progress. This is unquestionably a formidable objection, and what we shall have in the next lecture to consider is how the pluralists may attempt to meet it.

LECTURE IV.

THE CONTINGENCY IN THE WORLD.

We left Pluralism charged with the hopeless attempt of bringing order out of chaos. But the notion of chaos is after all altogether a myth: as much a bugbear as a chimaera. "No one," says Lotze, "who means to think clearly can form any idea of the existence of such an infinite agglomeration of countless possibilities.... [Such an] abyss of indefiniteness is unthinkable, and any attempt to set distinctly before ourselves the origin of natural forms must start from some definite primitive state, which—because it was this and no other—from the very first excluded from actuality much in itself possible, while of much else on the other hand it contained not merely the bare possibility but a more or less immediate and urgent positive ground for its realisation[1]." It is precisely such a definite primitive state that pluralism postulates, a totality of unique individuals each bent on self-preservation. But self here, we must remember, implies, not as in atomistic pluralism, a simple, unchangeable element that *ex hypothesi* must be conserved, though it does nothing and suffers nothing. What is here implied is a true self, whose

[1] *Microcosmus*, Bk IV. Ch. II., Eng. trans. Vol. I. p. 432.

feeling and action vary with, though they are not exclusively determined by, its situation relatively to the
rest. Such a definite situation will, as Lotze points out,
then and there exclude certain possibilities and lead
on immediately to the realisation of others. The
mechanical theory too must postulate a primitive collocation of atoms which its laws can never explain;
but, these atoms being unalterable, the laws that formulate their successive changes of position are regarded as also determinate and fixed. The individuals
of spiritualistic pluralism, on the other hand, are held
to be plastic and capable of development; and the
new relations that become established among them
are therefore regarded as the direct consequences of
such development. At the start then the order that
is to be has still to become : everything is inchoate,
but nothing chaotic, unless inexperience and innocence
are the same as anarchy and original sin.

The pluralists, we must remember, take all their
bearings from the historical standpoint and endeavour
to work backwards from the facts of human personality
and social intercourse. Their mode of thought is
frankly, though not crudely, anthropomorphic : hence
such titles as Personalism, Personal Idealism,
Humanism and the like, which one or other has
adopted. Now in this personal domain, whether
individual or social, we find orderliness and regularity
in plenty. From this orderliness and regularity we
may derive premisses, at once general and definite,
for practical syllogisms : it affords an ample basis of
reliable means for the realisation of the most varied
ends, and it makes education and further experience

always possible. But the whole of such development is the result of the conduct or the behaviour, severally or collectively, of the persons concerned : none of it existed previously as the presupposition of such behaviour. Other forms of order and regularity—we may call them lower forms—no doubt there were, but not these. Of such lower forms we may say that they were indispensable conditions of the higher forms that followed—indispensable conditions indeed, but not sufficient. The future is grounded on the past, it may be, but we cannot in history, as in science, infer the one from the other : we cannot anticipate the super-structure from a knowledge of the foundations, or prophesy whenever we can remember. Looking back then on the career of an individual or on the progress of a community we may distinguish, at any given point, on the one side the habits, tastes and dexterities already acquired or the customs, institutions and polity already established, and on the other the new and often unexpected development that followed upon these.

We may express the relation between the two by adopting—and adapting—the old scholastic distinction of *natura naturata* and *natura naturans*. What is done forecloses some old possibilities and opens up new ones : Vulcan, who had spent his youth at the forge, could hardly hope to charm Olympus with Apollo's lyre, though he made a suit of armour worthy of the god of war : the Semites worsted in their struggles with Rome could no longer aspire to the supremacy of the world ; though, scattered everywhere and yet united, they still remain its masters in finance. What is done, *natura naturata*—the decisions made, the habits formed, the customs fixed—constitutes at any stage the routine, the general trend of things, within which future possibilities lie. What is still to do, *natura naturans*, implies further spontaneity and growth ; new decisions to be taken, fresh experiments to be made, with their usual sequel of trial and error and possible eventual success ; happy thoughts or inspirations occurring to the individual ; and the rise of great men inaugurating new epochs for their race or for the world. Even Bacon, who was certainly sufficiently impressed by the supremacy of law, we find saying : *Super datum corpus novam naturam, sive novas naturas generare et superinducere, opus et intentio est humanae potentiae*[1]. How little this generating of new natures is to be regarded as the inevitable consequence of the antecedent routine is shown by the myths which attributed the earliest arts to the intervention of gods and heroes, Triptolemus, Prometheus, Athene, Apollo.

If now we were to contemplate an individual's career or a nation's progress at a later stage the same distinction could still be made, only that the line dividing the lifeless routine from the 'increasing purpose' would be drawn at a new point. The painful efforts and strange experiences of the past are now replaced by such masterly facility and perfect familiarity as can serve as 'stepping-stones to higher things'; the reforms and liberties, so hardly achieved, are now

---

[1] *Novum Organum*, Vol. II. I.   Kitchin's edn, p. 132.   On this whole topic see the brilliant article, 'Great Men and their Environment,' by that thorough-going pluralist, W. James, *The Will to believe*, pp. 216 ff.

unquestioned, and so open up possibilities of nobler
modes of life, with sweeter manners, purer laws.'   If,
on the other hand, we contemplate things at an earlier
stage than that with which we began, the converse will
hold.   What we then found consolidated into habit or
custom, as so much fixed routine, would still be fluent ·
and so to say adolescent ; alternatives then finally
determined would still be pending ; and much that
later will be commonplace, still a marvel beyond the
range of present surmise.   Now this characteristic of
the historical world the pluralist boldly generalises to
the utmost.   " All nature," to repeat a summary I have
made elsewhere, "is regarded as plastic and evolving
like mind : its routine and uniformity being explained
on the analogy of habit and heredity in the individual,
of custom and tradition in society ; while its variety is
attributed to spontaneity in some form[1]."   " The
one intelligible theory of the universe," a prominent
pluralist tells us, "is that of objective [i.e., I take it,
personal] idealism, that matter is effete mind, inveterate
habits becoming physical laws[2]."   Evidence of such
mechanization—that is, of what originally was spontaneous and tentative becoming eventually automatic
and regular—is forthcoming up to the very verge
of our knowledge of whatever can be regarded as
individual and unique at all.   But though individuals
other than conceptual ones are beyond the physicist's
ken, evidence has long been accumulating even here

---

[1] 'Mechanism and Morals.' Adamson Lecture, *Hibbert Journal*,
1905, p. 92.

[2] C. S. Peirce, 'The Architectonic of Theories,' *Monist*, Vol. i.
1890, p. 170. A similar expression used by Schelling. Cf. below, p. 143.

to strengthen the analogy between inorganic and organic evolution regarded *en bloc*[1].

It will be helpful at this point to recall a distinction too often ignored or confused in current expositions of causation—the distinction between efficient cause and occasional cause. The former leads us to say : Every event has a cause, an efficient cause, the latter finds its meaning in the generalisation : The same (occasional) cause is followed invariably by the same effect. Here in fact the notion of cause is transformed into that of law, for it is only on the ground of such regular recurrence that causal connexion is affirmed. Causal efficiency on the other hand is at once assured for us on a single occurrence, if that be our own act ; and though the occasion recur never so often, the act need never be repeated. With inanimate objects the occasion inevitably determines the result : this is the meaning of law. Hence, as Kant in substance put it, life is the death of all natural philosophy, for "life means the capacity to act or change according to an internal principle," means, that is to say, the presence of an efficient cause[2]. Now "chance," we are told, "is opposed to law in this sense, viz. that what happens according to law may be predicted and counted on[3]" : in the same sense the conduct of living beings, i.e. historical events, are opposed to law. Thus what one person might regard as due to chance may be really due to the act of another.

According to the pluralistic *Weltanschauung* then there are no laws antecedent to the active individuals

---

[1] Cf. e.g. Sir Norman Lockyer's *Inorganic Evolution*, 1900, Bk v.
[2] Cf. *Naturalism and Agnosticism*, 3rd edn, I. p. 177; 4th edn, p. 173.
[3] Fleming, *Vocabulary of Philosophy*.

who compose the world, no laws determining *them*, unless we call their own nature a law; and then indeed the world would start with as many laws as there are individuals[1]. Such a view of course involves throughout an element of contingency such as we find in all personal affairs[2]. Some pluralists, very ill-advisedly as I think, have identified this element with pure chance and even proposed to elevate it to the place of a guiding principle under the title of 'tychism,'—τύχη κυβερνᾷ πάντα. But every act of a conative agent is determined by—what may, in a wide sense, be called—a motive, and motivation is incompatible with chance, though in the concrete it be not reducible to law.

Possibly the objection will still be pressed that if, as all psychology teaches, the recurrence of like situations is essential to any advance in experience, it is difficult to see how without a previously established 'reign of law' experience could ever begin. In point of fact, even as things are now, with all the so-called laws of nature in full force, unless the range of an experient's distinguishable percepts and interests were restricted there could be no possibility of its advance in experience. We must postulate what I have called subjective selection, in other words we must assume that many of the changes that take place around it are for a given subject severally imperceptible and that to many that are perceptible it is entirely indifferent. Without such restriction the progress of science itself would be impossible. Thus, so far as our observations and means of measurement are concerned, the solar

---

[1] Cf. Lotze, *Metaphysic*, § 32.
[2] Cf. Supplementary Note I.

system is an isolated system : actually of course its motions are affected by those of all other stellar systems. But if the early astronomers had had to take these into account the complexity would have been beyond human powers to unravel. As it is, it has been remarked that if all the perturbations of the planets now known had been known to Kepler he could never have discovered the form of their orbits : as it was the problem proved one of colossal proportions and occupied him during ten years.

But from the pluralist standpoint the term imperceptible is not accurate: the whole universe is perceived by every percipient. But such perception may be confused, as Leibniz used to say, or undifferentiated to an indefinite extent. The presence of this indefinite background of confused or undifferentiated objects, though it is not attended to and determines no special response, is still of vital importance : for example, we do not feel the pressure of the atmosphere, yet its absence would be fatal. The development of experience however depends entirely on differentiated presentations and these in turn are commensurate to the position already attained. The shoeblack stationed by the Royal Exchange will welcome a muddy day, but is unperturbed by the fluctuations of the market; the *amoeba*, confined to a drop of stagnant water, has only to do with the tiny fragments that float within it, and need not bewilder itself about the weather forecast. So too the atom, if it be real at all, that is, anything for itself, has only to mind its partners in the dance and avoid collisions : as far as it is concerned, the continuity of things reduces all beyond its infinitesimally narrow field to a permanent background for it devoid of change : mechanically expressed, all its action is so-called contact action.

To resume then, the purposive act or deliberate intention of one agent may for the experience of a second be a mere happening or accident. It may befall contrary to all that the latter regarded as possible and independently of all his aims ; but it still remains the outcome of another's purpose, is neither causeless nor aimless. Though contingent to others it was not in itself a case either of chance or necessity[1]. But as bearing on the objection that we have been considering, there are two or three characteristics of a pluralistic world, a world partly fixed and partly fluent, partly *naturata*, partly *naturans*, which it may be well to emphasize as consequences of the contingency that such a world entails.

First, since for pluralism there are no natural laws so to say 'in force' from the beginning, but on the contrary all natural laws are evolved, there will be no rigorous and mechanical concatenation of things such as naturalism is wont to assume : the fixity, so far as it is real, will embody the result of experience ; so far as it is apparent, it will be due, as we have seen, to the statistical constancy of large numbers. But, again, in a world consisting of finite individuals no single individual and no community of such can foresee all the consequences of what they do : over and above what was intended much will result that was not intended. While chipping his flint instruments or polishing his weapons of wood the savage, it is supposed, may incidentally have generated the sparks or heat which he sooner or later turned to account for the

---

[1] Cf. Lectt. XIII. and XIV.

production of fire.   When certain Phoenician sailors
kindled a fire on the seashore, their sole purpose was
to cook their food, but among the dead embers they
presently discovered a mass of molten glass produced
by the fusion of the potashes and the sand; and so a
useful art arose.   When primitive men scratched rude
pictures on mammoth tusks they did not foresee the
passage of pictures into hieroglyphs or ideograms and
of these into phonograms or an alphabet.   Again, no
one deliberately excogitated such institutions as human
language, courts of justice or constitutional government.   Each step in the progress made realised some
unexpected advantage and made a new step possible;
but the progress as a whole involved no such practical
syllogism as the old theories of convention and contract
naïvely assumed.   The literal meaning of such words
as 'discovery' and 'invention' bears unmistakeable
testimony to the truth of this.   Such 'heterogony of
ends,' as Wundt has called it[1], the objective realisation
of adaptations that were never subjectively intended,
must have played a yet more conspicuous part in the
earliest phases of evolution.   As the result of what are
aptly called blind impulses, whether due to positive
pain or to mere restlessness, the successful individual
or race gradually raises itself in the scale of life,
shows a 'tendency to progression,' function perfecting
structure, though the end attained may never be foreseen.   As I have said elsewhere and anticipating
Wundt: "The tendency at any one moment is simply

---

[1] *System der Philosophie*, 1889, S. 337.   But the whole idea is
clearly formulated by Hegel: cf. his *Philosophie der Geschichte*, 1837,
S. 30.

towards more life, simply growth ; but this process of self-preservation imperceptibly but steadily modifies the self that is preserved.   The creature is bent only on filling its skin ; but in doing this as pleasantly as may be, it gets a better skin to fill, and accordingly seeks to fill it differently.   All that is required is that to advance to a higher level of life shall on the whole be more pleasurable or less painful than to remain behind.   Now this condition seems provided, without any need for a clear prevision of ends or any feeling after improvement or perfection as such, simply by the waning of familiar pleasures and by the zest of novelty[1]."

Since, as I have said, the pluralistic view of the world necessarily involves an element of contingency in its very idea of a finite Many mutually striving for the best *modus vivendi,* it must be allowed that the actual presence—*prima facie* at least—of such contingency in the world of our experience is so far an argument for the pluralist's position : absolutism leaves no place for this contingency.   Some amplification of this point seems then to be relevant and in order.   In the first place an instructive analogy may be drawn between the diversity in tools, weapons, and processes,

[1] *Psychological Principles,* 1918, p. 258 ; *Nat. and Agn.,* 4th edn, 1915, p. 293. However the Lamarckians and Darwinians may settle their differences, it is agreed on all hands that there are at any rate no really fortuitous variations or mutations. The pluralist, of course, holds that the ultimate explanation is to be found only in the conative impulses of sentient individuals. It is worth noting by the way that even Weismann at length so far agrees with this as to admit that "the direction of the variation of a part must be determined by its utility," cf. his article, 'Germinal Selection,' *Monist,* 1896, p. 267.

which different races of primitive men have devised for the same purpose, and the diversity in the natural adaptations, instincts or contrivances by which in different animals or plants the same functions are discharged. Thus among men centrifugal force is turned to account by some races who make slings, while others avail themselves of it in their use of the bolas or the lasso. Some shoot with bows, others with blow-guns, while yet others mainly use javelins, throwing-sticks or boomerangs. Canoes are made in various parts of the world from hollowed tree-trunks, from twigs and bark, from skins stretched over whale-bone, from a wooden framework covered with matting or with reeds, and in yet other ways. Exhilarating drinks are obtained in some cases by fermenting fruits —grapes, apples, dates—in others by fermenting grains, such as wheat, barley, rice; or again by fermenting honey or milk. And doubtless in the great majority of these instances the discovery or invention was the result of a combination of happy accident and happy thought rather than of deliberate design and fore-thought. But what we have specially to observe is the *identity* of the need and the *diversity* of the materials which in different cases are turned to account to meet it. The collocation of the two can only be regarded as contingent.

And the like holds good in numberless instances in the animal and vegetable kingdoms. Thus the bird owes its power of flight to those enormously developed scales with frayed edges, which we call feathers, that are attached to its hands and fore-arm. In the bat this apparatus is replaced by a stretched membrane

extending between vastly elongated fingers and fring-
ing the sides of its body.   In insects again the so-
called wings are only *physiologically* limbs : morpho-
logically they are but flattened folds of the integument,
so to say extemporized wings.   In the courting season
some animals attract one another by sounds that are
variously produced in different species—by voice, as
with frogs and song-birds, by stridulation, as with
crickets and the cicada, or by tapping on foreign substances, as with certain wood-peckers and the death-
watch ; some attract by their brilliant coloration, as in
certain apes and the peacock, or by phosphorescence,
as with the glow-worm ; and others by the production
of peculiar odours, as with the musk-rat and deer.
Some escape their enemies by the celerity of their
movements, others by death-like stillness ; some by
conspicuous coloration and a nauseous taste, others by
sombre hues resembling their inanimate surroundings ;
some by fetid exhalations, others by spines or a hard
encasement.   Plants in some cases trust to the wind
—as we aptly say—to disseminate their seeds, which
are provided with vanes or fluffy plumes, or are of
dust-like minuteness ; the seeds of others attach themselves by hooks or grapnels to the fur of passing
quadrupeds ; while those of others are violently pro-
jected by variously contrived springs.   Some again
pass through animals who have eaten their pulpy
envelopes, while others encased in a hard shell float
away on the water[1].

To suppose that all this variety should have been
directly created for variety's sake, 'almost like toys

---

[1] These and abundant like instances will be found more fully
described by Darwin, *Origin of Species*, Ch. VI. *et passim.*

in a shop, to use Darwin's phrase, is indeed, as he
urges, an 'incredible view,' as incredible as the view
would be that the similar variety we find in human contrivances was itself supernaturally preordained instead
of being the contingent result of differently situated
individuals having to work with different materials to
arrive at the same end. To make this analogy
clear it may suffice to consider the instance just now
mentioned, that of flight. The feathers of the bird
are homologous to, i.e. genetically connected with, the
lizard's scales : the subsequent modification of those
attached to the wings and tail so as to subserve flight
has no connexion with the original function of feathers
as a dermal covering, which remains their sole function
for the most part. It is just to the coincidence of
their special plasticity with the new conditions of
nascent bird life that their development is to be
attributed. Bats are scientifically called *Cheiroptera*
or hand-winged, but the fore limb in the adjacent
order, the *Insectivora*, is primarily adapted to running
or climbing, and again is modified in the moles, in
a direction the precise opposite to that of flight,
viz. burrowing. But the family of the *Insectivora*
nearest akin to the bats, consisting of the single genus,
Galeopithecus, and some of the rodents, the order next
adjacent, "are assisted in jumping by a kind of para-
chute, which consists of a cutaneous expansion, the
patagium, stretched between the limbs on each side[1]."
The bat's flight is but a development of this habit.
To secure this result the one means available was the
elongation of the fingers of the hand as a frame-

[1] Sedgwick, *A Student's Text-book of Zoology*, Vol. II. p. 642.

work for the greatly extended *patagium* or elastic
membrane, the original function of the hand being
sacrificed almost entirely.   The origin of the insect's
wings is, I understand, still something of a problem.
Professor J. A. Thomson writes about them :—" It
seems plausible to compare them to the tracheal outgrowths seen in some aquatic larvae, and to regard
them as primarily respiratory, and secondarily loco-
motor.   One may venture to suggest that the additional
respiratory efficiency derived from such outgrowths
would increase the total activity of the insect, and
more or less directly lift it into the air[1]."   And so,
mutatis mutandis, other instances of biological development may be explained.

"It certainly is true," as Darwin has said, "that new
organs appearing as if created for some special purpose, rarely or never appear in any being[2]."   Imagine
that a clock had been the first machine invented by
men and that all other machines had to be modelled
on this type.   As it is, mechanisms for very different
purposes *are* formed on this type, and human efforts, if
necessarily restricted to it, would doubtless in time
gradually devise many more by means of modifications
analogous to those which Nature displays in adapting
a given type of structure to very various conditions of
life.   Or again if we imagine that instead of a clock
some other machine, say a loom, had been that from
which the start was made, all subsequent machines
being modelled on that.   Many varieties of this form
of mechanism too already exist, and it is not too much
to assume that if necessary it could be indefinitely

[1] *Chambers's Encyclopaedia*, Vol. VI. p. 167.
[2] *Origin of Species*, 6th edn, p. 156.

varied. Such is in fact the picture that the organic world presents to us. As Darwin puts it: "All organic beings have been formed on two great laws —Unity of Type, and the Conditions of Life. By unity of type is meant that fundamental agreement in structure which we see in organic beings of the same class, and which is quite independent of their habits of life[1]." Let us consider for a moment two such types—say the arthropod and the vertebrate. Widely as these two types differ we find some species of each adapted to every condition of life in every variety of climate and locality, mountain heights or subterranean caves, the surface of the earth or the depths of the sea. We find creatures of each type flying, swimming, diving, or burrowing, active by night or by day, some sociable, some solitary, some preying upon specific living animals, others feeding more or less indiscriminately on the corpses of the dead; or vegetable feeders, some confined to specific plants, others to particular parts or tissues, and so on; for an exhaustive specification of the conditions of life to which these two types are alike adapted is impossible. Even when we take one of the leading modifications of each type—insects and birds, for example—the range of conditions is but slightly restricted.

A collateral consequence of this adaptation of a fixed type to various conditions of life is perhaps worth notice in passing. I refer to the awkward and grotesque, even the ludicrous and hideous forms of some plants and animals. The graceful shape and agile movements of the horse, the gazelle, the squirrel,

[1] *Op. cit.*, p. 166.

for instance, have been universally admired. Compared with them such creatures as the camel, the sloth and the wart-hog have been reckoned among Nature's abortions. But among less familiar animals there are many more ungainly or ill-favoured than these, as such scientific names as *Diabolus ursinus, Moloch horridus, Chimaera monstrosa,* suggest. These seeming anomalies did not escape the notice of the earlier naturalists. Buffon, for example, after the manner of Leibniz, imagines Nature setting before herself all possible forms and selecting first of all the most beautiful and harmonious, but "into the midst of this magnificent spectacle," he tells us, "some unfinished (*negligées*) products and some less happy forms, thrown like the shadows in a picture, appear to be the remnants of those ill-assorted designs and those disparate compositions which she has only allowed to remain in order to give us a more extended idea of her projects[1]." Theologians too have been exercised by these blemishes which seem everywhere to obtrude themselves, marring the beauty and detracting from the perfection of Nature. After an enumeration of a whole string of these 'veritably hellish shapes,' as they have been called—toadstools, thorn-apples, scorpions, rattlesnakes, &c. &c.—it has been asked:—"Can such an appalling, Callotesque fancy be attributed to God: can he be held capable of creating the ugly[2]?" The true cause of such

[1] *Histoire naturelle; Des Oiseaux,* t. VIII. 1781, à propos of the Stilt (*Himantopus candidus*). ~~Transfiguration~~

[2] Cf. Rosenkranz, 'Die Verklärung der Natur,' B. Bauer's *Zeitsch. f. spekulative Theologie,* II. 1837, p. 262.

deformities certain theologians have preferred to find in man's alienation from God and the consequent reaction upon nature, of which he was the crown and keystone, that his fall entailed. Whatever may be thought of their explanation of the fact of Nature's aesthetic defects, the recognition of the fact itself by such thinkers is noteworthy.

But the contingency in the world presents itself in a still more striking light when we follow out the consequences of the pluralist theory of the world. According to that, as we have seen, the world consists solely of finite individuals primarily dominated by private ends and for whom self-preservation is the first law of life. Each species develops for itself and never directly either for the advantage or the detriment of others; though such incidental consequences to one species may arise continually from the development of another, as we have already seen. In fact, evolution in large measure consists in adaptations to meet these consequences, so as to avoid or counteract as far as possible those that are harmful and as far as possible to avail of, or cooperate with, the rest. But such processes in the main and for long—so long, that is, as they are natural processes—are purely egoistic, not altruistic. Moreover the apostolic saying, God is no respecter of persons, turns out to be true of Nature in a way which seems entirely to disprove the cardinal maxim of the old natural theology that all the lower creatures exist for the sake of man. Man is undoubtedly 'the paragon of animals,' the highest link in a vast chain, but it is a chain in which one and the same right to live belongs to all. I recall a revolting sight that I saw in my youth, which rudely shocked my preconceived notions of the fitness of things. That man should slay and eat creatures lower in the scale than himself, that the song-thrush should feed on worms and snails or the gorgeously tinted kingfisher dart into the thick of a shoal of silly minnows to secure food for himself and his brood—all this seemed reasonable enough; for here the lower subserved the higher. But once I chanced to see three young rabbits playfully gambolling, heedless of a cold clammy snake who stealthily glided forward, and struck first one and then another till after a few momentary convulsions all lay stretched and dead; whereupon the sluggish reptile, without the faintest show of emotion, pleasurable or otherwise, proceeded slowly to suck down one after another these pets of my childhood—then indeed I felt that the world so far was neither well nor wisely nor beautifully ordered. Such an incident, however individually impressive, is, of course, utterly trivial compared with the terrible ravages, formerly regarded as the scourges of an offended deity, which we now know are wrought by the lowest forms of life with which we have any exact acquaintance, whereby not only our flocks and fields are continually devastated but millions of our fellow-men are painfully swept away. It is not however the physical evil, the dysteleology of all this that is now in point, but simply the fact that there is no necessary connexion between worth of life as we estimate it and fitness to survive in the evolutionist sense. In the physical struggle for existence worth does not count: distinguished men like Raphael, Howard, Keats and Hegel succumbed to microscopic bacilli, and it **is** conceivable that the whole human race might thus ignobly disappear. Such anomalies seem even *a priori* to be an obvious, almost an inevitable outcome of pluralism, and though perhaps not insuperable, still as far as they go, they are an argument in favour of the pluralist's and a difficulty for the theist's position.

But further the contingency in the world in general seems to involve that the existence of mankind at all is itself but a special contingency. In the case of other living kinds few persons would hesitate to admit this. According to the psalmist indeed God "causeth the grass to grow for the cattle...the high mountains are for the wild goats, the rocks are a refuge for the conies." But what is at all events immediately evident is rather the pluralist position, that these creatures are adapted to their conditions of life, not their conditions of life to them. The existence of grass does not depend on that of the cattle or goats or conies that browse upon it[1], but contrariwise these creatures are variously modified to derive their sustenance from the grass, according as it is found on plains, on crags or in hollows. Similarly it is argued that trees came into existence and continue to exist independently of the birds that there make their nests or of the various other creatures that live among their branches. So had there been no forests there could have been no apes, but the existence of forests is due primarily to the conditions of vegetable life and not to the needs of animals. Assuming man's simian ancestry—and assuredly, as Darwin has said, "if man had not been

---

[1] Cf. Lect. III. p. 62.

× Yes: but per contra this makes the phrase
" survival of the fittest " meaningless
or rather, without content "

his own classifier, he would never have thought of founding a separate order for his own reception"— then the mode of life of those climbing, chattering, inquisitive denizens of the woods gradually led up to his wonderful hand and erect posture, his power of speech and capacity for knowledge.   First the presence of trees made the *Quadrumana* or four-handed primates possible, and then the advance of the higher forms among these beyond the confines of the forest ushered in the two-handed primates or *Bimana* with their bipedal mode of progression.   Some fragments of one of the latest of the 'missing links' in this chain were said to have been discovered about ten years ago among some volcanic ash in the island of Java, the so-called *Pithecanthropus erectus*, and Professor Haeckel had previously thought it becoming to entertain his scientific readers with a fanciful picture of the family group under the title *Pithecanthropus alalus*.

No doubt it is the psychological gulf rather than any biological gap between the speechless man-apes and *Homo sapiens* that is most impressive : it is not the physical difference but the mental difference that is so profound.   This glaring psychological discontinuity between man and brute, as we know them, has led thinkers of every age and school to regard the origin of mankind and even of every individual man as something more or less supernatural, not wholly explicable by the ordinary processes that suffice to explain the nature and development of the lower animals.   In the Mosaic account of creation, "God said, Let us make man in our image, after our likeness" : here this difference is distinctly recognised.

It was this difference again that led Aristotle to regard the rational principle common to all men as not conjoined like sense and phantasy with bodily organs, not naturally generated like these, but as wholly separable from the body and divinely infused from without after the commencement of the bodily life. It was this difference that checked Descartes too from applying to man his famous automaton theory, which seemed to him adequate to explain the behaviour of brutes : in man alone he was constrained to allow that a soul is united with the animal machine. Even Leibniz, regardless of his cardinal principle of continuity, was driven to admit a difference in kind between the souls of animals and the spirits of men, a difference so great that he compares the relation of God to the animals with that of an inventor to his machine, but God's relation to men he compares to that of a prince to his subjects or a father to his children. At the moment of birth he supposed that God gave reason to each soul "by a special act or by a kind of transcreation[1].' Finally—to take one more example specially interesting in connexion with our present topic—we have Mr Wallace, whose name is so honourably associated with Darwin's, firmly maintaining that the theory of natural selection, which they independently promulgated, is insufficient to account for the development of man. As the existence of the poodle or the pouter pigeon is due to man's interference with the working of natural selection so, Mr Wallace assumes, the existence of man is to be attributed to a similar inter-

---

[1] *Théodicée*, § 91.

ference of some superior or supreme intelligence. In
short, as one of his ablest critics concisely puts it,
Mr Wallace's view amounts to saying that "our brains
are made by God and our lungs by natural selection"
and that, in point of fact, "man is God's domestic
animal[1]." Still this is something of a parody, and it
cannot be denied that Mr Wallace's hypothesis is a
perfectly legitimate one. But is it necessary?

In common with the other supernatural explanations
of man as rational animal, that of Mr Wallace recognises
the presence of the two factors which rationality and
animality imply; but all alike entirely refrain from
inquiring whether sociology may not account for the
one at least as completely as biology accounts for the
other. Reason is not correlated to an organ in the
way that sight and locomotion are: so far Aristotle
was right; it comes from without and is not generated.
Had the most transcendent genius been left to grow
up wild in the woods he would certainly never have
attained to reason On the other hand no biologist
would pretend to find in difference of organization the
equivalent of the vast interval between the genius and
the savage. The difference then between *Homo
alalus* and *Homo sapiens* is not a biological difference:
in short for biology there is no such species as *Homo
sapiens*. This is now generally allowed. But then so
far there is no case against the contingency of man's
origin biologically considered: not his lungs only but
his brain also or rather his entire frame may be regarded as equally the outcome of a pluralistic evolution.

[1] Cf. Wallace, *Natural Selection*, 1891, p. 205 n.

Let us now consider the sociological side. Cut off from society entirely the individual, we have seen, never attains to sapience at all; also the more advanced the social medium in which he lives the more advanced on the average his intelligence and humanity. Society of course presupposes language as the instrument of communicating and accumulating knowledge : without it a tribe of men would be no better than a pack of wolves or a herd of deer. But there are few nowadays who imagine that speech was directly imparted to our first parents by some supernatural instructor just as it was afterwards taught by them to their children. Though we have no precise knowledge concerning its original acquisition we know enough to be satisfied that it developed gradually out of cries and gestures. For curiosity, imitativeness and excitability even the existing primates exceed all other animals except man. As regards the sociological side of man's origin then—the advance from animality to rational personality through inter-subjective intercourse—there is, it must be confessed, *prima facie*, neither any definite evidence of, nor any absolute need for, supernatural interference. The progress of knowledge and co-operation shows, so long as we can trace it, the same contingency, the same 'heterogony of ends' that characterize biological development.

But if the existence of particular species, mankind included, can be regarded as *prima facie* contingent, still more obviously will contingency pertain to the existence of particular individuals, the great men who have often seemed to direct the course of human history also included. There is no need for detailed illustration here, but it is worth notice that this contingency is threefold; in respect, viz. of the individual's parentage, his nativity, and his survival to maturity. Those who breed and rear our domestic plants and animals take special pains to direct and control these circumstances, replacing nature's contingency by ideals of their own; and daring innovators like Plato and the late Sir Francis Galton have even proposed to apply the same 'eugenic' methods to the human race. Of "Eugenics," Galton recently said that it "dealt with what was more valuable than money or lands, namely, with natural inheritance of high character, capable brains, fine physique and vigour...It aimed at the evolution and preservation of high races and it well deserved to be strictly enforced[1]." Compared with those practices and this possibility it would, I believe, be hard to think of anything that sets the seeming contingency in the world in a more striking light. But history suggests endless similar reflexions, all trite enough to be sure yet none the less true. Had Letitia Ramolino not been so beautiful, some one has said, there would have been no Napoleon Bonaparte. The infant Isaac Newton, puny and prematurely born, was not expected to live many hours; how many potential geniuses, it may be asked, succumbed to the untimely death that he barely escaped?

But as regards the physical world at all events it was long supposed that a pre-established harmony, a complete unitary system could be safely assumed. Long after the Ptolemaic astronomy—with its primum mobile, its crystalline spheres, its firmament of stars,

---

[1] *Nature*, Vol. LXXI. p. 401.

the several planets with the sun and moon all revolving
in concentric circles round the earth—had given place
to that of Copernicus, it was still believed that there
was somewhere a great central sun round which the
entire stellar universe revolved. But this notion too has
been exploded. "So far as we can judge at present,"
writes Professor Young, "it is most likely that the
stars are moving, not in regular closed orbits around
any centre whatever, but rather as bees do in a swarm,
each for itself, under the action of the predominant
attraction of its nearest neighbours. The *solar* system
is an absolute monarchy with the sun supreme. The
great stellar system appears to be a republic, without
any such central, unique, and dominant authority.
Here perturbation prevails over regularity, and 'individualism' is the method of the greater system of
stars, as solar despotism is that of the smaller system
of planets[1]."

Turning from stars to atoms we find a similar change
of view. The five regular solids of Plato's cosmogony,
the hard, massy corpuscles of Lucretius and Newton,
the 'manufactured articles,' severally identical, ingener-
able, and immutable, of Herschel and Maxwell, are all
disappearing to make room for a theory of chemical
evolution, which recognises degrees of simplicity and
stability but finds no forms absolutely elementary or
absolutely permanent. The results of spectroscopic
investigations conjoined with the recently discovered
phenomena of radio-activity are, as Sir Norman Lockyer
says, "on all-fours with the geological record...We

---

[1] C. A. Young, *A Text-book of General Astronomy*, 1893, pp. 461,
514.

note the same changes of form, sudden breaks in forms, disappearances of old, accompanied by appearances of new forms; and with these we have to associate ...a growth of complexity...that is to say, the existence of our chemical elements as we know them does not depend upon their having been separately manufactured ...they are the result of the working of a general law, as in the case of plants and animals[1]."

[1] *Inorganic Evolution*, 1900, pp. 164, 166.

LECTURE V.

In spite of the contingency which pluralism leads us to expect, and which, in fact, we have found everywhere to characterize the world, there is at any rate one principle that from the pluralistic standpoint may be regarded as *a priori*. As a necessary consequence of the interaction of a plurality of individuals, intent on self-betterment as well as self-conservation, there should be a general tendency to diminish the mere contingency of the world and to replace it by a definite progression. And this, so far as our experience goes, we find to be in fact the case. Such progression we are wont nowadays to speak of as evolution.

But widely as the term 'evolution' is used, it is rarely defined; hence it is often without misgiving applied to processes that are diametrically opposed, to the differentiation of a unity and to the integration of a plurality. The history of this term is worth a moment's consideration. We begin with the literal sense, the unrolling of a scroll or volume, whereby what lies written inside it is no longer latent but laid bare—becomes patent and evident. This as a figure is then transferred to the processes of thought ; and we talk of evolving or explicating whatever may be implied or involved in a concept, an argument or a theory. We find it later applied with a similar meaning to the supposed unfolding of an organism regarded as completely pre-existing in miniature within the germ.   Such was the theory of biological evolution or preformation advocated by Leibniz.   And throughout the 18th century this was the prevalent view among biologists and philosophers alike; but now it is all but superseded by the very different theory of epigenesis or new formation; for which nevertheless the term evolution is still retained.   So different are the two theories in fact, that the earlier, strictly evolutional view would—unless essentially modified—render the Darwinian doctrine of the origin of species impossible.   For according to that earlier theory "the germ was more than a marvellous bud-like miniature of the adult, it necessarily included in its turn the next generation, and this the next—in short all future generations.   Germ within germ, in ever smaller miniature, after the fashion of an infinite juggler's box, was the corollary logically appended to this theory of preformation[1]."   The successive unfolding of such a system of *emboîtement* or involution, though the *ne plus ultra* of evolution literally understood, is then the direct negative of evolution as we understand it to-day. According to this later theory each new organism is not an 'educt' but a 'product,' to use Kantian phrases: its *parts* are in no sense present in the embryo but are gradually organized, one after another in due order, as the term epigenesis implies and as Harvey, who first used the term, prophetically maintained.—It is now known too that in this progressive integration the individual retraces the main stages through which the

---

[1] Geddes and Thomson, *The Evolution of Sex*, p. 84.

species has advanced: as Haeckel in technical language concisely puts it: Ontogeny recapitulates phylogeny.

Such a theory of evolution is in all respects conformable to the pluralistic standpoint. The diverging lines of phylogenetic ascent indicate the various directions by which different species have extended and improved their adjustment to the environment: here all is history, the result of effort, trial and error, here we have adventure and ultimate achievement; in a word *natura naturans*, as I said before. The successive stages of ontogenetic development, on the other hand, though each step is an advance for the individual and justifies Harvey's term epigenesis; yet from the point of view of the species it is mainly recapitulation, *palingenesis* as Haeckel has called it: here then we have on the whole only routine, heredity as the result of organic memory or habit, in other words, as *natura naturata*. The preformation theory on the other hand is only compatible with a singularistic, or as Professor James has called it, a block universe, in which

> With earth's first clay they did the last man knead
> And then of the last harvest sowed the seed:
> On the first morning of creation wrote
> What the last dawn of reckoning shall read.

Though this theory seems, so far as biology is concerned, to have originated in a certain faulty observation of Malpighi[1], the anatomist, it probably owed its long supremacy in large measure to the advocacy of philosophers, Regis, Malebranche, and especially Leibniz. For Leibniz indeed it was but a corollary of his

[1] Cf. Huxley's article 'Evolution,' *Ency. Brit.* 11th edn, Vol. x. p. 29 *d*.

doctrine of pre-established harmony, that hopeless theological pendant of his pluralism[1]. Such a theory of evolution is only appropriate to a singularistic philosophy, I have said ; but also it is the only theory of evolution which truly deserves the name. For evolution, strictly taken, presupposes a fundamental unity, in which all that is eventually evolved or disclosed was involved or contained from the first. Logic furnishes us with the clearest instance of evolution in this sense, and it was to the unfolding or explication of logical content that, as already said, the metaphor of evolution was first applied. The following passage from Hegel's *Encyclopaedia* is in point here :—" The movement of the notion is development : by which that only is explicitly affirmed which is already of itself present." The development of an organism was for Hegel the counterpart of this logical development, and he commends the so-called 'box-within-box' hypothesis of Leibniz and Bonnet for "perceiving that in the process of development the notion keeps to itself, and only gives rise to alteration of form, without making any addition in point of content[2]." But it was not the individual organism regarded apart but rather the entire universe that appeared to Hegel—Hegel the logician, that is to say—as just the realisation of such

[1] *Considérations sur le Principe de Vie*, Erdmann's *Leibnitii Opera*, pp. 429 ff.

[2] *Encyclopaedia*, i. § 161. Cf. also the following :—Die Weltgeschichte ist die Darstellung, wie der Geist zu dem Bewusstsein dessen kommt, was er an sich bedeutet; und wie der Keim die ganze Natur des Baumes...in sich trägt, so enthalten auch schon die ersten Spuren des Geistes virtualiter die ganze Geschichte. *Phil. der Gesch.*, Einleitung, p. 21.

a dialectical evolution. It is an immanent and self-determining process of explication of the Absolute One, setting out from and returning into itself. Duly to contrast it with this sublime idea of evolution, the progress that pluralism implies requires a distinctive name. It will be better at least at the outset to call the latter a process of integration and equilibration— terms which, it will be remembered, hold a prominent place in the synthetic philosophy of Herbert Spencer. Which is the truer view it is impossible, of course, to decide while the issue between pluralism and absolutism is still itself undecided. Whether the whole is prior to the parts or not, depends on the nature of the case. If the whole be a wood, then to the charge that he cannot see the wood for the trees, the pluralist may retort that at any rate the trees make the wood, not the wood the trees. But if the whole be a tree, it may be true that he fails to see the trunk because of the branches, and yet it is from the trunk that all these spring. Anyhow it is the parts, the many, with which the pluralist starts; the question, whether or no there is an absolute whole prior to—at once the logical and the real ground of—all the parts, is for him not the first question but the last. What we have now to do then is to consider this progressive integration that the Many imply, and in particular to ascertain the possible limits of the process[1].

The whole is more than the sum of its parts—that is the cardinal characteristic of evolution as understood by the pluralist. A unity that is not more than its constituent elements is no real unity at all : it is only

[1] Cf. Lecture IX.

a formal or mathematical whole. All real synthesis entails new properties which its component factors in their previous isolation did not possess. This statement many will hesitate to accept ; for a methodological distinction—that is, or was, commonly regarded as answering to a real difference in things—will, no doubt, occur to them : the distinction, I mean, between those concurring causes whose separate effects are said merely "to be compounded with one another," as in mechanical actions, and those, such as in chemical actions, "where the separate effects cease entirely and are succeeded by phenomena altogether different," by new and so-called ' heteropathic ' effects. This distinction—which the pluralist principle seems plainly to ignore, or rather, tacitly to contradict—is, according to J. S. Mill, whose account of it I have just quoted, " one of the funda-mental distinctions in nature." Not merely so, but the former case, that of the 'composition of causes,' as Mill terms it, is, he holds, the general one ; " the other "—perhaps the only one, certainly the chief ac-cording to pluralism—he declares "is always special and exceptional[1]." So it will seem so long, but only so long, as we overlook the essentially abstract character of the mechanical doctrine of the 'composition of forces.' If the causes compounded are purely quantitative, of course there can be no qualitative ' intermixture of effects.' But let all that actually happens in the real cases abstractly exemplifying such quantitative homo-geneity be taken into account and no one, I imagine, will deny that heterogeneity is also present. The motions that the astronomer describes, for example,

[1] *System of Logic*, bk III. ch. vi. § 2.

are far from being the only effects that the constitution of the solar system involves. Even if the various physical phenomena it displays should also eventually admit of mechanical description, such description would still remain abstract and general : it could never ear-mark the individuals concerned and follow their several histories.

Meanwhile it still remains an open question, as Mach has said[1], whether the mechanical view of things instead of being the profoundest is not the shallowest of all. One thing at any rate is certain, a strictly mechanical theory of the world, since it necessarily implies complete reversibility, can never explain what we understand by progress and develop-ment. Mechanism can always, life and experience can never, be made to move backwards : for the one composition and resolution are altogether on a par, in that they entail no change of either mass or energy; for the other there is the vital difference of value between organization and disorganization, sense and nonsense. The so-called conservation of mass and energy might be regarded as symbolising the initial state of the pluralistic world and as symbolising too the mere permanence and abstract being of its many units. But it is notorious that these concepts are the result of ignoring those differences of quality which alone convert units into individuals. Without these we may have *Erhaltung* but not *Entfaltung*, as a German would say : we may have conservation and

---

[1] Cf. his excellent chapter on 'The relation of mechanics to the other sciences': *Die Mechanik in ihrer Entwickelung*, ch. v. Of this work there is an American translation.

indefinite composition but not development and definite organization. In short, the concrete integration of experience is the diametrical opposite to the mechanical resultant of a composition of abstract units : it is a *creative* resultant or synthesis, to use Wundt's happy and striking phrase[1]. Evolution, then, for the pluralist is always synthesis, and all real synthesis is creative synthesis.

Of such synthesis experience furnishes instances at every turn. The timbre of a musical note is more than the sum of its constituent tones : a melody more than the sum of its separate notes. To an infant or a dog a picture may afford all the colour sensations that it does to us, but for lack of intellectual synthesis the picture is not a significant whole. We are ourselves only at this level when we first catch sight of an un-expected object which we momentarily fail to recognise, or when owing to lapse of attention we cease to 'take in the sense' or 'lose the thread' of what we hear or read. Again, to repeat an instance I have used else-where :—"A fish can feel, smell, taste, see, and even hear, but we cannot assume solely on that account that it has any percepts to which its five senses contribute, as they do to our percept, say, of an orange or a peppermint. Taking voluntary movements as the index of psychical life, it would seem that the fish's movements are instigated and guided by its senses not

[1] But to Lotze belongs the credit of first signalising the fact to which Wundt has given the name ; and even Lotze gets so far as to apply the term creation to this 'relating activity,' as he calls it. Cf. his *Metaphysik*, §§ 268, 271. It is, to say the least, surprising that Wundt nowhere refers to Lotze's unquestionable priority in this matter.

collectively but separately...To this inability to combine
simple percepts into one complex of a single object or
situation we may reasonably attribute the fish's lack
of sagacity[1]." It is just this difference between apprehending the parts and comprehending the whole that
distinguishes what we call intellect from mere sense.
It was the failure to appreciate this difference that
made the sensationalist doctrine *prima facie* plausible—
Nihil est in intellectu quod non fuerit prius in sensu;
as it was the failure to find the intellectually new
among the sensationally old, that eventually proved
this doctrine to be unsound. Spatial and temporal
perception are conspicuous examples of creative synthesis, the genesis of which sensationalists have failed
to explain and 'nativists' to explain away. By this
process at every stage 'objects of a higher order,' as
they have been happily termed, are attained; and these
in turn may serve as the constituents of a new synthesis.
So advancing, experience continually gains at once in
complexity and in unity.

The prime source of this synthesis the pluralist
leaves where Kant eventually left it[2]—in the activity
of the experiencing subjects; though it must be allowed
that the pluralist extends the concepts of experience
and activity far beyond the range of Kant's so-called
'synthetic unity of apperception.' The peculiarity of
each individual's syntheses again is regarded as due
primarily to what we call the individual's interest,

[1] *Psychological Principles*, p. 188.
[2] I say eventually, because in his Dissertation of 1770 Kant was
nearer to the Absolutist position. Cf. Caird, *The Critical Philosophy
of Kant*, I. pp. 209 ff.

giving to this term also a more extended meaning than it commonly receives. In other and plainer words perhaps, there is progressive experience at all because there are active individuals, severally *sui generis*, each from its own standpoint bent on working out a *modus vivendi* with the rest. And here we may remark the one-sidedness of the current concept of biological evolution as consisting simply in adaptation *to* environment, or even in adaptation *by* environment. For pluralism the adaptation is not rigidly one-sided but more or less reciprocal, a *commercium dynamicum*, to use Kant's phrase. The more experience advances the more there is of adaptation *of* environment as well as of adaptation *to* environment.

The synthesis by which experience is extended and enriched is then, we have to remember, not merely nor primarily knowledge. We begin by trying and end by knowing. Practice is the parent of theory and realisation the surest verification. We may be repelled by the idealist's paradox of the identity of thought and being, yet we insist that what we immediately experience is reality. If so, the reality, whatever it be besides, is this interaction of cognitive and conative agents : reality is experience. It is in this light that the pluralist seeks to interpret the fact of organization. Whereas naturalism, as we have seen, regards experience as the result of organization, pluralism regards organization as the result of experience : in other words, for the one the question seems to be how the body comes by its soul ; for the other, it is rather how the soul comes by its body. But in truth we know nothing of disembodied souls or of inanimate organisms : experience and organization appear always to advance together ; it will be more exact therefore to say that the naturalist makes function depend entirely on structure while the pluralist holds structure to be mainly determined by function. The opposition is not complete, for, as we have seen, a combination may present itself, which, from the point of view of the individual who turns it to account, is wholly fortuitous. Still even then it is entirely his action in selecting and utilising it that determines its function, and often leads to its further modification.—The multiplicity of parts of which a structure is composed is only a whole or organized when regarded in the light of the specific function which it subserves. This function is the new fact that is more than the sum of their properties, the creative synthesis that makes the parts an individual unity. The determination of structure by function is beyond question in the human affairs from which in the first instance all these teleological concepts of structure, function, organ, end and the like are derived ; and it is, of course, on this analogy that the pluralist's inter-pretation exclusively rests. Let us then consider the characteristics of what we loosely call evolution in this practical realm.

First then, to repeat, it is, proximately at all events, a process of synthesis or epigenesis, not one of strict evolution or preformation. It is needless now to dwell on this point. That the various forms of social organi-zation, political, industrial, academical or artistic, imply the cooperation and consensus of their several members is obvious. But there is another point worth notice in passing. We have called this synthesis creative ;

whereas the idea of potentiality, that is rarely long out of sight when development is in question, still suggests that the new was in some sort present, was in some sort, therefore, already preformed in the old— potentially there from the first. We owe this notion entirely to retrospective reflexion. Having seen one acorn in a suitable environment become an oak, we say of a second that it is potentially or virtually an oak already. Not only is such language, strictly speaking, indefensible[1], it is also worthless in so far as it throws no light on the process which it indicates, but does not even describe. Reality is entirely actuality : the potential, the possible, the problematic, on the other hand, belong exclusively to abstract thought. But that, while it always presupposes, is never commensurate with, reality. Actuality again is entirely experience : its factors are never abstract possibilities, they are living agents ; and the result of their interaction is a perennial epigenesis, the only creation that pluralism recognises. *Ex nihilo nihil fit* applies only to what begins to exist. In this sense creation out of nothing, thing supervening on no thing, is a contradiction, so surely as position, affirmation is necessarily prior to deposition, negation. But *e minimo maximum fit* is the truth which the notion of potentiality endeavours to express by inverting the process in idea after it has been realised in fact, realised directly by the creative synthesis for which pluralism contends.

[1] "The more a writer feels himself led naturally to have recourse to this phrase," says Mr Bradley, "the better cause he probably has for at least attempting to avoid it." Cf. his excellent remarks on the whole subject, *Appearance and Reality*, pp. 384–7.

In the next place, then, it will be granted that what synthesis creates in the practical world is not new entities but what we may call new values. As already said, whatever be the ultimate meaning to be assigned to mass and energy, we may allow the bare conservation of this: in respect of it the new would be only formative: there would be no new content. Even the manifold products of human art and industry, steam-engines and dynamos, looms and printing-presses, drugs and explosives, regarded in themselves, are but re-arrangements of so-called forces and elements. It is far otherwise when the human ends for which alone they were devised are taken into account. But most of all when we consider human achievements in litera-ture, science and art, the entire uplift of humanity from its rudest beginning to its present state of civilisation, the social, ethical and religious ideals that it has come to cherish and pursue, we need not hesitate to call all this inestimable store of new worth a veritable creation. Though there is no increase of energy there is an increase of directed energy: though there is no increase of mass there is an increase of determinate structure as the 'will to a higher unity' is realised. The good that is achieved tends not only to be con-served but to grow and advance to worthier forms and that without assignable limits.

But in a social organization there is no absolute opposition between structure and function. As in all organization, function is a unity depending on a com-plexity of structure. But in the structure the proximate parts are again complex, each having however a single function ; and so again of their parts in descending order. This characteristic the modern pluralist, as we have seen, following the lead of Leibniz, is prepared to extend indefinitely. What we have now to notice are certain consequences which this relation involves, consequences which our social and individual experiences plainly verify. The function of a general in the field, for example, is the direction of the campaign as *a whole*: the execution of his orders in *detail* he leaves to the several members of his staff in such wise, that they in turn have to issue further more specific orders to their various adjutants; and so on again and again, till at length thousands of private soldiers are set in motion[1]. But even the movements that these perform are carried out by a so-called 'psycho-physical mechanism,' to which the detailed co-ordination is left: of this they individually know nothing. And throughout, it is this gradual mechanization of lower functions by habit, that makes it possible to concentrate attention on higher functions. We have ample experience of this relief in our acquired dexterities, and it is assumed that the same principle holds good indefinitely.—Similarly if we order shoes we do not need to know how to make them, and the shoemaker in ordering leather has not to tell the currier how to tan it; but in earlier times we may suppose that everyone prepared his hides and made shoes for himself, doing both badly. In such a hierarchy of consentient functions as we are considering, each unit is—to use the Aristotelian phraseology— 'form' for the function below it and 'matter' for the function above it. Every form too is conditioned by its appropriate matter: soldiers cannot be effectively manœuvred till they have mastered their drill, nor

---

[1] Cf. an interesting passage in Horwicz's *Psychologische Analysen*, 1872, I. p. 13.

good shoes be made without good leather. Thus in all organization there is not only continuity throughout; there is also what the sociologist calls solidarity as well: the higher depends on the lower. And this relation according to pluralism will hold good however far the synthesis may go, however sublime the worth that may be attained. What we shall reach will never be a single unity independent of the plurality beneath, but only the harmonious coordination and consentience of these—ideally, an absolute harmony: in this sense at any rate the Many become more and more one.

But this dependence of the higher on the lower is only half the truth. As our individual and social experiences show us, the lower can also depend upon the higher, and this to an ever-increasing extent as we ascend in the scale of being. As we have already seen, there is according to pluralism no absolutely fixed environment: modification of environment is possible as well as modification by it. And this holds not only of the natural environment but—and still more—of the social environment as well. But for this power of directing it, the progress of development would be, to say the least, immeasurably slower than it is. In respect of this power man is manifestly superior to all creatures beneath him; and among men the civilised man and his community to the savage and his tribe. The drainage or irrigation of the land, the extirpation of tares and the cultivation of wheat, the domestication of useful animals and the destruction of their enemies— all these processes are strictly in line with the working of natural forces or natural selection, but they imply

a definite direction that does not appear in these.—
What the schoolmaster, the physician and the philan-
thropist effect for the amelioration of the masses needs
no description.   Here again we have definite direction
overriding the random and untrained impulses of the
natural man.   While the progress already made in the
physical and social amelioration of human life is inestimable, it is as nothing compared with what is still
possible.   Nine-tenths of our physical ills are due to
ignorance and perhaps a still greater proportion of our
social evils are due to selfishness.   Present scientific
knowledge is adequate to remedy a very large part of
the former and the ordinary prudential maxims of
utilitarian morality, if they were only observed as they
might be, would go far towards extinguishing the
latter: they would put at end to the worships of
Venus, Bacchus, and Mammon, if even they did not
establish peace and chain up the dogs of war for ever.
Social reformers and men of action, who seem to be
invariably optimists, have often drawn glowing pictures
of what this world might be if only all the knowledge
and the wisdom that it contains could be effectively
put into practice.   Before this can be they must be
shared by all, of course ; but on the other hand it is a
sublime though obvious truth, that these highest goods
are not diminished by being diffused.

Such millennial dreams are of very ancient date.
The Jewish prophet finely symbolizes his Messianic
vision as a time when " the wolf shall dwell with the
lamb, and the leopard shall lie down with the kid...and
a little child shall lead them...they shall not hurt nor
destroy ;...for the earth shall be full of the knowledge

of the Lord as the waters cover the sea." And the Christian apostle talks of the whole creation groaning and travailing in pain with us in earnest expectation that it also shall be delivered from the bondage of corruption. Fourier, one of the most celebrated socialist writers, believed that an attraction or sympathy, analogous to Newton's principle of gravitation between material bodies, existed throughout the universe and tended to bring about a complete harmony between society, animal life, organic life and so-called dead matter. His speculations and his prophecies as to the changes that were to ensue in the physical world as the socialistic reorganization of society approached perfection were doubtless fanciful in the extreme. Herbert Spencer's attempt to connect absolute ethics and cosmic equilibration, though seemingly more reasonable, is in fact more absurd. For, in making the physical aspect of things the only fundamental and complete one, he is logically driven to ignore the direction of the lower by the higher altogether. The universe for him is like a vast egg which hatches out perfectly by what he was once pleased to call a ' beneficent necessity.'

But if the extravagant fancy of many ultra-utopian visions of a final harmony among things 'seen and temporal' is reprehensible, not less so is the dearth of imagination that can picture nothing new under the sun. It is doubtless a mistake to attempt to forecast the further course of evolution in detail : so far as synthesis is creative this must be impossible save within comparatively narrow limits. But it is equally a mistake to ignore the tendency to progression, which we find not only to exist in fact, but also to follow as an *a priori* consequence from the fundamental character of the world as pluralism conceives it. As the world of the mere physicist tends towards a state of final equilibrium, so the world of the personal idealist tends towards a final harmony or equilibration. The Kantian 'principle of community' is applicable to both cases :— "All substances, in so far as they are coexistent, stand in complete community, that is, reciprocity one to another[1]." The nature of the *communio* or *commercium dynamicum*, as Kant called it, is, proximately at any rate, very different in the two cases. In a dynamical system, whatever be its initial configuration, there will be continual changes of configuration all tending towards the eventual equilibration of the whole. In a 'personal' system of sentient and conative agents the situation is more complex, even though we do not aim at more than a bare and abstract statement. Here the end of every action is the good : *quidquid petitur petitur sub specie boni*. But the good of each member is dependent on its relation to others, and at the outset involves, as we have seen, more or less blind and aimless struggle : this is the initial state of such a system on the pluralist view. For all members with like interests, however, there will be a common good and a common evil : so far their actions will tend as completely as possible to realise the one and to eliminate the other. If this were all, the case would be simple enough: the parallel between a dynamical system and a personal system would be very close. But the nature of individuality forbids that the immediate interests of any two indi-

---

[1] *Critique of the Pure Reason*, 1st edn. The Third Analogy of Experience.

viduals should ever be entirely identical. Still even
where individual interests collide a common interest in
their adjustment might be expected to arise, and did in
fact arise as soon as the social level was reached, and
it has grown with the progress of society and largely
contributed to that progress. Such adjustment is what
we call justice, 'the noblest among the virtues' as
Aristotle has said.

At the lower level of merely animal life, where
conscious cooperation is absent, justice is out of the
question. But even here some equilibration is secured
by subjective selection, whereby the general environment is, so to say, parcelled out and specialised : so
far in the apt words of Pope,

> All nature's difference keeps all nature's peace.

Within the same species there must however still be
competition so long as its numbers increase beyond
the resources of its peculiar habitat. Here we come
upon the Malthusian principle and its consequence,
natural selection. But again so soon as reason can be
brought to bear, an enlightened sense of justice can
operate to adjust population to the means of subsistence
and to secure the ends blindly attained through natural
selection by peaceful and painless means : the arts of
eugenics and hygienics may render the struggle for
existence unnecessary. Not so in the merely animal
world : here natural selection seems unavoidable. But
after all natural selection secures progress—of this
palaeontology affords ample evidence—and even equilibration in a certain wider sense, i.e. between species
and species. In concluding the *Origin of Species*
Darwin went so far as to say : "As natural selection

works solely by and for the good of each being, all corporeal and mental endowments will tend to progress towards perfection." Even if we allow this claim there still remains the fact that all the lower forms of life prey one upon another; and mankind takes its full share of such spoils. In this respect there seems to be no eliminating the struggle for existence. We have thus on the whole two principles at work—the ethical at the human level, where justice may be supreme ; and the principle that might is right, practically the *Helden-moral* of Nietzsche. We may call these respectively Rational Selection and Natural Selection.

But there is a vast difference between the individuals concerned in the two cases: a human being is a person, an animal is at best a chattel, in legal phrase. In looking at the world historically as pluralism does, we regard only species of plants and animals but we take account of individual men[1]. If we are content to stop at this division into natural and rational we can maintain a universal tendency towards progress and harmony or equilibration to be characteristic of the world as the pluralist conceives and regards it.

---

[1] It is interesting to note here the fundamental division of Ethics which Kant makes, grounded on the relation between the obliger and the obliged; according to this jural relations are denied between men and animals because these are "irrational beings devoid of power to oblige and towards whom no obligation can be constituted." *Metaphysik der Sitten*, Hartenstein's edn, VII. p. 38.

LECTURE VI.

THE PLURALISTIC GOAL.

We have now to face the question what sort of unity would be attained if the ideal were fully realised which the pluralistic interpretation of experience directly suggests. Such an inquiry brings us first of all to the problem, so much discussed of late by sociologists, as to the nature of society. Is society an organism? it is asked. That there are many analogies between society and an organism is certain, and impressive instances of their employment will at once occur to everyone, the fable of Menenius Agrippa, the parable of the vine, and St Paul's exhortation to the Corinthians, for example. But it is obvious too that if an organism must be literally either an animal or a vegetable, then, since society is certainly neither of these, it is not an organism: it lacks the physical continuity that they possess[1]. On the other hand, the more we lay stress on the co-operation of the several individual members and the adjustment of their respective functions, the more justification we shall find for the conception of what we may call sociological, as distinct from biological, organisms—organisms, that is to say, which imply a further and higher evolutional synthesis. In fact, if

---

[1] Nevertheless it has a continuity of a higher order, the continuity due to the mutual understanding and cooperation of its constituents. Cf. Fouillée, *Les Éléments sociologiques de la Morale*, 1905, p. 148.

with Kant and Hegel we define the living organism as a unity in which the whole and the parts are reciprocally ends to each other, such a definition seems even more applicable to society than it is to the biological individual, since the constituent members of the latter are not conscious, at least not self-conscious, and, moreover, are not coordinate.   This brings us to the heart of the problem that divides sociologists so hopelessly.   It is true that the individual man, for example, thinks and wills, and that his several organs—as ordinarily regarded —do not ; but, *per contra*, is it not true that while the several members of a commonwealth think and will the society as a whole does not ?   When Plato and Hobbes compare the state to a vast person and the individual man to a miniature state do they not overlook this essential difference ?   Is society then really a unity ; or is there in any exact sense a social spirit, a social will, a social end, a social conscience ?

Two radically different answers have been given to such questions by the so-called realistic and nominalistic sociologists respectively.   We are familiar enough with the latter in England : their standpoint is the thoroughly individualistic one characteristic of 18th century speculation in general and of English psychology, ethics, and economics in particular.   According to the nominalistic view, a society is a collection of individuals held together by the private interests that association promotes and which the social contract was deliberately formed to secure.   Between a collection of n independent persons, having each his own ends and aims, and the same number formed into a society with ends and aims in common, the only difference —great though it be in its consequences—is, it may be said, essentially an accidental or extraneous one : it is solely the result of a coincidence of interests. Some animals, like rooks or deer, find it advantageous to congregate together ; others, like hawks and tigers, to live apart. Man belongs to the sociable animals, and, owing to his superior intelligence, human society is more elaborate than any found among the lower animals. But in a human society of n units there is as little ground for regarding the society as an $n + 1$th unity with a distinct —and also superior—consciousness and will, as there would be in the humbler but otherwise parallel case of a colony of ants.

The other extreme, the 'realistic' concept of society, is well represented in Hegel's famous doctrine of 'Objective Spirit.' Whereas for the nominalistic extreme, society was the accident and the isolated individuals the substance, here the relation is completely transposed. It is this spirit, Hegel expressly says, that "has reality, and the individuals are but its accidents." If we "proceed atomistically, ascending from the *isolated* individuals [*Einzelnheit*] as basis" we shall never, he allows, attain to spirit as objective reality at all, but only to a combination or *Zusammenhang.* That amounts to saying : the nominalistic view is right in its conclusion but its premisses are false. "For [objective] spirit," Hegel continues, "is not an individual thing : rather it is the unity of the individual and the general[1]." As this is sometimes expressed nowadays : Society is a reality but an over-individual reality. Instead of calling the nominalistic premisses false, it would be more exact to say that they are ambiguous : the so-called individual is one being

[1] *Philosophie des Rechtes*, § 156.

out of society and quite another being in it.   A hand
severed from the living body is a hand no more,
Aristotle long ago remarked ; and no combination or
Zusammenhang of *disjecta membra* will ever make a
living whole. This is the truth that the whole 18th
century failed to grasp, and that the 19th has taught
us to appreciate fully.   The individuals whom Hobbes,
Locke, Rousseau and others imagined deliberately
contracting to form society were conceived as already
intelligent, and reasoning, i.e. as already social products.
—To ask which was first, a polity or man as 'a political
animal,' is no better than to ask the trivial question,
which was first, the hen or the egg.   If by man you
mean man as self-conscious and rational, then take him
where or when you will he is what he is only because
society preceded him.   Had your specimens chanced
to have lived the life of the legendary wild men of the
woods, they could neither have devised nor accepted
a social scheme at all.   Biologically regarded these
two kinds of men would be identical, psychologically
the difference between them would be profound.   The
first, the so-called 'natural man,' is not a man in the
second sense, is not a self-conscious, ethical person, at
all.   To suppose a group of the former should straightway constitute an organic unity of the latter is as absurd as to say that a handful of type is a set of verses.

And yet somehow or other the transition has been
effected, it will be said.   It has ; but the process
according to the pluralist's theory was an instance—
and the most important one—of that creative synthesis
which I have already attempted to describe.   As the
outcome of such a synthesis both the state and its several
self-conscious members are a new creation.   Neither the

one nor the other can be found in the primitive horde instinctively drawn together by mutual interests. *Pari passu* the two are evolved together: as the mere crowd of troglodytes become organized into a society they become differentiated as free persons; and again, in proportion as their rights and duties become more clearly defined they in turn attain to a clearer consciousness of themselves as rational and responsible individuals. But still the question presses : Granted that in becoming social the individual man becomes self-conscious and rational, still what exactly is meant when society is called a spiritual organism ? What at any rate is *not* meant is an $n + 1$th individual somehow superinduced upon the n individuals constituting its several members, any more than by an organism is meant an $n + 1$th organ additional to its complement of n organs. The objective mind, to use Hegel's phrase, is not something transcendent, existing aloof and apart: it is, on the contrary, the informing spirit immanent in the whole, whereby the several parts rise upwards towards a higher, common life : in this sense it is as he terms it 'the unity of the individual and the general.' To many such language may not seem to mean much or to be very illuminating. But we may perhaps find a helpful illustration by recalling the development of the *Metazoa* or multicellular animals from so-called 'loose colonies' or aggregates of *Protozoa* or unicellular animals, already referred to in an earlier lecture[1]—though the parallel is not exact, since society is not a biological organism. The several cells of a complex organism still retain their identity and continue their individual lives ; but if this were all they would remain a mere aggregate ; nor would they

[1] Cf. Lecture III. p. 58.

be more, if they differentiated independently. When however they differentiate, as it were in touch with each other, they become mutually complementary. In and with such consentient action there emerges that higher common life, which constitutes them into organs and the whole into an organism. As the unicellular organisms of the protozoan cluster become organs, the cluster becomes a new organism, a metazoan ; and *vice versa* as the cluster becomes an organism, the primitive unicellular organisms become organs. In other words the more intimate the unity of the whole the more complete the differentiation of its members. The two in short are strictly correlative, reciprocally cause and effect, means and end to each other. We should accordingly regard it as simply absurd to grant that the cells had become organs while hesitating to recognise that *ipso facto* the cluster had become an organism. If it does not seem equally absurd to allow that the individual man as a social unit is a rational and moral being—and stop there, that is only because familiarity has blinded us to what such an admission implies. Let us then pass on to its explication.

What now do reason and morality imply ? It will suffice to go at once to what is for us the main point : they imply what since Kant it has been usual to call 'objectivity.' The sensory and appetitive experiences of a given individual are altogether immediate, beginning and ending with himself, not merely exclusively and inalienably his, but also in their particularity peculiar to him and different from the immediate experiences of all others beside. Such are the characteristics of experience logically included together as subjectivity. Experience as objective is the precise opposite of this : it is never immediate, determined that is by sense or appetite ; nor is it either confined to the individual or contingent to him : on the contrary it is or it may become an unreservedly common possession by virtue of just those factors which we call reason and morality ; for these are alike for all and binding on the thought and action of each. In experience as sub-jective we find only the particular and contingent : in experience as objective we find always the universal and necessary. To subjective experience as such Leibniz's description will apply; it mirrors the universe from a particular and unique standpoint ; to objective experience as such on the other hand that description is not strictly applicable.

Objectivity cannot then be a characteristic of a purely individual experience, and to say that it is universal or common to all cannot mean that—like the blackness of crows, to use a trivial illustration—it is singly and separately developed in each. To God, it is true, Leibniz applied the old saying "that as a centre He is everywhere, but His circumference is nowhere[1]." Such language may be taken to imply an experience that is at once completely subjective and completely objective, at once altogether individual and altogether absolute. But such an experience entirely transcends our conception.—With this we may couple a well-known quotation from Aristotle's *Politics* ; " He who has no need of society because he is sufficient for himself, must either be a brute or a god." No wonder the transition from brute to man, from sense and appetite to reason and law, seemed inconceivable apart from special divine interference, so long as it was regarded

[1] *Principles of Nature and Grace*, § 13.

as taking place in each individual *singulatim*, as prior
to the dawn of evolutionary ideas it invariably was.
Still this long failure of individualism scientifically to
bridge the gulf between man and brute is strong testimony to the living unity of the social organism.
Through this objective mind, then, pervading all its
members, and not through any infusion from without,
each one in being social becomes human.   It is true
that society is wholly constituted by its members, and
is nothing apart from them, but it is equally true that
in forming it they *pro tanto* transfigure and at the
same time transcend their isolated selves.   By inter-
subjective intercourse they attain to the transsub-
jective or truly objective, both in knowledge and in
action ; and the more clearly they differentiate themselves from others the more distinct their own self-
conscious personality becomes.

This reference to self-consciousness brings us to a
new point well deserving of a moment's consideration.
It was Kant's great merit to have signalised the mutual
implication of self-consciousness and objectivity in the
higher or epistemological sense just defined.   " That all
the various elements of our empirical consciousness must
be bound together in one self-consciousness is," he says,
"the absolutely first foundation of our thinking at all[1]."
Such is the import of what he has made known as the
' synthetic unity of apperception.'   But in his exposition
of this principle in what he entitled the ' deduction (i.e.
justification) of the categories' Kant alternates between
two distinct inquiries, to the mutual confusion of both.
The one he calls the subjective deduction, the other

[1] *Critique of the Pure Reason*, 1st edn, Max Müller's trans.
p. 103 note.

the objective. The first is largely a psychological inquiry : it shows all the worst faults of the old psychology of ready-made faculties, and it is oblivious of all
questions of development. That it was defective,
Kant was from the first more or less dimly aware,
and he was driven by adverse criticisms in the end
practically to abandon it[1]. What he did not see
was that, from the nature of the case, his so-called
subjective deduction could not be conclusive. The
question really was, How does objective experience
arise ? and Kant in the first edition of his *Critique* set
himself to answer this question—very much as Locke
might have done—that is to say, by observing the
process in the working of his own mind as it was when
the genesis of all the functions or faculties concerned
was already complete. Or what comes ultimately to
the same thing, he adopted the analysis of 'the intellectual powers' provided ready to his hand in the
psychology then current, an analysis reached in the
usual individualistic fashion, and vitiated by the
psychologist's fallacy of attributing to the growing
mind the powers that only gradually emerge as its
development proceeds. It was as if an anatomist
should say that the eyes and hands were already
preformed in the embryo ; and as we have seen
anatomists did actually say this. In biology however
the hypothesis of literal evolution at length gave way to
the hypothesis of epigenesis and only lingered on in
psychology, where its fallaciousness was less palpable.
But in the *Prolegomena*, written five years later to

---

[1] Cf. Kant's preface to the 1st edn of the *Critique*, pp. xxvi f.,
and his preface to the *Metaphysische Anfangsgründe der Natur-
wissenschaften*, Hartenstein's edn, Vol. IV. pp. 363 ff.

obviate difficulties and meet criticisms, Kant made an important distinction between what he called judgments of experience, which have objective validity, and mere judgments of perception, which are only subjectively valid. He then proceeds to add:—"All our judgments are at first mere perception-judgments: they hold good simply for us, i.e. for our subjectivity. It is only subsequently that we give them a new reference, namely to an object, and intend (*wollen*) that they shall hold good for us not only at the moment but at all other times, and in like manner for all other persons." Again a couple of pages later he states this difference between the two acts of judgment as follows:—In the one "I merely compare the percepts and combine them in one consciousness of my own state," in the other I compare and combine them in one consciousness in general (*einem Bewusstsein überhaupt*)[1].

Within these statements there is room for all that we have to contend for. The so-called judgments of perception are the nearest approach to a true, explicit, judgment possible to the individual apart from inter-subjective intercourse. The observation of the lower animals and of children furnishes ample evidence of this, and nowadays it is, I believe, questioned by nobody[2]. Between the stage of these perceptive judgments and that at which judgments-proper arise—judgments,

[1] *Prolegomena* §§ 18, 20.

[2] Kant himself in another connexion had noted this fact some twenty years before he gave his *Critique* to the world; though even then he seemed to attribute the difference between man and the lower animals to reason as a 'heaven-sent faculty'—to use a phrase of Mr Bradley's—rather than to reason as the result of social development. (Cf. the paper 'On the false subtilty of the syllogistic figures,' *Werke*, Hartenstein's edn, II. pp. 67 f.)

that is to say, having an objective import, and which Kant was content to speak of merely as 'subsequent' —there intervenes the whole long process of social development. This is implied in their characteristic as judgments valid for consciousness generally, valid not merely for me and now but for all and always. Unless then I am not simply conscious of myself but conscious also of my community with others who are conscious of themselves and of me, I cannot so much as understand what objective validity means, to say nothing of affirming that it exists.

We come then to Kant's main position, the objective deduction, viz. that apperception—or that consciousness of objects which goes with self-consciousness—as opposed to perception, is the pre-condition of all intelligent and scientific experience. What we are here concerned about is not to call the principle in question but simply to indicate and emphasize the one point that Kant completely overlooked. It is a fact, at any rate, that 'the absolutely first foundation of such objective experience' is to be found only in society, in intersubjective intercourse, and not in 'apperception as a faculty' pertaining to the isolated individual mind[1]. But though Kant, and I may add, most of his commentators and critics, overlook this fact, they do not mean to deny it. Not only is it implied, as I have just said, in the necessity and universality which Kant assigns as the marks of judgments proper, or judgments of experience ; but it is more or less explicitly recognised in his various formulations of the moral law or categorical imperative: "Act only according to that

[1] Cf. the passage already cited, p. 124 above.

maxim which thou canst at the same time will should be a universal law," i.e. "Act so as to use humanity, whether in your own person or in the person of another, always as an end, never as merely a means[1]."

It is in this ethical connexion that Kant's most distinguished English commentator, E. Caird, insisted at some length on what he himself called the 'objective and social character of self-consciousness.' I will venture to quote some sentences, because they help, I think, to explain the general oversight which we have just noticed :—"It may be truly said that we find ourselves in others before we find ourselves in ourselves, and that the full consciousness of self comes only through the consciousness of beings without us who are also selves. Self-consciousness in one is kindled by self-consciousness in another, and a social community of life is presupposed in our first consciousness of ourselves as individual persons. It is true, indeed, that in his first return upon self, the individual is conscious rather of opposition to, than of community with, the other selves to whom he finds himself in relation....But we should not be misled by the self-seeking and self-will, which are the first manifestations of selfhood, so as to forget that the individual's consciousness of himself as an independent self *is* essentially a return upon self from the consciousness of others which it implies.... In the first instance the subject...does not reflect on the relativity by which this independent selfhood is mediated and especially on the social unity which it presupposes; and therefore

---

[1] *Groundwork for the Metaphysics of Ethics*, H.'s edn, Vol. IV. pp. 269, 277.

he can see no claim which other beings and things have upon him to be used otherwise than as means to his own ends[1]." That man's primitive egoism in practical life has helped to hide the social implications of self-consciousness seems to me a remark that is both new and true.   *But did not Aristotle see this long ago?*

There is still a further remark of some importance that may opportunely be made here.   It is often said that experience cannot actually " testify to anything more than the existence of the subject—the existence of a plurality of similar Ego's is an inference, a hypothesis to explain the phenomena[2]."   But drawing inferences and framing explanatory hypotheses presuppose a self-conscious intelligence already possessed of that objective experience, which by implying its own universality and necessity, implies also a plurality of selves.   On this assumption then we come to a deadlock or find ourselves revolving in a hopeless circle.   But the escape is simple, once we recognise that experience from the outset involves both subject and object, both self and other, and that the differentiation of both factors proceeds strictly *pari passu.*

We conclude then that society is truly a living reality, though a complex and over-individual one. To it belongs the objective mind that is at once immanent in and dominant over its several members, who thereby attain to self-consciousness and think and

[1] *The Critical Philosophy of Kant,* II. pp. 371 f.   Another writer who has done much to bring out the social character of self-consciousness is Prof. Royce : see, for example, his *Outlines of Psychology,* § 115.

[2] So said the late Professor Ritchie, for example, *Mind,* O. S. XIII. p. 258.

act as rational persons.   But societies as they actually
exist to-day are comparable to those less perfectly
developed *Metazoa* in which the differentiation and
unification of functions is still very incomplete and the
scope of life very restricted in its range.   Many of
these societies seem little more than reduplications of
similar parts without any supreme and central principle
or purpose, like certain organisms that are made up of
a chain of ganglionated segments and have little or no
brain.   Some indeed are so loosely organized as to
allow of division without much deterioration.   Even
the modern national states, that have attained to the
highest stage of civilisation so far known, are still in a
large measure mutually alien and exclusive, whereas
the society with which philosophy is concerned is
synonymous with humanity, nay it is even spoken of
as cosmopolitan.   It is happily true already that as
regards the higher life of man, society is wider than
any single political state, and its unifying spirit inspires,
though but partially and imperfectly, the whole civilised
world.

How far will this progress extend? To attempt to
forecast the future development of humanity in detail
would indeed be idle.   The element of contingency,
which the individuality of its ultimate factors introduces
into history, alone suffices to restrain the consistent
pluralist from all prophecies of this sort.   But, on the
other hand, his general *Weltanschauung* leads him—as
we have seen—to believe in a universal tendency
towards perfection as the very principle of life[1].

[1] Such tendency towards perfection was several times enounced
by Leibniz. As an instance may be cited the following: "Not only

The pluralist's view of the world leads him also to regard this progress as consisting in the advance towards a 'higher unity.' To set over against this, though the problem of evil is still serious enough, there is for the pluralist no 'evil one'—no *principle* of evil in the world ; and also no *pure* malevolence, no *radikale Böse*, as Kant called it, in the individual. All things in the main and in the long run, he holds, work together for good. Or, to put it otherwise, there is a conservation and a solidarity of the good such as does not exist for evil[1]. *Magna est veritas et praevalebit*: there are truths that wake to perish never, but errors never harmonize and tend inherently to refute one another. The memory of the just is blessed, but the name of the wicked shall rot.

Obviously if the hindrances to progress were insurmountable, there could have been no progress at all. But it might still be that the hindrances increased as progress advanced, that sooner or later a sort of 'law of diminishing return' would begin to operate. We are told however that even in the economic sphere of man's activity the law of diminishing return holds only of "the part which Nature plays in produc-

do immaterial things subsist always, but also their lives, progress and changes are regulated so as to attain to a definite goal, or rather to approximate towards it more and more, as asymptotes do. And though the movements are retrograde sometimes, like paths that have bends in them, yet the advance prevails finally and the end is reached." Letter to Queen Charlotte, *Philosophische Schriften*, Gerhardt's edn, VI. pp. 507 ff.

[1] That the essence of religion is 'faith in the conservation of value' is the main theme in Professor Höffding's original and interesting *Philosophy of Religion*.

tion," while "the part which man plays conforms to
the law of increasing return" and this part "tends to
diminish or even override any increased resistance
which Nature may offer to raising increased amounts
of raw produce[1]." There is then, we may say with
some confidence, no *a priori* ground for any analogy
between spiritual culture and agriculture in respect of
cumulative hindrances to progress. We have indeed
only to look closer at the two most serious obstacles to
social advance to see that they tend to be less formidable, in proportion, the further the advance proceeds.
I refer, of course, to ignorance and selfishness. It
may suffice to consider the last and worst—for society
and selfishness are in their very essence opposed.
The conflict of self-interest and duty to others has
long been a commonplace with ethical writers ; and it
has even been maintained that without extra-social
sanctions there is no means of bringing that wholly
imaginary person, the consistent egoist, to work for
the general good. Yet after all what keeps the selfish
man most in countenance is the selfishness of others :
he does to others as they in general do to him, not as
he would that they should do. But at least he cannot
will that the egoistic maxim should be a universal law.
He approves such examples of public spirit and philanthropy as he may see, though he does not follow
them ; and he is ready perhaps to support beneficent
schemes of legislation to promote ends for which he is
unwilling to make private sacrifices. This fortunate,
and—we might add—inevitable, inconsistency permits

[1] Prof. A. Marshall, *Principles of Economics*, vol. I. 1st edn,
p. 379.

social sanctions to stand out clearly and to become more efficient with every advance that better men effect. *Probitas laudatur et alget*, the satirist has said, yet in truth even bare commendation and approval do their part in quickening virtue into life. In short the objective mind or reason, in which the selfish share, divides them, as selfish, against themselves both individually and collectively, and leads them in their own despite to further its coherent ends :

ἐσθλοὶ μὲν γὰρ ἁπλῶς, παντοδαπῶς δὲ κακοί.

"This may be called the cunning of reason," said Hegel, "that she permits the passions to work for herself so that what they produce [for themselves] is forfeited and lost[1]." So again T. H. Green:—"Where the selfishness of man has proposed, his better reason has disposed. Whatever the means, the result has been a gradual removal of obstacles to that recognition of a universal fellowship which the action of reason in man potentially constitutes[2]." Such at least is the broad teaching of history so far.

Extreme as the selfishness of many may still be and rare as is any whole-hearted enthusiasm for humanity, yet the progress already made is amply sufficient to show that the direction in which it has moved and is still moving points towards the ultimate conciliation of self-interest and the common good. This progress may seem small, partly because to us the time it has taken looks immense, and partly because it still falls indefinitely short of the ideal that we entertain. But

---

[1] *Philosophie der Geschichte*, 1840, p. 41.
[2] Green, *Prolegomena to Ethics*, p. 230.

the problems that time involves do not much concern us in this connexion. *Der Weltgeist hat Zeit genug*, as Hegel once said, and in contemplating the world historically we have to accustom ourselves to regard a thousand years as one day. Compared with the age of the earth itself man's appearance upon it began but yesterday, and he has hardly yet emerged from the stage of infancy.

And now what has been the direction of this progress on its moral, that is its highest, side? We start from a state of natural selfishness, in which the life of the individual man, to use the memorable words of Hobbes, is "solitary, poor, nasty, brutish and short"; and we find ourselves in the era of Christian civilisation, where—to quote T. H. Green again—"'the recognition of the claims of a common humanity' is a phrase that has become so familiar...that we are apt to suspect it of being cant. Yet this very familiarity is proof of the extent to which the idea...has affected law and institutions[1]." This humanitarian idea then is operative now, though its full realisation is our still distant ideal. But if it is fully realisable, the fact that this realisation is a 'far-off event' does not, I would say again, very directly concern our present inquiry : for that, such eventual realisation is enough. "To any ethical student who finds its realisation difficult, I recommend," said Stuart Mill, "as a means of facilitating it, the second of M. Comte's two principal works, the *Système de Politique Positive*...It has superabundantly shown the possibility of giving to the service of humanity, even without the aid of belief in a Providence,

[1] *Prolegomena to Ethics*, p. 228.

both the psychical power and the social efficacy of a religion ; making it take hold of human life, and colour all thought, feeling and action, in a manner of which the greatest ascendancy ever exercised by any religion may be but a type and foretaste[1]." Kant, like Wordsworth and Coleridge, was inspired with a like confidence by what he describes as the moral enthusiasm for the ideal displayed in the French Revolution[2]. It cannot be said, however, that either Kant or Mill attempted anything like a philosophical deduction of this faith in human progress and perfectibility. Other modern philosophers in plenty have attempted this, no doubt— for example Lessing, Herder, Krause, Hegel, and many besides ; but always on grounds more or less definitely theological. But to the pluralist this tendency is clear in itself so soon as we allow that all at least *seek* the good and therefore tend to replace an initial state of comparative isolation and conflict by progressively higher forms of unity and cooperation. When the level of society and reason is reached, this tendency is no longer a blind impulse, it has become a conscious ideal. We emerge from the darkness, where we could only grope, into the light where we can see at least in which direction our ideal lies. "The practical struggle after the Better...makes the way by which the Best is to be more nearly approached plain enough" for further advance and also more feasible. This point has been worked out at length by T. H. Green. To the objection that it does not precisely define the course in which the advance is to be made we may reply in the

[1] *Utilitarianism*, p. 49.
[2] 'Streit der Facultäten,' *Werke*, Hartenstein's edn, VII. pp. 399 f.

. words of Professor Bosanquet :—"The difficulty of
defining the best life does not trouble us, because we
rely throughout on the fundamental logic of human
nature *qua* rational. We think ourselves no more
called upon to specify in advance what will be the
details of the life which satisfies an intelligent being as
such, than we are called upon to specify in advance
what will be the details of the knowledge which satisfies
an intelligent being as such. Wherever a human
being touches practice, as wherever he touches theory,
we find him driven on by his intolerance of contradictions towards shaping his life as a whole[1]." Reason
makes man master of his fate, and though slowly, yet
surely, urges him onwards to the accomplishment of
her perfect work.

We come at length then to the question, stated at
the outset, what sort of unity will the realisation of the
rational ideal secure? The answer may be very brief.
"Thy Kingdom come, Thy will be done on earth as it
is in heaven." To imagine this petition answered is
to imagine humanity animated by a single wise and
righteous will : every citizen would work harmoniously
with every other, each one doing the highest and the
best of which he is capable. The will of the Many
and the will of the One would accord completely. But
on the pluralist view the Divine will would only be a
reality as it was the ideal towards which the whole
creation moves, attained at length. The Kingdom
would take the place of the ideal King : there would
be a perfect commonwealth, but strictly no monarch,

[1] Cf. T. H. Green, *Prolegomena to Ethics*, Bk III. ch. iii. ;
Bosanquet, *The Philosophic Theory of the State*, p. 181 ; cf. Goethe :
Ein guter Mensch in seinem dunklen Drange
Ist sich des rechten Weges wohl bewusst.

other than 'the objective mind' sovereign in every
breast.

Such is, I believe, in the main a fair presentation
of the pluralistic *Weltanschauung*. The time it has
occupied may I fear have tired the patience of many
of you. It still remains to consider the objections
to which it is liable—many of which will no doubt
have occurred to you already—and the replies to
them which the pluralist can make. But first it will
repay us, I think, to take account of some underlying
affinities between the pluralist's position and that of
certain philosophers commonly regarded as singularists, which seems to be directly contrary to it.

LECTURE VII.

THE PLURALISM OF HEGEL.

The standpoint of pluralism in our day is, as we have seen, fundamentally historical. It is a philosophy of becoming rather than of being. It holds—as has been said of the philosophy of Aristotle—that "the ultimate metaphysical explanation of existence must be sought not so much in a *prius* out of which things emerge as in the goal towards which they move[1]." That goal, so experience seems to show, is indeed an ultimate unity, which however presupposes a real plurality: but no attempt is made to conceive the plurality as due to a differentiation of a unity pre-existing 'before the world was' and anterior to any conceivable experience. The three great singularistic philosophies of the nineteenth century however did venture on this bold enterprise, and it is, as we have seen, largely their conspicuous failure that has brought pluralism into vogue again. Now the last and chief of these, the philosophy of Hegel, is by common consent a philosophy of history in the widest sense, whatever it may be besides; and mainly, if not solely, as such is it generally acknowledged to be of great positive value. It will then be interesting as well as instructive to compare Hegelianism with pluralism in respect of their common historical ground. Such a

---

[1] Pringle-Pattison, *Hegelianism and Personality*, 1st edn, p. 82.

comparison will become more significant when it is re-membered, as Hegel's critics urge and his exponents allow, that the so-called dialectical development of thought as such, in which he attempts to find the unity that transcends the seeming plurality, is only distinct from the historical development by being abstracted from it after reflexion has revealed its presence there[1].

Regarding things historically Hegel found develop-ment everywhere, he found not a statical world like that of the Eleatics but a dynamical one like that of Heracleitus. His leading ontological concept was more akin to the active subject of the pluralist Leibniz than to the indifferent substance of the singularist Spinoza. No doubt he reached in the end a unity which he called absolute; but in his Philosophy of Nature and of Mind, where he first comes into touch with the real world, it is plurality that chiefly obtrudes itself. Yet, while recognising the "spectacle of a con-tingency that runs out into endless detail," Hegel treats it in the most contemptuous manner. The starry heavens that filled Kant with awe he thinks it fitting to call a "luminous rash...as little deserving of wonder as the rash on a human skin[2]." The wealth

[1] Hegel has himself described philosophy as 'thinking considera-tion of things' (*denkende Betrachtung der Dinge, Encycl.* § 2), and in his first systematic work, the Phenomenology of Mind, he undertakes to provide 'the ladder' by which the beginner may ascend into the 'ether' where the dialectic transfiguration enacts itself. But he so far overreached his purpose that, like theatrical managers at a fair, he has given us on the boards outside, as it were, a preliminary and more or less tentative outline of his whole system. Hence he also called the Phenomenology his voyage of discovery: in this bewildering adventure psychology and history play the leading part.

[2] *Naturphilosophie*, § 268, p. 92.

of forms, organic and inorganic, that Nature presents, ought not as such, he maintained, "to be rated higher than the equally casual fancies of the mind surrendering itself to its own caprices."   "Contingent determination from without has," he says again, "in the sphere of Nature its right place[1]."   But such language is mere *bravado* in the face of a serious difficulty, with which Hegel had not the patience to deal—or rather a difficulty with which a philosophy such as his could not have dealt at all.   As Professor Pringle-Pattison has well said: "A system of rationalism which talks of what 'is determined not by reason but by sport and external accident' [as Hegel has done] must fairly be held to acknowledge a breakdown in its attempt to grasp the whole of existence[2]."   The first point we have to notice then is, that in admitting our inability to eliminate contingency Hegel has also admitted our inability to . eliminate the plurality which it implies.   "This impotence of Nature sets limits to philosophy" he tells us.   Whether 'impotence' is the right name for the fact may well be questioned ; but the one point that concerns us meanwhile is Hegel's recognition of the fact itself.   Nature is for Hegel historically the first stage of the real world, and here at the outset he finds himself confronted and limited by the very plurality and contingency from which the pluralist too makes his start.   What he calls the 'impotence of Nature' is historically just that inchoate state of things which the progress of history is supposed gradually to straighten out.

---

[1] *Op. cit.* § 250, p. 36.
[2] *Hegelianism and Personality*, 1st edn, p. 138.

Taking this progress in its widest extent, the processes of what we call nature fall within it, and are to be regarded, Hegel himself tells us, as a system of stages leading up to Mind, which emerges from Nature like the phœnix from its ashes[1]. But though one of the stages proceeds from the other, it is not, Hegel goes on to insist, "*naturally* generated out of the other; on the contrary it [is generated] in the inner Idea that constitutes the ground of Nature[2]." In other words his meaning seems to be that the process is really timeless, or as Goethe put it

> Natur hat weder Kern
> Noch Schale,
> Alles ist sie mit einem Male[3].

Accordingly in a lecture-note to the passage quoted he adds : " The notion puts all particularity in a general way into existence at once." In saying all this Hegel seems plainly to be trying to take back with one hand what he has yielded with the other. Or, to put it otherwise, he oscillates between two different kinds of development—the dialectical, which is timeless as well as abstract and general, and the historical which involves time-process and deals primarily with the concrete and particular. For us at any rate the experience of this latter development is essential to our knowledge of the former, which—according to Hegel's

---

[1] *Naturphilosophie*, § 247, p. 24, § 376, p. 695.
[2] *Op. cit.* § 249, p. 32.
[3] This we might perhaps translate :

> Nature has neither shell
> Nor kernel,
> She's all at once in the eternal.

own teaching—belongs to its subsequent and latest
phase. Indeed he has said more than once of philosophy in general what in his introduction he has
expressly said of the Philosophy of Nature in particular:—both as regards its origin and its elaboration
it has experience for its presupposition and condition[1].
We might here fairly remind Hegel of a caution he
has himself uttered:—" In respect of Mind and its
manifestations [just as in the case of Nature] we must
be on our guard lest we be misled by the well-meant
endeavour after rational knowledge into attempting to
represent as necessary or, as the phrase is, to construct
a priori, phenomena to which the mark of contingency
pertains[2]." Even if it turn out that the dialectical
method holds good for the timeless development, yet it
is not a heuristic method; at the outset philosophy as
' the thinking consideration of things' has to begin with
its ' voyages of discovery.' The greater part of Hegel's
Philosophy of Nature and of Mind is of this sort[3].

And here in common with the pluralist he finds, as
we have already seen, plurality and contingency everywhere, and we have now further to note that he finds
also a gradual historical progress from nature to spirit,
from nature as a ' bacchantic God' to ' free spirit—the
truth that knowing knows itself'—a progress that in
all essential points corresponds with that which in the
exposition of pluralism I have already attempted to
describe. All this, we have to insist, antecedes for
us the timeless notional development which Hegel

[1] Cf. *Encyclopaedie*, §§ 6, 7, 12, 38, 246.
[2] *Op. cit.* § 145.
[3] Cf. such categories as Mechanism, Chemism, Life, &c.

attempts to blend with it. The problem of time in relation to the dialectic is one of the many that Hegel left wholly to his successors : it is perhaps the most serious aspect of that 'ugly broad ditch' with which Schelling taunted his quondam friend in a phrase embodying the most trenchant criticism the Hegelian philosophy has ever received.

We come to a new point. Things are not altogether contingent or progressive, though there is contingency and progress everywhere : what we find is 'uniformity flecked with diversity.' The uniformity in general we refer to nature as mechanical, and the diversity and progress to life or mind. This contrast too Hegel has noticed. "The changes in nature," he says, "indefinitely manifold as they are, exhibit only a routine that is ever repeated: in nature there happens nothing new under the sun....It is only in the changes taking place on the spiritual platform that novelty comes to the fore." Again he speaks of nature as "a system of unconscious thoughts, as an intelligence that, as Schelling said, is petrified[1]." Such language at once reminds us of the distinction between *natura naturans* and *natura naturata* as the pluralist interprets it. The former answers to nature as full of contingency, which is the very opposite of routine ; the latter to nature as mechanical and devoid of novelty, in itself but the 'corpse of the understanding,' as Hegel calls it ; the dead self on which we rise to higher things, as the pluralist maintains. The mechanization of habit, dexterity as consisting in making the body the uncon-

[1] *Philosophie der Geschichte*, 1837, p. 51. *Encyclopaedie*, § 24, Lecture Note 1.

scious instrument of the soul, in and through which it
expresses itself as if the body were the soul's work of
art, and so forth—all this Hegel recognises to the full
and describes in detail.   It cannot indeed be said that
he expressly traces back these psychological facts as
far as the pluralist attempts to do ; but it might be
fairly maintained that his view of nature justifies such
a procedure.

In the first place Hegel was no dualist : the whole
process of nature is to become spirit, and spirit it
is in itself or potentially from the beginning.   But
actually at the outset it is infinite isolation or dis-
memberment (*Vereinzelung*), and its unity is still to
seek.   It advances from this to the natural individuality
or particularity of physical bodies and finally to the
subjective individuality of organisms[1].   At this level
sentience emerges and we pass over into the realm of
mind, the individual existing for itself.   The earlier,
so-called inorganic processes pluralism explicitly interprets, in Leibnizian fashion, as also in some measure
sentient and conative.   In his *Philosophy of Nature*
Hegel was too much under the influence of Schelling
and dominated by his 'polarity myth' for this.   But
occasionally he comes very near to the Leibnizian
standpoint.   Thus he describes a soul as such, as "in
itself the totality of nature ; as individual soul it is
a monad ; it is itself the posited totality of its *particular*
world, so that this is shut up within it, is its content."
And again : " In contrast to the macrocosm of Nature
as a whole, the soul can be designated the microcosm,
in which the former is compressed (*zusammengedrängt*)

[1] *Naturphilosophie*, § 252.

and its externality thereby overcome[1]." This metaphorical language, by the way, looks very like nonsense : how the soul is going to condense the world
or how compression is to put an end to externality is
not evident. But what Hegel means, we may suppose,
is what Leibniz also meant: the world is for every soul
a presented, or—in the language of the first passage—
a 'posited totality'—or continuum. Now all this, it
must be remembered, is said, *not* of the higher stages
of mental development, which Hegel distinguishes as
spirit (*Geist*); it is said of what he calls the natural
and the sentient soul, the stage of obscurity (*Dunkel-
heit*) before the soul has attained to a conscious and
intelligible content[2]—the stage, in a word, of Leibniz's
'confused perception.' And who is to say how far
back this obscurity extends? All we know of it we
know because we do not begin with it but approach it
from the light and interpret it in terms of what it has
become. And this is the method of pluralism.

But now, it may be said, in the second place—
indeed it has been said by a thoroughgoing Hegelian
—that this principle of interpreting the lower on the
analogy of the higher was recognised by Hegel too.
Comparing the opposite processes of evolution and
emanation—or, as I have proposed to call it, devolution—both of which have been employed in the interpretation of nature, he expresses a preference for the
latter. "To proceed from the more perfect to the
less perfect is more advantageous," he says; "for then
we have the type of the completed organism before

---

[1] *Philosophy of Mind*, Encycl. III. §§ 391, 403. Cf. also § 352,
Zusatz, Encycl. II. [2] *Op. cit.* § 404.

W. 10

us ": albeit he held both methods to be 'one-sided
and superficial[1].' How then should we proceed, how,
in fact, do we proceed? "It is clear," said G. H.
Lewes, "that we should never rightly understand
vital phenomena were we to begin our study of life
by contemplating its simplest manifestations in the
animal series; we can only understand the Amoeba
and the Polype by a light reflected from the study of
Man." In quoting this passage the late Professor
Ritchie, the Hegelian I just now referred to, adds the
remark: "What makes it seem possible for the scientific
investigator 'to begin at the beginning' is the fact that
he is not doing so. The student of the Amoeba happens to be, not an Amoeba, but a specimen of a highly
developed vertebrate, and knows at least something
about the differentiated organs and functions of his
own body[2]." What we do then is by means of our
knowledge of the higher to interpret the lower, while
at the same time recognising that the actual process
has been a development of the lower upwards towards
the higher. With all this we may fairly say that
Hegel was in complete agreement, once we have disallowed his attempts to play fast and loose with the
two distinct kinds of developments—the historical and
the dialectic. He does interpret the lower by the
higher, he does admit an actual historical evolution,
and he does insist that Nature is potentially mental
from the first, so that the historical evolution is no

[1] *Naturphilosophie*, Encycl. II. § 249, p. 35.
[2] G. H. Lewes, *Study of Psychology*, p. 122; D. G. Ritchie,
'Darwin and Hegel' in the *Proceedings of the Aristotelian Society*,
vol. I. p. 59.

generatio equivoca. "The appearance," he remarks, "as if [the existence of] Mind were brought about through an Other, is disposed of by Mind itself; for this—so to say—has the supreme ingratitude to resolve and mediate that through which it seems to be produced, to reduce it to dependence on itself and to establish its own complete independence[1]."

Let us now look at Hegel's handling of this evolution a little closer.   His *Philosophy of History* is professedly little more than a philosophy of political history.   The progress that it traces is the progress of freedom as realised in the objective mind or society; but freedom, it should be observed, is regarded as identical with spiritual perfection generally; and so he describes 'world-history' as "the exhibition of mind as it works out the knowledge of what it is in itself." The realisation of this ideal, he explains, is the final end, the working principle, the informing notion of history.   But, as such, a principle is only general, abstract, and potential; in order to its realisation a further factor is essential: in history proper this factor is the activity of human beings.   But an end for which I am to be active must be in some sense my end: even if it have other aspects that do not concern me, still it is my own satisfaction that makes it interesting to me. He concludes then "that absolutely nothing is brought to pass without the interest of those who actively cooperated in it:...that *nothing great in the world* is accomplished without passion[2]."

Reason the card, but passion is the gale.

---

[1] *Philosophy of Mind*, Encycl. III. § 381, p. 23.

[2] *Philosophie der Geschichte*, 1837, p. 28.

The history of the world in the widest sense, however, goes further back than this; and though Hegel
regarded it as neither fitting nor worthy of philosophy
to take up the story before rationality comes upon the
scene, he nevertheless has some introductory remarks
concerning the pre-historic.   These are important as
further bearing out what has just been said about the
spiritualistic continuity of the whole process of evolution as Hegel conceived it, and as making clearer
the pluralistic basis that it implies.   Having insisted
that "nothing happens, nothing is accomplished save
as the individuals actively concerned in it secure their
own satisfaction," he continues : " But the world's history does not begin with any conscious end, such as
we find in particular centres of men.   The simple
impulse to live together has already the conscious end
of security for life and property, and so soon as this
life in common is attained the end is [further] enlarged.
The world's history begins only potentially (i.e. as
Nature) with its general end, the full realisation of
the notion of spirit.   That end is its inner, nay its
inmost unconscious impulse, and the entire business of
the world-history is the labour of bringing it to consciousness.   Thus making its appearance in the form
of natural beings, natural wills, what has been called
the subjective side [of history] is straightway present
for itself[1]."   Translated into pluralistic language this
amounts to saying : A plurality of conative beings at
first casually interacting in pursuance of their several
particular and immediate impulses gradually come to
have ends and continually widening ends in common,

[1] *Op. cit.* p. 29.

thereby advancing towards the complete realisation of the one objective end of history that is now to be regarded as its potential principle from the first.

We are not then surprised to find Hegel too describing and illustrating—as we have already done under the title 'heterogony of ends[1]'—the fact that in the course of the world's history the actions of mankind are continually realising ends that they neither intended nor foresaw. But the explanation which he seeks to give of this fact is very different from that of the pluralist. He regards human interests and actions in the first instance simply as instruments and means. Through them the absolute final purpose of the world's history is carried out, but carried out as something beyond and external to them—just as a house is erected by means of natural forces and elements that have no concern with its inner end, which in fact is to keep *them* at bay. But this illustration, which please understand is Hegel's own[2], at once and very pointedly raises the question : Where in the case of the world's history is the guiding and controlling mind to be found that corresponds to the architect in the case of the house ? It must have a place somewhere in one or other of the three great divisions of Hegel's philosophy. But where ? Obviously not in the *Logic,* for that lies on the other side of everything like historical and natural development, as Hegel expressly

---

[1] Lect. IV. above, p. 79.

[2] *Philosophie der Geschichte,* 1840, p. 34. This illustration was omitted by Gans, the editor of the 1837 edition, who professed to follow Hegel's own revision ; but it was inserted in the second edition by Hegel's son Karl, Gans having in the meantime died.

maintained. It is the realm of pure thought, not the realm of ends. In the *Philosophies of Nature and of Mind* the *Logic* is applied; but their contents, as such, do not enter into it or concern it. Perception, imagination and the like, which belong to self-conscious mind, are to be as completely excluded from logic as are the forms of space and time and the phenomena, inorganic or organic, which fill them out. The 'notion' is not to be regarded as an act of the self-conscious, subjective, intellect: even the term 'objective thought' is awkward as applied to it, for *thought* is usually referred only to mind or consciousness, and *objective* in like manner primarily only to the unconscious[1].

Let us turn next to the *Philosophy of Mind*; for in his *Philosophy of History* Hegel often refers to the 'world-spirit' as that which directs and controls the actions of men to subserve its own supreme end. But what does Hegel himself tell us in the *Philosophy of Mind* about this 'world-spirit'? "This movement," he says referring to the course of history, "is the way, whereby the spiritual substance is liberated—the deed, whereby the absolute final purpose of the world is accomplished in it, [whereby] the spirit that at first exists only *potentially* (*an sich*)...becomes the world-spirit[2]." Actually then, it would seem, the world-spirit corresponds to the realised plan of the house rather than to the architect who shapes and controls the materials. A plan does not ordinarily carry itself out. Still, it may be urged, a mere illustration is not to be pressed. That, of course, is true; but on the

---

[1] Cf. *Logik*, III. pp. 21, 18; *Encyclopaedie*, § 24.
[2] *Philosophy of Mind*, Encycl. III. § 549 *init.*

other hand it is to be remembered that, according to Hegel's own statement, the world-spirit is only potentially present at first, only gradually attains to "consciousness and self-consciousness and so to the revelation and reality of its perfect nature, its nature [*Wesen*] as it is in and for itself"—a position which, as we may see presently, carries important consequences. It has to be remembered too that Hegel, as we have already seen, makes a point of insisting that the plan or principle or end of history needs means and instruments in order to its determinate realisation and is in itself only 'general, abstract, not completely real.'

But at this juncture some disciple of Hegel may refer us back to the *Logic* for the true meaning of teleology. There Hegel tells us "we may say that in teleological activity the end is the beginning, the consequence is the ground, the effect is the cause, a case of becoming is a case of what has become, in it only what is already existing comes into existence, and so forth[1]." Afterwards, in the corresponding section of the so-called *Smaller Logic*, he expresses himself still more strongly. "As a matter of fact," he here says, "the object is potentially [*an sich*] the notion; and so when the notion, as end, is realised in the object, this is only the manifestation of the inner nature of the object itself. Objectivity is thus, as it were, only a covering under which the notion lies concealed....The consummation of the infinite End, therefore, consists merely in setting aside (*aufheben*) the illusion [which makes it seem] as if the end was

[1] *Logik*, III. p. 228.

not yet accomplished.   It is under this illusion that
we live, and at the same time it is this illusion alone
that stirs us to activity [*das Bethätigende*] and on
which our interest in the world depends.   The Idea
in its process makes for itself that illusion—posits an
Other over against itself—and its activity consists in
setting this illusion aside[1]."   The serpent with its tail
in its mouth is an ancient mystic symbol, and if Hegel,
like Herbert Spencer, had bethought himself of a
book-plate to adorn *his* theory of evolution, doubtless
it is this that he would have chosen.   Moreover a
devoted disciple has provided the motto :—*Serpens
nisi serpentem comederit non fit draco*[2].   It would be
needless for our purpose to spend time in discussing
the validity of a position that cannot even be stated
without contradicting itself : it is sufficient to observe
that an illusion that embraces the whole range of
experience and is declared to be the source alike of all
truth in theory and all zest in practice is no illusion
for us.   This appeal to the *Logic* then does not help
us in our search : it only confronts us once more with
the problem as to the relation of the dialectic to time.

Coming back now to the historical again—which
the employment of means and instruments to accomplish with much pain and labour a superhuman end,
in any case implies—there is only the *Philosophy of
Nature* left.   In Nature, from or in which the world's

[1] *Encyclopaedie*, i. § 212.   In the phrase 'sets an Other over
against itself,'—*setzt ein Anderer sich gegenüber*, Hegel, like Fichte
before him, seems to be trying to read his own philosophy in the
German word for object, i.e. *Gegenstand*.

[2] J. E. Erdmann, *Geschichte der neueren Philosophie*, Bd iii.
Abth. ii. p. 841.

process begins, can we find the guiding executive whose working consummates itself in the fulness of time? But if it be true that even in the realm of mind the world-spirit works at first underground like a mole, to use Hegel's own simile, and only at length emerges into consciousness and self-consciousness, surely we cannot expect to find it enacting the part of a supreme and intelligent director in Nature, where contingency runs riot like a bacchantic god and its impotence sets limits to philosophy, which that cannot overcome[1]. In his explication of the notion of mind Hegel begins: "Mind has *for us* Nature as its *presupposition*, the *truth* of which and so the *absolute first* of which it [nevertheless] is." Again, speaking of its development, he says: "Mind is preceded not only by the logical Idea but also by external Nature. For the *knowledge* already involved in the *logical* idea is only the notion of knowledge that we think, not the knowledge that is there for itself, not actual mind but merely its possibility. The actual mind, which alone is our object-matter in the science of mind, has Nature for its proximate, as it has the logical Idea for its primary, presupposition[2]." This very oracular language is another instance of the seemingly double-dealing of Hegel's circular theory of development, and once again we must claim to distinguish sharply between the dialectical development—where "the Idea thought in its repose is indeed timeless"—and the historical development, where the Idea as concrete appears to be "not at rest but an existence progressing in time[3]." What

---

[1] Cf. above, p. 140.   [2] *Philosophy of Mind*, § 381.
[3] Cf. *Geschichte der Philosophie*, I. p. 46.

Hegel's explication comes to then seems to be this : Nature is 'Mind out of itself' from the abstract standpoint of the Logic ; but it is Mind not yet 'come to itself' from the concrete point of view of historical development. Seeing that in the Logic we have not actual mind, not knowledge but only its possibility, it may well be questioned whether this mere possibility can become actual by passing out of itself : it may even be doubted whether mind out of itself can be called mind at all. No wonder, then, that thinkers largely in sympathy with Hegel—as, for example, von Hartmann, and still more, Volkelt—regarded his system as really a philosophy of the unconscious ; or that others, trained in the Hegelian school, like Strauss and Feuerbach, resolved it into a refined naturalism. From such constructions there seems to be no escape unless we take Hegel's unconscious nature in the Leibnizian or pluralistic fashion. And the continuity of the Hegelian historical evolution, which we have already noted, may be held to favour such an interpretation.

No doubt the objection will at once occur, that for Hegel Nature is *essentially* a unity that only *appears* as a plurality. But is that after all so clear as at first sight it seems—assuming, of course, that we ignore the desperate leap from the Logic to Nature, in other words disallow any continuity between the dialectical and the historical evolution ? Not only does the contingency of Nature imply plurality, as already said, but Hegel repeatedly lays emphatic stress on what he calls the externality (*Aussereinander*) of Nature, not simply in relation to mind, but to itself ; and on

its infinite separation (*Vereinzelung*) where the unity
of form is still ideal, potential, and therefore still to
seek, Nature remaining meanwhile an 'unresolved
contradiction.' "Its differences...," he says, "are
existences more or less independent of each other;
through their original unity indeed they stand in
relation with one another, so that no one is conceivable without the rest; but this relation is for them
in a higher or lower degree external[1]." Even when
he has advanced so far as the *Philosophy of Mind*
he represents the soul as at first only natural, not yet
sentient or actual; and *à propos* of this earliest stage
he remarks :—" As the light breaks up into an infinite
multitude of stars, so also the general Nature-soul
breaks up into an infinite multitude of individual souls;
only with this difference, that, whereas the light has
the appearance of existing independently of the stars,
the general Nature-soul attains to actual existence
only in the separate souls[2]." This comes very near
to presentationism or the 'mind-dust theory' and would
more than satisfy the pluralists of our day.

So far we have been considering Hegel's interpretation of that heterogony of ends which in common
with the pluralists he recognises throughout the course
of the world's history. He attributes it to what he
was fond of calling 'the absolute cunning of reason'
or the world-spirit in ensuring that the contingency
of all things finite shall subserve its own supreme end.
This end so far we have found him regarding as

[1] Cf. *Philosophie der Natur*, §§ 247, 248, 252; *Philosophy of
Mind*, § 381, Zusatz.
[2] *Philosophy of Mind*, § 390.

external to, and independent of, its instruments ; and even as directed against them, as a house is built by means of the forces of nature in order to set them at defiance.   But we have been unable to find in Hegel's philosophy any evidence of this world-spirit in its *rôle* of superintending overruler.   We have found the house in progress, but no architect ; or rather we have found the whole metaphor bursting its bounds, as Hegel would say ; for the completed house is to be the architect.

Does the house then build itself ?   So the pluralist would say ; in so saying, however, he refuses to regard the finite agents in history as simply means and instruments to purely alien ends.   And Hegel after all does likewise : as instance, the following :—— "If now we are content to see individuals, their ends and the satisfaction of these, sacrificed, their happiness generally abandoned to the dominion of chance, to which it belongs ; if we are content to consider them in general, as falling under the category of means, still they have one side which we hesitate even in comparison with the Highest to regard only in this light... viz. their moral and religious side."   But he goes much farther, and presently continues :——"If we speak of a means we imagine it in the first instance as only external to the end and as having no part in that. In fact, however, natural things generally, let alone what is higher,—nay, the commonest lifeless objects that are used as means—must be so constituted as to answer to the end or have something in them that they share with it.   Men least of all stand in that entirely external relation as means to the end of reason...on the contrary they have a part in that end

of reason and are, just because of this, ends of themselves[1]." Now we must here, I think, admit that
a very close approximation to the pluralist's theory
of evolution is at least implied. Such approximation
appears still closer when we take into account what
Hegel has said *à propos* of the 'absolute cunning of
reason'—how it stands aside and leaves things to interact according to their own nature ; letting them rub
together and frustrate each other, while it never itself
directly interferes ; how it allows full scope to human
passions and interests, paying the tribute of transient
existence (*Dasein und Vergänglichkeit*) not out of itself
but out of them, while it foresees the result to be not the
accomplishment of these designs but of its own[2]. This
very deistic account of an assumed spectator of the
world's history, whether called Reason or God or Providence—and Hegel in turn calls it all three—we may
leave entirely aside, for we have been able to find it
only as the culminating Idea of the dialectical development and as the goal of the historical. All that
immediately interests us is the near approach that
Hegel here makes to the pluralistic position. This
position, as we have seen, is that all the agents at work
in history, from the lowest to the highest, are not
primarily means to external ends, not primarily things
but persons in the widest sense[3], who by their mutual
interaction and striving—since all seek the good—

---

[1] *Philosophie der Geschichte*, 1837, p. 33.

[2] *Encyclopaedie*, I. § 209, and elsewhere.

[3] In saying this I have in view an interesting book written mainly
from the pluralistic standpoint, which I have only just come across—
Person und Sache by L. W. Stern, 1906.

gradually eliminate the contingency, which their comparative isolation—Hegel's primitive *Vereinzelung*—
at first entailed, and so gradually bring about the reign
of reason and right.   And this position could hardly
be more concisely stated than in words that are Hegel's
own :—"The history of the world shows only how
spirit comes gradually to the consciousness and will
of the truth : this dawns upon it ; [then] it discerns
the chief features ; eventually it attains to the full
consciousness of it[1]."   The long introduction to his
Philosophy of History is full of similar passages which
suggest not a preconceived plan steadily carried out
by a single overruling mind employing passive instruments, but a living organization slowly and tentatively
achieved by the long and painful efforts of generations
of struggling individuals.   *Der Trieb der Perfecti-*
bilität ist die Bestimmung der Menschen, Hegel has
said, and all that history shows is this *Trieb* at
work.

But the unity of the whole is the last word of
philosophy : "All philosophy is nothing else than the
study of the determinations (*Bestimmungen*) of unity...
always unity, but in such a way that this is always
further determined" said Hegel.   And so too says
the pluralist to-day : how far the two agree about the
determination we must consider in the following lectures,
when we shall have to look closer into this aspect of
pluralism itself.

[1] *Philosophie der Geschichte,* 1837, p. 51.

LECTURE VIII.

THE HEGELIAN UNITY.

We have seen that there is a strong undercurrent of pluralism running through the whole of Hegel's philosophy regarded as 'the thinking consideration of *things*' in distinction from his attempted 'dialectical development of pure *thought*.' But of course every philosophy must recognise both plurality and unity in some fashion, the important question then still remains: Is the unity with Hegel, as with the pluralist, result, or is it ground and presupposition; historically is it the starting-point or is it the goal: in other words Is there a unity differentiated into a plurality or is there a plurality organized into a unity? Here again I think we shall find much to justify us in affirming the second alternative. No doubt there is something to be said on the other side; of that the disruption of the Hegelian school within five years of the master's death is sufficient evidence. The thinkers on the Hegelian right held that Hegel had taught the absolute priority of the unity as personal Creator and Providence. It is true that he had said in so many words that the content of philosophy and of religion is the same, the difference lying only in their form; the form of the one being logical (*Begriff*), that of

the other being figurative (*Vorstellung*). It is true
that he had found speculative interpretations for the
Christian dogmas of the Trinity, the incarnation, the
atonement, and even the sacraments. Nevertheless
the verdict of succeeding generations has been given
almost unanimously in favour of the thinkers of the
Hegelian left. But they disavowed altogether Hegel's
attempt to incorporate the leading tenets of Christianity
into his philosophy of absolute idealism, and maintained its essentially pantheistic structure. Indeed it
would nowadays seem needless to refer to any other
interpretation, were it not that the leading exponents
of Hegel amongst us have been till lately members
of the right. The appeal to Hegel's doctrine of the
Trinity as evidence of the theistic character of his
philosophy is particularly unfortunate. So long as the
Christian dogma is—so to say—read into it between
the lines, it might pass as such. But taken, as it
ought to be, with the context of the Hegelian philosophy as a whole, the doctrine is obviously and transparently pantheistic. In place of a triple personality
there is no personality at all. The Trinity is simply
equated to the main triad of the Hegelian system,
Logic, Nature, Spirit as severally Thesis, Antithesis
and Synthesis. Let us briefly consider each in turn.

In an important and often-quoted paragraph defining the nature of Logic, Hegel concludes :—" Logic
accordingly is to be understood as the system of pure
reason, as the realm of pure thought. This realm is
the truth as it is unveiled in and for itself. We can
therefore say that this content sets God before us as
he is in his eternal essence before the creation of

Nature and finite spirit[1]." God the Father then, or rather what Hegel describes as the Kingdom of the Father, answers to this realm of pure thought, this 'realm of shadows,' as he proceeds a few pages later to call it. All the unity we can expect to find here then is an ideal unity. But no, the orthodox Hegelian may reply, within the Kingdom of the Father we find, according to Hegel's own teaching, the generation of the Son and the procession of the Spirit : we have the archetype of all community, divine love. "In friendship, in love," Hegel himself has said, "I give up my abstract personality and by so doing win it back as concrete personality. The true in personality then is just this, to gain personality through this absorbing and being absorbed in the other." Yes, but in the case of the Trinity what exactly is this other ? Had Hegel been content to leave this 'silent mystery' as he calls it still fermenting in the thoughts of men as he professed to find it, or had he been content on religious grounds to accept it as the directly revealed truth, which Christian theology proclaims it to be, we should have nothing to say. Nothing at least, unless it were to protest against a philosopher meddling with what is avowedly either mystical or 'revealed.' But he essays to explain it. "The relation of father and son is taken from organic life and is only figuratively used...and so never entirely corresponds with what ought to be expressed." Philosophy alone is competent to put the truth in adequate form and this form is the dialectic development through the moments or functions of the so-called Subjective

[1] *Logik*, I. p. 35.

notion, through universality and particularity to individuality. In Hegel's fearfully laboured expositions this is the only thing that stands out clearly.

The so-called Kingdom of the Father is, it is true, itself a triad within the first moment—universality; and though the notion becomes increasingly adequate and concrete as we advance, still the whole movement falls within the realm of pure thought. Even this triune God, if we like so to call it, is still without the world and so not God, as Hegel himself has said in so many words. The terms which in the course of a few pages he applies to the first person of the Trinity are conclusive so far. "The eternal Idea that is not yet posited in its reality but is itself still the abstract Idea"; "God as simply the Father is not yet the true"; "The abstract God, the Father, is the universal"; "This universal implies the complete Idea, but also only *implies* it, is only potentially Idea." In keeping with such language are the various—chiefly neo-Platonic—attempts to reach the truth, which Hegel thought deserving of recognition; in the course of which we come across such phrases, as for example, the Ὄν, the Abyss or Deep, that is as good as to say, what is as yet empty; the προπάτωρ who is a Father only mediately, the προαρχή, He who was before the beginning; and so on[1]. The 'process' within this universal Hegel describes partly in biological, partly—as we have already seen—in ethical, language, partly, that is to say, as life, partly as love. "Life," he says,

---

[1] *Philosophie der Religion*, 2te Aufl. 1840, Bd II. p. 244, Eng. trans. by Speirs and Sanderson, III. p. 30. Though references are given to this the translations in the text have been made independently.

"preserves itself, preservation means passing into difference, into the struggle with particularity, means finding itself to be distinct over against inorganic nature. Life is thus only a result, since it has generated itself; is a product that in the second place again produces :...what is produced is already there from the beginning. The same holds true in love and love returned[1]." Obviously this is the figurative language appropriate to religion, which for Hegel was but one remove from art : for philosophy such forms are still inadequate. Accordingly Hegel has no sooner elaborated his comparisons than he proceeds to tone them down. For the divine life there is no external; and so here, "the process," he says, "is thus nothing but the *play* of self-preservation, of making sure of one's self[2]." So again, having described love as between two persons, he then characterizes the divine love, as involving "this distinction and the nullity of this distinction, a play which is not in earnest, the distinction being just posited as abolished[3]." In the end then we find Hegel coming back to the realm of pure thought as alone furnishing an adequate account of this process as he all along maintained. Here, he says, it is manifest "that every definite notion is this— to set itself aside (*sich selbst aufheben*), as being its own contradiction, consequently to become its own difference and to posit itself as such. And thus the Notion itself still retains this one-sidedness or finitude, that it is something subjective; the determinations, the differences are posited only as ideal, not in fact as differences. This

---

[1] *Op. cit.* II p. 241, E.t. III. p. 26.
[2] *Op. cit.* II. p. 241, E.t. III. p. 27.   [3] *Op. cit.* II. p. 227, E.t. III. p. 11.

is the Notion that objectifies itself[1]." But again the question recurs : What exactly is this objectification ?

Passing so to the Kingdom of the Son we come upon the Other, Difference, the Objective, as fact and not merely as thought : this is the region of 'infinite particularity' not of 'total particularity' or universality. Here plurality precedes unity. Referring back to the Kingdom of the Father—wherein the differentiation "is only a relation of God, of the Idea to itself, only a play of love with itself, in which it never attains to the seriousness of Other-being, to separation and dis-union (*Entzweiung*)"—Hegel remarks "that we have not yet got to difference in its completeness, in the form that peculiarly belongs to it (*in seiner Eigenthüm-lichkeit*)....In order then that difference may *be*, and in order that it may come to its rights, Other-*being* is requisite, so that what is differentiated may be Other-being as *beënt* (Seyendes)[2]"—to use Dr Hutchison Stirling's term. This Other, let go as something independent, is the World in general, that is Nature and finite minds. But now comes the difficulty : how are the Son and the World related ? How does the playful, ideal differentiation, which amounts only to abstract difference in general, stand towards the com-plete and actual differentiation of a World let go in deadly earnest, in such wise 'let go' that Hegel, like Schelling, can even refer to it as *der Abfall der Idee*, wherein the Idea is 'estranged from itself' ? This is again the question we raised just now : what exactly is the Other ?

---

[1] *Op. cit.* II. p. 232, E.t. III. p. 16.
[2] *Op. cit.* 2nd ed. II. p. 249, E.t. III. p. 35.

If we stop at the Other in the Kingdom of the Father, we have not gone far enough; but if we advance to the Other in the Kingdom of the Son, we seem to have gone too far. In the one we have merely what, stripped of all more concrete metaphors, Hegel can only describe as 'a movement' in the realm of pure thought: in fact, however, when we look closer, it is hard to see how we can have even this. For though it be true that every 'definite notion' implies negation, it is not easy to see why or how the 'pure notion, the notion apart from all limitation,' should imply it[1]. However even granting that this dialectical movement is in itself conceivable, the only point that interests us is that in it difference does not—to use Hegel's own phrase—"get its rights, the right of diversity (*Verschiedenheit*)" or plurality, as, in view of the context, we may I think render it. Now it is in the Kingdom of the Son, he tells us, that this "advance to further determination takes place :...We thus enter into the sphere of determination, i.e. of space and the world of finite mind[2]." And here Hegel, as I have said, has too much on his hands. And he is far from oblivious of the fact.

---

[1] We may talk of 'subjective need' in a finite life, a finite friendship; but to suppose that the content of the 'divine notion,' the first person in the Hegelian Trinity, implies anything analogous to this must surely appear meaningless, when we recall how that content is described. Well, then, may a critic describe this "life in the categories as the most inconceivable thing in the world" (A. Drews, *Die deutsche Speculation seit Kant: das Wesen des Absoluten und die Persönlichkeit Gottes*, 2te Ausg. 1895, Bd 1. p. 248). It is certainly the veriest travesty of the Christian doctrine of the Trinity.

[2] *Op. cit.* II. pp. 250 f., E.t. III. pp. 37 f.

Two very different 'movements,' or processes, are clearly implied, but Hegel feels bound to show that these two are somehow one. So he refers to them as two moments in the analysis of the Son, which are kept apart and yet both contained in Him. The difficulty is really the old one of getting across the famous 'ditch.' How much at a loss Hegel is is shown by the fact that he thinks it illuminating to refer to Jacob Boehm's description of 'the transition' between the two moments of the Son: how "the first only-begotten Lucifer imagined himself in himself, advanced to being and so fell; and how immediately the eternally Only-begotten took his place[1]." On the strength of this piece of utter mysticism Hegel proceeds to refer to "a state before time was when the angels, God's children, sang his praises," and then more exactly defines this 'state' as the relation of thought to its object. Apparently then not only was there a Trinity in the eternal realm of pure thought, the Kingdom of the Father, but a complete and harmonious choir of ideas as well, reminding us of Plato's ideal world. Apparently too the world in space and time was after all not 'freely let go' but, in advancing to its rights of Other-being and plurality, really revolted and fell. Without attempting to resolve this difficulty as to the *Abfall der Idee* and two Only-begotten, we may content ourselves with noticing that it furnishes Hegel with an additional reason for distinguishing the two

---

[1] This passage calls to mind Goethe's account of his early theological speculations, in *Dichtung und Wahrheit*, bk VII. He too speaks of Lucifer 'believing that he found himself in himself' and of the creation and fall that resulted.

and keeping them apart; for otherwise the false position would arise "as *if*," to quote his words, "*the eternal Son of the Father*, the Godhead existing objectively[1] for itself, were the *same* as the world, as if by that only this were to be understood[2]." And yet, notwithstanding all, he still maintains that the two are implicitly the same : the Idea, that is to say, is in itself the same, merely the form is different : it is only figurative thought (*Vorstellung*) that holds the two apart as two wholly diverse spheres and acts. More explicitly, Hegel's final solution of the difficulty—in spite of all that he has said about divine history as the process of self-differentiation, of God without the world not being God, and much beside—is simply to sweep away time and declare the world of finitude to be only the ἕτερον, limited, negative etc., that as such has no truth. Regarded from the point of view of time, "it is merely an instant (*Augenblick*), like the gleam of the lightning-flash, which in its appearing has immediately disappeared. But what we have really got to do is to get rid of every time-determination, whether duration or the now....The world as temporal is just the region of contradiction, the Idea in a form inadequate to it[3]." The one Other then has two forms, one true and the other untrue ; the unveiled, eternal Other of the realm of pure thought, the Kingdom of the Father, and the phenomenal, half-concealed, half-revealed Other of the Kingdom of the Son ; the Other that makes no difference in the unsullied light of the divine self-identity

---

[1] But has Hegel ever made this 'objective existence' clear?
[2] *Op. cit.* II. p. 251, E.t. III. p. 39.
[3] *Op. cit.* II. p. 252, E.t. III. p. 40.

and the Other that refracts and disperses it in endless
particoloured beams ; God in his eternal essence and
the world of infinite particularity, of subjective consciousness and ordinary thought, that is the world
of experience, the historical realm of ends.

Now surely in all this we may say that one thing
at least seems clear : what Hegel undertook to explain—the transition from the Kingdom of the Father
to the Kingdom of the Son—"how this Idea passes
out of its universality and infinity into finitude" proves
to be inexplicable. The Kingdom of the Father, then,
to which the Son as the eternally Only-begotten belongs, is thus—as I attempted to show in the second
lecture—the undiscovered country from whose bourn
no traveller returns. The Absolute cannot be the
startingpoint of real knowledge,—it may be the ultimate goal of philosophical speculation. Experience
may lead us to frame the idea of the Absolute, but it
will not enable us to deduce the world of the Many
from it. Among the opening sentences of his exposition of the Kingdom of the Son, Hegel has the
following which comes near to admitting the truth
of all this :—" First there was the Idea in the element
of thought : this is the foundation and with it we have
begun ; [for] the Universal and therefore more abstract
must precede [all else] in science[1]"; but in fact "it is
the later in existence ; it is the potential (*das Ansich*)
but it comes later to consciousness and knowledge[2]."
That is to say the Idea in the element of thought, to

[1] Hegel uses 'science' here in a Fichtean sense, that is as
equivalent to philosophy.
[2] *Op. cit.* II. p. 247, E.t. III. p. 33.

which Hegel has relegated the persons of the Christian Trinity, lies behind existence and experience: as he goes on immediately to say, "the *form* of the Idea comes to appearance as *result*, but this [result] essentially is *potentiality* (*das Ansich*)." Clear in itself, such language is nevertheless not a little confusing in view of the context, that we were just now discussing, in which it occurs. For there the whole finite world of our conscious experience is declared to be illusory, inadequate, and untrue, and the movement within the realm of thought to be verily reality, truth, infinity. But there still, of course, remains the Kingdom of the Spirit, in which this estrangement of the Idea, which constitutes the inadequacy of the finite world, is finally overcome.

This estrangement is puzzling not only for the reasons we have already considered, but also in yet another respect. Thus, at the end of the *Logic*, Hegel describes the Idea as impelled to realise itself beyond the confines of pure thought and pictures it as freely but with absolute self-confidence taking the plunge into another sphere. This, as we have seen, is a difficult situation to conceive, but the result is equally bewildering. For the plunge, when made, has at once to be undone: the Idea, dissipated and out of itself, has painfully to collect itself again and rise anew to its pristine unity. Fortunately it was not let go as a whole: it is only the second element or moment, that of particularity, that answers to Nature, and the externalisation which was the work of the first moment is internalised anew through the third. This Kingdom of the Spirit we have presently to consider: I anticipate it here because the continuation of the sentence just now quoted is somewhat clearer when this is taken into account. The whole sentence runs :—"The *form* of the Idea comes to appearance as *result*, but essentially this [result] is *potentiality* ; as the content of the Idea is such that the last is the first and the first the last, so is what appears as result, the presupposition, the potentiality, the foundation[1]." This is the cardinal principle of Hegel's doctrine of development, to which I have already several times referred : the end is the beginning, for the beginning is its presupposition, and out of this nothing comes but what is already there. There is a sense in which this paradox may be true and have a meaning : there is a sense in which it is not true but self-contradictory. It may be justifiable when we are dealing with essence and its explication, with a dialectical movement : it is not true of existence and of historical evolution. The plausibility—but also the falsity—of Hegel's position lay in identifying the two. Bare potentiality, the bare idea of an end to be accomplished, however sublime, however completely explicated in respect of its essential import, will never become actuality.

But is it so certain, it may be urged, that what according to Hegel philosophy places first of all is not the supreme reality? Unquestionably if we could suppose that what he meant was simply that—though we only gradually attain to a knowledge of God, yet when we do—we may believe that God is not merely the *ratio essendi*, but is also the personal creator and conserver of all, we should have less difficulty. But

---

[1] *Op. cit.* II. p. 247, E.t. III. p. 33.

the whole trend of his system is against such an interpretation. Now Spirit for Hegel, it will be remembered, falls into the triad of subjective, objective and absolute Spirit. In keeping with such an interpretation, then, as Lotze has remarked, " we should have expected that absolute spirit...would have returned,...only with greater depth of meaning and perfection, to the form that spirit possessed in the first stage of this development, the form that is to say of personal, individual Spirit[1]." But as we are aware, Hegel's Absolute Spirit, the counterpart of the Absolute Idea in the *Logic*, was something wholly different from this. What Hegel places first is then neither a single substance nor a single subject. As the latest and one of his ablest commentators, Kuno Fischer, has said, " the main theme running through the whole of his philosophy is the development of the world in accordance with reason. What is developed is rational consciousness, spirit, the self-knowledge of humanity." All actual development of course presupposes its own possibility, and it is just this that Hegel places first as potential end and aim. He declares thought and being to be identical and yet places abstract thought at the beginning and then fails to effect its union with actual being again. Let me quote another commentary : " It may be all very well to declare that the life of

---

[1] "Of course," Lotze adds, "we could then properly regard the whole series of philosophical notions, that were to lead up to this climax, not as furnishing a history of the development of God himself, but only as the history of our ideas concerning his nature. In so far as this interpretation of it is impossible the dialectical exposition must be changed." *Geschichte der deutschen Philosophie seit Kant*, 1882, pp. 71 f.

God and the divine knowledge is a play of love with itself; [but] such an idea sinks to the devotional or even to insipidity, if the seriousness, the pain, the patience and labour, of the negative are lacking in it. *In itself* that life, it may be, is undisturbed harmony and unity with itself, in which there is no concern about other-being and its estrangement, and as little about overcoming this estrangement. But this [life] *in itself* (*dies Ansich*) is abstract universality, wherein its nature, to be *for itself*, is ignored." But 'nature,' let me parenthetically remark, implies process. This commentary is Hegel's own, and occurs in one of the very last paragraphs that he revised for the press. After another sentence or two he continues: "The true is the whole. The whole however is only the essence completing itself through its own development. Of the Absolute it is to be said that it is essentially *result*, that not till the *end* is it what it is in truth....What though the embryo be *potentially* man, it is still not *actually* so: it is that only as matured reason, which has *made* itself to what it is potentially[1]." The true inwardness of Hegel's paradox that the Idea must first make itself to what it is, that its end was its aim from the beginning, so that like the circle it only completes itself in returning into itself— should now be clear.

The difference between the actual and the potential is regarded not as a difference of existence but as what Hegel somewhat oddly terms a difference of form. Here is an example that he gives · "The man who is

---

[1] Cf. *Phaenomenologie*, pp. 15—17.   Prof. Baillie's translation
I. pp. 16 ff.

potentially rational has advanced no further when he is actually rational. The potentiality (*das Ansich*) is conserved and yet the difference is quite enormous. No new content has emerged, yet the form is an enormous difference. On *this* difference all the difference in the world's history turns[1]." This reminds us of his former allegory of the house : it is as if one said, the house and the plan of it are logically the same. When we have both we have a difference of form, or what he calls a duplication : we have the plan and the plan out of itself. But suppose the house became self-conscious : it would, Hegel assumes, in that case recognise the identity between itself and its plan : the duplication would yield to identity, and the end coincide with the beginning. Yes, logically or ideally perhaps ; but still there is 'the enormous difference.' A conjuror throws up a picture and it comes down a watch : how are we going to account for that, especially how, if we have no conjuror ? But in truth it turns out that it is after all not a plan, a picture or an idea with which we begin, but a germ and an impulse. " The potentiality determines the course of the development "—so we say after the event—but it does not provide the motive. There is besides an impulse towards self-development, something " that cannot endure to be only potential " : this is 'the germ' that is thus already partly actual. " The impulse," says Hegel, " is the contradiction, that it [the germ] is only potential and yet ought not to be so. The impulse puts forth into existence[2]." This is the point where Hegel essays to ford his ditch : the impulse in historical development

---

[1] *Geschichte der Philosophie*, 1833, I. p. 34.   [2] *Ibid.* p. 35.

and the contradiction in dialectical development are identified; and the former, as temporal and phenomenal, is, as much as may be, suppressed.

To recognise this 'monstrous' ὕστερον πρότερον, as Schopenhauer called it, of Hegel's panlogism is to recognise that in his zeal for thoroughness he over-reached himself. In order to make doubly sure of his foundation, and start without presuppositions he sundered what he could not afterwards unite. The unity which he places at the beginning, so far from being suppositionless, is but 'the shadow' of the unity that by means of the historical method he reaches in the end—the slowly and painfully achieved unity that rests on plurality. The so-called transition to the Kingdom of the Son, from the Idea to Nature, turns out to be no veritable transition at all, to be not the spiritual in alienation from itself, but the spiritual at the outset of its development. The Kingdom of the Spirit is not the return of finite spirits to the eternal Father from whom they have wandered nor to the universal source whence they emanated: it is simply the advance of humanity towards an absolute consciousness of its own unity. Passages in support of this assertion might be quoted from all parts of Hegel's works. Here are some: "The consciousness of finite spirit is concrete being, the material for the realisation of the notion of God[1]." Again, "In the higher speculative consideration it (Spirit) is *the absolute Spirit itself*, which in order to be for itself the knowledge of itself, differentiates itself *in itself*, and thereby posits the finiteness of spirit, within which it becomes the

---

[1] *Philosophie der Religion*, 2te Auf. II. p. 551, E.t. III. p. 365.

absolute object of the knowledge of itself. Thus it is
the absolute Spirit in its community (or church),—the
actual Absolute as Spirit and knowledge of itself[1]."
Again, "God is God only in so far as He knows
himself: his self-knowledge is, further, his self-
consciousness in man, and man's knowledge *of* God
which proceeds to man's self-knowledge *in* God[2]."
Once more, contrasting religious faith with historical
evidence, he says of the former: "This rather than that
is the rise of the community, is the community itself,
the existing Spirit, the Spirit in its existence, God
existing as community." And a sentence or two later
on, in referring to the three persons of the Trinity :—
"The first was the Idea in its simple universality for
itself....The second was the Idea in its externality, so
that the external phenomenon is brought back to the
first, is known as divine Idea—the identity of the
human and divine. The third is this consciousness,
God as *Spirit*, and this Spirit as existing in the
community[3]." Finally, "God is infinite, Ego finite:
these are false, objectionable expressions, forms that
are inappropriate to the Idea, to the nature of the
fact....God is the movement to the finite...in the Ego,
as that which is annulling itself as finite, God returns
to himself, and only as this return is He God. Without the world God is not God[4]." The full significance
of these and many more passages of like import[5] only

---

[1] *Æsthetik*, I. p. 122.   [2] *Philosophy of Mind*, Encycl. III. § 564.
[3] *Philosophie der Religion*, 1ste Auf., 1832, II. p. 261.
[4] *Op. cit.* 2te Auf. I. p. 194, Eng. trans. I. p. 200.
[5] Several of which will be found in Drews' *Deutsche Speculation
u.s.w.*, vol. I. pp. 260 ff. and in McTaggart's *Studies in the Hegelian
Cosmology*, pp. 208 ff.

becomes apparent when we remember that, according to Hegel, God before this realisation in the finite, this existence as the community, this self-consciousness in man, this return to Himself, is only this very result ideally regarded as its own presupposition. God comes to consciousness only in humanity, and otherwise is not God, not Spirit, but only Idea. But an Idea is not conscious, though it implies consciousness : hence God as Idea is either the unconscious, as Schopenhauer and von Hartmann maintained, or an abstract essence that 'comes later to existence,' as Hegel himself by turns concedes and denies as he alternates between the historical and the dialectical.

But much more impressive than any string of quotations is the whole drift of Hegel's *Philosophy of Religion* and especially of the long section devoted to the so-called Kingdom of the Spirit. In the latter referring to the divinity of Christ he says it is "clear that the *Community* of itself produces this faith.... Whereas grateful peoples have placed their benefactors only among the stars, the Spirit has recognised subjectivity as an absolute moment of the divine nature. The person of Christ has been decreed by the Church to be the Son of God[1]." Miracles, the *words* of the Bible, Councils and such like have nothing to do with it. "The true Christian content of faith is to be justified by philosophy, not by history." Not by history as ordinarily understood Hegel means, but taking the philosophy of history in its widest sense, then by that and nothing else. It is all 'divine history,' 'development in conformity with reason,'

---

[1] *Op. cit.* II. p. 328, Eng. trans. III. p. 121.

Hegel affirms. Yes, but chequered and distorted by contingency to an indefinite extent, emerging gradually out of superstition and phantasy, out of sorrow and disappointment. "The sorrow of the world," he has said, "was the birth-place of the impulse of Spirit to know God as spiritual in universal form and stript of finitude. This want was begotten through the progress of history and the development of the world-spirit." Hercules was deified by the Greeks, the Roman Emperor was revered as God; and Christ was decreed to be the Son of God only by the same effort of Spirit as that which lies at the basis of those earlier forms and can be recognised as present in them. "Out of the ferment of finitude as it changes into foam Spirit exhales its fragrance[1]."

When we pass from Hegel's *Philosophy of Religion* to the *Phenomenology of Spirit* we find there a record of the same gradual process and the same ultimate result—an account which runs closely on all fours with that which the pluralist would give. It starts with mere sentient experience, which advances towards self-consciousness, as the subject, in shaping and controlling its environment, realises its own independence as an agent. Finally it reaches the stage of reason, as such incipiently self-conscious agents enter into social relations and become fully self-conscious; then too they develop a system of law and order and also begin to realise the spiritual world of art, religion and philosophy. I know of no better summary of this wonderful but terribly intricate work than the following given by Windelband in his *History of Modern*

---

[1] *Op. cit.* 2nd ed. II. p. 330, Eng. trans. III. 124.

Philosophy:—"Hegel's aim is to...build up the whole of philosophy out of the continuity shewn in the historical development of the human mind. Man's self-consciousness is the world-spirit that has come to itself. The evolution of the human mind is the conscious self-apprehension of the world-mind, and the essence of things is to be understood from the process which the human mind has passed through in order to grasp its own organization and thereby the organization of the universe itself. The Hegelian philosophy regards itself as the self-consciousness of the entire development of the culture attained by the reason of the human race, and in this it sees at the same time the self-consciousness of the Absolute Spirit as it unfolds itself in the world. Thus this philosophy becomes on the one side a thoroughly historical view of the world (*Weltanschauung*) but on the other lapses over into a completely anthropocentric speculation about the world (*Weltbetrachtung*), that is to say, it looks upon the development of the human spirit as the development of the 'world-spirit'[1]."

In the light of this summary the famous sentences with which Hegel concludes his *Phenomenology* become more or less clear:—"The way to the goal, absolute knowledge, or spirit knowing itself as spirit, lies in the memory of minds"—the solidarity of heredity and tradition, I suppose we might say—"as they are in themselves and as they accomplish the organization of their realm. Their conservation on the side of their free existence manifesting itself in the form of contingency is History, but on the side of their organization in notional

---

[1] *Geschichte der neueren Philosophie*, 4te Aufl. 1907, II. p. 329.

form (*begriffenen*) it is Science manifesting itself as knowledge. Both together, *history in notional form*, constitute the memory and the Golgotha of the Absolute Spirit, the actuality, truth and certainty of his throne, without which he would be the lifeless Solitary; only

> 'From the chalice of this spirit realm
> Sparkles his Infinitude'[1]."

The reference to Calvary recalls the negative element, the sorrow of the world that spiritualises it, on which Hegel had previously dwelt. With this we may compare a similar passage giving the 'result' of the *History of Philosophy* :—" The struggle of the finite self-consciousness with the absolute self-consciousness, which appeared for that to be beyond it, ceases. [For] the finite self-consciousness has ceased to be finite; and thereby on the other hand the absolute self-consciousness has acquired the actuality, which it previously lacked. In general the entire history of the world so far, and in particular the history of philosophy, is simply the exhibition of this struggle. And now they seem to have reached their goal, where the absolute self-consciousness, of which they had a presentation (*Vorstellung*), has ceased to be something foreign, where, that is to say, the spirit as spirit is actual.... The Spirit produces itself as Nature, [and] as Society (*Staat*). The former is its unconscious action,... in the deeds and life of history as also [in the works] of art it brings itself forth consciously,...but only in science "—i.e. in philosophy—" does it know itself as absolute spirit, and this knowledge alone is spirit, is its veritable existence[2]."

---

[1] An inaccurate quotation from Schiller's poem *Die Freundschaft*.
[2] *Geschichte der Philosophie,* III. pp. 689 f.

Everywhere, then, in all his works, Hegel reaches unity as the result of a development, and everywhere emphatically declares it to be a result. Surely therefore it is reasonable to believe that he means what he says. When, however, he adds that this result is itself the beginning, he does not say what he means. What he means is itself result—the speculative inversion of the concrete development in the mirror of the so-called Logic : he himself compares it to standing on your head[1]. Even the Absolute Idea itself is so far a result that the notion of it is described as ' an object in which all differentiations have coalesced[2].' As to the actual unity that is its correlative—in spite of occasional passages in which Hegel refers to it as ' having personality,' it can hardly be called a person in the strict sense. This, I think, is evident from Hegel's account of the State or Society. Much the same language as he used in describing the religious community is repeated here. The state is "the ethical spirit, the substantial will that thinks itself and knows and what it knows accomplishes"; "it is the spirit that is stationed in the world and there consciously realises itself, whereas in Nature it is only actualised as its own Other, as sleeping spirit." He even calls the idea of the state ' the actual God[3].' But we have still to see how far Hegel's actual unity is from deserving the title Absolute ; and this will bring us round again to Pluralism, in which there is the same shortcoming.

----

[1] *Phaenomenologie*, p. 21; E. t. p. 24.   [2] *Encyclopaedie*, § 236.
[3] *Philosophie des Rechtes*, 1ste Aufl. § 257, pp. 312, 318, 320.

LECTURE IX.

What after all, we have now to ask, was Hegel's actual unity? It was entirely geocentric and anthropocentric. The earth, he says, is the truth of the solar system, just as animal nature is the truth of vegetable, and this the truth of the mineral. The earth is *the* planet: the sun has neither produced it nor thrown it off; but sun, moon, comets, and stars are only conditions for the earth (*Bedingungen der Erde*) which they serve. Among the continents of the earth, Europe, in virtue of its physical characteristics, forms its consciousness, its rational part, and the centre of Europe is Germany[1]. With his own philosophy, he had the sublime assurance to think, the history of philosophy closes; and in the restoration of Prussia under Stein he thought the culmination of the world's history was attained. It is however not so much this unique anticlimax that now concerns us; but rather the general position that there are not 'more worlds than ours,' which Hegel shared with the fifteenth century ecclesiastics. They, it will be remembered, had burned Giordano Bruno alive, who was one of the first in modern times to proclaim this doctrine; and

---

[1] *Encyclopaedie*, §§ 249, 280, 339.

they regarded even Columbus as verging on heresy. "As the planet, the *earth* is the body of *individual* totality...its characteristic as organic is to digest the entirely general astral powers, which as heavenly bodies have the illusory appearance of independence, and to bring them under the control of its individuality, in which these Titanic members sink to moments.... From a quantitative standpoint one may regard the earth as 'a drop in the sea of the infinite,' but magnitude is a very external determination." The earth "is our home, not as physical, but as the home of spirit[1]."

This seems to be about all that Hegel had to say concerning the existence of a plurality of worlds. He appears never to have thought seriously of controverting it : it was too completely beyond his purview for that. The question :—To what end then all the rest of the universe ? which vexed the soul of old Böhme—why, Höffding asks, did it never trouble Hegel ? His contempt for Nature was too extreme, we reply : the man who compared the starry heavens to a 'light-rash' or 'a swarm of flies' was hardly likely to have troubled his head further about them. Had he done so, facing the facts with an open mind and without *parti pris*, he would have found the realisation of the Absolute Idea as the Kingdom of the Spirit a far more serious problem than from his purely geocentric and anthropocentric standpoint it proved to be. It would have been impossible then to call the earth '*the* home of spirit' *par excellence*. Now this is precisely the problem with which pluralism is on one side confronted. So far as our experience goes we seem unable to

---

[1] *Op. cit.* § 280.

conceive how a plurality of worlds can ever become a single Realm of Ends, such as might fitly be called absolute.

But the plurality of worlds seems not only to stand in the way of that complete consummation of the will towards a higher unity, which is the pluralist's ideal: it also presents difficulties for the Christian theologian. The continuity between natural and moral evil is so close that it can hardly be seriously maintained that the advance from a state of merely animal innocence to a 'knowledge of good and evil' has not frequently, perhaps invariably, entailed actual sin and error and misery. If so, then for other worlds as for ours, what Hegel has called a 'Golgotha' would be essential; and thus, if we are not to charge God with the arbitrary partiality of an oriental potentate, we seem driven to assume that 'the plan of salvation,' the divine progress from the manger to the cross, has been reenacted in worlds innumerable. Sir David Brewster apparently was prepared, if need be, to assume this; but theologians, so far as I know, have been less presumptuous. Two other alternatives then present themselves. The existence of a plurality of worlds might be simply denied, as it was by John Wesley, by Whewell—in his famous anonymous essay—and as it has been denied again recently by Dr Alfred Russel Wallace. Both these later writers rely mainly on a use of the argument from probabilities, which seems clearly fallacious. If a given effect can only result from the cooperation of a single group of independent causes we may proceed to inquire about the probability of their concurrence elsewhere; but if the given effect can result in manifold other ways, then the absence of all the conditions present in a given case proves nothing. It may be true that a fauna and a flora analogous to ours are possible nowhere else, that human beings could only exist on this one planet. But metabolism, stimulation, and spontaneous direction may be possible in a protoplasm very different from that with which we are familiar, and evolution might progress indefinitely on quite other lines than those that have obtained for us[1]. Viewed from such more general standpoint the probability is not against, but enormously in favour of, a plurality of worlds, as men of science almost unanimously allow. We come then to the other alternative.

Granted that in the one universe there are many worlds, the Christian theologian has the strongest grounds for believing that they are spiritually and historically, and not merely physically, interconnected. It was 'the infidel Tom Paine,' a quondam Quaker, who first made the plurality of worlds a serious stumbling-block for Christian believers by his once famous work, the *Age of Reason.* To meet his objections without denying his premises, Andrew Fuller and afterwards Chalmers—mainly on the strength of isolated texts from the Old and the New Testament—sought to establish "the position," as the latter puts it, "that the history of our redemption is known in other and distant places of creation, and is matter of deep interest and feeling amongst other orders of

---

[1] The protoplasm of our planet has determined once for all the possible foods and the possible senses of all its organisms; but quite other protoplasms are perfectly conceivable.

created intelligences[1].". The nature of such a connexion is the problem that pluralism in our day has to consider. We may call it the upper limit of pluralism.

It seems obvious that unless some supreme spiritual unity is found the universe will remain in the highest sense an absolute plurality, if such a term is allowable. Such a universe would be a merely sporadic manifold of realms of ends having a common physical basis but devoid of all teleological continuity; like so many village communities without a supreme federation, geographically neighbours but strangers politically. As society lifts the individual to a higher level, so we feel that a supreme unity would increase the worth of this universe both intellectually and morally. Such a unity is an ideal that we feel ought to be real. Can we conceive it more definitely or find any evidence of its existence? The theological writers—as the words just quoted from Chalmers show—rely on the Christian doctrine of a hierarchy of angels to render the connexion of a multitude of otherwise isolated worlds intelligible. Angels are to be regarded not only as the ministers of Providence but as spectators of universal history. Such a conception is entirely in keeping with the general standpoint of pluralism, as I have tried to describe it. The principle of continuity indeed almost forces us to posit higher orders of intelligence than our own; and the fact[2] that *we* are able to control and modify the course of evolution suggests that if there are higher intelligences they can exercise this power in a still higher degree.

[1] *Christian Revelation in connexion with Astronomy*, Disc. iv. 1st edn, p. 145.

[2] Cf. Lecture v. p. 111.

This latter possible function of intelligences of a higher order does not directly concern our main problem, that of an ultimate and supreme unity; but it bears on it indirectly, in so far as any evidence of such control would be evidence of the existence of those superior beings; and their existence again would strengthen the assumption of a still higher unity in the plurality of worlds. Is there then we may inquire any evidence of this sort? Evidence, I mean, of a purely objective and scientific kind, not merely evidence which could satisfy only persons with certain subjective convictions lying outside the purview of science proper. For on the lines of our present inquiry it might be held that we cannot fairly appeal, for example, to the specially religious evidences in support of theophanies, incarnation, inspiration and the like. At the same time it should not be forgotten that spiritualistic pluralism, unlike naturalism, can have no *a priori* objection to the 'supernatural' in this sense[1].

We have an instance of the sort of evidence we are seeking in Dr Russel Wallace's arguments, already

[1] These remarks will of course suggest to everybody a topic which is in fact fundamental to the whole subject we are considering—the question, namely, of religious faith and religious experience. Such an experience implies a consciousness of the presence of a higher spiritual being—a consciousness which is wholly distinct from the belief in other selves which we reach by the ejective interpretation of what is externally presented. It is in such wise that to earnestly religious minds 'the evidence of things unseen' is certain, immediate and practically verified. For them the problem of the unity of the many is already essentially solved. But their certainty after all is primarily subjective: it *is* faith, not knowledge. It cannot compel assent on purely scientific or merely speculative grounds. Hence I think we do well to follow Kant's example and for the present to leave it aside.

noted in an earlier lecture, to show that man's appearance on the earth is due to such supernatural interference.
After enumerating a number of human characteristics,
such as naked skin, a brain largely in excess of animal
needs, musical voice, moral sense, etc., he proceeds :—
" The inference I would draw from this class of
phenomena is, that a superior intelligence has guided
the development of man in a definite direction, and
for a special purpose, just as man guides the development of many animal and vegetable forms.   The
laws of evolution alone would, perhaps, never have
produced a grain so well adapted to man's use as
wheat and maize ; such fruits as the seedless banana
and bread-fruit; or such animals as the Guernsey milch
cow, or the London dray-horse.   Yet these so closely
resemble the unaided productions of nature, that we
may well imagine a being who had mastered the laws
of development of organic forms through past ages,
refusing to believe that any new power had been
concerned in their production, and scornfully rejecting
the theory...that in these few cases a controlling intelligence had directed the action of the laws of
variation, multiplication, and survival for its own
purposes.   We know, however, that this has been
done ; and we must therefore admit the possibility that,
if we are not the highest intelligences in the universe,
some higher intelligence may have directed the process
by which the human race was developed, by means
of more subtle agencies than we are acquainted with."
In a note he adds :—" Angels and archangels...have
been so long banished from our belief as to have
become actually unthinkable as actual existences, and

nothing in modern philosophy takes their place. Yet
the grand law of 'continuity,' the last outcome of
modern science…cannot surely fail to be true beyond
the narrow sphere of our vision, and leave such an
infinite chasm between man and the great Mind of the
universe. Such a supposition seems…in the highest
degree improbable[1]." As I have already said[2] there
is no denying the formal soundness of this reasoning,
even if we hesitate to go further. It at least serves to
set the continuity argument in a telling light.

A similar, if less impressive argument is perhaps
to be found in the prodigality in nature of beautiful
colours and forms, which natural selection on grounds
of bare utility seems altogether unable to explain.
Take for example the gorgeous coloration of humming-
birds or the so-called 'ball and socket' ornament in
the secondary wing-feathers of the Argus pheasant[3].
In reply to the late Duke of Argyll[4], one of the few
writers who have dwelt at any length on this particular
'mystery of creation,' Darwin admitted that natural
selection was powerless to account for such facts, but
he thought that sexual selection would suffice. Dr
Wallace, who at first agreed with him in this, has since
recanted; and now, I take it, he would agree rather
with the Duke of Argyll that "love of beauty is equally

---

[1] *Natural Selection and Tropical Nature*, 1891, pp. 204 f.

[2] Cf. Lect. IV. p. 91.

[3] Of Tennyson his friend Edward Fitzgerald relates that "picking
up a daisy as we walked and looking close to its crimson-tipt leaves
he said: 'Does not this look like a thinking Artificer, one who wishes
to ornament?'" *In Memoriam*, A. W. Robinson's excellent edition,
p. 255.

[4] *Reign of Law*, 1st edn, p. 236.

a purpose which we see fulfilled in Nature," and so implies some superior control. At any rate he concludes his chapter on the colour-sense by saying :— " The emotions excited by colour and by music alike seem to rise above the level of a world developed on purely utilitarian principles[1]." This whole subject of what we might call Natural Aesthetics seems to be a fruitful field of inquiry that, so far as I know, has been strangely neglected[2]. The subject no doubt is beset with difficulties, and there are many *pros* and *cons* to weigh before the intervention of such superior and disinterested principles can be maintained with any confidence. Still, if their presence were credibly ascertained it would add greatly to the antecedent probability that, to repeat Dr Wallace's words, " the grand law of continuity cannot fail to be true beyond the narrow sphere of our vision."

This 'grand law' then encourages the pluralist to assume, though lacking sufficient direct evidence, that there exist individuals of a higher order, or rather a hierarchy of such orders—a speculative view with which Leibniz and Fechner have made us all familiar. But human beings owe their pre-eminence on this planet to social organization, which we regard as not merely an aggregate but as an over-individual unity. The law of continuity then would seem to suggest that individuals of a higher order in like manner are organized into over-individual unities, and so on — possibly *ad indefinitum*. This view would thus lead

---

[1] *Op. cit.* p. 415.

[2] August Pauly is an exception. Cf. his *Darwinismus und Lamarckismus*, 1905, pp. 272 ff.

up to a society rather than to a person as the Supreme Unity of all. But—apart from other difficulties that we shall have presently to consider—it might readily be brought into line with the Christian doctrine of a tri-personal God. The objections that have recently been brought against theism by Dr McTaggart—from the standpoint of what may fairly be called a Hegelian pluralism—might perhaps in this way be met. It is noteworthy that it is those theologians who have been most influenced by Hegel, who insist the most on what is technically called the 'essential trinity' ($\tau\rho\acute{o}\pi os$ $\acute{v}\pi\acute{a}\rho\xi\epsilon\omega s$) of the divine nature in opposition to the Sabellian heresy of an 'undifferentiated unity,' which only assumed a triple form in its revelation to mankind, a so-called 'economic trinity' ($\tau\rho\acute{o}\pi os$ $\acute{a}\pi o$-$\kappa a\lambda\acute{v}\psi\epsilon\omega s$). Thus Martensen in his *Christian Dogmatics* writes :—"Without the Son the Father could not speak of himself as I, for the first-personal form, apart from an objectivity distinct from the Ego (a not-I, a Thou), is unthinkable." "When then," he remarks, "we teach with the Church the eternal preexistence and independence of creation not only of the Father but also of the Son and the Spirit, we thereby affirm that God, in order to be the self-revealing, self-loving God, must eternally differentiate himself into I and Thou, and just as eternally unite himself with himself as the Spirit of love that proceeds from the relation of contrast[1]." At the same time there is no logical incompatibility between pluralism and the assumption of a single personality as the Supreme Spirit of the world. In fact Leibniz refers to God in this wise as *la monade*

[1] *Christliche Dogmatik*, §§ 56, 55.

primitive, a phrase which is precisely equivalent to the *Monas monadum*, which Giordano Bruno and others had previously used.

But as I have already observed[1], such supreme unity, whether triune or not, could from the pluralistic standpoint be regarded only as supreme, only as *prima inter pares*, not as absolute. A supreme monad or society, that is to say, would necessarily imply a certain relativity and limitation consequent on the existence of other monads and societies also possessing some spontaneity and initiative. For a strict and absolute pluralism moreover such limitation would not be self-imposed; not an act of will on the part of one supreme being but an actual characteristic of the nature of things, of the absolute whole consisting of such Supreme and the rest of the world. The ordinary notion of creation—viz. that at a given moment there was no world and at a subsequent moment the world was there—is rejected as having no sort of analogy with experience, and as therefore unthinkable. On the other hand the notion of creation as eternal and continuous seems to involve an essential implication of God and the world—limitation on the one side, dependence on the other. But these relations hold good also of the finite spirit. The world is the object of my experience : in Leibnizian language it is mirrored in my experience from that unique standpoint which makes me what I am as regards capacity and opportunity. The world limits me in manifold ways, but it is also dependent upon me. For I am not wholly passive and inert : I am able to react upon it and do

[1] Cf. Lecture II. p. 29.

in fact in some measure modify it : apart from me it would not be all in all just what it is. On the strength of the principle of continuity then the pluralist would assume the like to hold good of the highest. The world is the object of God's experience, God is the subject that *has* this experience, not the abstract totality in which the distinction of subject and object disappears. Like every other spirit God must have his unique standpoint ; but it is unique in a quite special way : it is the highest.

But if now, as theism commonly does, we regard this highest as infinitely transcending ourselves, we should be prepared to find such difference of degree really amounting to a difference of kind. Take, for example, a circle : its circumference, a curved line, meets a diameter, a straight line, at two equidistant points and bears to this the ratio commonly represented by the Greek letter π. If however we let the diameter become infinite, the circumference ceases to be curved ; and if now, from one extremity of the diameter we imagine three bodies travelling, one along the diameter itself and the two others in opposite directions along the circumference to its other extremity ; then the further they go the further they will be apart, although, if we are dealing with a circle, we must also imagine all three eventually meeting. But in truth we are no longer dealing with a circle but with something generically distinct, that is to say with the limit towards which we approach—but which we never attain—when the diameter of the circle increases indefinitely. We regard the circle as a closed figure, but in passing to the limit in this wise we leave definite enclosure behind us. Now what we have to note is that whereas the theist passes beyond the series, the pluralist remains within it. Both may recognise a Supreme Being surpassing all our powers of conception ; but for the theist the superlative is absolute and transcendent, for the pluralist it is relative and immanent. When the theist says that man is made in the image of God and then proceeds to describe God as infinite and absolute, it needs but a very slight acquaintance with the meaning of these attributes to realise that both statements cannot be literally true. For the pluralist on the other hand, if there be a Supreme Spirit at all, as he may reasonably suppose, that Spirit is still genuinely a member of the realm of ends, albeit the highest and, so to say, the central member[1].

But there is still a mark of relativity clinging to any ideal of the Supreme Spirit that pluralism as such can entertain, which must ever distinguish this ideal within the realm of spirits from the unconditional Absolute of so-called philosophical theism. For the standpoint of the pluralist is historical : he contemplates the world exclusively as a world of life and experience and

[1] As such there must be attributed to Him powers and capacities that would not be adequately represented if we attempted to combine and magnify indefinitely the powers and capacities of the most exalted human beings just as, for example, our human nature would not be adequately represented if we imagined the social ascidian, one of the earliest progenitors that the zoologist assigns to us, picturing a human being as a sort of social ascidian *in excelsis*. In particular it would, I think, be reasonable to suppose, as I have already remarked, that mutual communication between this Supreme Spirit and ourselves—and even between other superior beings and ourselves— would be possible of a more immediate, so to say more internal nature, than that which alone holds between ourselves and our fellow men.

W.

13

therefore of process and change or, as we are wont to say, under the form of time not under that of eternity[1]. As immanent in this world God must, it would seem, so far be conceived as subject to its fundamental conditions. Conformably with what I said just now, we may suppose his time-span to exceed ours indefinitely, we may credit him with thoughts that are intuitive and adequate where ours are only discursive and symbolic : he may know all truth *sub specie aeternatis*. But all this is hardly life. As the World Spirit *par excellence*, interested and active throughout the universe, how can he be a living God wholly apart from the world's evolution and history ? Even if philosophical speculation after many vain attempts should at length succeed in explaining time as in some way 'the moving image of eternity,' as Plato poetically expressed it, still this would not alter the case. *Mutatis mutandis*, unless the world of experience were reduced to an impossible illusion, the relations temporally prefigured would still remain and have a meaning. A Supreme Spirit confronted and conditioned by free agents certainly does not correspond to the notion usually entertained of the Deity. Such a 'finite God' many would disown as a manifest contradiction in terms ; yet beyond this it does not seem possible for the pluralist to go. It is however a sign of the times that there are not a few theologians who have been led by the problem of freedom and the problem of evil to entertain the pluralistic conception. Later on we shall have, of course, to consider the question further in connexion with these problems[2]. But so much for the present

[1] But see Supplementary Note iv.   [2] Cf. Lectures xiii.—xvii.

concerning what I have called the upper limit of pluralism. Let us now turn to what in contrast we may term the lower limit.

Resuming our example of a circle or sphere : just as when the radius becomes infinite we have no longer a figure occupying space, but simply the whole of space itself ; so when the radius is zero we have a figure no more, but simply a point in space which has position but neither parts nor magnitude. As the principle of continuity will not carry us to a transcendent upper limit, neither will it carry us to a transcendent lower one. The naked, slumbering monads of Leibniz, the monads whose so-called perception is absolutely con-fused or undifferentiated, are as much an abstract ideal as the mass-points of the physicist. Body without extension and a subject without consciousness are limiting concepts, not known realities within experience. If we attempt to trace the evolution of the world back to such an ideal beginning, as Spencer for example did, what becomes of our Many ? Though eventually some are dominant over others, still—if evolution is to be thorough-going and complete—can we suppose that they begin by dominating ? But if all are at first unconscious and slumbering, how is the awakening to begin ? If all mirrored the same universe in the same as yet absolutely undifferentiated fashion, all would be so far homogeneous ; and according to the principle of the identity of indiscernibles, which Leibniz himself had formulated, all would be one, all would have the same content which effectively would be no content ; and there would thus be no ground for change and as little possibility of it. So then it would seem that as

13—2

the unattainable upper limit of pluralism points towards an absolute and unconditioned Being transcending the Many, so the unattainable lower limit points towards an indeterminate Being, an ἄπειρον, that affords no ground for the discrimination of individuals at all.

Again we may proceed in a different way only to reach a similar result. The goal of the pluralistic world at any stage in its progress is, we say, higher unity between its constituent monads and systems of monads —advance in organization both individual and social. We have left it for the present an open question whether the highest term is strictly an individual or an over-individual, a person or a society of persons. But the lowest can only consist of individuals ; unless indeed anyone should think it worth while to call the primitive Many a society in the loosest sense, on the ground that it is in some sort a unity. When we advance to an organism as a complex of individuals or monads we assume the presence of a dominant monad, or what Leibniz called a *soul*. Its dominance must be regarded as due in part at least to its innate or essential superiority, not solely to the accident of its position : such absolute tychism could not conceivably be made to work. But if evolution as a historical process is to be thorough-going there must be a stage at which this dominance is not yet realised but remains so to say 'potential,' awaiting the fulfilment of its complementary conditions. Agamemnon and the men he was to lead were all much on a par as infants together in their cradles. And the fact that as evolution advances diversity increases suggests that all the differences that eventually emerge were originally latent. Such absolute origin as the lower limit of evolution is as much beyond all experience as the absolute beginning of his own life is beyond the conscious experience of any individual among us. Such antitheses as nature and origin, form and matter, are for us always but relative.

Either way then if we attempt to regress to the lower limit we seem only to reach the illegitimate notion of pure potentiality; there is no *natura naturata*, and in order that the process, the *nasci*, may begin we seem to require a *Primum movens* that is not one of the nascent Many. Otherwise the nearer we approach to the beginning the more inconceivable the beginning becomes. We are thus led to regard our two limits as really related, as they are in the cosmogonies of Plato and Aristotle for example; that is to say, we are led to regard God as quickening the bare potentiality of a world into actual motion and life. We approximate too to the theism of Leibniz, who was likewise driven beyond the limits of his monadology proper. Not as *Monas monadum*, but as transcending all monads, God according to Leibniz as 'infinite intellect' contemplates the absolute totality of possible worlds and gives reality to that which his goodness has selected as the best.

In truth however all this rests, it is urged, on an outside, not an inside, view of the pluralistic position. The philosophies of Plato and Aristotle, which have determined the main trend of all subsequent speculation till comparatively recent times, shew a marked bias towards what is nowadays called Intellectualism. According to this, cognition is the primary factor in experience and pure contemplation the most perfect state. Even for Leibniz activity was dependent on perception in such wise that confused perception and complete passivity were synonymous.

What is called Voluntarism however inverts all this. Conation, not cognition, is regarded as fundamental to life : it is the blind impulse to live that leads on to knowledge, just as it is for the sake of life that knowledge is valued ; not *vice versa*. This doctrine of the primacy of the practical first definitely announced by Kant, repeated and extended by Fichte, was still more emphatically proclaimed by Schopenhauer, the very title of whose chief work, *Die Welt als Wille und als Vorstellung*, is but the complete formulation of the doctrine already adumbrated by Kant. The things *per se* in the world are will, the things we know are but their appearance. For voluntarism an 'unconscious' world would not be either a dead material world or the bare potentiality of a living world only to be made actual by some fiat from without. On this view experience does not begin with sensation as a purely passive state ; it presupposes activity ; and cognition with its distinction of subject and object is a consequence of this. In the absence of that distinction this activity is called unconscious.

To be sure Fichte and Schopenhauer were singularists. But so far as the assumed relation of will to presentation is concerned, this seems more readily conceivable if there is a multiplicity of wills which interact, than if there is only a single will and nothing beside. In fact we seem then driven to assume a really inconceivable fractionation of the one unconscious will into many, in order that consciousness may arise.

Modern pluralists are, I think, almost invariably
voluntarists, or as some of them prefer to call themselves, pragmatists. As such, while they admit the
impossibility of regressing to the beginning of evolution, they deny that evolution requires a transcendent
Prime Mover distinct from the Many : for the Many
they hold are all prime movers, and so far *causæ sui*.
I say ' so far,' because the term *causa sui* is generally
construed as equivalent to absolute ; but what is here
meant, I take it, is only that each has an unconditional
existence over against the rest while none has an
unconditional *experience*. They are aware of each
other in virtue of their own interaction : they interact
in virtue of their inherent spontaneity. Will is the
ratio essendi of presentation, presentation the *ratio
cognoscendi* of will. Will is the logical *prius*, but as
absolute beginnings are beyond us there is no question
of chronological priority. The efficient causation in
the world then is just this totality of prime movers, its
final causation their organization into a higher unity.

Bearing this distinction in mind, an obvious objection made by von Hartmann, which would otherwise
be a fatal objection, loses some of its force. "The
aseity of the [one absolute] Substance," he says, is "for
our discursive understanding, restricted [as that is] to
the category of causality, the problem of problems ;
because it implies only the negative statement that this
being is no more the effect of an other. When however
the understanding still persists in applying the usual
causal category in this case too, then it terms the
[absolute] Substance its own effect and its own cause,—
the understanding thereby only making a mockery of
itself. That the [absolute] Substance groundlessly is

and not is not, that is for us the wonder of all wonders."
A system of philosophy, he then goes on to urge,
which multiplies this wonder innumerable times, as
pluralism in his opinion does, stands self-condemned[1].
It might perhaps be replied that wonderfulness is
inversely proportional to frequency. So far then
v. Hartmann would be convicted of subtly begging the
question. But pluralism, in fact, does not maintain
that a world of *n* monads is a world of *n* absolutes.
The totality may be called absolute, if there is nothing
to condition it from without, but no one individual
within it can be called absolute. Whether in the
abstract an absolute totality of individuals or an absolute
individual be the greater problem or the greater wonder
is surely an idle question. The only real question is
the question of fact. If pluralism is self-consistent and
self-sufficient it does not become a problem, merely
because it is wonderful. And the like again, of course,
would hold true of singularism.

But there is this difference between them, we start
with the Many as given: so far they do not need to be
'deduced.' With the One we do not thus start. At
the same time it must be allowed that pluralism cannot
furnish, has never attempted to furnish anything deserving to be called a philosophical justification of
itself—it is, as William James called it, radical empiricism; whereas for singularism in the abstract there
have been ontological and *a priori* arguments in plenty.
Pluralism, as Kant long ago remarked, is confined
exclusively to cosmological arguments[2]. It starts with a
discrete Many, severally related and therefore severally

---

[1] *Kategorienlehre*, p. 528.

[2] Cf. his remarks on the thesis of the fourth antinomy.

comparable, and beyond this its cardinal principles of continuity and evolution will not enable it to go. Neither by regressing can it reach a lowest limit or origin, in which all diversity is latent; nor by progressing can it reach a highest limit or goal in which all plurality is transcended. This, the pluralist's extremity, will doubtless be regarded as the singularist's opportunity. But the latter so far has never succeeded—without doing violence to the facts—in advancing beyond a more or less covert dualism of the One and the Many, of God and the World. The connexion of these two, that is to say, remains a problem. Thus in the latest and one of the most important expositions of singularism, its author, Mr Bradley, tells us:—" The fact of actual fragmentariness, I admit, I cannot explain. That experience should take place in finite centres, and should wear the form of finite 'thisness,' is in the end inexplicable. But"—he adds—" to be inexplicable and to be incompatible are not the same thing[1]." Here we have the whole matter in a nutshell. If pluralism is 'infected with contradictions,' as Mr Bradley affirms, we must turn, he contends, to singularism, that is to say, to Absolutism. If such an Absolute Being as he supposes, is possible, then, in view of the said contradictions, it must be declared actual. If, as we maintain, it is not possible, then we are reduced to scepticism, unless the asserted contradictions can be resolved. Even though not compelled by contradictions altogether to abandon pluralism, we ought to prefer Theism if that systematizes more and disappoints less. The difficulties of pluralism then must be our next topic.

[1] *Appearance and Reality*, 2nd edn, p. 226.

LECTURE X.

PSYCHOPHYSICAL AND METAPHYSICAL DIFFICULTIES IN PLURALISM.

There is one difficulty which the exposition I have attempted to give would so readily suggest, that it is perhaps best to mention it at the outset. The goal of final harmony and unification on which the personal idealist counts as—a far-off event, it may be, but still as—a rational possibility may yet never be attained, however rationally possible, because of what we ordinarily call physical hindrances. Let these consist, if you like, of the actions of inferior—sentient it may be—but still irrational monads : the disaster would be none the less appalling on that account, nor is its possibility for that reason very seriously diminished. For we have had meantime to allow that millennial dreams of a liberation of Nature from the thraldom of so-called physical evil are as fanciful as the legends of this subjection as a consequence of moral evil. It is true there are modern pluralists, Renouvier certainly and probably Dr Howison, who still defend such views of the solidarity of the cosmos. But if we smile at Fourier when he imagined that, so soon as we have learnt to dwell in brotherly love together, the whales will seize our ships by their cables and tow them to their destinations over seas no longer briny but pleasant to drink, must we not regard it as still more

extravagant to picture finite minds taming the earth-
quake and the tornado, to say nothing of checking
the stars in their courses and staying the clash of
worlds? For what to all appearance are physical
set-backs, sometimes involving whole worlds, certainly
exist. But they are the exception, not the rule. It
may be that with time they will become rarer still. It
may be too that as death is held to be but 'the covered
way that leads to life,' so these catastrophes do but
open up an unseen order, which we can only dimly
surmise. All that the pluralist can safely do is still
to assert the spiritual possibility of harmony among
rationals; and for the rest he can only maintain that
the difficulty raised is one that also besets the theist's
position. But there is this difference, the belief in an
unseen world has a warrant, if theism is true, which
pluralism alone cannot furnish: *per contra* the difficulty
is graver for the one than it is for the other. On the
whole then it will be best to defer these difficulties,
which affect any theory of the world as a realm of ends,
till they meet us again in our discussion of theism[1].

One remark, before passing for the present from
this topic, may however here be made. It is a well-
known opinion widely held by scientific men that
the second law of thermodynamics, otherwise called
the law of the dissipation of energy, points conclusively
to universal death as the final goal of all. The
pessimist von Hartmann professed to see in this
law the chief consolation that science brings to men.
But one recent pluralist makes an ingenious attempt
to rebut the argument, that seems at least theoretically

[1] Cf. Lect. XVI.

sound. The process of degradation, he urges in the
first place, is only asymptotic ; it will therefore never
be complete[1]. And in the next place he maintains that,
since in psychophysics it is the difference of intensities
not their absolute amount that is significant, therefore
life will always be possible[2]. But in truth the most
effective reply is much simpler. The second law of
thermodynamics is entirely statistical : it is not binding
on the interaction of individuals at all. For the philosophy of personal idealism this law is so far then of
no account.

Another difficulty that besets pluralism, and one
again from which theism is not altogether free, relates
to the past and future existence of individuals beyond
the range of our direct experience concerning them.
How are we to interpret what we know as the birth
and the death of a given L or M ? According to the
pluralistic, as according to the Leibnizian view, all the
individuals there are have existed from the first and
will continue to exist indefinitely[3]. Birth and death,
then, cannot really be what they seem to be. But it
still remains true that every man, as we know him,
came at a certain date upon this world's stage and,
after playing his several parts for a brief interval, will
presently pass off. Is he born and does he die but once,

---

[1] In this he had been already anticipated by Prof. Poynting.
See *Naturalism and Agnosticism*, 3rd edn, 1. p. 321 ; 4th edn, p. 593.

[2] L. W. Stern, 'Der zweite Hauptsatz der Energetik u.s.w.,'
Zeitschrift f. Philos. u. philos. Kritik, Bd 121, 1903.

[3] Pluralism, at all events, must assume that every monad relatively
to every other is self-existent ; for obviously, if one were the ground
of the existence of others, they and it would be related as Creator
and created and could not belong to the same ontal series.

or has he births and deaths innumerable ? The latter alternative, that of metempsychosis in various forms, most of them very extravagant, has long prevailed in the eastern world, while the other alternative, that of a single birth, has been current almost universally among the civilisations of the west. For many singularistic philosophies, of course, the beginning of a soul-life, like everything that pertains to the Many, is nothing more than a phase or moment of the One. But Christian theism has always striven, however inconsistently, to see more in it than this. The doctrine known as creatianism attributes the independent existence of each human soul to a definite creative act; while the opposite doctrine, called traducianism, holds that all souls are generated from other souls in the same way and at the same time as bodies from other bodies. Neither of these positions, between which theologians seem continually to have wavered, is compatible with strict pluralism. The pluralist, in fact, seems shut up to some modification of Leibniz's doctrine that all souls have preexisted 'always in a sort of organized body,' which at the time of generation undergoes a certain transformation and augmentation. But the Leibnizian doctrine of *emboîtement*, that, for example, all mankind preexisted in Adam, modern biology, as we have seen, will not allow him to accept. Again, as we have also seen, he is not compelled to adopt the view to which Leibniz inclined, that reason is imparted to human souls at the time of birth 'by a special operation or by a kind of transcreation[1].'

But the pluralist may fairly be expected to come

[1] *Théodicée*, pt i, § 91.   Cf. Lect. iv. pp. 90 ff.

to closer quarters with the problem of heredity than Leibniz either did or could do. Here in the first place one point seems clear: what is metaphorically described as heredity—as if there were a bequest from one organism to another—is rather so much habit or memory, which pertains to the offspring in virtue of its original continuity with the ancestral stem. The process of regeneration, whereby an organism restores a lost part, and the process of budding, whereby it produces a new whole, are simply instances of such continuity. Even sexual reproduction, in spite of the important preliminary preparation that the maturation of its two constituents requires, seems to be essentially nothing more than the union of two buds. But in none of these processes, so far, is there any individual to be found that can be called the heir, and therefore no ground for calling their result a heritage. All we can say is that what has been done myriads of times is done once more: in regeneration or asexual reproduction the old routine is repeated precisely; and in sexual reproduction there is the joint result of two compatible routines that are similar but not entirely identical. As evidence of the continuity of the process and the completeness of its routine we may appeal to the so-called biogenetic law or principle of palingenesis —that ontogeny recapitulates phylogeny. But is the new individual nothing but 'a chip off the old block,' nothing but a new specimen of the species regarded as self-repeating? The lower the form of life that we consider the less ground have we for assuming more: there seems to be almost as much routine in the conduct of the simplest organisms as there was in their

construction. Contrariwise the higher the form of life
we take note of, the more we seem driven to assume
that the organism has a director, and is not a mere
automaton. It is here that we are led to talk of an
heir and to regard the body as his heritage. This
heir is the soul or dominant monad. But where does
it come from and how does it get possession of this
body ? These questions however implicitly contradict
the pluralist's assumption, that souls do not get bodies
but always have them. The biogenetic law is then a
psychophysical law ; in other words, it has a psychological side ; hence to say that the genetic history
of the individual summarizes the life-history of the race
would better express this.

One essential difference between the two is, of
course, that the life-history of the race is original, is
a long process of gradual acquisition by way of trial
and error, in short, answers to what we have identified
with *natura naturans* ; whereas the genetic history of
the individual is a derivative, rapid and, so to say,
substantially invariable process, in a word, is routine
or *natura naturata*. This difference is apparent again
in the dependence of the primary process on immediate
commerce with the environment and the independence
of the derivative process of any such intercourse. The
eye which in the race has been developed in contact
with the light is reproduced in the individual in darkness. The higher vertebrates, whose history has led
them through the most varied environments—first
water, then land, then water again, as in the case of
the whales—complete their embryonic life directly
shut off from environmental changes altogether.

According to Haeckel the life-history of the human race can be biologically marked out into sixteen stages of steadily increasing complication. "The entire succession of men, throughout the whole course of ages," Pascal has said, "is to be regarded as one man always living and always learning[1]." I have myself, to meet the needs of psychological exposition and yet leave aside the problem of heredity, made use of a similar idea. It will help us forward, I think, if I may be allowed to quote a passage from what I wrote years ago on this point:—"We know that in the course of each individual's life there is more or less of progressive differentiation or development. Further, it is believed that there has existed a series of sentient individuals beginning with the lowest form of life and advancing continuously up to man....But what was experience in the past has become instinct in the present. The descendant has no consciousness of his ancestors' failures, when performing at once by an 'untaught ability' what they slowly and perhaps painfully acquired. But, if we are to attempt to follow the genesis of mind from its earliest dawn, it is the primary experience rather than the eventual instinct that we have to keep in view. To this end, then, it is proposed to assume that we are dealing with one individual who has continuously advanced from the beginning of psychical life, and not with a series of individuals, all of whom, save the first, 'inherited' certain innate capacities from their progenitors. The life-history of such an individual, then, would correspond

---

[1] *Pensées et Opuscules*, edit. Brunschvicg, p. 80: quoted by Prof. Sorley, *Ethics of Naturalism*, 2nd ed., p. 249.

with all that was new in the life of a certain typical series of individuals, each of which advanced a stage in mental differentiation[1]." Let us now suppose our imaginary immortal to be set back once more to the beginning but to retain the memory of his former experiences. We may be sure that in that case he will make good the ground lost in much less time than he required at first, and also without following all the windings of the tentative route into which his previous inexperience had led him: his route the second time will be routine. Illustrative instances in plenty will occur to everyone at once.

But the situation we have supposed is exactly that of a new organism. It does repeat with no hesitation or uncertainty so much of the ancestral experience as had become habitual, secondarily automatic or organized, and it does so because it is continuous with the organisms to which this work had been previously delegated[2]. To understand this we must regard the organism, in Leibnizian fashion, as an orderly hierarchy of monads and not as merely a vastly complex physico-chemical mechanism. The acquisition of new experience by commerce with the environment, the process that is to say of development through

[1] Article 'Psychology,' *Ency. Brit.* 11th edn, vol. XXII. pp. 555 f. *Psychological Principles*, p. 74.

[2] But, it may be objected, between the new organisms and the old there is always more or less 'variation': the two then are not strictly continuous. This we must allow, but on the other hand we may not assume that variation is ever independent of experience taken in the wide sense which the pluralist gives to it. In this way we can understand the fact that variations are vastly greater in sexual as compared with asexual reproduction.

W. 14

experience—in which clearer and distincter percepts, wider and exacter adjustments are attained—is to be conceived as a process in which subordinate monads are drilled and manœuvred: here it is that, as we say, function perfects structure. We may call it biotic as distinct from genetic organization. We know directly by observation that the memories and dexterities that are acquired latest are the least engrained and the first to fail. Entirely in keeping with this we observe too that it is specific characters rather than the generic characters, upon which they are superposed, that are liable to variation[1]. The transmissibility of acquired automatisms is then proportional to their persistence. To say that no acquired characters are transmitted would be tantamount to saying that nothing is transmitted ; and to say that the automatisms accomplished in a single lifetime are not in any degree transmissible is to say that transmission can never begin. In this gradation in the persistence of organic differentiations we have, it would seem, the key to the genetic history of the individual or ontogeny: till the lower and earlier automatisms are evolved there is no *métier* for the higher and later, which depend upon them, to which they stand in the relation of matter to form.

But a viable organism, after it has developed, continues to grow or augment. It thus becomes possible at length not indeed mechanically to divide it, but still to divide it, so to say, selectively. Herein seems to lie the possibility of a new organism. In what way the sifting out, collecting and enrolling of supernumeraries is effected we can at present hardly even

[1] Cf. Darwin's *Origin of Species*, 6th edn, pp. 121 f.

conjecture. The pluralist must at all events maintain
that these processes depend in some way on the
sentience and appetition of the several monads concerned and also on the affinities and antipathies which
their natures determine. Provided some procedure
on these lines is conceivable, that is sufficient to make
his position tenable. Now that far at any rate we are
able to go, helped, as in other cases, by the analogy
of what we know of the higher phases of living intercourse. Indeed it is not too much to say that on
these lines a far simpler hypothesis is conceivable
than Weismann's of the continuity of germ-plasm,
for example. But there still remain difficulties.

Thus it is assumed that the supreme monad or
soul of the system is within it from the first, but its
dominance is manifest only towards the close of the
genetic process; but how is it attained? How in
particular, in sexual reproduction, when two colonies
unite? Is there here a rivalry or conflict between
two potential monarchs? Or is there possibly after
all, as some psychologists suppose, no unity at all
beyond that of the system: is that only a commonwealth and not a monarchy? But such a view, though
by no means devoid altogether of justification, seems
inconsistent with pluralism; for, rigorously followed out,
it would altogether destroy the notion of dominance
on which the entire doctrine of monadism is built[1].
On the whole it seems best to regard the organism on
its psychical side as simply the *Anlage* or primary

[1] And this by the way, it may be incidentally remarked, suggests
an analogical argument in favour of a supreme world-spirit.

14—2

medium of the soul's life : this is its heritage but how it comes by it we do not know[1].

We come now to the difficulties besetting the pluralistic interpretation of death. Why, it may be asked, should there be death at all, why should not the individual enjoy that prolonged existence which we have imagined only for expository purposes ? I do not propose however to enter upon the far-reaching inquiry which this question opens up, since the difficulties that more immediately concern us are of another sort. Death, as the more or less complete dissolution of the organism, means that the soul in consequence, so far as it is thus deprived of its *locus standi*, is, to use Leibniz's phrase, in the position of a deserter from the general order. Temporarily it is in a like position during sleep ; and death for Leibniz was but a longer and profounder sleep : in neither case did he believe that the continuity of the individual's life was completely broken. Still the amount of personal continuity between its successive lives might in general be extremely slight. In fact if the notion of a merely bodily resurrection was incredible in Leibniz's day it is more incredible still in our own. Who expects to see trilobites and ammonites, the pterodactyle and the diplodocus come to life again ?—No doubt we find the passage back from the organic to the inorganic barred on every side. Nature has no crematorium : she turns dead sheep and oxen into jackals and crows it may be, but not into ashes. Such facts would almost suggest that the best thing to befall a dying man would be to be eaten by such of his younger

[1] Cf. below, Lect. XVIII.

contemporaries as liked him, and according to Professor
Tylor personal affection was one among other motives
for cannibalism[1].   At any rate 'metempsychosis' in
some form seems an unavoidable corollary of thorough-
going pampsychism[2], so long as we look broadly at
the facts of life as a whole.

We have just noted in the economy of nature a
tendency to conserve the organic : is there also some
principle of 'conservation of value' tending to prevent
rational, self-conscious spirits from lapsing back into
merely animal souls ? This question Leibniz answered
with a decided affirmative. Thus in a letter to Arnauld,
after substituting what he called metaschematism,
change of body, for metempsychosis or change of soul,
he continues :—" But spirits are not subjected to these
revolutions, or rather it must be that these revolutions
of bodies subserve the Divine economy in relation to
spirits.... They must always keep their moral qualities
and their memory in order to be perpetual citizens of
that universal all-perfect commonwealth of which God
is the monarch, which can lose none of its members
and the laws of which are higher than those of
bodies[3]."   Apart from its theological standpoint this
is obviously a purely dogmatic statement. But the
idea of a higher spiritual order, as we have already
seen, is perfectly compatible with pluralism and—
though it lack adequate empirical evidence—is directly

[1] This practice, so-called endophagy, is "intelligible enough on
the principle that 'the life is not allowed to go out of the family'."
Chambers's Encyclopaedia, s.v. It is referred to by Herodotus.

[2] Cf. above, p. 205.

[3] Lettre à Arnauld, *Philosophische Schriften*, Gerhardt's edn, II.
pp. 99 f.

suggested by the principle of continuity, against which the Leibnizian theology more or less offends[1].

But without this idea and 'the conservation of values,' the *Weltanschauung* of pluralism is sadly far away from the heart's desire. The biologist pictures for us the gradual evolution of the human species onwards from some primitive moner, and the sociologist the gradual advance of humanity from savagery to civilisation. But what of all this progress if we are forced to say of all the individuals concerned that one labours and another reaps the reward? The individual, it may be, that falls out of the ranks for a time is not dead but only sleepeth, yet if he return not as the same identical person but only, so to say, as the same metaphysical entity; and especially if, as the chances are, the higher his former position the more likelihood that he will start again in a lower one, what —we are forced once more to ask—what worth or meaning is there in such revolutions? And when we remember that whole species become extinct, we may be told that at least the fittest survive. But then it is only in what we may call the ascending phase of things that the fitter is the better: when this earth enters upon its inevitable decline the fitter will be the worse. But every winter turns to spring, it is replied, and old worlds are continually rejuvenated. Yes, but once more we urge that if there is no personal continuity between the old constituents and the new, if as with the individual beginning a new life, a world entering upon a fresh evolution cannot start where it left off and may even begin in less favourable conditions

---

[1] Cf Latta, *Leibniz, The Monadology &c.*, p. 265 note.

than before, what ground have we to expect progress
on the whole? In a word, without such spiritual
continuity as theism alone seems able to ensure, it
looks as if a pluralistic world were condemned to a
Sisyphean task. *Per aspera ad astra* may be its
motto, but *facilis descensus Averno* seems to be its fate.

Let us turn now to metaphysical difficulties. There
is one such objection to pluralism that will at once
occur to every student of Lotze's philosophy, one that
is all the more impressive because Lotze—unlike most
who maintain the doctrine of an Absolute One—
starts as we have done from the side of the Many,
which seems to confront us at first. He finds however
that the concept of causal interaction or 'transeunt
action' as he terms it, which we ordinarily employ
alike in everyday life and in our scientific expositions,
is really unthinkable. He is therefore driven to
postulate an absolute substance, of which the Many
are in truth but states or modifications. Moreover
such a fundamental unity of things was, it seemed to
him, analytically involved in the facts of what we
conceive as reciprocal action. But what is strange is
that Lotze, who was never a dualist, who from first
to last was clear upon one point, viz., that there are
no things that are things and nothing more, should
nevertheless have discussed this problem of causation
in connexion with physical action. He is aware, of
course, that for the scientific investigator who is content to stop at 'occasional causes' there is no problem
at all; he has indeed himself emphasized the methodological utility of occasionalism in its modern or positivist

guise. But for philosophy the question, how or why,
when the state of a certain thing A changes to a, that
of another thing B should change to β, has been a
serious problem since the days of Hume at any rate.
Assuming that A and B are independent things, Lotze's
argument in its barest outline is simple enough. Since
attributes cannot be separated from substances, "no
state can detach itself from the thing A, whose state
it was, so as to subsist even for an infinitesimally small
moment between A and B, as a state but yet nobody's
state, and then connect itself with B so as to become
its state[1]." The facts themselves not being in question
the only conclusion according to Lotze is that A and
B are not independent substances, that is not substances at all, but only different modifications of the
one absolute substance, which we may call M. The
state of the universe at the one moment he represents
by the equation $M = \phi(ABR)$ and that at the other
as $M = \phi(a\beta R)$; that is to say he regards the Absolute
as compensating one change of state, that of A into a,
by the other, that of B into β; the rest of the universe,
represented by R, being, for simplicity's sake, regarded
as in the particular case remaining unaffected.

But considering so-called 'things' apart, this doctrine
of Lotze's seems very closely to resemble Berkeley's

---

[1] It was long assumed that this difficulty only applies to 'action
at a distance' and not to 'contact action.' And so far as perception
or the constructions of abstract mechanics are concerned this may
be true. But actual bodies are not ideal solids; they are more like
clouds, or swarms of particles in motion. Moreover absolute contact
implies a common point or surface (interface), in fact no longer
contiguity but continuity. Cf. *Naturalism and Agnosticism*, 3rd edn,
i. pp. 122 ff.; 4th edn, p. 118.

well-known doctrine of sense-symbolism. The entire physical world, 'the whole choir of heaven and furniture of earth,' is but the medium, divinely constituted and sustained—as it were the language and the instrumentality—whereby finite spirits communicate and interact. Now it seems *prima facie* perfectly possible to adapt this doctrine to the pluralistic standpoint: in fact in some way or other the pluralist must regard all perceptual objects as the manifestation of subjects or ejects. There would be important differences of detail, no doubt; for example, as we have already said, we should begin with a Babel and have to achieve 'one language and one speech.' In short the equation by which Lotze typifies the 'self-conservation' of his Absolute seems so far to answer simply to what would be better called its behaviour in sustaining the intercourse of free agents, if such a medium were necessary, as he for the most part inclined to doubt. His equation amounts in fact merely to the doctrine of physical conservation.

When however A and B are not things but persons, can we still say that they are merely modifications of the Absolute? When A changes to a—when the child, feeling hunger, wants food, let us say, and B his father, let us suppose, thereupon changes to β, that is, gives him bread—are we to believe that the persons here are not beings for themselves but only so-called things, that they are nothing but modifications of an Absolute, that adjusts one to the other solely on its own account? Such an interpretation of personal intercourse is clearly untenable and Lotze did not seriously entertain it. The description that he has given of personal intercourse, regarded from the side of the Many, differs entirely from the conceptual framework by which science summarises what is called physical interaction. There is here no constant equation involving rigidly concatenated variables, no network of relations of which individuals are but the *termini*, no lines of direction subsisting between them along which in some mysterious way actions and passions are interchanged. The spatial metaphor of influences, energies or forces transferred and transformed, which makes up the concept of transeunt action, is no longer applicable even as a figure to personal intercourse. The doings and sufferings of persons are both alike immediate: what brings them into relation is a 'sympathetic *rapport*' or interest that rests upon cognition. All that is strictly personal in social intercourse is of this nature. It entirely consists, in the first place, of the apprehension or the knowledge on the part of one person of the 'attitude,' the feelings and intentions displayed or announced by other persons; secondly, in their cooperation or opposition, actual or prospective: and finally, following on this, in the new feelings and intentions of the person interested, to which this knowledge leads. We can readily imagine situations in abundance that are altogether of this sort, into which—even when life itself is at stake—no physical constraint whatever directly enters. Think, for instance, of all that the phrase '*noblesse oblige*' implies, of Regulus returning to Carthage, of Socrates refusing to fly, of the Hindoo *suttee*, which means, I understand, 'virtuous wife,' or of the Japanese '*hari kari*' or 'happy despatch'; or again

of the wiles of the hunter and the angler, who have
to count simply on the behaviour of their game till it
brings itself into a position to be dealt with, so to say,
as a thing. It is, however, as needless as it would be
tedious to picture out such cases in detail.

But usually in these cases there is, in addition to
the conduct of those primarily concerned, that of subordinates and accessories, upon which they can safely
count—the law and the police, impartial spectators,
servants and retainers; and again dogs, decoys, stalking
horses and the like. All this we may call social environment in a wide sense: upon it we rely and depend, much
as we rely and depend upon what we call the physical
environment. And we have seen already that this
social environment, so far as habit and custom enter
into it, tends to approximate to the character of the
physical environment: nay that very character, which
we express by such terms as law and order, subject
and attribute, is, we know, so much metaphor borrowed
from the world of persons. For the pluralist, however,
it is more than metaphor. If the Leibnizian assumption, that there are no beings entirely devoid of
perception and spontaneity—which Lotze too accepted
—is otherwise sound, then the objections to transeunt
action between *things* become irrelevant. For these
objections do not apply to personal interaction based on
mutual *rapport*, which is all that the pluralist requires.
On the contrary the very fact that this suffices for
his view of the world is so far an argument in its
favour.

But there is still another objection to pluralism,
likewise urged by Lotze, that is more serious.

Granted that sentient and conative beings can shape their conduct relatively to each other—in so far as they are clearly aware of each other's presence and attitude—without the need of another being distinct from them all to play the part of a go-between, still the fact that such 'sympathetic *rapport*' exists is in Lotze's opinion nothing less than an 'inexhaustible wonder.' Nay the mere fact that all the Many are comparable and commensurable, that no individual, however unique, is altogether disparate and isolated from the rest, though undeniable, is such a wonder: only extreme familiarity leads us to take it for granted as a matter of course. Lotze is content to press only this second broader and simpler issue, which he regards as a form of the cosmological argument[1]. The first which approximates rather to the teleological argument he seems content to waive. Still it may be well to look at both.

Let us begin with the argument in its more detailed form. We can readily imagine a case sufficiently analogous to bring out the point of the argument, how very far the actual relatedness of things is from being self-evident or self-explanatory. Let us suppose that we had a sack of type continually shuffled, which differs however from ordinary type in one respect. When letters forming syllables come together we will suppose that their arrangement remains comparatively stable, that when syllables forming words come together this arrangement is still more stable, and similarly of words forming sentences and so on; that generally the more meaning the more stability. Under such

---

[1] *Microcosmus*, Eng. trans. vol. II. pp. 668 f.

circumstances the more 'sense' the final arrangement presented the more we should be inclined to believe that we had been dealing from the first not with a random collection but with a definite selection, with what, in fact, was all along really a whole and not merely an aggregate. And should the final arrangement be complete and perfect without one redundant or deficient letter, this presumption would amount to certainty.

No doubt the better fitting arrangements of our world are to be regarded as the more stable arrangements. The Many however are not, like type, moulded unalterably once for all: on the contrary they must be regarded as more or less plastic and adaptable, as mutually moulding each other in a greater or less degree. The round man, to be sure, avoids the square hole; and yet if circumstances force him into it, he usually contrives to adapt it or to adapt himself. The limpet shapes its shell to fit the rock, the Pholas shapes the rock to fit its shell. And after all, the teleological harmony to be found in the world is not such as to force on us the conviction that it is due solely to a single underlying or overruling principle. "Taken alone," Lotze himself allows, "it would more easily lead to the polytheistic view of a plurality of divine beings, each dominating a special department of nature as its special genius, their diverse modes of adminis- tration agreeing too so far as to attain to a certain general compatibility but not to a harmony that is altogether complete[1]." But then is it not strange to maintain that the pluralistic view, which is admittedly suggested directly by the facts of the world, is yet

[1] *Op. cit.* vol. ii. p. 667.

really inconceivable, and that the opposite view, which the facts seem at first sight to negative, is nevertheless the only view that is not self-contradictory? This, however, is what Lotze does: let us next examine this position somewhat more closely.

The Many are all related: they interact. This interrelation is at once the *ratio essendi* and the *ratio cognoscendi* of their comparability. No two are altogether different, for all are conative and cognitive to some extent. Such is the familiar pluralistic doctrine. And now, says Lotze, because all this is so, the Many are substantially *one*, are *only* different modifications of a single Being that we designate the Absolute[1]. The Many are either severally comparable or they are not. If they are not, there can be no knowledge of their plurality: if they are, then they are fundamentally and ultimately one. Such is Lotze's short and easy method with pluralism. It yields, I fear, only a 'cheap and easy monism.' There can be no experience of a plurality, whether of beings, qualities or events, that are absolutely disparate and disconnected—that is certain. All experienced diversity implies some identity; and, for the matter of that, all experienced identity some diversity. All this is so much logical commonplace. From this it follows that to every known or knowable Many there will be some common term applicable to them all, which *logically* unifies them all. But it leaves the question of their real unity untouched. Ice, water, steam, is a plurality which turns out to consist only of varying states of one substance. Gold, silver, copper, is a plurality which has not been thus unified: logically it belongs

[1] Cf. *Grundzüge der Metaphysik*, 1883, § 48.

to the one class, metal. The class is logically one, but we do not say there *must* be a single prime and ultimate metal. The Many of pluralism are in like manner a logical whole: they constitute the class of entelechies or persons in the widest sense, beings, that is to say, who are something for themselves, conative and cognitive individuals bent on self-conservation and seeking the good. To resolve the logical universal itself into a personal individual, of which the several persons that it denotes are but modifications, so far from explaining the facts denoted, seems flatly to contradict them. Yet this is what Lotze does. To be sure the Many are more than a logical whole: they are a real unity, but a unity of another order, just as a regiment is a unity though it is not a soldier. This other unity answers to the fact—a fact, it is important to notice, which perception and appetition imply—viz., that the Many are severally related by their mutual interaction: for each, as subject, the rest constitute an objective continuum. We have not, I repeat, two distinct and separable facts, first the Many existing in isolation, and then their interaction, either subsequently intervening as a real *mutuum commercium* for them or else preestablished as a merely 'ideal' harmony independently of them: the former answering to the Herbartian, the latter to the Leibnizian pluralism. For modern pluralism the universe is the totality of monads really interacting; and this is one fact: the plurality implies this unity, and this unity the plurality. But this fact, says Lotze, is an inexhaustible wonder. Unquestionably: the universe *is* an inexhaustible wonder. Still after all a wonder is not a contradiction. Returning then to Lotze's formula,

$M = \phi(ABR)$ or $\phi(ABR) = M$, for the mere equation gives no priority to one side over the other; if it can be shown that M is more than the name we give to a plurality of reals A, B, C,..., whose functional relation is symbolised by ϕ—that M is in fact itself the one absolute reality, and ϕ the relation which 'its individuality as a self-conserving unity' imposes upon its several differentiations or modes A, B, C...—all well and good. But the mere formula will not accomplish this. Taken as an abstract formula it may suggest either alternative, but taken as a description of the universe or *mundus*, M, regarded empirically or *a posteriori*, it is no longer equally ambiguous. From this immanent standpoint M does not resolve the wonder, it merely names it. If we are to get any further we must assume that M is transcendent, an *ens extramundanum*, to use Kant's phrase; and this all theism does that is worthy of the name. Then, however, A, B, R will no longer be merely modes or states of this M. But to express the relation of this transcendent Being to the world of experience no equational formula seems either appropriate or adequate. Theism, however, promises to effect much in resolving the difficulties of pluralism, and to the careful discussion of theism I propose to devote the second part of these lectures. Meanwhile I think we must insist that the way cannot be cleared in any summary fashion by convicting the pluralist's *Weltanschauung* not merely of incompleteness but of actual contradictions. In fact, if it were radically infected with contradictions, we have seen, I trust, that the way to theism would be hopelessly barred; for from pluralism speculation really always has and always must begin.

PART II.

THEISM.

LECTURE XI.

THE IDEA OF CREATION.

We have seen that modern pluralism is, on its own confession, 'radically empirical.' It makes no attempt to deduce the universe from a single absolute principle, or indeed to deduce it at all. The world is taken simply as we find it, as a plurality of active individuals unified only in and through their mutual interactions. These interactions again are interpreted throughout on the analogy of social transactions, as a *mutuum commercium*; that is to say, as based on cognition and conation. To the speculative mind *pur sang* there is nothing satisfactory about such a view unless perhaps its frankness.

But then, on the other hand, there are objections to all attempts to proceed altogether *a priori*. It seems obviously puerile to ask, for example, for a sufficient reason why there is something rather than nothing. This notion of being absolutely thoroughgoing, of building up a metaphysic without presuppositions, one that shall start from nothing and explain all, is, I repeat, futile. Such a metaphysic has its own

w.   15

assumption, and that an absurd one, viz., that nothing is the logical *prius* of something. Well at any rate, it may be said, if we must start from something, let us at least start from what is absolutely necessary, or rather let us not stop till we reach it : let us not rest in what is merely actual, for that can only be contingent. But, paradoxical though it may sound, necessary being is but another aspect of such 'contingent' being; for within the limits of our experience only that is called *really* necessary which is inevitably conditioned by its cause, and is thus contingent on this, that is to say, follows from it. In other words real as distinct from formal necessity is synonymous with causation ; and moreover, as Kant said, this real or causal necessity "extends no further than the field of possible experience, and even then does not apply to the existence of things as substances ; because such substances can never be looked upon as empirical effects or as something that happens or comes to be[1]." Thus to talk of absolutely necessary being as the *foundation* of the universe, so to say, is only to be guilty of the fallacy of Locke's poor Indian philosopher, the fallacy of applying to the whole a concept that is applicable only to the part. "The favourite notion of the philosophers," said Schopenhauer with wonted bitterness, "of 'absolutely necessary being' involves a contradiction : the predicate 'absolute,' which means 'dependent on nothing else,' removes the characteristic through which alone 'necessary' is thinkable and has any sense[2]." The absolute totality of being has no cause, it simply is. To attempt

---

[1] *Critique of Pure Reason*, M. Müller's trans. p. 198.
[2] *Vierfache Wurzel, u.s.w.* § 49.

to reflect causation back on itself as in such phrases as *causa sui*, aseity, or being through self, really adds nothing to our bare recognition of this being. But if there is no sense in calling the absolute totality of being necessary, there is none in calling it contingent. Within it there is necessity and contingency in plenty : every part is related to the rest : but the whole, we have again to say, simply is.

If then the whole simply is, those philosophers have only deluded themselves, who have essayed by the royal road of pure thought to determine *a priori* what it must be. The only *a priori* statements concerning the world that are beyond challenge are purely formal statements ; yet the entire body of logical and mathematical truths would not yield us the faintest anticipatory gleam of what the actual world would be, even if it were possible to know such truths in advance. But this supposition too is only a delusion : for validity implies reality and is otherwise meaningless. The two are distinct but they are not absolutely separable. The notion of a sort of antecedent logical fate determining all subsequent existence is psychologically explicable as the result—not of the supremacy of our reason—but of the limitations of our imagination. We distinguish relatively to a particular case between form and matter. But when we make the distinction absolute, pure form and pure matter both alike become empty abstractions. We find the logical to be in every case necessary, the empirical in every case contingent ; but we are guilty of a sort of *fallacia compositionis* when we imagine that the totality of the empirical on the one side is conditioned by the totality of the logical on the other[1]. The enormous labour that Kant is known to have spent in deducing his table of categories from his logical table of judgments is perhaps the most disastrous instance of mistaken ingenuity to be found in the whole history of philosophy ; for to that in very large measure may be traced the daring but hopeless enterprises of his idealist successors, Fichte, Schelling and Hegel. Nobody ever has, nobody ever will, derive the categories of substance, cause, end, or any other concept concerning reality, from any source altogether independent of experience.

All ontology alike then has to begin with the question : What is Reality[2] ? And nowadays pluralist and singularist alike answer : It is Experience. But the difference between them is that the pluralist is content to stop at the totality of finite experiences, whereas the singularist, or at all events the theist, with whom we are now primarily concerned, maintains that beyond the universe of the Many there is a single transcendent experient, who perfectly comprehends the whole.

The superiority of the theistic position, if it can be sustained, seems indisputable : it will then be, to use Kant's words, "an ideal without a flaw." Well, in the first place, it is superior in respect of its unity. On the pluralistic view every one of the finite individuals is related to all the rest but only for himself. In

[1] Cf. Lotze, *Microcosmus*, ii. p. 705 and *Metaphysic*, § 88 *fin.*

[2] This may entail a preliminary inquiry into the nature of knowledge, but epistemology is after all only a preparation for ontology.

Leibnizian language each mirrors the whole from a unique standpoint, and therefore *not* the whole, but only an aspect of the whole. The pluralistic whole, then, is a whole of experiences, but not a whole experience, a whole of lives but not a living whole, a whole of beings but without a complete and perfect being. Is such a whole really a unity at all : is it more than a totality ? We have a type of a higher unity than this in our own experience as self-conscious subjects. Here there is a unity which is more than the related objective continuum, a unity to which all this belongs and refers. Now remove from such an experience the relativity which 'standpoint' implies and you approach the theistic ideal of an absolute experience, the experience of a living and acting Spirit whose 'centre is everywhere, whose circumference is nowhere,' an experience complete at all points and including every one. The pluralist's universe in the light of this transcendent Being would thus have a unity which it would otherwise lack.

Not only so, but in the second place the pluralist's universe would itself be immeasurably enriched if the theistic idea of God's relation to this universe were accepted. For according to that God is not simply a transcendent Being, existing aloof and apart from the world, he is also immanent, and active within it. And such active presence of the One Spirit, who alone knows all, affords—manifestly—an assurance that the pluralist's ideal will be attained, an assurance which we have had to allow must else be wanting. For it would be extravagantly arbitrary to assume that this one transcendent Being alone would be more devoid of

X what is the Pluralist's "ideal"? see Pf. 117 ff

benevolent purpose than finite beings are.   At any
rate the theist believes that this God who knows all
loves all.   And so in the third place it is evident that
the theistic idea not merely adds to our confidence
in the eventual realisation of the pluralist's ideal but
it enhances the character of that ideal by all the
ineffable blessedness that the presence of God must
yield.

But to determine what is reality, we have agreed,
is the first business of philosophy.   Can we then prove
the existence of God ?   Attempts innumerable to prove
this have been made—as of course we know—all of
them reducible to one or other of the three forms called
respectively the ontological, the cosmological and the
teleological argument.   The fatal defects of all these
have, it is almost universally conceded, been clearly
exposed once for all by Kant.   The ontological
argument, as he has shown, involves the common
metaphysical fallacy of hypostatizing an idea ; the
teleological argument does not carry us beyond
pluralism ; and the cosmological only does so by
implicitly assuming the ontological.—But though demonstrations of the existence of God are unattainable,
it by no means follows that the idea is theoretically
worthless.   It has even in this respect—to say nothing
of its practical value—a 'regulative use' as what Kant
called a *focus imaginarius*, a use which he declared to
be not only admirable but indispensable.   What Kant
meant by a *focus imaginarius*, it may be worth while
to illustrate by an example.   Suppose the earth were
wrapt in cloud all day while the sky was clear at night,
so that we were able to see the planets and observe

their movements as we do now, though the sun itself was invisible.   The best account we could give of the planetary motions would still be to refer them to what for us in accordance with our supposition would only be an imaginary focus, but one to which was assigned a position identical with the sun's position.   The pluralist's universe, according to Kant, answers to the wandering orbs that we see and God to the sun, which we are supposed not to see, but merely to conceive as giving to their motions both reason and unity.   It behoves us then, especially in view of the acknowledged difficulties and incompleteness of the pluralistic scheme taken alone, to examine this sublime conception with reverence and with care.   Is the theistic ideal verily without a flaw ?

One thing is at once clear: theism is not simply the possible crown and completion of pluralism : such a transcendent addition will, it may be expected, change all.   It introduces one essential modification, at any rate, viz., the idea of creation.   It does not, that is to say, assume merely that one transcendent Being exists above and beyond the whole series of the Many, however extended ; but it assumes further that this one Being is related to them in a way in which none of them is related to the rest : they do not simply coexist along with it, they exist somehow in it and through it.

In this idea of creation there are two sides to consider, its relation to the world and its relation to God.   As to the first—it cannot be said that the world as we know it involves the idea of creation as a fact. If it did, we should have direct and tangible evidence of God's existence. "The heavens declare the glory of God and the firmament sheweth his handiwork," sang the Psalmist long ago. Possibly it is so, but there is nothing in all our physical experience that *compels* us to admit it : on the other hand there is nothing that would justify us in denying it. Further, the metaphor of making, of handiwork, which is the sole empirical content of the term 'creation,' is inadequate : *making* out of nothing, in short, is a contradiction. But then this is not the meaning of creation : it is not a making or shaping at all. The idea is, in fact, like the idea of God, altogether transcendent. It is impossible therefore that experience should directly give rise to it at all.

But, it has been urged, the universe cannot have existed for ever, since in that case, at any assigned moment, an infinite time would be completed, and that is impossible. The universe must then have had a beginning and so must have had a First Cause. Well, if this argument were valid, it would apply equally to the existence of God. If *per impossibile* we could transcend experience and contemplate the world from without we might, it has been thought, find that the world had a beginning : but then we should be there and as what should we have to be reckoned ? Keeping within experience we can only endlessly regress with no prospect of ever reaching the beginning or of forming any concept of what it was like. On the contrary, say certain physicists, we have empirical evidence of a beginning. But in all cases it will be found, I think, that the beginning affirmed is a purely relative one ; and moreover that its affirmation assumes

In calling God the creator, what are we mean t express in the world's dependence on Him

modern science to be exactly and absolutely, and not merely approximately, true[1].

There is equally little to support the view of creation as an event that occurred at a finite date in the past, when we attempt to regard it from the side of God as creator. Whatever the reason or motive for creation may have been—and some motive or reason the theist must assume—it seems "absolutely inconceivable," as v. Hartmann put it, "that a conscious God should wait half an eternity content without a good that ought to be." If creation means anything, it means something so far involved in the divine essence, that we are entitled to say, as Hegel was fond of saying, that "without the world God is not God." In calling God the creator then it is simply the world's dependence on Him that we mean to express. If so, it seems clear that this dependence is not, as commonly maintained, a causal dependence strictly understood. For causation relates to change in existence; but creation regarded from the side of the created is not a change in anything existing. To speak of it as a change in nothing, whereby nothing becomes something, is once again— it seems hardly needful to say—mere thoughtless absurdity. Creation in other words is not to be brought under the category of transeunt causation. Nor can we, regarding it from the side of God, bring it under the category of immanent causation, as being a change in Him, unless indeed we abandon the

[1] Cf., e.g., *The Unseen Universe*, 2nd edn, § 116 and Clifford's criticism, *Lectures and Essays*, 2nd edn, p. 156; also the article by Professor Arrhenius, 'Infinity of the Universe,' *Monist*, vol. XXI. 1911, pp. 161 ff.

God is the ground of the world being.

position that God is God only as being creative. To say that the world depends on God is tantamount to saying that could God cease to be, the world too would cease to be ; or that if the world should cease to be, it would be because God had ceased to be. In other words God is the ground of the world's being, its *ratio essendi*. The notion of ' ground,' it will, I assume, be conceded, is wider than that of cause, which is only one of its special forms.

But we have not yet brought out the full meaning of creation as the theist conceives it. Spinoza, for example, also conceived God to be the ground of the world, but interpreted this relation in a way which the theist cannot accept. Spinoza, as his phrase *Deus sive Natura* shows, identified the world and God as completely as he identified the properties of a triangle with the triangle itself : the reality of the One meant so much that there was no reality left for the Many at all. For pantheism God is the immanent ground of the world, for deism he is the transcendent ground, for theism he is both. How are we to conceive this twofold relation ? The most hopeful attempt perhaps is that which is nowadays associated with the name of Kant, though it is really, I believe, as old as Plato and recurs continually in ancient and modern philosophy alike. I may call it the theory of intellective intuition. Our knowledge according to Kant has two stems, both requisite to complete our experience. The one, sensibility, is receptive and passive ; but taken alone it is blind, that is to say it furnishes only the material of knowledge. The other, understanding, is active but yields only the form of knowledge : taken alone it is

Kant + the 2 stems of Knowledge. a) Sensibility – receptive + passive b) + understanding active.
a) + b) together yield phenomenal knowledge.
God on the other hand "Knows" by creative intellectual intuition

empty, its content is abstract. But together these two sources yield what we call phenomenal knowledge ; so far we may, according to Kant, be said to shape Nature though we do not create it ; our objective knowledge, in other words, is the joint result of the manifold data that we receive and of the discursive synthesis of these which our thought achieves. Reality is first there, is given, and our work—all we are capable of—is to understand it. But now we are to imagine our sensory and passive perception replaced by an active, intellective 'position,' our discursive synthesis by an original thesis or intuition. The Being to whom this intellective intuition belongs will be creative ; its objective experience will contain nothing that is merely given to it, but only what is ultimately ' posited ' by it : its objects will be not phenomenal but noumenal, not independent manifestations of an Other but the creation of itself.

But the world as presented to us is veritably an Other ; hence the passivity in our perception : we know the world only in this its external relation to us, not as it is in itself ; hence it is phenomenal. Here the distinction, the duality, of subject and object is real. But in intellective intuition all real difference between being and knowing, thought and thing, seems to have vanished. Such intuition, in fact, implies far more than we ordinarily understand even by omniscience[1]. For as our relative and imperfect knowledge does not *partially* constitute the being of its object, so absolute and perfect knowledge, if merely knowledge, would not, we seem entitled to say, constitute its object completely.

[1] Omniscience, literally taken, is still science, not intuition.

Our partial knowledge of a thing is knowledge of its utterances, attitude and behaviour as they are for us: hence we call this relative knowledge. But a knowledge of all such characteristics of all things in all their interactions would still only be absolute as knowledge: i.e., it would be as absolute or complete as knowledge can be, which, by its very nature, is essentially relative. It would leave the things themselves still independent as regards their existence, and so would fall short of this intellective intuition wherein, it is supposed, they are not merely known but whereby they exist. Thus then the idea of a transcendent experient, whose standpoint, so to say, is ubiquitous, does not reach to the still more transcendent idea of a creator, of one who is the ground of the objects that he 'knows.'

. Moreover immediate experience of another subject is beyond any knowledge that we have or can conceive : in fact it might, I think, be fairly maintained that the very idea involves a contradiction. If now it be further allowed that the actions of free and advancing intelligences make new beginnings possible, imply real initiative, it would follow that even complete and absolute knowledge (or omniscience), as knowledge is ordinarily understood, would still leave every finite subject in the position of an eject : each would be known completely as regards its utterances, its objective relations with the rest, but not as it is in itself. But more than this, it will be said, is implied in the divine so-called omniscience as theism understands it: "the Lord seeth not as man seeth ; for man looketh on the outward appearance, but the Lord looketh on the heart." And why? "He that keepeth thy soul doth not he

know it[1]?" Such 'omniscience' in a word presupposes
creation ; thus it is only for creative intuition that
the knowing and the being of objects could be said
to be in any sense the same.

But then, so far—on the principle of the identity of
indiscernibles—is not this so-called knowledge or intuitive thought of the object as such itself just the
object, and is not the object just this so-called knowledge
or intuition ? In that case what becomes of the divine
transcendence on which theism lays such stress? Do not
theism and pantheism after all come to the same thing:
God is the world and the world is God ? But identity,
if it is to mean anything, must imply some difference :
there is no point, for example, in saying ' This is the
same ' unless I refer to something experienced previously. The bare, and therefore meaningless, identity
of God and World simply leaves us with God only, as
in the acosmism of Spinoza; or with World only, as in
the ' polite *atheism*' of Schopenhauer. But, it is urged,
there is, after all, a difference and one which our own
self-consciousness enables us to understand. Here the
knower and the known are one and the same, and yet
are distinct in so far as the subject is its own object.
Moreover self-consciousness is the only form of knowledge that can be in a sense absolute. Knowledge of
an Other, so long as the Other is veritably such, must
ever be relative and incomplete ; whereas we cannot
call our consciousness of self merely phenomenal.
True, but—as I have already urged in the second
lecture[2]—throughout our experience the consciousness
of self involves the consciousness of not-self : the two

---

[1] I Sam. xvi. 7 ; Prov. xxiv. 12.   [2] Lect. II. pp. 30, 41.

being always correlative and coordinate. It does not surprise us then to find certain of the philosophies of the Absolute represent it as coming to self-consciousness in and through consciousness of the world. From such a view it is but a step to a philosophy of the Unconscious, such as v. Hartmann and others have constructed mainly on a Hegelian basis. And we may note by the way, as an odd illustration of extremes meeting, that v. Hartmann's 'clairvoyance of the Unconscious' or 'Over-conscious' is but a bad setting of the old idea of intellective intuition[1]. The attempt, therefore, to equate creation regarded as intellective intuition with a pure or absolute self-consciousness—if this were conceivable—will not avail for theism : it leaves no room for the divine transcendence and without this the distinctness of God and the world and the dependence of the world on God both alike disappear. Our result so far then is simply this : neither absolute knowledge nor absolute self-consciousness can take the place of the idea of creation ; and therefore, if the notion of intellective intuition or intuitive understanding is to help us, we must find more in the activity which it after all implies than thought or knowledge of any sort will cover ; and also more than such identity as self-knowing and self-known implies.

We may discern perhaps a faint and distant analogy, one suggesting a better interpretation, in what we are wont to style the creations of genius. We never apply this phrase to the most marvellous discoveries in science or the most fruitful inventions in

----

[1] Perhaps too Bergson's *élan vital* is but another variant of this idea.

the technical arts : nobody, I fancy, would say that Newton created gravitation or that Gutenberg created printing. If Newton had not discovered gravitation some one else would, and as for printing we know that it was invented more than once. But it is common to speak of such works as the *Antigone* of Sophocles, Shakespeare's *Hamlet*, Michael Angelo's *Moses*, Raphael's *Sistine Madonna* or Beethoven's *Ninth Symphony* as creations; and we feel pretty confident that if their authors had not produced them they would never have been produced. This approximation to the divine that we find in the originality of genius leads us often to speak of its 'creations' as inspired. In the case of discoveries and inventions we realise that sense and intellect, the receptive and active factors, are both concerned ; but the immortal works of art, the things of beauty that are a joy for ever, we regard as rather the spontaneous output of productive imagination, of a free spirit that embodies itself in its work, lives in it and loves it[1]. Yet however much the man of genius loves his work and lives in it, he is still distinct from it, still greater than it. On the other hand, however dependent on him is his production, though he knows it through and through, yet it too is distinct from him : from its first inception, even in the full tide of his activity, he feels that it is working itself out and sees that it is good ; in other words he finds himself expressed in it and he respects his work.

Yet after all, as we have allowed, this analogy is very imperfect, and it is just in the important point where it fails that our difficulties with the idea of intellective intuition begin. Between what we may

[1] Cf. Aristotle, *Nic. Ethics*, IX. vii. 4, and Grant's note, vol. II. of his edn, p. 296.

call relative creation, the origination of something relatively new within the world, and the absolute creation
of the world itself there is an impassable gulf.   The
one presupposes experience previously acquired, the
other is coeval and identical with the divine experience
itself.   God in short is the Absolute Genius—the
World-Genius, as he has been called.   Any analogy
drawn from our experience must then be inadequate to
such an experience : God's ways are not as our ways
nor his thoughts as our thoughts.   But the difference
lies simply in transcending the limit to which our
experience points but can never attain : it need not
imply utter disparity.   We may perhaps safely assume
that the distinction of will and presentation is applicable to the divine experience as well as to our own ;
and also that there too they are equally inseparable.
At any rate we cannot say that volition precedes
presentation nor that presentation precedes volition ;
that the subject is first nor yet that the object is ; nor
finally that both are originally undifferentiated[1].   If so,
we cannot then represent creation as starting with a
blind will to create followed by a discursive selection
of the best possible plan of creation ; nor as starting
with a dialectic development of the only possible plan
followed by the resolve to let it be.   It is at once 'pure
activity ' and ' original insight,' idea and deed, life and
light.   God is transcendent to it, for it is not God, but
his utterance and manifestation ; and yet, because it is
his utterance and because he ever sustains it, he is
immanent in it, it is his continuous creation.

So then at last the theist is bound to admit that

[1] Cf. Lect. ix. p. 199.

this conception of God-and-the-world is beyond us : we can assign it no beginning and so we say it is 'eternal': we can find no ground for it and so we say it is the Absolute. At the same time we have to remember that the pluralist's position is no better, nay we must acknowledge, I think, that it is not so good. He too has to assume an endless regress for the world. For him too there is something groundless and therefore absolute, but it is the totality of a Many in their inter-action regarded as the ultimate reality. Of this plurality in unity he can give no account beyond saying that it is just this, and that it is there. As I have already said this position cannot—so far as I see—be charged with inherent inconsistency ; but it is incomplete and un-satisfying. A plurality of beings primarily independent as regards their existence and yet always mutually acting and reacting upon each other, an ontological plurality that is yet somehow a cosmological unity, seems clearly to suggest some ground beyond itself. The idea of God presents itself to meet this lack. The Many depend upon God for their existence though still dependent on each other as regards their ex-perience. The idea of God would then be meaningless, unless God were regarded as transcending the Many ; so there can be no talk of God as merely *primus inter pares.* On the other hand it would be equally meaning-less to talk of God apart from the Many. A God that was not a Creator, a God whose creatures had no independence, would not himself be really a God. Herein theism differs from thorough-going singularism or absolutism. A theism that is reached through pluralism can never end in an Absolute in which God and the World alike were absorbed and lost : the only Absolute then that we can admit is the Absolute which God and the World constitute.

And yet the tendency of theism to pass over into singularism is notorious and we have noted it again and again. How may we account for this ? It follows partly, no doubt, from the besetting sin of speculative thinking to hypostatize abstractions—hence the so-called 'abstract monism' or acosmism, of which Spinoza furnished the type. Partly it is the result of a religious spirit of self-abasement, self-abnegation, as in certain forms of Indian and Christian mysticism. But in large measure it is due to the difficulties in the idea of creation itself. We say God and the World constitute the Absolute ; but if God is the absolute ground of the World is not God alone after all the real Absolute ? In this question there lurks perhaps the error of concreting abstractions just now mentioned. If there were no world, God would cease to be the ground of it. He would still be the potential ground, it will be replied perhaps. But if he were only this, do we not require some further condition—some restraint to be withdrawn or some external impulse to supervene before the world can become actual[1]? Or, if not that, are we not then driven to conceive God as not actually being all that it is his nature to be—if such an expression is allowable ? But no, the

---

[1] "'Tis an established maxim...that an object which exists for any time in its full perfection without producing another, is not its sole cause ; but is assisted by some other principle, which pushed it from its state of inactivity." Hume, *Treatise of Human Nature*, Green and Grose's edn, vol. I. p. 378.

creation implies limitation or at least self limitation

objector may persist, if God is the absolute ground of
the world—even granting that his creation has no
time limits, still—the world cannot possibly, without
ceasing to be created, share with him the title of
Absolute. The more clearly we realise the entire
and complete dependence that creation implies the
more flagrantly absurd will such a claim appear. Even
the potter may find the clay not ideally plastic; indeed
the artistic creator at his best meets with some limitation in his material. For God there can be none,
which is all that is meant by the phrase 'creation out
of nothing.'

To this we may reply :—No theist can pretend that
the world is coordinate with God : the divine transcendence is essential to the whole theistic position.
No theist again assumes that creation involves external limitation. But the point is that if creation is
to have any meaning it implies internal limitation. It
is from the reality of the world that we start : if this is
denied, the divine transcendence becomes meaningless,
nay, God, as the ideal of the pure reason, sinks to a
mere illusion within an illusion. On the other hand, if
the reality of the world be admitted, then this reality
stands over against the reality of God. God indeed
has not been limited from without but he has limited
himself.

But now new difficulties emerge. Self-limitation
seems to imply a prior state in which it was absent,
whereas a limitation held to be permanent—as we hold
creation to be—suggests some ultimate dualism rather
than an ultimate unity. Such an objection is in keeping
with our ordinary experience confined as that is to

temporal processes, but it is not applicable to the notion of an absolute ground ; as a trivial example may suffice to show. The sides of a triangle are independent of its angles only if regarded merely as lines, and yet they are the ground of the angles ; also in forming these they limit themselves in so far as they thereby determine their several ratios. We do not say that God comes into being with the world, but only that as ground of the world he limits himself : duality in unity is implied here as in all experience, but not dualism.

But how, it may be asked, can self-limitation be involved in creation, if creation is pure activity and original intuition, if God is all life and all light ? How can God be omnipotent, as theism ordinarily assumes, and yet be limited ? Well, in the first place, we might reply, an omnipotent being that could not limit itself would hardly deserve the name of God; would, in fact, be only a directionless energy of unlimited amount. At the same time the Mosaic notion that God must needs rest from his labour and even Tertullian's bold assertion that his glory was the greater on this account, nobody nowadays, I suppose, would seriously defend. It is not any limitation of this sort that we have primarily in view. *All* determination is negation, that is limitation, we must say with Spinoza. But if God were what Hegel described Nature as being, *ein bacchantischer Gott, der sich selbst nicht zügelt und fasst*, then indeed we might regard him as an Absolute notwithstanding possible creational vagaries, but he would be the absolutely Indeterminate. But God according to the theistic idea does not repudiate but owns and respects his world, a world that is cosmic, not chaotic, from the first, and through which we may believe that one increasing purpose runs   Even men abide by their pledges, cherish their offspring, show steadfastness and consistency in their purposes, and in manifold other ways limit and determine themselves by their own deeds.   By their deeds, yes ; but not by their dreams.   We surely then cannot suppose that God is less earnest, less steadfast than his creatures : rather we regard him as without variableness or shadow of a turning.   Again, to argue that unless the world is merely a divine phantasy, God is determined by its existence, does less than justice to the pluralist's position : it is from the reality of the world that we start.   Apart from this, I must again insist, we have no basis for our ideal of God at all.

  There still remains of course the difficulty, which from the outset we have allowed to be insuperable : *how* God creates the world and thereby limits himself we can never understand[1].   The idea of creation, like the idea of God, we admit is altogether transcendent. But—paradoxical though it may seem—this admission in a sense explains and removes our difficulty.   Even if the idea of creation be valid, we must necessarily fail to understand the process, just because that *cannot* fall within our experience ; on the other hand any process that we could understand could not be the creative process, because it *would* fall within our experience.   This may sound very like a final surrender ; for what, it may be urged, is the use of a hypothesis that can never be directly verified ?   Nevertheless this objection rests on

[1] See Supplementary Note II.

a complete misapprehension as to the function of philosophy. A scientific hypothesis is directly verifiable;
because the facts which it is framed to unify, simplify,
or explain, do fall within experience, which is sure
therefore sooner or later to furnish a crucial test of its
validity. But philosophy is not science—though it is
bound to be systematic and methodical—for it deals
not with parts or aspects of experience in isolation but
with experience as a concrete whole. To this whole
it must appeal to justify its 'ideas'; and they are
justified in proportion as they enable us to conceive
this whole as a complete and systematic unity. The
radical pluralist halts at the Many and their interaction:
he declines to go further because he finds no direct
warrant for so doing. But if the idea of creation will
carry us further, and if nothing else will, then that
idea, it is maintained, is rationally justified though it
be not empirically verified.

LECTURE XII.

THE COSMOLOGY OF THEISM.

The idea of creation, we have allowed, must in any case lead to modifications of the pluralistic *Weltanschauung*. But it is questionable if these modifications need to be as radical as most theists assume. To these differences and their possible reconciliation we have now to turn.

Pluralism and theism are—nowadays at all events—both monistic : for neither, is the distinction between person and thing, matter and mind, an ultimate distinction. For both alike, material phenomena are only the manifestation of minds, of so-called ' things *per se.*' These however are not literally things at all, but beings that are beings for themselves, i.e.—in the widest sense of the term—persons, who are conative and cognitive in varying degrees. But whereas pluralism regards all material phenomena as due to the direct interaction of such persons or monads, reduces the entire course of the world, in short, without reservation, to such interaction ; theism usually attributes material phenomena to the direct and orderly intervention of God, who in this way provides a medium and instrumentality for the mutual intercourse and understanding of his creatures. Of the former position we have taken the Leibnizian monadology as the type, discarding however the doctrine of 'pre-established harmony,' as Wolf and others did, who attempted to systematise Leibniz's philosophy. Of the latter position we have typical instances in the occasionalism of Berkeley or of Lotze in his later views; they agree in referring matter or the so-called mechanism of nature to the immanent activity of God himself. Such theism then, it will be readily seen, assumes two apparently quite distinct forms of divine activity: first, the creative and sustaining activity, whereby the finite Many exist, and secondly the continuous mediation whereby they are brought into living relation with each other. In proceeding then to examine what we might call the Cosmology of theism, the general theory of occasionalism comes up for consideration first of all.

This theory, originated to bridge over the gulf that the Cartesian dualism had made between mind and matter, contributed in the end to that denial of the independent reality of matter altogether, which is common to all forms of spiritualistic monism or idealism and was in fact implicit in the teaching of Descartes himself. At first all that was asserted was, that since the utter disparateness of matter and mind rendered any direct influence of one on the other impossible, their seeming interaction must be due solely to the 'assistance' or intervention of the Creator of both. It was however still assumed that bodies causally and immediately affected each other. But as the consequences of the entire inertness assigned to matter came to be realised, and our own voluntary activity came to be regarded as the prime source of our sense of power, the theory of occasionalism underwent a corresponding change. The idea of God as mediating between mind and matter gave place to the simpler idea of God as mediating between finite minds, the so-called material world being regarded no longer as the means by which this mediation was effected, but rather as the actual fact of this mediation itself. This is the form of occasionalism that was maintained by Berkeley and Lotze. This also we find already in germ within Descartes' own system[1]; and it was so far developed by the Cartesian Malebranche that a disciple of his, Arthur Collier, is said by his biographer to have anticipated the Berkeleian position by several years[2].

At the outset too, as its name suggests, occasionalism implied the continuous interposition of the Deity in each and all of the innumerable cases of apparent interaction ceaselessly occurring throughout the entire universe. Against such a view Leibniz brought the charge of perpetual miracle, of irrational recourse to a *Deus ex machina*; and the objection is commonly regarded as fatal. Well, no doubt intervention in the affairs of a multitude of distinct and unique beings does for us imply a corresponding multiplicity of separate acts; and the thought of such a multiplex— so to say discursive—intervention is to us utterly bewildering. But for God, who is to be conceived as omniscient, the case is altogether different. For God, as its common Creator, the world is one whole: however much differentiated, it never for him loses its meaning and therefore never lacks its intuited unity.

---

[1] Cf. e.g. his sixth Meditation.
[2] Cf. Fraser's edition of *Berkeley's Works*, 1st edn, vol. I. p. 252.

For God there is no exclusive standpoint and therefore no need to hurry hither and thither, attending now to this, now to that. Further, since continuity is the common characteristic of the growth and development of all his creatures alike[1], his compensatory adjustments, the supposed means of their interaction, will also be continuous and orderly. They may exhibit the regularity of increasing purpose rather than the rigidity of fixed mechanism, but at least they will be compatible with the idea of Law, of orderly control.

But to talk of a *Deus ex machina* in such a case is to assume that there is some independent system to get tangled up into knots, to forget that Nature for the theist just is this continuous mediation of the Divine and not a mechanism independent of it. Again to call this a perpetual miracle, if that means more than a subject for perpetual wonder and admiration, is equally absurd. The fact is that Leibniz's own theory of pre-established harmony does not differ so much from occasionalism as is often supposed. Bayle pointed this out long ago and the resemblance has often been

---

[1] Thus it cannot be objected that a man might, for example, will to fly, and that therefore there could be no orderliness in the world if God simply gave effect to whatever might be willed. In truth, however, a man cannot will to fly, and the mere *wish* to fly entails no change of attitude, no actual conation. Still he might possibly try to fly; but then his first attempt would start from his *status quo*. But what can a finite being will to do, more generally what is such a being always striving for? For self-conservation and self-betterment, we say; but this again carries us back to the *status quo*. There will then be a certain continuity in the actions of each and all such beings, and so there will also be a corresponding continuity in that mediating activity of God which we ordinarily summarise as the uniformity of Nature. *Natura non facit saltus.*

noticed since. If we figure to ourselves two badly-made clocks ('*horloges méchantes*'), and imagine the clockmaker continually interfering to correct their faulty adjustment—and this is Leibniz's caricature of occasionalism—then indeed the objection to miraculous meddling would be in place. But the whole point is that there are not two clocks. To call Nature—the only clock there is, if there is a clock at all—a perpetual miracle is to ignore the fact that a permanent miracle is a contradiction in terms. For theism, when it is thought out, there is however not even one clock : to attribute to God the need or even the use of organs or instruments is but childish anthropomorphism[1]. "Il n'y a point d'autre nature, je veux dire d'autres lois naturelles, que les volontés efficaces du tout-puissant," said Malebranche.

Nevertheless the term occasionalism will always tend to suggest the part played by a broker, middleman or 'go-between' in human affairs ; and this, it will be felt, is no worthy *rôle* to assign to the divine being. And yet such an objection is due simply to misunderstanding. It would be just as reasonable to maintain that to create finite beings at all is unworthy of the Infinite. So long as creation implies mediation—and this is the usual theistic position—the two activities, however distinct, are in fact inseparable, the one being consequential on the other, and both together resulting in one complete cosmos. We find the life and intercourse of finite beings to depend on two things, first on their organisms, and secondly on their environments : these together make up the one whole we commonly

[1] Cf. *Naturalism and Agnosticism*, 3rd edn, II. pp. 274 f. ; 4th edn, pp. 564 f.

speak of as the physical or material world. And so in virtue of the continuity between any given organism and its environment—i.e. eventually, the whole so-called 'material' world—we may regard this as itself the organism common to all living things alike, the universal matrix within which their several individual organisms are differentiated but not separated. Again, as the several individual organisms, as the very term itself implies, constitute the instrumentality of the sentient agents or persons to whom they belong ; so we may say that the entire material world is in like manner the common possession or medium of life and intercourse for them, the only truly active beings. According to the cosmology of theism, in short, the physical world is simply a system of means provided for the sake of the realm of ends : it is only to be understood as subservient to them, and apart from them is alike meaningless and worthless.

But though the existence of the material world is not dependent on us but is rather on this view the medium on which we ourselves depend, though it is indispensable as a system of means for us, we cannot from this conclude that it is in the same sense indispensable for God. We are not, in other words, justified in assuming that the realm of ends is created conformably to a prior system of means, life being primarily adjusted to matter, not matter to life. The creations of finite minds are, it is true, subject to material trammels, the exigencies of rhyme and metre, the small range of luminosity in pigments, the intractable nature of marble or bronze, and so forth. But we cannot suppose either that the divine creation is necessarily beset by limits of this kind or that God has arbitrarily limited the world of living forms by a pre-ordained world of lifeless stuff. The creative activity is then, the theist holds, only the condition of, not at all conditioned by, the mediating activity; and the unity and purpose of the former as a realm of ends involves and determines the law and order of the latter as a system of means.

But do we need thus to distinguish between ends and means, between creative activity and mediating activity? Does the idea of creation necessarily imply what we may call a unified and systematic occasionalism? If the interpretation of interaction towards which pluralism seems to tend is possible and sufficient, we certainly may answer this question in the negative. There may, in fact, be such a divine system or economy embracing and encircling the living agents of the world, furnishing, as it were, the properties and the scenery in which these *dramatis personae* of history enact their parts. Such subsidiary aids, I say, may exist, but according to the pluralist view they are not necessary. But can the pluralist position be thought out? Why can it not, it may be replied, if it requires nothing more than the sort of mutual understanding or *rapport* which we daily observe in the personal intercourse of our fellow-men? "As in water face answereth to face so the heart of man to man." Of course such mutual understanding is approximately complete only between persons similarly situated and similar in their interests and pursuits, who can thus become—as we aptly say—intimate with each other. It tails off rapidly in our intercourse with strangers, and tends to dwindle away altogether as we pass to creatures further and further removed from us in the scale of being. You may train a dog to fetch and carry, but it is useless to tell a fly not to settle on your nose : like Milton's mariner disembarking on the leviathan's back, he takes you to be *terra firma*. Yet the flies understand each other and glide about in airy mazes without colliding.

But it will be said, both flies and men have organisms, and without these their mutual adjustments of behaviour would be altogether inexplicable, and it is just this interaction by means of physical organization that is the problem[1]. This is true and the pluralist is fully aware of it. It was Leibniz himself, the founder of modern pluralism, who said that "a disembodied soul would be a deserter from the general order, which implies matter and movement and their laws[2]." But the question is: What is matter? More exactly stated: What is the simplest concept of matter to which we are led, setting out from the realm of ends as the reason of its existence? We note then, first, that for Leibniz, as for his modern successors, any given organism itself consists of organisms, which for it are organs, having special functions and working consentiently together as members of this one whole. This however implies an indefinite—Leibniz even said, an infinite—regress. But for the modern pluralist all it means, I take it, is that we cannot assume any given organism that seems simple, to be so really. Yet, none the less, since the complex involves the simple, bare—or as Leibniz called them, naked—monads may well exist. And now

---

[1] See Supplementary Note III.
[2] Cf. *Philosophische Schriften*, Gerhardt's edn, vol. VI. p. 546.

how are we to conceive such a bare monad? It cannot
be a dominant monad, for this would imply subordinate
monads : it cannot therefore have a body distinct from
itself. In some sense then, it would seem, it must
be its own body or disappear altogether from the
universal connexion of things. But we must not
understand this to mean that apparently all mental
characteristics are gone and only material characteristics
are left. The true solution seems rather to be that we
have reached the limit of both. The physical concept
of such a limit is the dynamical concept of a mass-point ?
as a centre of force. The corresponding psychological
concept answers to what Leibniz happily described as
mens momentanea seu carens *recordatione*[1].

Some elucidation of both these concepts is requisite
before we can attempt to formulate the conclusion to
which this regress points. Leibniz spoke of monads
generally as "the *real* atoms of nature, and in a word,
the elements of things." Such language, which seems
specially appropriate to his naked monads, should be
sufficient to put us on our guard against identifying
them with the mass-points of the modern physicist—
which Leibniz held to be only phenomenal. They
are more analogous to Boscovich's centres of force[2]:

[1] *Theoriae motus abstracti Definitiones*, Gerhardt's edition of his
philosophical works, vol. IV. p. 230.

[2] It is worthy of remark, that notwithstanding this analogy, to
which Boscovich himself refers, he was so far from identifying
monads and centres of force as to maintain that the 'seat of the
soul' is more or less extended. Cf. his *Philosophiae naturalis Theoria*,
Venice, 1763, Appendix, *De Anima et Deo*, §§ 536 ff. It is also
worthy of passing notice that it was through Boscovich that Priestley
was led to his so-called materialism.

although they differ from these in being all qualitatively distinct, or unique, like Herbart's reals, not all qualitatively the same, as Boscovich's elements were[1]. But they resemble these in another respect and that a very important one. Boscovich conceived his simple atoms as acting at a distance, which—paradoxical though it sounds—really means interacting directly without any intervening medium, doing, in fact, what according to the Newtonian mechanics is inconceivable. This immediacy of interaction is held to characterize the bare monad of the modern pluralist, the monad that is, so to say, its own body. Such interaction implies what Lotze called a sympathetic *rapport*.

This brings us to the psychical nature of the bare monad, and here again immediacy is the thing we have specially to note. This immediacy answers to what psychologists now call pure sensation, an ideal limit to which *our* simplest experiences never descend: our sensations correspond rather to complexes or syntheses of the elemental sensations or '*petites perceptions*' of Leibniz. Moreover, for *us* it is true that all cognition is recognition, implies assimilation, and therefore memory in the widest sense, i.e. the retention of what has been either inherited or acquired. Pure sensation or cognition is the 'momentary consciousness' of some *datum*, the perception or recognition of which, on the other hand, would presuppose previous experiences that still in some sense endure. Clear evidence of such a 'psychical' or enduring present is only found in connexion with comparatively complex organisms, and

---

[1] Cf. *op. cit.* § 3, quoted also by Fechner, *Atomenlehre*, 2nd edn, p. 240.

this range in time is found also to increase as the biological differentiation of the organism increases. When then, on the contrary, we imagine this complexity decreased without limit, we reach the concept of the bare monad whose organism, so to say, reduces to a point, and its present to a moment ; which can only react immediately and to what is immediately given. In other words such monads deal directly with their common environment and, so long as they gain nothing by experience, so long, that is, as they remain bare monads, they severally deal with it always in the same way. The existence of an indefinite number of such monads would provide all the ' uniform medium ' for the intercourse of higher monads that these can require, without any need for such divine intervention as occasionalism assumes.

The precise details of this psychical intercourse the pampsychist is unable to specify. But it is questionable whether—notwithstanding this—the occasionalist with his apparent psychophysical interaction is not in a worse position ; for he only dispenses with the need for any specification by assuming what we may call a 'dualism' in the divine activity, and that to many minds will always appear too cumbrous and, so to say, unscientific, to be intellectually satisfactory. And after all the main outline of the pampsychic alternative can be clearly stated. The relation of a dominant monad (*A*) to any monad of its organism (or of its brain, when its organism is so far differentiated,) is different in kind from the relation to the same monad of the dominant monad (*B*) of another organism. The one relation we may call an internal, functional, or vital, the other an

external, foreign, or physical, relation. The totality of
these internal relations at a given time answers to *A*'s
objective experience at that moment. Certain changes
in this whole are, so far as *A* is concerned, initiated
by certain of the subordinate monads : these changes
answer to *A*'s sensations, and as to these it is receptive
or passive. Certain other changes, on the other hand,
are due to *A*'s active initiative : these entail sensations
in certain subordinate monads, and their response is
what we call *A*'s movement[1].

But the monads of *A*'s organism are not, we have
said, related solely to it and to each other. If that were the
case, the organism would fail altogether of its purpose
and meaning: its existence at all would be inexplicable,
unless it were—what it certainly is not—an absolute whole
and self-maintaining. In fact, however, these subordinate monads are related also to the environment,
which we have called the common matrix of all monads.
This in the last resort is conceived as consisting of
bare monads, which have only external relations to
one another, or rather for which, as the limit of our
regress, the distinction of internal and external ceases
to hold. What is true of *A*'s organism is true also of
B's. So we can understand how *A*'s acts may give
rise to sensations in *B* through this double mediation
of organism and environment and how *B*'s acts in
turn may give rise to sensations in *A*. Presently as
like sensations (or recepts) recur they become gradually
more and more assimilated with previous experiences
of them and the advance to definite percepts is made.

[1] See Supplementary Note III.

What, then, were originally only immediate sensory data
have now a meaning[1]; *A* and *B*, that is to say, are *en
rapport*. *Pari passu* with advancing experience we find
also increasing complexity of organization : functions
that were originally discharged by the dominant monad
then devolve upon its subordinate organisms or organs.
And thus habitual or secondarily automatic processes,
which for the dominant monad lapse into subconscious-
ness, arise and extend.   The process of mediation, then,
once begun, tends continually to increase ; and so, as
the range of an individual's experience extends, he
knows more and more of the external world, and yet is
ever further removed from that immediate relation with
it which psychologists call pure sensation.

Both the pampsychist and the occasionalist alike
agree, as we have seen, in holding all real existence to
consist in experients and their experience ; they agree
too, we may assume, in accepting the current psychological analysis of experience into presentation, feeling
and action.   But in interpreting presentations as subjective modifications, assumed to be due directly to the
divine activity, occasionalism becomes hampered with
all the epistemological difficulties of what is known as
subjective idealism, difficulties which made the existence of the external world such a hopeless problem for
modern philosophers till Reid began to clear the way
by his criticism of the Cartesian 'theory of ideas.'

---

[1] Thanks to the 'creative synthesis' which the processes of
recognition and perception imply. (Cf. Lect. v. pp. 104 f.) But
in so far as they affect their subject even bare sensations always have
a meaning, i.e. a value as pleasurable or painful. This is 'meaning'
in a most vital sense.

Leibniz's famous paradox that, although they mirror the universe, the monads have no windows, is but another way of stating this theory. Modern pluralists on the other hand maintain that all monads have windows—more literally stated, that presentation is a relation among monads not a subjective state in a single monad. And this 'natural realism,' as Hamilton called it[1], is certainly the simpler hypothesis—if that can be called a hypothesis which claims to be the bare statement of the facts. So much simpler that—we may say with some confidence—occasionalism would never have been heard of but for the Cartesian dualism of matter and mind and the Cartesian theory of ideas as subjective states. That God should have created the monads without windows and taken on himself the function of supplying their place—whether continuously, as the occasionalists assumed, or once for all, as Leibniz held—seems then a needless complication.

Nevertheless, since we cannot actually verify the indefinite regress which the existence of bare monads implies, and since we cannot show that the indirect mediation of our finite intercourse is not a fact, we have no means of deciding empirically between the two alternatives. The most we can say is that the pluralist alternative is the *prior* as well as the simpler, and it seems adequate. To the objection that it reduces theism to the level of mere deism and leaves the world once started to go of itself, it is sufficient to reply that this supposed tenet of deism is really inconceivable. As we have already seen, the idea of creation by simple

---

[1] Albeit in his own version of it he halts and trims in very half-hearted fashion.

' fiat ' at a definite epoch will not work ; but deism on any other view is reduced to atheism.   If there is a Creator at all he can never stand aside and wholly apart from his world.   As Lotze has well said, such a proceeding " is intelligible in a human artificer who leaves his work when it is finished and trusts for its maintenance to universal laws of Nature, laws which he did not himself make, and which not he, but another for him, maintains in operation "; but " the picture of God withdrawing from the world," the sole ground of which is himself, is incomprehensible[1].

But, it may be urged further, the sense-symbolism of Berkeley serves not only as a medium of intercourse for God's sentient creatures but it is also at the same time a revelation of God himself, is the language wherein he addresses us[2].   Granted that as an independent argument the appeal to the teleology of Nature is not decisive, still if there is a Creator, as we are now assuming, he must surely somehow manifest himself.   But may we not reply : Surely if there is a Creator, the world of his interacting creatures will itself be a clearer manifestation of him than a mere medium of intercourse, alike available for very diverse ends and alike indifferent to all?   The two seem to stand in

---

[1] But the ascription of such a tenet to deists generally—to the English deists of the 18th century, for example—is a grievous misrepresentation.   What they denied was not the divine immanence *in toto*, but only such occasionalistic interference as miracles, special revelations and special providences imply.   They were in fact what we should now call rationalistic theists.

[2] Physical catastrophes are a serious difficulty for the theist on this view.   Cf. a striking article by Professor Howison, 'Catastrophes and the Moral Order,' *Hibbert Journal*, vol. I. 1902, pp. 114-121.

much the same position as grammar to literature.
Accordingly the theists who set out by distinguishing
the realm of Nature from the realm of Ends allow that
it is the latter that reveals God the more clearly and
impressively. If so, the case for theism can hardly be
impaired should this distinction turn out to be unnecessary. But after all, it will be rejoined, your analogy
between language and literature is rather unfortunate,
since literature presupposes language. In the abstract
perhaps it does, but not in actual fact, in so far as
all utterance has some meaning. It is precisely the
absolute distinction of means and ends that is denied.
So far then we seem entitled to conclude that while
both alternatives are compatible with theism the
thorough-going pampsychism of the pluralist which
dispenses with a distinct medium of intercourse is, as
simpler, so far preferable to occasionalism for which a
mediating activity is essential.

But as yet we have considered mainly the structural
or, as the favourite phrase used to be, the statical
aspect of the world: let us now turn to consider more
directly its functional or dynamical aspect. Here
again the pampsychical or Leibnizian seems preferable
to the occasionalistic alternative. We must in any
case admit that what we commonly call inorganic or
physical processes precede and underlie those which
all alike recognise as the processes in which life and
mind are undoubtedly manifest. We must, that is to
say, acknowledge that Nature is *die Vorstufe des
Geistes*, the prelude to Mind, in so far as so-called
physical processes invariably introduce those that are
distinctly psychical. If so, then, when life and mind

appear, have we not a break in the course of evolution
—have we not that *generatio æquivoca* of something
wholly new, to which the most infelicitous name imaginable is often given, viz. 'the spontaneous generation'
of the living by the lifeless? But this naturalistic
assumption is rejected by the theists who accept the
occasionalistic distinction between nature and spirit.
" I should certainly never," says Lotze, " set any one
the task out of ten elements to make an eleventh arise
equally real with them "—a curious understatement, by
the way, of the enormous assumption involved in the
naturalistic theory of life. " It is not from them "—
the inorganic elements, Lotze continues, "that...the
substance of the soul would spring ; nor would it arise
above them or between them, or by the side of them,
out of nothing. It would be a new creature, produced
by the one encompassing Being from its own nature as
*the supplement of its physical activity there and then
operating*[1]." In thus speaking of the Absolute as
"giving to every organism its fitting soul" Lotze
seems to invert our ordinary notions of the relation of
the two in the very way to which we had just now to
object[2]. We do not talk of fitting inhabitants to their
houses but of fitting houses to their inhabitants. Lotze's
language reminds one of Herbert Spencer's view that
when the organism becomes too complex to work
automatically consciousness comes to its rescue. Yet
Lotze was perfectly clear as to the relative importance
of the two, as the following sentence may suffice to
show : " Nor again is it out of nothing that the soul
is created...; but to satisfy the phantasy we may say,

[1] *Metaphysic,* § 251 *fin.* Italics mine.   [2] Cf. above, p. 252.

it is from itself, from its own real nature, that the Absolute sets free (*entlässt*) the soul, and so adds to its one activity, the course of nature, that other which, according to the prescriptive meaning of the Absolute, is its completion[1]."

Now for the downright dualist, who ascribes reality to matter and to mind alike, this priority of the course of nature to the evolution of life and mind, which it somehow helps to bring about, is conceivable at the outset at any rate; and it is moreover what facts themselves in the first instance suggest. That such dualism turns out to be eventually an unworkable hypothesis is in the meantime nothing to the point. But for the monist—who is aware of the *impasse* to which dualism leads and who is therefore prepared to recognise in the so-called course of nature, as distinct from the realm of ends, " only a system of occasions or means for producing presentations in spiritual beings[2]"—for the monist, I say, to suppose nevertheless that this system is maintained by the divine activity, when as yet there are no spiritual subjects to benefit by it; nay, to suppose further that this system is actually itself not so much a means adapted to them but rather a means to which they are adapted—surely this is a ὕστερον πρότερον not easy to match. It seems to imply a need for instrumentality, which—as I have already said—contradicts the whole notion of a Creator. May we not then conclude that when in Hegelian fashion people talk of *die Natur als Vorstufe des Geistes*, what is meant is not that there is a breach of evolutional continuity but simply that the level of *self*-conscious

---

[1] *Op. cit.* § 246 *fin.*   [2] Lotze, *op. cit.* § 97.

existence, of Spirit in the narrower sense, is reached
continuously by development through earlier stages
of more or less conscious life ?

The question then which we have next to raise
concerns what in an earlier lecture was called the
lower limit of pluralism : in other words : What do we
ultimately reach when we try to trace the process of
evolution backwards ? And our chief concern will
now be to ascertain, if we can, the theistic interpretation
of this initial situation or ideal limit, to which we
attempt to regress. Herbert Spencer, it will be remembered, maintained that what we should ultimately
reach would be a state of homogeneity and that from
such a state, in consequence of its essential instability,
all the heterogeneity that we now find has been
gradually evolved. And, on the supposition that
evolution will explain everything, he reasoned correctly
enough ; for, since what we now observe is continually
increasing heterogeneity, this seems fairly to suggest
an original state in which there was no heterogeneity
at all. Leibniz and the modern pluralists on the other
hand, as we know, while admitting homogeneity in so
far as no two monads are altogether different, yet contend for the presence of heterogeneity throughout : no
two monads or ' reals,' according to them, are or ever
were altogether alike. If now we try to imagine all
these in their initial condition we seem to reach a world
of bare monads, since all the processes of organization
fall within the scope of evolution, not of origin. But
bare monads, we have seen, are described as having
only a momentary consciousness without memory and
as so far incapable of acquiring *by* experience : how then

from such an initial condition can the evolution of experience ever begin ?   Can the bare monad acquire experience ?

The pluralist, like Herbert Spencer, starts with a certain initial instability.   But he gives a better account of it : describing it not in terms of matter but in terms of mind.   Even his bare monads are conative, that is are feeling and striving subjects or persons in the widest sense, not inert particles or things.   Even so it would be conceivable, of course, that every one existed in a certain neutral state that called for no efforts of self-conservation ; and then, unless we could credit some at least with impulses towards self-betterment, nothing would happen.   Anyhow, as a matter of fact, some things have happened.   In the course of these changes, it is assumed that certain monads come into relations that, as mutually helpful, they tend to maintain.   At the same time to this comparative intimacy within a group there corresponds a comparative differentiation—for each member of it—between such group and the world of monads at large ; and with this differentiation within the present there arises *pari passu* an increase in the range of what is known as the 'specious present.' So change is experienced, and plasticity tends to become memory.   It is needless to reproduce in further detail the pluralistic *Weltan-schauung*, already described in earlier lectures.   What now interests us is the interpretation or modification that theism has to impose.

But first it will be well to recall what theism as such in any case implies, viz. that the initial state, from which pluralism seeks to start as a fact, finds in God its ground and reason. The bare existence of reality in the plural, it may be argued, seems no more to demand a ground than its bare existence in the singular. But when the Many, regarded as existentially independent of each other, are found to be mutually complementary, conspiring, as it were, to realise an intelligible organic whole, then the presence from the first of an underlying unity suggests itself. Why should the Many tend towards one end unless they had in the One their source? Otherwise, the further we attempt to regress must we not allow that the more inconceivable a supreme end becomes[1]? Those who decline to accept theism may either leave such questions unanswered, maintaining that for the world's evolution as ultimate there can be no sufficient reason other than the fact itself; or they may fall back on an Absolute in which the distinction of God and world disappears. The former of these alternatives ignores two things: that we as rational beings are part of the world's evolution, and that the demand for a sufficient reason is thus a demand that the world itself has raised. The latter reduces the world to an inexplicable appearance which, somehow seeming to be there, it can only explain away.

There is indeed another possible course, viz. to deny that things show any tendency towards the realisation of an organic whole or that the world is a single realm of ends at all. Chance, it may be said, would suffice to account for all the mutual compatibility that we find : in a manifold of indefinite extent we might expect indefinitely many coincidences. In such a supposition there is a covert appeal to the unknown

[1] Cf. Lect. IX. p. 197.

that is specially out of place in such ultra-radical empiricism.   In the world that we know there is, as the pluralist himself assumes, that amount of unity which every plurality in order to be known necessarily involves.   This world, moreover, in the course of its development has already advanced some way towards what we have called a higher unity, and at the stage of self-conscious reason has adopted this unity as its ideal goal.   For these facts the theistic hypothesis furnishes an adequate explanation and so far no other or better is known or even wanted.   We may then resume our inquiry : how does theism interpret that lower limit, towards which the pluralist attempts to trace all evolution back ?

There can be no doubt, I think, that the hypothesis of evolution was foreign at any rate to modern theories of creation.   Thus we find even the deist Voltaire preferred to account for the fossil shells found on mountain slopes by supposing passing pilgrims to have dropped them, rather than admit the theories of the new science of geology.   " Nothing of all that vegetates, nothing of all that is animated," he wrote, " has changed : all species have remained invariably the same : it would indeed be strange that the grain of millet should have conserved its nature eternally and that the nature of the entire globe should have varied[1]." But nowadays theism professes to accept the evolution hypothesis.   To accept it, but in what sense ?   Only I fear in the literal and original sense of merely unfolding what is there all along, not in the scientific sense of epigenesis or creative synthesis, described in an earlier

---

[1] *Les Principes de la Philosophie,* vol. III. § 45.

lecture.   If so, all the difference there would be between
creation without evolution and creation with it would
be in the method not in the result ; it would be such
a difference as, to take a simple example, there is
between starting with a binomial, say $(a+b)^2$, and
starting with its expansion $a^2 + 2ab + b^2$.   Creation in
either case must be through and through determinate
and complete, embracing both all that is and all that
happens ; only in one case its content would at first be
explicit, in the other only implicit.   Thus we have
found Hegel saying : " The history of the world is the
exhibition (*Darstellung*) how spirit comes to the consciousness of what in itself it means ; and as the seed
carries in itself the whole nature of the tree,...so too
the first traces of spirit virtually contain the whole of
history[1]."   This is the literal evolution in which everything is predetermined if not foreordained, a drama of
which the book of final judgment constitutes the play
and the history of the world just its representation
(*Darstellung*), as the astronomer-poet of Persia had
said centuries before Hegel was born.   Up to this
point the reconciliation of pluralism and theism seemed
possible, but here the disagreement threatens to be
radical : an evolution that is essentially dialectical
demands more than pluralism, resting on the *prima
facie* evidence of experience, can accept ; while evolution
as epigenesis seems even more clearly to conflict with
the ideas of theism generally current.   We come in
fact upon the old problem of ' fixed fate, free-will, foreknowledge absolute ' : intractable as it has proved we
must needs try to discuss this problem with open minds.

[1] Cf. above, Lect. v. p. 100.

LECTURE XIII.

FREEDOM.

In our endeavour to reconcile or combine pluralism and theism we have reached a point at which they seem hopelessly to diverge, viz., in the interpretation of evolution. For theism, as ordinarily understood, evolution is literally the mere unfolding or expansion of what is implicitly present from the first: in creating the world God is held to know and ordain all that from our temporal standpoint is yet to be. The theist is not content with saying that not a sparrow now falls to the ground without God knowing it, but he insists that the very hairs of our heads were eternally numbered by divine ordination. Creation in reality is once for all and for ever complete : it is not only a *totum simul* but it is a *totum sempiterne* : a *nunc stans* in which all the past and all the future alike eternally exist. For us who move through it there is change ; but for God, who is omnipresent in what we call time as well as in what we call space, and who therefore does not move and is not moved, for him there is no change.

To the pluralist on the other hand, as we have seen, the so-called evolution of the world is really epigenesis, creative synthesis ; it implies continual new beginnings, the result of the mutual conflict and cooperation of agents, all of whom, though in varying degrees, act spontaneously or freely.   For the pluralist, in short, these agents are themselves creative ; and if they were not they could never come to entertain the idea that they are creatures too.   God may have made man in his own image, but it is from the image that men reason back to God as their maker.   But the notion of making, the potter notion, is anything but apposite, and the pluralist will have none of it.   God's creatures are not manufactured articles, and if we must have a figure to represent what utterly transcends us, that of generating the living is far apter than that of kneading clay.   Singularist philosophers are fond of speaking of the world as the differentiation of the Absolute.   But if this Absolute be verily spirit, then its differentiation into conscious automata, now pleased, now pained, by their pre-established movements, must strike us, however wonderful, as still but a very poor performance.   If this Absolute be not spirit, then it may possibly correspond to the union of spirits, but in that case to call spirits its differentiations would be almost meaningless.   "*Unless creators are created,*" says one impassioned pluralist, "nothing is really created[1]."   The pluralist then may allow that God is the sole ground of there being a world to evolve, but he cannot admit that God, as many theists maintain, determined 'before the foundation of the world' everything that shall ever be done in it : for then nothing would verily be *done* in it at all.   But it was not till deeds were done that men talked of fate ; then, falsely projecting the fixity of the past into the future and

[1] Howison, *The Conception of God*, 1902, p. 97.

thence reflecting it back again, they denied the very source of the idea of fate itself by denying real freedom or personal initiative altogether.

But quite apart from the difficulty of reconciling finite freedom with divine foreknowledge, the reality of true self-determination is questioned on more empirical grounds. It is obvious then that this question concerning the so-called 'freedom of the will' must engage our attention first of all. This phrase, freedom of the will, however, is a very misleading one : Locke long ago protested against it, and we shall do well, as far as possible, to avoid it ; though it is so firmly established in common thought that its complete elimination from controversy is hardly practicable. And yet it will not be denied that whenever we talk of freedom or liberty, we always—unless these words are metaphorically used—refer to a person or persons. Again it will not be denied that by will we mean not a person but a faculty or power that is attributed to a person. Finally it will not be denied that this concept of a power or faculty called will—like all such concepts— is but a generalisation based on actual instances of volitions or acts of willing. There is thus no will that wills but only a person or subject that wills. To quote Locke : "We may as properly say that it is the singing faculty sings, and the dancing faculty dances, as that the will chooses[1]." The real question then is what is meant when it is asserted or denied that in willing a man is free ?

Again this question is not clearly stated when described, as it often is, as concerned with the alternative

---

[1] *Essay concerning Human Understanding*, vol. II. ch. xxi. p. 17.

issues, determinism or indeterminism; when the question, that is to say, is supposed to be, whether a volition has a cause or ground or has not. The determinist, confident that for every event there is a cause, assumes that he must therefore deny that the person in willing is free. The indeterminist, confident that this freedom is a fact, supposes that he must therefore deny that a volition has a cause[1]. It is possible that each may be right in what he affirms, and wrong only in what he denies—possible that volitions have causes though these causes are free. That in some sense a volition is caused can only be disputed by one who is prepared to allow a positive reality to absolute chance, and to regard praise and blame as entirely meaningless and out of place; to deny in fact at once, if he is an idealist, the existence alike of order and morality altogether. On the other hand, that in willing the agent is in some sense free can only be disputed by one who is prepared to maintain that a like necessitation applies both to the events of the so-called physical and to those of the moral world; but that would be tantamount to denying any distinction between them. It seems plain then that there is some complexity in the subject-matter of this perennial controversy, which the bare antithesis—either determinism or indeterminism—does not resolve: in other words it seems still possible to maintain that a volition is in one sense determined and in another not determined. To ascertain and analyse this further complexity is what we must now attempt.

We may begin with the concept of cause. Its source and primary meaning we find unquestionably in

---

[1] Spinoza denied 'free will' in this sense even of God. *Ethics*, I. xxxii. n. 2.

ourselves as active or efficient. Hence we derive the phrase ' efficient cause,' to which ' effect,' the name we give to the result of our activity, is strictly correlative ; so that, without an efficient, an effect is meaningless or impossible. To the question how an efficient or determining cause produces its effect no answer has been, or seemingly can be, given that will enable us to resolve our sense of activity into simpler elements. The title bestowed by Aristotle on this form of causation, ἀρχὴ τῆς κινήσεως, is perhaps instructive here : it is not itself a movement but what produces movement[1]. Again we find efficient causation used in two senses : we speak, that is to say, of a transeunt cause and also of an immanent cause. Thus we say a man eats his dinner and smokes his pipe ; and we say too he wakes, he breathes, he walks, and so forth. Metaphorically we also apply the concept of immanent causation to inanimate objects, as when we say that the sun shines or the tide rises. But inasmuch as whatever is inanimate is regarded also as inert and therefore incapable of changing of itself, the supposed immanent causality of mere things is resolved into transeunt causality. The sun's shining is resolved into molecular motion, the result of preceding mass motions ; and the tide is found to rise only because of the motions of the earth, the sun and the moon.

Once more, even if we can give no answer to the question how we are active, we find that an answer to

[1] In the case of physical causation, on the other hand, the so-called cause is itself a motion, consequent on a precedent motion and so on in indefinite regress ; so that the notion of efficiency also recedes indefinitely.

the question why in any special case we act at all, can usually be given. This reason for acting is what Aristotle called the final cause, and identified with the good as the end alike of all process and all motion. But science does not and, it may fairly be said, cannot take so wide a view. In dealing severally with the facts of the so-called material world, such ideas as final causes and the good are out of place : like vestal virgins, as Bacon said, they are here fruitless and so useless. Summing up then as regards the concept of cause, we may say that in the case of conative subjects it implies both immanent efficiency and purposiveness, but that in the case of inanimate things it implies neither. What it does imply in this case is still in large measure to seek.

And so we come next to the idea of necessary connexion according to law, or the uniformity of nature, as it is otherwise called, for it is this, nowadays at any rate, that is meant first of all when the term causality is scientifically used. Thus Helmholtz, for example, says "the principle of causality is in fact nothing more than the presupposition that in all natural phenomena there is conformity to law (*Gesetzlichkeit*)[1]." But now in what sense can this regularity or uniformity of nature be called also a case of necessary connexion? There is no logical necessity about a law of nature : it is neither in itself intuitively certain nor is it logically deducible from premises that are themselves intuitively certain : to doubt or deny it entails no contradiction. Granted, it may perhaps be replied, the necessity is not formal or logical, it is real or natural necessity.

---

[1] *Ueber die Erhaltung der Kraft*, Ostwald's edn, p. 53.

But what does this mean? When we speak of a fact or event as real what we primarily intend to assert is its presentation to sensory perception. Such assertorial or categorical judgments are for the percipient not less necessary and inevitable than so-called apodeictic judgments[1]. I am quite as little able to deny the fact of daylight, when at noon my eyes are open, as I am at any time to deny the truth that $2 + 2 = 4$.

The grounds of the necessitation in the two cases are different, no doubt; but that for the present does not concern us, save as it may lead us to repeat that causal necessitation is not of the apodeictic sort. The same real necessitation, so to call it, which constrains me to affirm that it rains, when I am caught in a thunder-shower, constrains me also to affirm that the thunder-clap followed the lightning-flash; for all this is perceived. What I am not constrained to affirm, for that is not perceived, is any real connexion between the two events. But though all that we perceive is the *post hoc* we no doubt frequently assert the *propter hoc* as well, and that too on the strength of a single instance. Such a venture is however purely anthropomorphic: it rests entirely on the analogy that we observe between our own behaviour and what we regard as the behaviour of some inanimate thing. The primitive and popular concept of transeunt causation is altogether anthropomorphic in this wise; as the whole structure of human speech amply shows. Thus the more completely thought is confined to the standpoint of immediate experience, the more causality implies the connexion of *efficiens* and *effectum*, or real necessity;

[1] Cf. on this point Sigwart's *Logic*, § 31.

but then the less, in the same proportion, does it imply of uniformity or law. The transition from the one standpoint to the other falls almost entirely within the period of modern thought, and in our day may be said to be at length complete. But as I have discussed this at some length elsewhere it is needless to enlarge upon it here[1].

If then neither logical necessity nor necessity in the sense of effectuation is involved in the scientific concept of causality, what necessity is there left? Only the hypothetical necessity of Helmholtz's 'presupposition.' The scientific principle of causality, in short, is a necessary postulate : scientific knowledge—in other words, knowledge expressed in general propositions concerning matters of fact—is possible only on the assumption that events actually happen with strict and uniform regularity. Now there is one theory of the world, and one only, which would justify this assumption completely, and that one is the mechanical theory. Accordingly the postulate of the uniformity of nature is frequently converted into the theorem that nature is a mechanical system ; and thus a methodological principle becomes an ontological dogma.

We can now see, as we suspected at starting, that to say an event is determined still leaves the nature of the determination an open question, and is so far ambiguous. When the wayfarer says, I am determined to go on against the wind, and the man of science says, It is determined that the dust will always go with it,

---

[1] Cf. *Naturalism and Agnosticism*, 3rd edn, I. pp. 62 ff., II. pp. 241 f.; 4th edn, pp. 58 ff., 531 f. An excellent exposition of this transition is given by Dr Venn in his *Empirical Logic*, chs. ii. and iv.

this ambiguity is at once apparent. In the first case determination implies efficient causation, self-direction and purpose : it does not imply any uniformity such that in all like circumstances a like determination always has recurred and always will. In the second case, on the other hand, this is precisely what is implied ; whereas here nothing is implied as to efficient causation ; also self-direction and purpose are either denied or treated as meaningless.

But at this point the determinist may interpose, insisting that, to say nothing of habitual actions, there is abundant evidence of uniformity in human conduct even when most deliberate. There is unquestionably ; but for all that the two forms of determination remain as different as ever : moreover the uniformities in the two cases are also altogether different. In every instance of deliberate conduct, though the agents decide alike, each is still conscious of self-determination, of purpose, and of effort in the pursuit of it, conscious of that 'action' contrary to the line of least resistance, which in the case of inanimate things is impossible. And though in like situations there is often a corresponding likeness in the agents' conduct, often there is not ; there is here then no warrant for any such generalisation as natural law implies. If we ask a man why in a new and strange situation he acts as he does, it will hardly occur to him to explain his conduct by describing to us the immediately preceding situation. The answer he is likely to give, and that we naturally expect, will consist rather in describing the end at which he aims and the value that it has for him, as the reasons for his determination. But if we ask the physicist to explain an unusual phenomenon he can do so *only* by discovering its antecedents, tracing these to their antecedents, and so on indefinitely : in other words he can explain it only on the assumption that it is determined by its place in a single rigorous mechanical system.

Prima facie then the two forms of determination are distinctly different: whether the difference is ultimate, and if it is not, which form is the more comprehensive—these are further questions. At all events the difference runs very deep. The one form, that of self-determination—implying such teleological categories as personality, utility and worth—dominates all our interpretations of the world as a realm of ends. The other form, that of determination according to fixed law, implying in the last resort only the categories of mechanism, underlies our scientific description of the so-called realm of nature or world of things. The one has been called the ethical postulate of freedom, the other the epistemological postulate of necessity[1].

But in truth self-determination extends beyond the self-conscious and rational autonomy that we find only in the ethical sphere, and is besides not simply an ideal or moral postulate. The contrast with which we have to deal then is the wider one between spontaneity or individual activity as *prima facie* a *fact* on the one side and the scientific *concept* of inert matter as a constant quantity on the other[2]. Individuality is

---

[1] So far the old distinction of Libertarianism and Necessitarianism is really clearer and therefore, *pace* J. S. Mill, also 'fairer' than that now in vogue of Indeterminism and Determinism.

[2] As already remarked (Lect. I. p. 8) the negative *concept* of inertia or inactivity presupposes the positive *fact* of activity.

inseparable from mind and altogether foreign to matter, which loses nothing by disintegration and gains nothing by integration ; whereas to divide one mind into many or to aggregate many minds into one is meaningless and impossible. But for all that, the more individual minds cooperate the higher they rise and the more they achieve severally and collectively. Hence the steady advance in the efficiency of the world of ends, which Wundt has called the dominant law of spiritual life and entitled 'the increase of spiritual energy' in contrast to the energy of the physical world that is held neither to increase nor to decrease[1].

Wherein then does the difference between them lie? Perhaps if we say that it lies in the different meaning given to direction in the two cases, the contrast we are considering will be made clearer on another side. When we regard the world as a realm of ends, direction implies guidance and control, and therewith activity ; but when we regard it as a physical whole, direction has simply its literal, spatial meaning. We describe the inertia of a moving body by saying that it cannot of itself change its direction or its velocity. And whenever by the so-called 'action' of another body either of these components of its motion is altered there will also, according to the mechanical theory, be a compensatory alteration in the components of the motion of that other body. Then generalising, and agreeably to the notion of inertia, we have the principle known as the Conservation of Momentum, a principle which perhaps expresses as clearly as any that the

[1] Wundt, 'Wachsthum der geistigen Energie,' *System der Philosophie*, 1889, p. 315.

so-called uniformity of nature completely excludes all ideas of spontaneity and guidance.

Yet that such guidance *prima facie* exists is no longer seriously disputed : every movement of every living thing is an instance of it. Nevertheless the fact of guidance is, by the very terms of the mechanical theory itself, a fact outside the range of that theory. Moreover, primarily for the sake of such guiding control, and largely by means of it, the theory itself has been elaborated. And those who know it best only claim that it tells us what will happen so far as things are left to themselves, but not that it can show how guidance is possible or when it will occur[1]. As often as it does occur then, we have an event which does not lie within the sweep of the so-called uniformity of nature regarded as a system determined throughout by mechanical necessity, determined in such wise that all its uncontrolled working admits of rigorous calculation. Every such event, so far as the system is concerned, is a new beginning to which, as inert, the system simply submits, and yet for which it, as inert, cannot possibly account. It is just the continual accumulation of such unique events and the conservation of their values that distinguishes the historical evolution of experience from the steady downward trend of the physical world conceived as independent of experience. The course of the one, its final equilibration, is theoretically calculable from the beginning ; the course of the other, the final harmony of the realm of ends, is not.

[1] Cf. an excellent article by Professor J. H. Poynting on 'Physical Law and Life,' *Hibbert Journal*, 1903, pp. 728 ff.

Much as Plato found the characteristics of justice more conspicuous in the state than in the individual, so perhaps we find that in the broad contrast between nature and history the difference we have been seeking to analyse and elucidate is more apparent than it is when we confine our attention to the individual alone. But for all that, the solution of our problem—and that of Plato's too—ultimately turns on the reality of individual existence. Efficiency and spontaneity, purpose and worth, these ontological and teleological categories are more and more ruthlessly extruded from the description of nature as a phenomenal whole the more that description succeeds in attaining to scientific precision. Yet these are the categories that in the main define what we mean by an individual or a person. The course of history we refer to self-determinations, the course of nature science regards as due to mechanical necessitations.

But are these alternatives, determination by personal agency and determination according to universal law, really mutually exclusive? We picture the course of history as continually foreclosing genuine alternatives, and the course of nature as throughout completely determined : the future in the one case cannot, we believe, but in the other certainly can—theoretically at least—be deduced from the present. But there are many who think otherwise and who include the doings of men as well as the motions of matter under the phrase 'uniformity of nature.' These we may term thorough-going determinists; for there is no ambiguity in the meaning they assign to determination. It is simply the (hypothetical) necessity of

Hobbes 'that classic determinist'

science. Still whether such a position is compatible with the existence of a plurality of really conative agents remains to be seen. We must first examine the position itself.

Hitherto we have not attempted to analyse the process of voluntary action itself, but as the contention of the thorough-going determinists turns upon this analysis we must now follow them. Their procedure in the main is to regard motives as forces, between which—in deliberation—there may be a varying conflict till at length one proves itself the strongest, whereupon the action, that it is said to determine, ensues. The man meanwhile seems to play the part of a simply passive spectator. How little *he* determines the result according to this view is shown, for example, by the reiterated statements of that classic determinist, Hobbes : " In deliberation there be many wills, whereof not any is the cause of a voluntary action but the last," "Will therefore is the last appetite in deliberating." Now there is no doubt that motives in relation to each other have a certain analogy to forces or to weights in a scale, whence indeed the word 'deliberation' is derived. But the relation of motives to the subject deliberating is not at all that of independent forces applied to an inert object, albeit Hobbes treats of them under the head of Physics[1]. Appetite and aversion, that is to say conation, implies something that seeks and shuns, a subject that actively strives according as it feels and as long as it lives. Psychologists do not ordinarily talk of motives save in connexion with deliberation, which in strictness is an

---

[1] *English Works*, Molesworth's edn, vol. I. p 408.

intellectual rather than a conative process ; but for the purpose of our present discussion it will be convenient, and need not mislead, if we regard motives not as pleas or reasons for acting but as impulses or tendencies to action. So regarded their characteristic is not, that like external forces they move or tend to move the subject, but that they are themselves the subject moving or tending to move, or more accurately, acting or tending to act.

We say indeed that hunger makes a man eat, but we do not interpret this statement as we should the statement that heat makes a glass crack. In both cases we have a certain situation, but in the one case the active subject changes the situation ; in the other the situation changes the passive object. Again in what we may call physical situations, where several forces concur, the change is always their resultant and each, strong and weak alike, produces its full effect. In psychical situations, on the other hand, where several motives are said to conflict, the eventual action is determined in accordance with one only, the so-called strongest motive : the rejected motives, if they tell at all, do so simply as testing steadfastness of purpose. It is perhaps hardly needful to say that strength does not here, as in the case of a force, imply any reference to an external standard. In a certain situation, which they share in common, so far as two persons can ever be situated alike, one will say : This motive weighs most with me, and the other, This the most with me.

The analogy then between the relation of forces applied to an inert object and the relation of conations to an active subject seems to fail in all essential points.

So long as the subject does not act but merely 'deliberates or ponders' how he shall act, there is some resemblance in his procedure to that of using a balance to determine weights, and the suggested metaphor is as old as Plato; but it is only a metaphor after all. When, however, we consider the facts in their active rather than their cognitive aspect the disparity between the psychical and the physical seems complete. Forces, though distinct, combine their effects only because they converge on one body: motives, though distinct, conflict only because they diverge, so to say, from one subject. The forces, that is, are applied to the body, the motives spring from the subject. The body moves in the one path which the forces collectively determine, the subject moves in the one path which it selectively determines. The magnitude of a force is referred to an objective standard, the strength of a motive depends on its subjective worth: the sufficient reason is in the one case mechanical, in the other it is teleological.

Nevertheless, the thorough-going determinist will doubtless rejoin, these differences are comparatively superficial, and when we think the matter out what we come down to at last is in both cases alike the same necessitation; the same complete determination of the consequent by its antecedents. We speak of a man's path through life as well as of a body's path through space, and this, however intricate it may have been, we know was throughout perfectly definite and at every point inevitably determined. Now what is true of the motions of a body is true of the doings of a man. Well, it is certainly true always that whatever is once determined is inevitably determined and that in this sense the complete antecedents uniquely determine the consequent. But is this a reason for ignoring the difference between the circumstances that determine the rolling of a stone and the volitions that determine the movements of a hero? Or can anyone seriously maintain that we get to the bottom of things by thus ignoring it? If the said difference is merely an accidental accessory, what is the essential characteristic supposed to pertain alike to the physical event and to the voluntary act? It is, the determinist will repeat, that the antecedents in both cases, in the rolling of the stone and in the willing of the man, are beyond control: as Hobbes has said, " The will is also caused by other things whereof it disposeth not[1]." If we ask for further explication, as we well may, we get two answers, more or less connected, which it will be best to consider in turn.

First, it is said, a man's volitions depend on his nature, and that is not a matter of his choice. If it be urged that often they depend rather on the character which he has acquired, a character which may control his nature; it is replied that acquired character is due to modification of nature induced by circumstances, so that after all we come back to nature or original character in the end. But what real distinction, we may ask, can anyone find between a subject and its nature or character[2]? As to what an individual subject

---

[1] ' Liberty and Necessity,' *English Works*, Molesworth's edn, vol. IV. p. 274.

[2] It is not of course with such specific attributes as a subject shares with others of its kind, but with its own peculiar traits that we are here concerned.

is, there may be room for much metaphysical dispute. But at least we are certain that it is not an indefinite 'this,' or an abstract entity, having only an extrinsic connexion with its so-called nature. Thinking is relating, and we are sometimes led in consequence to talk as if reality were altogether resolvable into relations. It is this same habit of thought that leads the indeterminist to talk of the freedom of the will apart from motives, and that leads the determinist, as Priestley does, to talk of "motives as the proper causes of human actions, though it is the man that is called the agent[1]." The efficiency and initiative that

---

[1] "No writer," says Schopenhauer, "has set forth the necessity of voluntary acts so thoroughly and convincingly as Priestley in his... *Doctrine of Philosophical Necessity*." I trust I shall be excused then, if I venture to give a specimen of his reasoning. It occurs in one of the most important sections of his work, in which he is arguing against his Libertarian friend, Price. "Suppose," he says, "a philosopher to be entirely ignorant of the constitution of the human mind, but to see, as Dr Price acknowledges, that men do, in fact, act according to their *affections* and *desires*, i.e. in one word, according to *motives*, would he not as in a case of the doctrine of chances, immediately infer that there must be a *fixed cause* for this coincidence of motives and actions? Would he not say that, though he could not see into the man, the connexion was *natural*, and *necessary*, because *constant*? And since the motives, in all cases, *precede* the actions, would he not naturally, i.e. according to the custom of philosophers in similar cases, say that the motive was the *cause* of the action? And would he not be led by the obvious analogy to compare the mind to a balance, which was inclined this way or that, according to the motives presented to it?...Therefore," he presently concludes, "in proper philosophical language, the motive ought to be called the *proper cause* of the action. It is as much so as anything in nature is the cause of anything else"—sentences which Schopenhauer thought it worth while to quote. (J. Priestley, *Disquisitions*

the indeterminist seems to find in the man apart from his character the determinist professes to find in the character apart from the man. But whereas it is certain that there cannot be less in the concrete self than we know, there may very well be a great deal more ; and therefore, while it may be possible to clear indeterminism of its seeming paradox, it is not possible to reconcile thorough-going determinism with our actual experience.

We certainly have no experience of events without causes, but we experience determination in both the forms which make up the two sides of causation : the effect as determined, the cause as determining ; and we experience both, not objectively as presentations of what is not self, but subjectively as immediate states of self. We have moreover no ground for regarding the one as a whit more real than the other : if pleasure and pain are verily subjective feeling or affection, conation is verily subjective activity or effectuation. What we are here calling a motive implies both ; and essentially distinct though they are, both arise together in certain situations. But not even the feeling, still less the conation, can be described as caused by the situation, if that is regarded simply as any science except psychology would regard it. Psychologically the situation must be interesting ; but this is not a quality pertaining to the situation as such, it is a character that the subject as such gives to it. And gives why ? Because the subject is not, like an inanimate thing, indifferent

relating to Matter and Spirit, 1782, vol. II. pp. 64 ff.) I fancy, if I had myself put this forward as a presentation of the determinist's case, it would have been condemned at once as an unfair travesty.

to circumstances, but has ends and aims to realise, and therefore assumes a different attitude towards its environment according as this helps or hinders it in the pursuit of its purposes—purposes which conform to no general law save that of self-conservation and betterment. Its *own* character determines the character that it gives to objects, and its behaviour towards them is so far essentially self-determination. To deny all this is tacitly to deny the reality of the self or subject of experience altogether.

This brings us to the second answer, a psychological analysis of experience in much favour with thorough-going determinists, wherein this denial is openly made. Hume, it will be remembered, described the mind as "nothing but a bundle or collection of different perceptions, which...are in a perpetual movement or flux." In this bundle his successors signalised appetites and aversions, which are also in perpetual flux. They agree then with him in maintaining that "it cannot therefore be from any of these impressions," as he calls them, "or from any other, that the idea of self is derived, and consequently there is no such idea[1]"—so that, speaking plainly, there is no such reality. If there were, said Bain, "a fourth or residual department [of psychology] would need to be constituted, the department of 'self' or Me-ation, and we should set about the investigation of the laws (or the anarchy) prevailing there, as in the three remaining branches [Emotion, Volition, Intellection]." "I cannot," he continues, "light upon anything of the sort;

---

[1] Hume, *Treatise on Human Nature*, Green and Grose's edition, vol. I. pp. 533 f.

and in the setting-up of a determining power under the name of 'self,' as a contrast to the whole region of motives...I see only an erroneous conception of the facts[1]."

The hopeless shortcomings of this doctrine—variously known as Sensationalism, Associationism, Presentationism—have been often exposed, and it is doubtful if in the present day there is a single psychologist who would defend it. We might then fairly content ourselves by saying that thorough-going determinism finds at once in this sensationalism its logical outcome and its refutation. But the reasons of its failure can be put very briefly. In the first place, determinism and sensationalism alike, in common with all naturalistic thinking, set out from the objective standpoint, as if it were absolute. The subjective factor in all experience, which the natural sciences can safely ignore, can, they assume, be ignored by the moral and historical sciences too. The category of 'attribute or property' which implies possession is metaphorically used of things, though these, albeit qualified, in reality *possess* nothing. "Without property no person," Hegel has said: but we may convert this and say, Without a person no property. Experience is in this sense property: it is always owned. Percepts and appetites that nobody has are not percepts and appetites at all. To talk of motives conflicting of themselves is as absurd as to talk of commodities competing in the absence of traders.

---

[1] *The Emotions and the Will*, 3rd edn, 1875, p. 492. To 'contrast' self and motives in this fashion is indeed just that 'erroneous conception of the facts' referred to above, p. 286 *fin.*

Again, if there is only a bundle of percepts and
motives, but no self to determine or control, it is
obvious that there can be no self to be determined
or controlled. But since presentationism cannot consistently regard presentations themselves as purposive,
there can be no purpose in the Many at all. Finally,
since the only causality naturalism recognises is the
hypothetical regularity of sequence, there is no place
left for efficiency either : the world is resolved into
mechanism, and so experience is explained away.
Such a *reductio ad absurdum* is surely an indirect
proof of the reality of that self-determination which
we directly experience.

LECTURE XIV.

FREEDOM AND FOREKNOWLEDGE.

We may perhaps claim to have found that the thorough-going determinism, which denies self-determination and self-direction *in toto*, refutes itself by overshooting the mark and proving too much: by resolving the subject of experience into an abstraction it denies the reality of experience altogether. But there are those who profess to admit freedom in the sense of self-determination, in common with the Libertarian, and who yet maintain necessity in the sense of natural law, in common with the Necessitarian. I am thinking, of course, of Kant and his solution of this antinomy between the demands of pure science and pure ethics as he conceived them—a solution which Schopenhauer praises as among the most admirable and profound achievements of human genius. The self is here noumenal and its freedom transcendental, but its active manifestations are phenomenal and necessarily determined. Though many besides Schopenhauer have been impressed with the amazing ingenuity of this Kantian doctrine, he, almost alone, seems to have had the courage or the hardihood to accept it completely[1]. At this time of day then it would be unprofitable to begin by discussing it at length, though it may repay

[1] Fichte and Schelling ought perhaps to be included.

us presently to consider whether after all beneath this splendid failure there does not lie a great truth. But it is Schopenhauer's exposition that more immediately concerns us. Adopting the scholastic principle, *Operari sequitur esse*, he says :—" It has been a fundamental error, a ὕστερον πρότερον of all times, to assign the necessity to the *esse* and the freedom to the *operari*. On the contrary freedom pertains to the *esse* alone; but from this and the motives the *operari* follows of necessity; and from what we do we know what we are[1]." And "necessary" he defines as "that which follows from a given sufficient ground[2]."

So far and at first sight there seems nothing here incompatible with self-determination as the Libertarian understands it : a being that in a given situation is itself the sufficient ground of what it does is all that we mean by a spontaneous or free being. The only such beings that we know or can conceive are conscious, that is to say conative and cognitive, subjects. But we find no such restriction of freedom in Schopenhauer's doctrine. The freedom that he allows is not confined to conscious beings; and on looking closer we shall see that consciousness has essentially nothing to do with it. It is the inner essence of each thing, he maintains, whether it be physical force or vital force or will, that determines its characteristic reaction. The law *operari sequitur esse* applies alike to all : as its reactions disclose the nature of a chemical substance, so his volitions disclose the character of a man. "*Objectively*

[1] *Sämmtliche Werke*, 'Freiheit des Willens,' Frauenstädt's edn, vol. IV. p. 97.
[2] *Op. cit.* p. 7.

considered, a man's behaviour," he tells us, "like the action of every natural essence, is recognised as falling necessarily under the causal law in its utmost rigour: *subjectively* on the other hand everyone feels that he always does only what he *wills*. This however only amounts to saying that his action is the pure outcome of his own peculiar nature : even the meanest thing therefore would feel the same, if it could feel at all[1]." What all this comes to then is substantially and briefly as follows :—The *esse* of everything is noumenal and is will or energy of a definite kind, the kind differing for all the so-called physical forces, for all organic species and for all individual men. The *operari* of everything is phenomenal, and involves two factors ; (1) the original *esse*, i.e. force or will, and in addition to this, (2) the determining condition or occasion, answering to what in physics we term causes in the narrower sense, to what in biology we call stimuli, in psychology motives. All that these so-called causes account for is the when and where of the manifestations (*Aeusserungen*) of the primitive things *per se*, which— themselves beyond explanation and causation—are the principles of all explanation and the source of all causation. As such a thing *per se* or noumenon, man according to Kant and Schopenhauer alike is free— free as a cause that is not in turn an effect.

And now what is the result of all this freedom of the noumenal world? A phenomenal world of cast-iron necessity ; and since this is the only world we know about, the determinist, so far as objective experience extends, is completely in the right. But how from such

---

[1] *Op. cit.* pp. 57, 98. Cf. Spinoza's *Letters*, lviii. (earlier edns lxii.) which Schopenhauer quotes, *Welt u.s.w.* § 24.

complete liberty does this rigorous necessity come about?
Because the essential nature or character of everything
is unalterable : what is conscious and what is not are
in this respect, according to Schopenhauer at any rate,
completely on a par. In like manner Kant affirms that
"all the acts of a man, so far as they are phenomena,
are determined according...to the order of nature, and
if we could investigate [them]...to the very bottom,
there would not be a single human action which we
could not predict with certainty and recognise from its
preceding conditions as necessary, just as we do an
eclipse of the sun or the moon[1]."

It is not, however, this assignment of freedom to a
purely extra-phenomenal 'nature' that is at variance with
the pluralistic interpretation of evolution, although it is
against this that most of the objections to the Kantian
doctrine have been directed. On the contrary, as I
shall attempt presently to show, in this respect it
contains, as I have already hinted, a great truth. But
if the characters of men, say, are fixed and immutable,
just as the qualities of the chemical elements are assumed
to be ; and the course of history therefore is as amenable
to calculation as the movements of the planets, then—so
far as experience goes—we may as well accept at once
'the firmly rooted conviction of the ancients concerning
Fate,' as Schopenhauer was prepared to do[2].

We must inquire, therefore, in the first place
whether the statement so often made by determinists
is really defensible, viz. that persons and things are so

[1] *Critique of Pure Reason*, 1st edn, p. 550, M. M.'s trans. p. 474 ;
Practical Reason, Hartenstein's edn, vol. v. p. 104.
[2] *Op. cit.* p. 60.

far on a par that from a complete knowledge of a man's present 'empirical character' all his future actions could be foretold. It is obvious however that more than this would be needed; that in fact a complete specification of all the circumstances in which the man is hereafter to be placed would be equally indispensable. It is obvious again that nothing short of a complete knowledge of the characters of all his contemporaries as well would suffice to render such complete specification possible. But, once more, the thoughts and deeds of contemporaries on the one hand and physical events on the other obviously could not be regarded as two independent series; for conduct is unquestionably affected by natural changes, while at the same time certain natural changes are the result of human interference.

What we should have to deal with then would be one vast predetermined series. The idea of such a rigorously concatenated system is just what the thorough-going determinist understands by the Uniformity of Nature. All the same, when the man of science proceeds to picture out this uniformity, he does so only on the supposition that the whole is a mechanism, whose ultimate constituents are qualitatively alike and differ only quantitatively, in respect of mass, configuration, acceleration, and so forth. Given a complete knowledge of the *whole* of such a system at two successive instants and its state at any assigned date in the future or in the past is ideally *calculable*. Men also interact and affect each other, in so far as they are members of a social system; but then their characters and interests are not alike, and therefore for each the world, though objectively the same, is different too. The words of

Terence, *Quot homines tot sententiae*, are here to the point. As Oliver Wendell Holmes has somewhere humorously put it, whenever two persons M and N converse together there are six individuals concerned, M as he is, M as he thinks himself to be, M as N thinks him to be; and a like trinity as respects N. While it is true that we find no two individuals of our acquaintance entirely alike, it is true also on the other hand that we know no one completely: indeed adequate knowledge about the individual is allowed to be logically impossible. So far Professor Royce is right in his emphatic contention that an individual—however intimately known—is, as known, but an instance of a type: that M or N is the only instance we know does not make him essentially unique[1]. If on the strength of this partial knowledge we venture to predict his future conduct, we are generalising, following, that is to say, the hypothetical procedure of science, as truly as when we affirm that he will die.

But in certain circumstances the one prediction would be as justifiable as the other, since both alike would be instances of the 'uniformity of nature,' viz. when the man's action, like a forced move in chess, is externally constrained; or when again, like some trick of manner, it is secondarily automatic, a case of mechanical routine, the outcome of the dead self, the woodenness of the man as distinct from the growing life. The cases to which Schopenhauer so triumphantly appeals are in part of this sort. And even in the rest we find our confident expectations often belied: the most humdrum mortals rising to great occasions, and

---

[1] *The World and the Individual*, vol. I. pp. 292–4.

others, in whom the hue of resolution seemed native and ingrained, growing pallid in the supreme crisis and finally renouncing their cause. But the literature of conversions and counter-conversions, of which Professor James in his Gifford Lectures has given such an admirable selection, is amply sufficient to turn the flank of Schopenhauer's position. Moreover not only Kant but even Schopenhauer, the more rigorous determinist of the two, is inconsistent enough to recognise these radical changes of character. To be sure they regard them as 'mysteries,' cases of regeneration or new birth, manifestations not of 'nature' but of 'grace'; but it is enough for us now that they admit their possibility. If the appeal then is to be to facts, can anyone soberly maintain that it is even *ideally* possible to forecast what he, still less what another, will think and do a week hence? Besides, even if the forecast could be made it would take the week to make it; for none of the intervening thoughts and deeds could be safely omitted; nor could their rate be accelerated unless a like acceleration held throughout the world—and then we should be relatively just where we were before. The so-called forecast in a word would be after the event[1]. Surely if there is an empirical common-place beyond dispute it is this, that no man knows beforehand even his own possibilities completely, to say nothing of those of another.

So far as experience goes what we find is not simply uniformity and routine, *natura naturata*, but also innovation and variation, *natura naturans*. Hence while it is possible to publish *Bradshaw's Guide* as

---

[1] Cf. Bergson, *Les Données immédiates*, 2me edn, pp. 140 ff.

well as the *Nautical Almanack, Zadkiel's Almanack* is
a fraud, and other forms of clairvoyance an absurdity, in
spite of Schopenhauer's confident appeal to them.   But
after all his thorough-going determinism—or 'noumenal
freedom'—was not based on experience.   Further his
definition of necessary as "that which follows from a
given sufficient ground" does not justify him in assuming
that the ground is once for all fixed and unalterable[1].
That is an assumption which he simply took over
straight from Plato's theory of ideas and grievously
misapplied.   If on this assumption there could be
events, their rigorous concatenation would, of course,
be inevitable.   But though the fixed and unalterable
character of the 'free,' noumenal, grounds of nature
would necessitate a phenomenal world fast bound in fate,
we cannot till we have found this *infer* that.   To *assert*
such a character of the noumenal, and thence to deduce
what the phenomenal, world must be, is mere dogmatism.

   Nevertheless it was to this solid mechanism or
'nature-necessity' as he called it that Kant appealed in
support of his 'empirical' determinism.   And most inconsistently, for he has himself allowed that this miscalled
'necessity of nature' neither logically nor really deserves
the name.   The 'uniformity of nature' is indeed so far *a
priori*, as being part and parcel of the postulate that the
very possibility of any empirical forecast at all implies.
But now postulation is a practical not a theoretical matter:

---

[1] What, we wonder, would Schopenhauer have said of the *Kea*,
the New Zealand parrot that has developed the extraordinary habit
of picking holes in the back of the living sheep ; or of other instances
of changed habits which Darwin gives? (*Origin of Species*, 6th edn,
pp. 141–3).

what then in the last resort does it really mean? Experience itself being practical, and theory the result not the presupposition of experience, we can put the matter most simply by saying of experience what Helmholtz has said:—*Hier gilt nur der eine Rath: Vertraue und handle!*

> *Das Unzulängliche*
> *Dann wird's Ereigniss*[1].

This then is our postulate reduced to its lowest terms, and with this the progress of experience entirely agrees. The Many have all alike had to trust and try, sometimes succeeding, sometimes failing, but on the whole always learning and so gradually achieving the order that determinism assumes to exist *a priori.* This established order or *natura naturata* then implies free causes, (as Kant and Schopenhauer maintained,) for it is the work of these; but why suppose that by their very first stroke they forge for themselves adamantine chains? Yet this is what Schopenhauer certainly assumed[2] and what Kant seems to assume. Such a supposition, so far from making experience possible, would rather make it impossible; for if the nature or essence of all agents were irrevocably fixed, how could —nay why should—there be any evolution at all? A Spinozistic world, existing *sub specie aeternitatis* but really devoid of progress, is all we could expect.

Nevertheless, as I shall now try to show, the Kantian distinction between intelligible and empirical character is of real importance; although, of course, we must take it to mean not that a subject has two characters, one noumenal the other phenomenal, but

---

[1] *Handbuch der physiologischen Optik*, 2te Aus. p. 594.
[2] Cf. *Sämmtliche Werke*, Frauenstädt's edn, vol. II. p. 598, vol. IV. p. 97.

simply that in the latter we have sundry manifestations of what the subject's character really is : *operari sequitur esse*, as Schopenhauer said. But Kant, I think, never meant to regard the free subject as Schopenhauer did, that is, as related to its acts as a logical essence is to its predicates. When therefore he speaks of it as out of time he does not mean to exclude process and change in the sense in which logic excludes these : that he postulates immortality in order to the attainment of perfection is enough to show this. What then does he mean ? What he really means is, I think, far more clearly expressed in his distinction of *homo noumenon* and *homo phenomenon.* As phenomenal, 'when we are merely *observing*[1]' a man, he is an object simply, not a subject. Like all observed objects, he is so far conceived as merely part and parcel of that continuous whole we call nature ; and the successive states through which he is observed to pass are conceived as regularly linked in with those of other phenomena in this one unbroken continuum. It is to this regular succession of phenomenal events that the category of causality as used in science applies.

But besides this causal relation to other phenomena everything phenomenal is related, on the one hand to the subject to whom it appears, and on the other to the 'transcendental object,' of which it is the appearance. Whether consistently or not with the main position of his critical philosophy, it is at all events a fact that Kant never dreamt of questioning the existence of things *per se* as the ground of the phenomena that we observe externally. It is equally certain that

[1] Kant's phrase. Cf. the context of first passage quoted above, p. 295.

he regarded the 'transcendental subject' or the ground of the facts that we experience internally as also such a thing *per se* ; and that not simply from the standpoint of practice but also from that of theory. In a word the experience of phenomena, whether 'external or internal,' implies the existence of corresponding 'things *per se*' as their grounds or causes ; as Leibniz, Herbart and Lotze maintained. *Wie viel Schein so viel Hindeutung aufs Sein* was as true for Kant as it was for them. But the causality in this case is not the phenomenal and relative causality of science, but the noumenal and absolute causality that pertains solely to the ultimate efficiency of the thing *per se.* To man conceived as noumenal this absolute or free causality belongs. The reasonable in thought and conduct affords the most adequate instances of such causality ; for "reason," as Kant says, "does not yield to the impulse that is given empirically and does not follow the order of things as they present themselves as phenomena, but frames for itself, with perfect spon- taneity, a new order according to ideas to which it adapts the empirical conditions[1]." But he also gives the following simpler example :—" If at this moment I rise from my chair with perfect freedom, without the necessarily determining influence of natural causes, a new series has its absolute beginning in this event, with all its natural consequences *ad indefinitum*[2]."

The phenomenal world then we may compare, as Lotze has done, to a continuous texture or fabric con- sisting entirely of the joint effects produced, the overt

---

[1] *Critique*, 1st edn, p. 548, M.M.'s trans. p. 473.
[2] *Op. cit.* p. 450, M.M. p. 392.

deeds done, by innumerable things *per se* or agents. The pattern of this texture is what we call filled time, and the process of filling-in is, as we know, ever going forward.   So far as we are merely cognitive, we are confined to observations, past and present, of this process and to such more or less probable inferences concerning the future as these suggest.   As a matter of fact our inductions frequently turn out right, and they prove to be more reliable the more methodically we proceed.   It is so ; but as already said there is no necessity, either logical or real, about it.   " For we could quite well imagine," Kant himself allows, "that phenomena might possibly be such that the understanding would not find them conformable...: all might be in such confusion that nothing would be found in the succession of phenomena which could supply a rule of synthesis corresponding to the category of cause and effect, so that this category would therefore be altogether null and void and meaningless[1]."   Thus it is simply to the ideal of a ' rule' of succession, which the weaving of the phenomenal texture *de facto* suggests, that we apply the concept called by Kant ' causality of nature.'

Entirely distinct from this phenomenal or empirical causality is that which Kant calls 'causality of freedom ' —intelligible or noumenal causality.   So different are the two that positive science fights shy of the terms, ' cause and effect,' because of their association with this efficient or noumenal causality, the existence of which positive science ignores and naturalism dogmatically denies altogether[2].   But to the grounds

---

[1] *Critique of the Pure Reason.*   Analytic § 13, M.M. p. 80.
[2] Cf. *Naturalism and Agnosticism*, vol. II. pp. 241, 247.

for assuming its existence we need not now return. At all events, as the very causality that produces the pattern in 'the context of nature'—Kant's phrase by the way—this noumenal causality obviously cannot be identified with the phenomenal causality—so-called—that the pattern itself displays. The essential characteristic of the latter is objective time-order according to universal law : the essential characteristic of the former is subjective initiation. Since it freely inserts those 'links in the chain of nature' it cannot, I say, be a part of the time-order that it makes. As compared with the phenomenal solidarity or continuity that they jointly produce, these independent, real, causes may then be said to be out of time. Their acts are not 'events' that seem to come out of (*evenire*), or to follow from, what has preceded in the time-process: they are rather 'interventions' that appear in this process and constitute its further evolution. Accordingly in reference to them and them only 'ought' has a meaning ; for, as Kant truly says : "If we look merely at the course of nature, 'ought' has no meaning whatever.... It expresses a possible action, the ground of which cannot be anything but a mere concept," cannot be a phenomenon[1]. This concept, as we should say now, is the axiological concept of worth or of the good, whereby the realm of ends in which it obtains is still further differentiated from the realm of nature in which it is meaningless. In the one, events appear as determined by preceding events ; in the other, actions are initiated to secure future ends.

But can we then say that the realm of ends is out

[1] *Op. cit.* p. 547, M.M. p. 472.

of time ?   Certainly not, as I have already maintained, in the sense that it is, like Plato's world of ideas, an eternal world of immutable essences, a logical world but not a real world at all.   In tending to equate 'intelligible character' to mere *essentia + existentia*, as Schopenhauer expressly did, Kant's procedure is indefensible as well as inconsistent.   But what is the time, beyond which, so to say, free agents are said to exist ?   It is that time which Kant conceived as yielding an exact science of chronometry, the pendant of geometry the exact science of space.   It is time as a continuous quantity of one dimension, and so far comparable to a line, save that its points or parts are not simultaneous but successive.   Succession in this time is conceived as constant ; in other words this time is regarded as homogeneous and so as measurable, divisible into intervals of equal length.   In a word it is the abstract time of science in which we imagine the successive states of the whole phenomenal world to be plotted out, suggesting, as Bergson has admirably put it, the substitution for the complete world of experience of a set of kinematographic pictures.

What then is left out of this abstract or empty time ?   Paradoxical though it appear, what is left out, we shall find, are the mutually implicated facts of duration and change.   An interval of time is not the same as the experience of duration, and the two different states situated at its extremes are no equivalent for the experience of change.   But these problems of time which we have here broached are far too complex for discussion now.   The only farther elucidation I can offer is to raise one more question and content myself with a very summary answer. How do we come by this schema of time ? We come by it solely because our experience involves both duration and change ; and thus, as has been well said, "time is in us though we are not in time." But for experience duration is not something objective, is not a homogeneous linear quantity that is abstracted from a multiplicity of successive presentations. What the term duration ultimately represents is our subjective experience as actively striving and wearing on: it implies the actual living, which only is actual in so far as it is not homogeneous and empty but full of changes endured or wrought. And change again as experienced is not merely a temporal succession, *a, b, c*..., where *a* is not when *b* is, and *c* is not till *b* is no more. Such a schema would never yield experience : it answers exactly to that *zero* limit of experience that, as I have already remarked, Leibniz ascribed to bodies, when he said *omne corpus mens momentanea est*. But experience yields that schema ; and empirical psychology affords us a fairly complete analysis of its constituents and a fairly probable account of their genetic synthesis. Experience however yields that schema only because experience, as living, is the *natura naturans* that leaves behind it, as it were, the *natura naturata* to which the schema entirely belongs. Between the intemporal world of ideas and the temporal world of phenomena free agents then have their place[1].

[1] Cf. Bergson, *L'Évolution créatrice*, p. 391. "The feature in Professor Bergson's contribution to the philosophy of experience which distinguishes it fundamentally from the views of previous thinkers, is his new conception of time as concrete time, or what

The necessitarian position is not then, we seem entitled to conclude, empirically warranted. As an argument from experience it rests on the assumption that phenomena are the whole ; that there is, in other words, nothing but filled time : whence and how time is filled, it does not inquire. Once this foundation is found faulty, all the empirical arguments that rest upon it may be overturned. Nor, with one exception, are the supposed *a priori* arguments more satisfactory. That every event must have a cause we may allow to be axiomatic, but not that the same cause—the same efficient cause, that is—must always produce the same effect. Again to identify such a cause with an essence, to equate it, as it were, to a reason was the mistake of rationalism, which Kant completely exposed in his important pre-critical paper on *Negative Quantities*.

he calls Duration" (D. Balsillie, *Mind*, 1911, p. 357). I think however that I may fairly claim to have anticipated him to some extent. In 1886, three years before the publication of Professor Bergson's *Données*, I had written a long paragraph on this topic, containing *inter alia* the following :—"Thus...there is an element in our concrete time-perception which has no place in our abstract conception of time. In time, conceived as physical, there is no trace of intensity ; in time, as psychically experienced, duration is primarily an intensive magnitude" (*Ency. Brit.* 'Psychology,' 11th edn, p. 577). I should probably have taken an earlier opportunity of mentioning this point, if I had known before, that one of Professor Bergson's compatriots had already called attention to it—of this however I only became aware quite recently. Cf. M. G. Rageot in the *Revue philosophique*, t. LX. 1905, p. 84. In a reply to him Professor Bergson (*ibid.* p. 229), while establishing his own independence, strangely misses the point of resemblance, which is not, as he supposes, between my 'presentation-continuum' and his *durée réelle*, but between this and my analysis of time as concrete.

On the main question see further in Supplementary Note IV.

20—2

But if we start from theism the case is quite other-wise : then indeed the necessitarian position appears to be axiomatic[1].   It is, I think, generally allowed that in the long theological controversies, which for cen-turies have raged round our problem, logic has been on the side of those who, like Augustine, Aquinas, Calvin and Edwards, have maintained the doctrine of divine predestination, the doctrine "that God orders all events, and the volitions of moral agents amongst others, by such a decisive disposal, that the events are infallibly connected with his disposal[2]"; or otherwise put, that second causes in nature are incompatible with the admis-sion that there is only one cause, the First Cause. What however does this start from theism imply ? It implies a supposed knowledge of God that is independent of experience—partly as innate, partly as revealed.   It im-plies further that knowing what God is apart from the world we infer what any world that he creates must be. The absolute omniscience and omnipotence of God are regarded as beyond question; and from these follow as a corollary the absolute and eternal decrees.   As Jonathan Edwards concisely put it : " All things are perfectly and equally in his view from eternity ; hence it will follow that his designs or purposes are not things formed anew, founded on any new views or appear-ances, but are all eternal purposes."   But there is another corollary equally evident from which those intent on theism at any cost seek in vain to escape. There is—as already said—no room left for other

---

[1] So we come round again to the divergence between pluralism and theism from which we first set out. Cf. Lect. XIII. *init.*

[2] Jonathan Edwards, *Enquiry*, 4th edn, 1775, p. 406.

causes, other purposes, no room for a real world with
such a God at all. As a Scottish professor of divinity
has said :—"If God is thus the real cause of all that is,
the universe would seem to be merely God evolving
himself, and there has been no true creation, no bringing
into being of wills separate from his own[1]." In a word—
as I attempted to show in the second lecture—starting
from the One there is no arriving at the Many. If we
attempt to conceive of God apart from the world there
is nothing to lead us on to the idea of creation. On
the other hand, if we start from the Many, it has, I
trust, become more and more clear as we have advanced, that we find there no justification for the notion
of a 'block universe'—as Professor James called it—a
universe, that is, in which every detail is decreed, in
which real initiative, evolution as we understand it, is
impossible. But, in fact, we *have* to start from the
Many, and accordingly always do—this too I trust has
been made clear. Moreover, if thorough-going determinism were true, we should, it has seemed equally
clear, never attain to the idea of a Creator at all. For
if ourselves devoid of all originality what meaning could
that idea have for us ?

The doctrine of predestination has been for theologians a hopeless and insoluble problem as well as a
source of bitter strife largely because of this opposition
between *a priori* speculation and actual experience.
"That in the actual passage of events something should
actually come to pass, something new which previously was not; that history should be something more
than a translation into time of the eternally complete

---

[1] Rev. Marcus Dods, *Ency. Brit.* 9th edn, s.v. Predestination.

content of an ordered world—this," said Lotze, "is a deep and irresistible demand of our spirit, under the influence of which we all act in life. Without its satisfaction the world would be, not indeed unthinkable and self-contradictory, but unmeaning and incredible[1]."

But though I have used that ominous word 'predestination' I am not going to attempt to adjudicate the theological differences of Augustine and Pelagius, Arminius and Calvin. It is the wider issue—that of reconciling pluralism and theism—that alone concerns us. Nevertheless there are two or three points connected with the purely theological controversy that are worthy of notice. First, in its most rigid and, as it seems to me, its most logical form—in what is called Supralapsarianism—the dogma of predestination has always appeared so shocking, so 'excruciating' as Augustine said, to ordinary humanity, that it has not only been charged on moral grounds with *tending* to atheism, but it has been used either openly or covertly to promote atheism. Readers of church history will remember the fates of Gottschalk and Vanini. But, secondly and as more important, we may notice the attempts that have been made to tone down the extreme rigour of the Calvinistic dogma—as represented, for example, in Jonathan Edwards's classical treatise— by distinguishing between the divine prescience and the divine purposes. The text of all such attempts is to be found in a famous saying of Origen :—"God's prescience is not the cause of things future, but their being future is the cause of God's prescience that they will be." To the relations of finite beings this dis-

[1] *Metaphysic*, § 65, E. t. p. 117.

tinction is certainly applicable. I may confidently expect what another will do, without any responsibility for his deed ; but in proportion as he has become what he is through my deliberate influence and effort the distinction lapses : so far, what I expect is just what I intended. If then the divine decrees and the divine prescience are coeval, if God is the sole cause of all that is and foresees infallibly all that can ever happen, *a fortiori* it seems futile to attempt to discriminate between what he decrees and what he merely permits.

The philosopher Reid, who in opposition to Priestley attempted to reconcile divine foreknowledge and human freedom, made the extraordinary blunder of comparing foreknowledge of the future with memory of the past. He practically assumed that because memory of the past is memory of what was once both future and contingent, the fact remembered remains contingent though it is future no more. Nothing is easier than to turn this analogy against him with fatal effect, as his own disciple Hamilton has actually done. "*Factum infectum reddere, ne Deus quidem potest*, has been said and sung in a thousand forms," says Hamilton. The past that is to say is necessary : if then God's prescience resembles our memory, it is only because the past and the future are both alike to him : as the past is not contingent so neither is the future[1].

But notwithstanding his exposure, Hamilton still sides with Reid, not with Priestley. And this brings to our notice another attempt to save the Divine Sovereignty, as it is called, without surrendering the

---

[1] *The Works of Thos. Reid*, Hamilton's edition, p. 631 *n.*

freedom of man ; and that is the simple declaration
that the problem is transcendent.   The conciliation of
divine foreknowledge and human freedom is, said
Hamilton, "one of the things to be believed, not
understood": all "attempts to harmonize these anti-
logies by human reasoning to human understanding"
are to be rejected as "futile...'vain wisdom all and
false philosophy.'"   But what if antilogy is only a
euphemism for contradiction, and what of the logical
cogency of the predestinarian view, about which,
however repulsive, there is nothing obscure or inconceivable ?   I do not think Jonathan Edwards
overstated his case, when he said :—"There is no
geometrical theorem whatsoever, more capable of
strict demonstration than that God's certain Prescience
of the volitions of moral agents is inconsistent with
such a contingency of these events, as is without all
Necessity[1]."

The pluralist then, it would seem, has no alternative
but either to deny the complete prescience of the One
or to abandon the self-determination of the Many, and
thus wholly surrender his own position.   There is
however still an old attempt at conciliation, recently
set forth anew by a former Gifford Lecturer, which we
perhaps ought not to pass altogether without notice.
"Foreknowledge in time," says Professor Royce, "is
possible only of the general and of the causally predetermined, and not of the unique and the free.   Hence
neither God nor man can perfectly foreknow, at any
temporal moment, what a free-will agent is yet to do.
On the other hand, the Absolute *possesses a perfect*

[1] *Op. cit.* p. 182.

knowledge at one glance of the whole of the temporal order, present, past and future. This knowledge is ill-called foreknowledge. It is eternal knowledge[1]." But I fear that even eternity will not afford a secure refuge from the difficulty. It is noteworthy that, while it is of God that Professor Royce denies perfect fore-knowledge, it is of the Absolute that he asserts eternal knowledge. There is here more than an accidental difference of expression. Professor Royce in fact, like only too many theists, is guilty of that vacillation between God and the Absolute which Mr Bradley we found quaintly comparing to the futile attempts of a dog to follow two masters[2]. The Absolute must be in every respect all-inclusive, but God, if his creatures are free, is so far not all-inclusive. As I have already said the Creator together with his creatures may be called the Absolute ; but unless the creatures—said to be made out of nothing—verily remain themselves but nothing, God is, no longer at any rate, the Absolute. To God we may attribute personality and therefore experience and knowledge ; since for him the world is a Not-self, although his own creation. But we cannot attribute personality to the Absolute, for there the duality of Self and Not-self is necessarily tran-scended. We cannot then speak of the Absolute as knowing ; but since it is all-inclusive we may perhaps say that it 'possesses knowledge'—a vague phrase that will mean too little to help us much[3].

---

[1] *The World and the Individual*, vol. II. p. 374. Italics the author's.

[2] Cf. Lect. II. p. 44.

[3] It would be equally true to say, as Mr Bosanquet has observed, that it possesses colour.

But if now we turn for a moment to consider what Professor Royce understands by an eternal knowledge that takes in 'at a glance'—the expression is odd— the whole temporal order—again an odd but significant expression—we shall find that in fact we are not helped at all. He distinguishes two senses of present, an exclusive—as when we hear or apprehend a musical air note by note, where each note excludes the rest from coexistence with itself—and an inclusive—as when we take in or comprehend the melody as a whole and appreciate it. In this latter case the whole melody is present, included at once in what I have called a time perspective. The range of such inclusive present, or time-span, is for us extremely limited, but within such limits we experience a sort of temporal ubiquity. As I have already had occasion to observe, when this limit is reduced to zero, there is strictly no experience. Now, on the other hand, imagine all limits withdrawn and you have the sort of experience Professor Royce calls eternal knowledge. Comparing the whole temporal order to an infinite symphony, he holds that the Absolute knows it at once as we might know one brief rhythm. But now, we ask, when is it that we grasp this rhythm as an ordered whole? When it is complete—*a parte post*. And here surely the fatal defect of Professor Royce's solution for our purpose is evident. No wonder he talks of ' the temporal order' as if it were fixed! If the Absolute takes in at a glance the whole temporal order of the world, it can only be, according to Professor Royce's analogy, because, as Hegel supposed, the world's evolution is for it merely a rehearsal after the symphony is composed.

But such an absolute One, as we have seen many
times over, has no need and leaves no room for a
real Many at all.   Further, it seems contradictory to
attribute to it the limitations of the temporal standpoint along with the perfection of the eternal[1]: the
composer can never be a mere auditor too.

This remark brings us back to the pluralist's
solution, and raises an obvious difficulty.   Is God
then not the composer it will reasonably be asked: are
we not assuming that the world is his creation?   Or
has he only devised an Æolian harp and left the winds
of chance to call the tune, being himself then only an
auditor?   Such questions suggest two extremes, neither
of which is compatible with pluralism ; between which
however there lies a *via media* that may be.   *All* is
not decreed : the world is not created like a symphony.
Again, all possibilities are not left open : the Many
have not severally unlimited freedom, that 'freedom of
indifference' which is indistinguishable from chance.
God's creatures are creators, the pluralist maintains :
their 'nature' is partly his doing, partly their own :
he assigns the talents, they use or misuse them.
Not everything that is possible is possible to any,
yet some initiative is open to every one : none are
left with no talent at all.   The *total* possibilities then,
however far back we go, are fixed ; but within these,
contingencies, however far forward we go, are open.

"An infinite Mind, with prevision thus extended
beyond all that is to all that can be," said Martineau,
"is lifted above surprise or disappointment...yet, instead of being shut up in a closed and mechanized

[1] See Supplementary Note iv.

universe, lives amid the free play of variable character and contingent history. Is this a *limitation* of God's foresight, that he cannot read all volitions that are to be? Yes, but it is a *self limitation*...: lending us a portion of his causation, he refrains from covering all with his omniscience...." "There is no absurdity in supposing," said Dugald Stewart, "that the Deity may, for wise purposes, have chosen to open a source of contingency in the voluntary action of his creatures, to which no prescience can possibly extend." "God who is everything," said Jowett, "is not really so much as if He allowed the most exalted free agencies to exist side by side with Him." "Free will," said Tennyson, "was undoubtedly the main miracle, apparently an act of self-limitation by the Infinite, and yet a revelation by Himself and of Himself[1]."—A much longer catena of passages similar in purport could easily be provided. As a consequence of the growing acceptance of the pluralistic standpoint, this admission of what is very inaccurately styled the 'doctrine of a finite God[2]' has become widely prevalent of late. It has its difficulties, no doubt, as the idea of creation for us must always have. But, on the other hand, by means of it, the problem of evil, to which I propose to invite your attention next, is greatly simplified.

[1] *In Memoriam*, Robinson's edition, p. 260.
[2] Cf. below, Lect. xx.

LECTURE XV.

THE PROBLEM OF EVIL AND PESSIMISM.

The problem of evil has been recently called 'the crux of theism': the phrase serves to emphasise how thought has moved on since Leibniz, the philosopher and courtier, in obedience to royal orders wrote his famous Theodicy—a piece of 'superficiality incarnate,' Wm James has ventured to call it. Nowadays it is asked: How is the evil in the world compatible with there being a God at all? For Leibniz the existence of God was demonstrable: thus for him the problem was simply to show that this world is the best possible. Whether he succeeded or not, it may fairly be maintained that, his main premises granted, no other reasonable supposition is possible. God would not be God, if his world were not the best. Even Hume explicitly admitted this. "There are," he says, "many inexplicable difficulties in the works of Nature, which, if we allow a perfect author to be proved *a priori*....become only seeming difficulties for the narrow capacity of man, who cannot trace infinite relations." And again, after a lengthy summary of the circumstances on which natural evil in the main depends, he continues: "Shall we say that these circumstances are not necessary and that they might

..ly have been altered in the contrivance of the ..niverse? This decision seems too presumptuous for creatures so blind and ignorant. Let us be more modest in our conclusions. Let us allow that, if the goodness of the Deity....could be established on any tolerable reasons *a priori*, these phenomena, however untoward, would not be sufficient to subvert that principle; but might easily, in some unknown manner, be reconcilable to it[1]." And in fact this position is one continually adopted. Lotze, for example, holds fast to the goodness of God and so—while frankly admitting that for our finite wisdom the problem of evil is insoluble—rests satisfied that there is a solution, though we do not understand it[2].

But if we start from the evil that for our immediate experience seems really beyond question, it may be contended that the solution should come first, and that without this the theistic position is not only beyond proof, but impossible. It now becomes utterly futile to represent evil as essentially negative and unreal, however forcible in other respects this time-honoured argument may be. For immediate experience what is evil is just as real and positive as its contrary good. Again, from the pluralistic point of view it seems a useless mockery of the Many not a vindication of the One to put Leibniz into verse, as Pope did, and declare 'all partial evil universal good.' So long as the evil that I suffer brings no good to me, furthers nothing that I approve, so long God will not be God for me; on the other hand in proportion as I

---

[1] *Dialogues concerning Natural Religion*, Green and Grose's edn, vol. II. pp. 412, 451; cf. also pp. 444 ff.

[2] Cf. *Microcosmus*, Eng. trans. vol. II. p. 717.

discern a soul of good in things evil I may bless and trust him though he slay me. Complete certainty one way implies complete certainty the other : God and Evil, in a word, are contraries : if the problem of evil is altogether insoluble, there is an end of theism : if God exists, there is nothing absolutely evil.

But it is important here to bear in mind a distinction on which Kant was wont to lay much stress : failure of proof is very different from disproof. It may be that in this life we shall ever fall as far short of a triumphant and definitive theodicy as we have of a rigidly demonstrative theology. But scepticism is not atheism : where there is room for doubt there is 'room for faith.' At any rate one thing seems clear : whatever be the details of the divine vindication it must show that at least the possibility of evil is essential to the world's perfection ; and even if we cannot show this completely and in every case, yet to prove the contrary, it may be maintained, is equally impossible. Now at the outset of our inquiry we came to the conclusion that the theistic ideal, if it can be sustained, would add immeasurably to the worth of the world as pluralism alone has to conceive it. But we have found no theoretical proof of the divine existence and cannot therefore directly outflank the so-called enigma of evil as an empirical problem. The problem then for us seems to formulate itself in this wise :— Granting that if there is a God, this world must be not only good but—so far as it is his creation—the best possible, have we any certain evidence that it is not ? Keeping strictly on the defensive the only theodicy we can attempt is to require those who accuse to prove their indictment.

The pessimists with their contention that the world is the worst possible or absolutely bad confront us first. A distinction is sometimes made between those who are pessimists by temperament and those who are pessimists on purely theoretical grounds, as the result of dispassionate inquiry and conviction ; but in truth I doubt if there has ever been a pronounced pessimist who could be placed in the latter class alone. Schopenhauer and Mainländer, who are accounted philosophers, were every whit as morbid as Byron or Leopardi. The pessimist sees the world not by the dry, objective light of reason, but rather looks out upon it through the subjective humours of his own sickly 'pity for himself.' This leads him to magnify or even enjoy whatever misery, to minimize and perhaps envy whatever happiness, he finds without[1]. How can we accept the evidence of such diseased and pusillanimous souls, or trust the theories they propound ? But the temperamental optimist, it may be said, is at least as one-sided, and the theoretical optimist is far more superficial. Not only is that true, but it is true further, as has been often urged, that the jubilant and fatuous optimism of the eighteenth century helped to bring into vogue the pessimism of the nineteenth, and even justified it as at least a salutary reaction. When the actual evil in the world is compared to the shadows in a picture, or to the dissonances in a sonata, that only enhance the aesthetic perfection of the whole, it is surely reasonable

---

[1] "I rejoice to discover more and more the misery of men and things, to touch them with the hand and to be seized with a cold shudder as I search through the unblessed and terrible secret of life." Leopardi, quoted by Sully, *Pessimism*, 2nd edn, 1892, p. 27.

to insist on the one thing immediately certain, the inherent badness of these blemishes and discords as such. It is surely reasonable too to argue that if the actual evil of the world is part of its perfection as a whole, then to replace it by good, to change actual misery into happiness, actual vice into virtue, would only diminish not increase the world's perfection—a *reductio ad absurdum*, if ever there was one[1]. No wonder that such shallow formalism should strike earnest men as insincere[2]. "I cannot refrain from declaring," said Schopenhauer, "that to me optimism appears not merely as an absurd but as a positively wicked way of thinking, a bitter mockery of the unspeakable suffering of mankind—anyhow," he continues, "let no one perchance suppose that the teaching of Christianity favours optimism; for on the contrary in the Gospels 'world' and 'evil' are used almost as synonymous expressions[3]." Yes, but world in the New Testament does not mean the whole sum of things but only 'the things seen and temporal,' the natural without the spiritual.

And here we touch upon the point in which optimism and pessimism are equally at fault. The one seeks to show that this world is, to use Wallace's phrase, 'a felicific institution,' the other has no difficulty in showing that it is not; and therefore, since both start from the

---

[1] Cf. H. Rashdall, *The Theory of Good and Evil*, 1907, vol. II. pp. 242 f.

[2] Several writers have maintained that Leibniz was not sincere and one even went so far as to say that Leibniz both in writing and in conversation admitted as much. Cf. O. Willareth, *Die Lehre vom Uebel bei Leibniz*, Strassburg, 1898, p. 12.

[3] *Die Welt als Wille und Vorstellung*, Bk III. § 59.

same eudaemonistic premises, the pessimist claims to have won his suit, and disposed of the old theodicies and theologies altogether.   Pessimism has certainly shown, as Wallace said, " that he who makes happiness the aim of his life is on the wrong tack," but then rational ethics, which is not pessimistic, also allows that.   In bringing home to our modern consciousness the hopelessness of the hedonistic theories of this life that had dominated the thinking of the eighteenth century, pessimism then, we must admit, has been of lasting service.   But deliberately, as Schopenhauer does, to endorse Byron's petulant stanza,

> Count o'er the joys thine hours have seen,
>   Count o'er thy days from anguish free,
> And know, whatever thou hast been,
>   'Tis something better not to be;

to maintain, whatever a man is, that in proportion as his life fails of pleasure it fails in worth, is to make a great assumption which experience does not bear out. That a world of happiness unalloyed, were it possible, would be the best—though so widely held—is just the position that we must presently carefully examine. But before we attempt to discuss this dogma common to optimism and pessimism alike[1], it will be worth our while to subject the subsequent steps in the pessimist's argument to some criticism.

Optimists were fond of saying that pleasure is positive and pain negative : Schopenhauer's first step is to assert that, on the contrary, pain is positive and pleasure negative.   Perfect and continuous happiness would then have the value zero : there would be no pain.   "Whatever is opposed to our will, thwarting

---

[1] Cf. below, Lect. XVI. pp. 337 ff.

and resisting it, that is, whatever is displeasing and painful—of all this," he says, " we are directly sensitive, at once and very distinctly : [on the other hand] we do *not feel* the healthfulness of our whole body, but only the one spot 'where the shoe pinches'; so also we do not think about the state of our affairs in general, so long as all goes perfectly well, but only about some insignificant trifle or other that annoys us. On this ground," he continues, " is based the negativity of well-being and happiness in contrast to the positivity of pain, upon which I have so often insisted[1]." Pessimism based on the crumpled rose-leaf we might say : could anything be more perverse! We cannot indeed forget the harrowing pictures that Schopenhauer loved to draw of all the vast and varied ills of life. But this after all is not the point. He tells us, for example, that "if we could even approximately conceive the sum of want and pain and misery of every sort on which in its course the sun daily shines, we should acknowledge that it would have been better if the earth like the moon had been but a lifeless mass[2]." But he forgets that such a conclusion would only be forced upon us if we accepted his assumptions. Grant that all the good the sun sees counts for nothing, lies below the threshold, as we now say, and that only the evil is positive for us ; then we might agree with him.

Nay, if his psychology of will is sound, we must in any case do so. For "all volition," he maintained, "springs from want, implies defect and therefore suffering." Yet lasting satisfaction and contentment

---

[1] *Parerga und Paralipomena*, Bd II. § 150.
[2] *Op. cit.* § 157 *init.*

are impossible, since fresh wants and new disappointments arise continually. From the lowest stages of its manifestation to the highest, the will altogether lacks any definite end or aim : it is simply ever striving after something, for in such striving its whole essence lies. To look for meaning or progress in life or history is then absurd. "So the subject of volition lies permanently on the revolving wheel of Ixion, pours for ever into the Danaids' sieve, is Tantalus eternally yearning[1]." In a word, *Alles Leben ist Leiden.* Whether Schopenhauer has succeeded better in proving the good in the world to be negative than Leibniz in proving this of the evil in it, is a question. Certainly if the rosy pictures of the one are not decisive neither is the gallery of horrors of the other. But till Schopenhauer's psychology of feeling and will is established, so long his pessimism will lack the foundation upon which he himself professed to rest it. This is the point on which I would now insist, the point which Schopenhauer's readers, carried away by his masterly delineations of human ill, are only too apt to overlook.

His follower, von Hartmann, however allows—what indeed there is no denying—that pleasure and pain are alike positive, and also that there is progress and development in the world : he even takes some trouble expressly to refute Schopenhauer's teaching in these respects. Nevertheless he holds Schopenhauer's pessimism to have been in the main justifiable ; for he claims to show that there is a preponderance of evil in the world, a preponderance too that steadily increases as the world's evolution

[1] *Welt als Wille und Vorstellung,* §§ 38, 56.

proceeds. He professes to prove this, first inductively as a fact, from an exhaustive survey of experience ; and secondly deductively, as a necessary consequence from established psychological and ethical principles.

The empirical survey he regards as essentially a matter of accounts : just as we might proceed to ascertain whether there are more apples or more pears on a given table, so, he says, we must proceed to strike a balance between the amount of pleasure and the amount of pain in the world at a given time ; and then, comparing successive balance sheets, we shall see which way the world is tending. Here again as with Schopenhauer we notice the failure to distinguish between pleasure and worth : the contented pig is after all better off, it would seem, than the aspiring philosopher, since he suffers less. However, leaving this all-important distinction aside and keeping strictly to the question immediately raised—Is the algebraic sum of pleasure and pain in the world positive or negative ?—we have to ask how this sum is to be worked out. It is not simply a question of counting, as Hartmann's trivial reference to apples and pears assumes, it is a question of measuring. How are we to find the quantity that admits of common measure ? I can think of but one way. "Like brain vibrations," says Hartmann, "call forth in all individuals like sen_ sations." At any rate there is a fundamental continuity in all protoplasm, so that like functions have everywhere like characteristics. Regarded from this side pains are but the subjective concomitant of disturbed function : already the physiologist can frequently estimate the amount of this disturbance, and as knowledge advances physiology will doubtless become more and more a quantitative science. All the pain in the world seems unquestionably correlated to physiological process, of which protoplasm is the common basis. Here then, I say, there does seem to be some chance of working out Hartmann's hedonistic balance sheet. But again from the physiological standpoint it is unquestionable that pain as disturbance of function is abnormal, the exception rather than the rule. Pleasure in general tends to enhance and promote life, pain to diminish and extinguish it. If the abnormal really preponderated, were in fact the normal, the world could hardly have advanced so far. The most hopeful method for his purpose then can hardly justify the conclusion to which Hartmann professes to be led.

But he preferred to work from the subjective standpoint: here, however, he acknowledges two undeniable difficulties. Let us see how he meets them. First, the estimate of the pure pleasure-pain total of two subjective states is more uncertain the more diverse they are. Accordingly he proposes 'as far as possible' to leave such comparisons aside and to be content with 'a special balance' for each class of feelings separately. "If now," he winds up by saying, "it turns out that every one of these classes apart yields a negative result, all need for an estimation of one against the other is entirely avoided: *since* all the negative special results simply add up to a negative total." *If* all turn out as supposed this is beautifully simple, of course: there seems no need even to add; and, by the way, adding is still impossible without a common unit. But then, so far as I can learn, neither Hartmann nor anyone else has ever so much as attempted to work these special sums[1]. But secondly, there is 'the still greater difficulty' of estimating the sensations of different subjects, one against the other. To avoid this, however, we are told again, is easy : "one strikes the personal balance of his life for every individual, and *since* all come out negative, one has only to add them up to reach the universal world-balance." The preliminary 'if' is here dispensed with and the result straightway assumed. Identifying the supposed solubility of the question with its actual solution in favour of pessimism, Hartmann expresses surprise that empirical pessimism is nevertheless combated so much. But this opposition is partly explicable, he thinks, 'from the psychological motives and the sources of error incident to the working out of each one's own balance[2]!' A good specimen this of that charming *naïveté*, for which Hartmann is unsurpassed. Remembering that Hartmann elsewhere has thought it advisable to "meet the suspicion that his pessimistic proclivities are due to a gloomy personal experience, by means of a pleasant little sketch of his home life, lit up by the presence of a sympathetic wife, of a beautiful engaging boy...and of a few congenial friends[3]," one naturally wonders how far 'psychological motives,' how far the inevitable 'errors' contributed to

---

[1] The superficial character of the summary which Hartmann's disciple, A. Drews, gives of this 'empirical proof' of pessimism is noteworthy. Cf. his *Eduard von Hartmann's philosophisches System im Grundriss*, 2te Ausg., 1906, pp. 320–2.

[2] "Zur Pessimismus-Frage," *Philosophische Monatshefte*, XIX. 79 f. Italics mine. This article is republished in Hartmann's *Philosophische Zeitfragen*.

[3] Sully, *Pessimism*, 1st edn, p. 114.

perturb *his* balance.   At any rate he provides himself
with an interesting dilemma.

We may now inquire whether Hartmann is more
convincing when he attempts to deduce pessimism
from psychological principles.   Here he is substantially
at one with Schopenhauer and we may deal with both
together.   Both alike on the one hand confound all
psychical activity with will and on the other identify
will exclusively with desire.   In the first sense both
presentation and feeling would presuppose will, since
they both imply psychical activity or life.   But the
converse would be true when will is restricted to the
narrower sense of desire.   Desire does not merely give
rise to feeling; it also presupposes it; we do not want
and then feel pain, but rather feel pain and then and
there want its removal.   Further and more important—
so far as feeling is antecedent to pursuit—there may
be pleasurable feelings which cannot be what Schopenhauer called negative, the mere filling up of a want, for
they may come without our striving and be wholly
unforeseen.   We do not need to cite only such rare
cases of good fortune as unexpected legacies or sudden
unearned increments : there are few lives without any
agreeable disappointments, any halcyon days, golden
opportunities, or runs of luck.   It is not only the lilies
of the field that are clothed, though they toil not neither
do they spin.   Finally—and as the fundamental fact
in the whole matter—spontaneity and an unimpeded
energy, that is for a time at least self-sustaining, are
sources of pleasure and well-being to most creatures
during a large part of their lives, quite apart from desire
or antecedent pain.   In a word absolute privation, like

absolute negation, is unthinkable : the world cannot begin in utter bankruptcy without any assets. Hartmann's initial state of the Absolute as *empty* will is the most glaring contradiction of a writer who has perpetrated more absurdities than any other writer of repute that I know. How, it has been often asked, can the Absolute lack anything ? And how too, we may add, can the finite Many, if parts of the Absolute, lack everything ? Only to him that hath can be given : we cannot therefore equate life with privation, resolve all activity into desire or all pleasure into the mere cessation of the pain to which unsatisfied desire gives rise.

But it is not even true that wherever there is desire there is pain. The huntsman, for example, only desires to catch the fox because of the pleasure of the pursuit ; and, in general, we account that man happy who can follow his favourite pursuit ; for "it is not the goal, but the course which makes us happy," as Jean Paul Richter said. Still without 'progressive attainment' there would be no pleasure in pursuit[1] ; and if will were nothing but desire, we should be as much at the mercy of vain desires, as Schopenhauer and von Hartmann suppose. But grown men are not the slaves of endless whimsies, they are not ever crying for the moon like a spoiled child. Again, strictly speaking, to will is not to desire but rather to control desires : its sphere is possible action and its essential characteristic, even according to Schopenhauer, is not want but energy. "We *exist* only as we energise ; *pleasure* is the reflex of unimpeded

---

[1] To have insisted on this point, overlooked by Sidgwick, is a merit of Professor Mackenzie's *Manual of Ethics*; cf. ch. vi. Note 1.

energy ; energy is the *means* by which our faculties are
developed ; and a higher energy the *end* which development proposes. In *action* is thus contained the existence,
happiness, improvement and perfection of our being[1]."
These words of Hamilton are but an echo of the teaching of Aristotle, with which the teaching of Kant and
Fichte had much in common. But now it was from
Kant and Fichte that Schopenhauer and von Hartmann
derived their doctrine of the primacy of will, a doctrine
incompatible, as we have seen, with the identification
of will and desire. Unless this identification is true,
the pessimism is groundless, which they rest upon it.
The question of its truth or falsity is one for psychology,
and I can only say that I do not know of a single
psychologist who would uphold it.

In spite of pluming themselves on the inductive
and scientific character of their method, Schopenhauer
and von Hartmann have perhaps surpassed the most
'romantic' of their countrymen in the wildness of their
metaphysical speculations : here, if anywhere, we have
mysticism and mythology *in excelsis*. And it is in
these metaphysical speculations that their identification
of will with blind desire, and the consequent complete
separation between will and idea, work out their own
refutation. Let error but develop *à outrance* and it
explodes itself. This truth, which, as we shall see, is
for Hartmann the golden thread of his pessimism,
applies—as perhaps it ought to do—to his own metaphysics. "If will as such is *blind* how shall it in
willing come by *sight*? If as will it is endless, irrational
impulse, how shall it in willing be other than just as

[1] Sir W. Hamilton, *Discussions on Philosophy*, etc., p. 40.

endless and irrational? How shall what is aimless set
to work to give itself an aim[1]?" These are the questions which Hartmann addresses to Schopenhauer, and
which he rightly enough maintains Schopenhauer did
not and could not answer.

Let us see how he answers them himself. Schopenhauer, he says, failed to reach the rational; Hegel, to
reach the real. By combining the *Panthelismus* of
the one with the *Panlogismus* of the other, Hartmann
claims to have corrected the one-sidedness of both;
and thus, in place of an Absolute that is only Will or
only Idea, to reach an Absolute Spirit of which both
will and idea are the attributes. The only objection
he finds to calling this Absolute Spirit God, as Spinoza
did, "lies in the exclusively religious origin" of that
term. Such an all-powerful, all-wise Being could, if
he would, we should suppose, create a world that is
not only the best possible but absolutely good, not a
world, that, though the best possible, is irretrievably
bad. How came Hartmann, who seems to begin by
agreeing so far with the optimist's views concerning
God and the world, nevertheless to end by siding with
the pessimist? Unlike Leibniz and theists generally,
Hartmann, as is fitting in a romantic philosopher,
starts his philosophy not with a theology but with a
theogony. Here we shall find the answer to our questions. Before time was—filled time that is to say—
Thought or the Idea in the Absolute was only '*latent*'
and could not of itself pass over into actual existence,
and Will was only potential, had only the *capacity*

---

[1] "Ueber die nothwendige Umbildung der Schopenhauerschen
Philosophie," *Philosophische Monatshefte*, 1867, II. p. 465.

of willing or not willing 'according to circumstances.'
How there can be circumstances where there is no
actual being we will not stop to inquire. Actual
willing requires a content and this only the Idea can
give—the *sine qua non* of actual willing thus lies outside
of the Will as such. But in that case how with only
pure latency on the one side and only pure potentiality
on the other did actual willing ever arise? A single bare
possibility cannot advance to reality, how is the case
mended if there are two?

Here is the Achilles' heel of all Absolutist speculation as it appears in the speculation of Hartmann. The
jump into existence that he denies to Hegel's Idea is,
he thinks, less of a jump in the case of Will, to which,
after all, 'initiative' essentially belongs. Between the
state of rest—and blessedness—of the mere potentiality
to will or not and actual, determinate, willing with a content, there comes 'empty willing,' the mere initiative
of willing to will—a state of "absolute unblessedness,
torment without pleasure and without pause." And
now, since Will and Idea are both but attributes of
the same Absolute Spirit, the Idea cannot for a
moment withhold itself or escape when the empty
Will lays violent hands upon it. But if the empty
Will can thus secure its object the instant the impulse
arises, why lay stress on its ceaseless and infinite pain,
what ground is there for extending pessimism even to
the Absolute? It is in answer to this question that
Schopenhauer speaks through Hartmann. Will is
everywhere infinite, so it is necessarily insatiable;
since a completed infinite is logically impossible, is
a content therefore that the Idea cannot supply. Let

the world be never so good, and it is the best possible,
yet beyond the world, for God himself, there is only
absolute pain and unblessedness. This can only cease
when the willing to will itself ceases.

It is God then who more even than the world
needs deliverance from evil. Even granting, as
Hartmann maintains, that this willing to will on the
part of the Absolute was a piece of absolute stupidity—
and if stupid at all, we must perhaps assume that the
Absolute is absolutely stupid—still, since it is just as
truly absolutely wise[1], will it then not at once retrieve
the blunder ? At least it *will* retrieve it, Hartmann
assures us. But how often do we find that a momentary
folly on the part of one person takes another years to
undo ! The Absolute is in a like predicament : the
whole world must run its course before the divine fall
can be redeemed and the blind aimless will cease from
troubling and be again at rest. This purely negative
outcome is the supreme goal of the world as a realm
of ends. But " how shall what is aimless set to work to
give itself an end?" was, as we have seen, the question
Hartmann proposed to Schopenhauer.

And now at length we reach his own answer: Were
the Absolute only Will the thing would be impossible ;
but it is also Idea and as such provides the end. Like
Hegel he believes in the 'absolute cunning of reason.'
The Idea is powerless to resist the sort of rape, which
he supposes the will to perpetrate, but it takes care

---

[1] The remark that used to be made of Charles II., "he never
said a foolish thing and never did a wise one," seems true also
of the Absolute, according to Hartmann. As Will it is absolutely
stupid, as Idea absolutely wise.

that at least the offspring shall be such as to put a term to the paternal folly. For though "the world gets its 'that' from the father, its 'what' and 'how' come from its mother" says Hartmann, adopting an old conceit of Goethe's, which Schopenhauer professed to explain[1]. It does not concern us now to examine in detail this process of deliverance from evil, 'evolutional optimism' as Hartmann had the effrontery to call it: enough to note that its one essential feature is the evolution of self-conscious beings whose wills are *not* blind and aimless. These, as they advance in intelligence, must realise more and more distinctly the irrationality of the positive will to be, and—as negative will not to be—must finally suppress it. Hartmann is frank enough to confess that no apocalyptic vision of the final scene has been vouchsafed him; so he can only vaguely conjecture under what conditions it would even be possible[2]. One preliminary, however, is certain: the world must first be reduced to a state of rational despair. From beginning to end suffering has preponderated to an ever increasing extent, God himself or the Absolute Spirit being the greatest sufferer of all. Only through this climax of despair is release possible;

[1] *Philosophie des Unbewussten*, 6te Aus. 1876, p. 796.

[2] Needless to say, the supposed conditions are improbable in the extreme. Hartmann has dilated at length on 'the three stages of illusion' through which the intelligent world must pass before it realises that positive happiness is unattainable. His one remaining consolation, that at least the world can then will itself out of existence, has been aptly called by a rival pessimist, Bahnsen, 'the fourth stage of illusion.' But for Hartmann, who begins by setting aside the first half of the old ontological maxim, *Ex nihilo nihil*, there can be no difficulty in setting aside the second, *In nihilum nil posse reverti*.

and the world with this as its goal was devised by the divine Wisdom as the one means of effecting its own deliverance.

And when the end comes, what then ? The will of the Absolute is reduced again to the state of pure potentiality to be sure, but it has learnt nothing ; for it is altogether devoid of intelligence. It may then instantly repeat its former *faux pas* : also it may not. In place of the existing certainty of evil, there will be an even chance of its non-recurrence ; and this, says Hartmann, is " a gain not to be despised." When a cheerful medieval sinner was being borne away by the devil at the end of his earthly career, he is said to have exclaimed :

> Even so, of course, it might have been yet worse:
> For, though now, as you see, he's carrying me,
> An it pleased old Harry, I'd had him to carry.

An optimist of this sort was the pessimist, Eduard von Hartmann.

It is but a step from the sublime to the ridiculous ; and this pessimism would certainly strike the stoutest heart with terror if it did not at once strike every sane mind as nonsensical. The very superfluity of its naughtiness embarrasses the critic. But one point at least stands out clear : the supposed *faux pas* of the Absolute is simply Hartmann's own *faux pas* ; and, as I hinted at the outset, the one like the other is its own undoing Hartmann has *not* synthesized Hegel's Absolute with Schopenhauer's : he has simply set them over against each other in irreconcilable conflict, so soon and so long as they are at all. Only while they are bare possibilities and actually nothing can they be said to agree. Anyone, to whom it does not seem meaningless, may regard them in this non-existent state as 'subsisting' in a single substance, but the moment they exist their incompatibility makes any real unity impossible, to say nothing of unity in one and the same spirit. The subtlest modal distinction or *secundum quid* will not avail to bring contradictories into simple unity, least of all the unity of an absolute Spirit who may be called God. Hartmann's God *qua* willing and absolutely irrational and his God *qua* thinking and absolutely rational may be two Gods perhaps, or God and something else; but one God simply it cannot be. Instead of *le Dieu méchant* of Manichaeism, what Hartmann gives us, as Secrétan happily put it[1], is the still greater absurdity of *un Dieu bête*. The dualism into which he is driven in spite of himself comes out clearly in the fine ethical appeal that he makes to us to sympathize and co-operate with God in effecting his redemption and our own. But surely we cannot sympathize with a God who is the source of all evil; certainly we cannot cooperate with such a God. Moreover Hartmann makes a point of maintaining that for the existence of the world a "God as such" is not responsible: in this, he says, lies the superiority of his philosophy over that of the ordinary theist. That a mind daring—or shall we say, rash—enough to start from nothing or the other side of being and show how God came to be could not manage to reach a better theogony is surprising. Nevertheless Hartmann maintains that his speculation has a scientific basis. The truth is that

---

[1] *Revue philosophique*, 1883, xv. 395.

it rests on the bad psychology of will which he inherited from his master, Schopenhauer; and, as I have said, in developing that error *à outrance* he has furnished the most telling refutation of their common pessimism : he has imitated his Absolute's suicide, as Bradley would say.

The odd thing is that almost at the close of his chief work Hartmann explicitly recognises the truth that he began by implicitly denying. " There is no doubt," he says, " that a *particular* volition in man..... can be suppressed by the influence of conscious reason," not indeed directly but by the suggestion of counter motives[1]. And without this truth, as he expressly allows, his whole scheme of redemption would become quite impossible. But *all* volition is particular volition : volition of nothing in particular or empty volition is surely a veritable chimaera. If the imperfect reason of man can sometimes control the will, why should this never be possible for the all-perfect reason of God ? Because God is the Unconscious, perhaps one might expect Hartmann to reply. But no, God is omniscient, possessed of an intellectual intuition equivalent to an absolute clairvoyance not only of this world and all that is therein but of all possible worlds besides. *Only* to differentiate this ' Over-consciousness ' from all such consciousness as we can conceive is the term ' the Unconscious ' ' temporally ' applied to it. It is the absolute Initiative of the primordial Will that prevents the divine Reason from influencing it. The fateful deed is done before that Reason emerges from its pristine latency. By what good fortune then, we may ask, does this Will, ' unenlightened by a single

[1] *Op. cit.*, p. 768.

ray of rational intelligence' out of all the possible worlds lying latent in the Idea, realise precisely that one that is the best? This is substantially the question already mentioned, which Hartmann addressed in vain to Schopenhauer, and it now becomes clear that he can give no satisfactory answer to it himself. The fact that there is a world at all he attributes, as we have seen, to absolute chance. The fact that it is the best possible can have for him no better ground, so long as he refuses to extend to reason that influence over will in the creation of the world, which he allows is essential to its evolution when created. In a word intellectual intuition and a blind will cannot be conjoined. Again as severally but possibilities they can effect nothing. It is an error long since exploded that bare possibilities can precede all actuality. So then there is no *empty* will; and no will with a content can be called blind. Thus we are entitled to conclude that, while their empirical pessimism is not proven, the so-called 'metaphysical pessimism' of Schopenhauer and Hartmann has no basis in experience and is but a bad dream.

LECTURE XVI.

THE PROBLEM OF EVIL AND OPTIMISM.

The two leading systems of pessimism, which on account of their wide vogue, seemed to challenge our attention, deserve—most of you, I think, will allow—the title of irrational philosophies, which Windelband, a very fair and able historian of philosophy, has recently assigned to the chief of them. We may, then, now turn from these to consider whether other and less sweeping indictments against the constitution of the universe can be better sustained.

First of all it is especially important, not only as bearing on our present problem, but also for the sake of our whole discussion, to examine the dogma, already referred to as the basis of optimism and pessimism alike—the dogma, I mean, that an ideally perfect world would be one in which from first to last, permanently and universally, there was unmixed happiness; in which physical and moral evil were alike unknown. But only if complete happiness were the sole end of the world would its continuous and universal presence prove that the world was perfect; and perfect simply because of that. Here then there is a manifest assumption, for if happiness *per se* were the one supreme good, any conduct that conduced to it would be so far

justified and would be otherwise without any justification.   The only standard of right would be the hedonistic one.   That happiness is involved as a positive
constituent of the supreme end, only the thorough-
going pessimist would have the hardihood to deny.
But that happiness *per se* is not the end as such,
hedonists themselves unwittingly allow in accepting
what Sidgwick called the 'fundamental paradox of
hedonism.'   "The impulse towards pleasure, if too
predominant, defeats its own aim," he says[1].   Pleasure
may come unsought but to get it we must forget it.
But now by 'aim' or end in this connexion—practical
end, that is to say—we mean something that we *aim*
at, that we actively strive to accomplish, the consummation of some definite purpose towards which we
direct our efforts.   Hence the literal meaning of sin
as ἁμαρτία or missing the mark, on which theologians
love to dwell.   Grant that pleasure is not the mark,
but only the satisfaction felt on attaining it, and there
is no paradox; but insist that pleasure is verily what
we aim at, then to maintain that we are not to aim at
what we are all the while really aiming at is surely
something more than a paradox.

Clearly too in that case, as Sidgwick somewhat
naïvely observes, "if we started with no impulse
except the desire of pleasure, it might seem difficult
to execute the practical paradox of attaining pleasure
by aiming at something else[2]."   It might indeed; but
I think we may go further and say that with such a
complete inversion of the order of nature the difficulty

[1] *Methods of Ethics*, 6th edn, p. 48.
[2] *Op. cit.* p. 137.

would, in fact, prove insuperable. The anticipation of a state of feeling that would be the same, no matter how it was attained, could never give rise to definite acts at all. Thus a subject animated solely by the 'mere desire of pleasure' would never get under weigh ; but such a being is quite inconceivable. For experience, as already said, could never begin from a state of absolute privation, nor with the representation of something in the future while as yet there was nothing definite in the present. Yet Sidgwick was of opinion that "even supposing a man to begin with absolute indifference to everything but his own pleasure, it does not follow that if he were convinced that the possession of other desires and impulses were necessary to the attainment of the greatest possible pleasure, he could not succeed in producing these." Unfortunately Sidgwick makes no attempt even to suggest hypothetically how such a being, who obviously could not be a man, would set about this task[1].

Sidgwick contents himself with saying : " But this supposition is never actually realised. Every man, when he commences the task of systematising his conduct...is conscious of a number of different impulses and tendencies within him, other than the mere desire of pleasure... : so that he has only to place himself under certain external influences, and these desires and impulses will begin to operate without any effort of will[2]." To the biologist or the psychologist

---

[1] Such a being would closely resemble the blind will of Schopenhauer or von Hartmann and doubtless would end by being a pessimist. Indeed we may say that it was the underlying hedonism of Schopenhauer and von Hartmann that led to their pessimism.

[2] *Op. cit.* p. 137.

even this statement must sound like a parody of the real facts of life. A mere aggregate of organs does not make an organism, nor does a number of merely different functions or impulses make life. Again a living being does not first exist aloof from its environment and then 'have to place itself under external influences' in order that its life may begin. When a man 'commences the task of systematising his conduct on principle' he is already a definite individual, already organically related to a definite environment : in a word his life is already a 'system,' so that in advancing from the natural plane of behaviour to the rational he only develops further what is already there. There is meaning and system in his behaviour at both levels : can we then suppose that there is no sort of connexion or continuity between the two ? And if there is any connexion or continuity between them how can the psychological character of their ends be fundamentally distinct ? This is a point that it will repay us to consider a little more closely.

Since the publication of Butler's famous sermons on *Human Nature*, if not before, our moralists have admitted what rightly understood is indisputable, viz., that on the lower plane of animal life, the various springs of action are severally 'extra-regarding or disinterested' and in a sense, 'blind'; but that in proportion as a 'self-regarding and interested' spring of action develops, controlling these—such as self-love so-called—a higher level of life is attained, one characterised by rational insight and unity of purpose. The implication is that whereas those various 'propensions' are, so to say, automatic and spontaneous, self-love is autonomous and deliberate: *they* suggest a sentient organism, *this* presupposes a controlling and self-conscious mind.   But the terminology employed is apt to mislead.   On the one side we have a number of extra-regarding, blind, and mutually indifferent impulses; on the other a single self-regarding, foreseeing, and interested person: on the one side, objective ends without a self; on the other, a self without any objective end. Now surely in all this there is too much antithesis, the contrasts are too extreme; so that not only the *advance* from the one level to the other, which nowadays at any rate is conceded, becomes altogether inexplicable, but both as *they stand* are beset with contradictions.

We may see this best by starting from the higher. The end of self-love is said to be happiness, a continuous subjective state of pleasant feeling.   But the self that we love is presumably the self that we know, and that certainly does not live by feeling alone.   Nor is it absolutely identical with the self that loves, in such wise that—disregarding grammar—we might say I love I, or—concealing the breach of grammatical concord—John loves John.   Here, as elsewhere, out of barren identities nothing can come.   The self that I love, that is the self that I know, is *my* self holding intercourse, having reciprocal relations, with a community of *other* selves and with an environment to an indefinite extent resolvable into selves.   So essential are these relations of other selves to my self, of the objective to the subjective, that without them not only would the all-important possessive 'my' disappear for lack of its correlatives, but the possessing I too would become as meaningless as the centre of a circle that had no circumference. With no 'content' to be conscious of, it could know nothing, feel nothing, and do nothing: such a bare I would thus be worth nothing. Consciousness or experience then is not purely subjective, is not simply a state. It implies also an objective factor, that is certain; and it implies further the reciprocal interaction of subject and object, self and not-self.

But till one's knowledge of others has advanced some way self-consciousness, the knowledge of one's self, cannot begin. Definite objective knowledge in turn arises only along with definite subjective interests, so that apart from such interests there would be no knowledge of self and so no interest in self, such as self-love or the desire of one's own happiness assumes. Briefly then, self-consciousness or knowledge of self presupposes consciousness or knowledge of objects, and this again presupposes interests in objects. We may call such interests extra-regarding not self-regarding, so far as they are distinct from the interest in self. But here two points are important. First, interest in self is secondary and presupposes these primary interests; alone it would be empty and meaningless. Secondly, as interests *of* the self, without which there could be no interest *in* self, these primary interests cannot be called disinterested in the literal sense of unselfish: interests without a self would again be a manifest contradiction. They are then the interests of a self, though a self as yet without knowledge of itself, and so without any reflex interest in itself, in other words, without any self-conscious interest

in its interests. These primary interests or ends
are objective, but not in the sense in which the end
of a watch—to use Butler's illustration—is objective ; they are not merely the ends of another, they
are the ends of a conscious self. So then the end of
the *self*-conscious self in controlling and extending
these objective ends must obviously be itself objective
too. In fact a subjective end without an object and
an objective end without a subject are both alike contradictory. The psychological character of all possible
ends of conduct is then fundamentally the same, and
so the advance from the lower or natural plane to the
higher or the rational is conceivable. But, and this
for us now is the main point, *in neither is pleasure ever
itself the end,* but always simply the satisfaction consequent on the accomplishment of ends[1].

Nevertheless, the hedonist will reply, it is obvious
that we must distinguish between means and ends ;
and since the attainment of all objective ends would
be worthless without happiness it is obvious too that
this alone is intrinsically desirable, that this subjective

---

[1] At first blush it seems conceivable that at any rate a self-
conscious being could adopt pleasure as his end, and the ideal
voluptuary is supposed to be such a being. In him, as Mr Bradley
has said, "the feeling of self-realisation is the end, which calls for
reality, without respect for anything in which the self is to be
realised, except as a means. It is not necessary to say," he continues,
"that the abstract feeling of satisfaction, as an end, contradicts the
very notion of an end and must fail to satisfy ; nor is it necessary to
add that the voluptuary as the man who consistently pursues that
end, is an impossible character" (*Ethical Studies*, p. 245). Such an
abnormality certainly could not be called a rational being nor could
a society of such hold itself together. History affords proof enough
of that.

end is the only ultimate end, in relation to which the so-called objective ends are in reality only means. Let us examine the following important passage from Sidgwick's *Methods of Ethics*, in which this position is clearly stated. "It may be said that...we may take 'conscious life' in a wide sense, so as to include the objective relations of the conscious being...and that from this point of view we may regard ['Virtue, Truth, Beauty, Freedom'] as in some measure preferable alternatives to Pleasure or Happiness...." But Sidgwick continues: "to me at least it seems clear after reflection that these objective relations of the conscious subject, when distinguished from the consciousness accompanying and resulting from them, are not ultimately and intrinsically desirable...that, when (to use Butler's phrase) we 'sit down in a cool hour' we can only justify to ourselves the importance that we attach to any of these objects by considering its conduciveness, in one way or another, to the happiness of sentient beings[1]." Now, first of all, is there not here a radical confusion—one to which we are all too prone —the confusion, I mean, between analytical distinction and actual separation? To say that "we may take conscious life in a wide sense as including objective relations" implies that we may also take it in a narrow sense as excluding these. But the psychologist assuredly has no such choice: he must take what he always finds. No reflexion will enable him to take the consciousness *accompanying or resulting from* objective relations apart from these relations themselves; for there is no consciousness, or as we had

---

[1] *Methods of Ethics*, 6th edn, pp. 400 f.

better say, no experience, unless these form an integral part of it.   It is clear, from the context, I allow, that what Sidgwick here meant by consciousness was pleasure (or pain).   But it is equally clear that feeling alone, a purely subjective state, though always an element in consciousness or experience, is never the whole of it.   We cannot then talk of pleasure or happiness or, to speak generally, of pure feeling as in any measure an *alternative* to the cognitions or actions from which it is inseparable.   And yet Sidgwick not only admits this inseparability, but even urges that " if we finally decide that ultimate good includes many things distinct from Happiness[1]," hedonism becomes ' entangled in a vicious circle.'   But if the inseparability be admitted, how is that decision to be avoided ?

Why then does he still argue as if pleasure by itself could be a subjective end and the only ultimate end ?   Regardless of the fact already insisted upon, that a purely subjective end is a psychological contradiction, Sidgwick's main contention, we shall be told, is not that pleasure is a ' thing' we can experience apart from ' things' which are pleasant, but that these other ' things' are only means to it.   But this we remark in the second place is like saying, to use a trivial illustration of Mill's, that one of the blades of a pair of scissors is a means to enable the other blade to cut : it is to ignore that subject and object are both essential to all conscious life, desirable or undesirable. If one is a means then the other must be a means too, and as cutting is the end of a pair of scissors so

[1] *Op. cit.* 1st edn, p. 376

happiness becomes the end for the sake of which subject and object alike are only means: the pure feeling of pleasure, though a state of one of them, is the ultimate *raison d'être* of both[1]. All that matters is the capacity for pleasure in the one and the fitness to produce it in the other. Maximum pleasure being the end of the world, it would seemingly be indifferent whether the number of conscious individuals were increased and their capacity *pro tanto* diminished, or *vice versa*: in any case the attainment of the end would be the solution of the quantitative problem :—The greatest possible sum of pleasure wanted : how is it to be got[2]? When all the objective interests of life are emptied out of it as only means and not meaning, this is the one question that remains.

[1] But Sidgwick used a different illustration, which he doubtless thought more apposite. Green's contention that "pleasure as feeling in distinction from its conditions, which are not feelings, cannot be conceived" (Hume, vol. II. p. 7) he said "is neither more nor less true than the statement that an angle cannot be conceived apart from its sides" (*Mind*, O.S., II. p. 36). He then proceeds to urge that this does not hinder us from comparing one angle with another without comparing their sides. But surely as regards the main contention this is irrelevant. The pursuit of an end may be aptly enough represented by the direction of a line, but without ends we have no lines and therefore no angles. Again, whereas directed lines enclose an angle of definite magnitude, this as purely quantitative can never determine definitely directed lines, two pairs of lines, though oppositely directed, having *e.g.* the same angle. How then can maximum angle, if it have any meaning, be the end?

[2] Cf. Sidgwick, *op. cit.*, 6th edn, p. 415: "The point up to which, on utilitarian principles, population ought to be encouraged to increase, is ...... that at which the product formed by multiplying the number of persons living into the amount of average happiness reaches its maximum."

But now we may regard life as a series of processes, and in these, as in all processes, the mere means either disappear and are left behind as the process advances; or they become so far worthless when the process is complete and its end attained. Moreover there is no ultimate advantage in means as such, and in fact we always seek to shorten and simplify such intermediaries as much as we can. But that the objective interests of life are not means in this sense is conclusively shown in parasitism, where many of them are dispensed with, *but where too degeneration invariably* follows. The literal meaning of *happy* in our own language and of its equivalents in others—as, for example, εὐδαίμων, *felix, glücklich, heureux*—more or less distinctly implies the favour of fortune but contains not a hint of successful striving. That the favourites of fortune often show the degeneracy of parasites is proverbial. Far fuller is the life of self-reliant effort for the worthiest ends, and far fuller too the blessedness and content that crown its achievements. The thoughtless may envy the easy life of the favourites of fortune, but this is not the life that wise men praise. A world in which unalloyed pleasure was meted out to every sentient being would then be very like a world of parasites and so far from being the best of worlds would, because of its inevitable vapidity, *ennui* and unprogressiveness, be almost the worst—a contradiction, of course, and yet, so far as we can see, a necessary consequence. But this only serves to show that such a world is not possible at all.

We can now move on a stage. If this conclusion is sound, it follows that much at any rate that we call evil is only relatively such. The term evil in such cases is, in fact, ambiguous ; since what is in one sense an evil is in another sense a good. "The world (it has been said) is, what for an active being it must be, full of hindrances[1]." Invincible obstacles that barred all progress would indeed be absolute evils, but not so the hindrances that can be overcome, for only in surmounting such is solid advance possible. As to these, it has been said again, a man may "bless God for the law of growth with all the fighting it imposes upon him," evil in this sense, "*i.e.* what it is man's duty to fight, being one of the major perfections of the Universe[2]." Again, in another way this relativity of many so-called evils is apparent : in relation to the past, as marking progress, they are really good ; only in view of future progress which they may delay do they become evil. So far it is true to convert the French proverb and say *Le bien est l'ennemi du mieux*: not only true but truer, so surely as progress is better than stagnation. "If a man has not wants, he will make no efforts," says Professor Sorley, "and if he make no efforts his condition can never be bettered. Thus social reformers have often found that the classes they have tried to elevate did not feel the evil of their lot as their benefactors saw it ; and they have had to create the consciousness of wants before attempting to satisfy them[3]." The new position we reach then is, that a world whose fundamental characteristic—now at any rate—is

---

[1] Vauvenargues, quoted by Eucken, *Geistige Strömungen der Gegenwart*, 4te Aus. p. 288.

[2] C. S. Peirce, *Hibbert Journal*, VII. p. 107.

[3] *Ethics of Naturalism*, 2nd edn, p. 250.

evolution cannot at any given stage of its development have that perfection towards which it is still only moving, which it can only have by acquiring. It is childish and futile to ask if the world might not have been created perfect at once; to question whether an evolving world is the best. We cannot form the dimmest idea of what experience in a 'ready-made' world would mean, if experience, as I have ventured elsewhere to define it, is the process of becoming expert by experiment. So far as we can judge, a world perfect—in the sense of finished and complete at once—is a contradiction.

But at any rate the question may be raised whether the sort of evolution that we observe in this world is ideally the best. Granted that in an evolving world there will be the imperfection or incompleteness that all becoming implies, need there be besides such positive defects as physical suffering, error and sin? As we have first the blade, then the ear, then the full corn in the ear and can conceive each to be faultless, can it be impossible to conceive the development of a world in like manner? And if that is not impossible, how can this world with its manifold physical, intellectual and moral defects be the best? This objection we must now in the next place endeavour to meet.

The term evolution we have found used in two senses; in the strict sense, for the gradual unfolding of what is implicitly present from the first, and again in a looser sense for what is better called epigenesis or the continuous creation of what is essentially new. The initial possibilities would in the one case virtually include the actual course of the process throughout the future, in the other they would only exclude indefinite abstract possibilities as not compossible, to use Leibniz's phrase, that is to say, as actually impossible. In both cases certain possibilities would give place to actualities as the evolution advanced ; but in the latter new possibilities would continually arise, in the former they would not. In the one there would be from the first a unity and harmony which in the other were only eventually achieved. The one would be what William James called a block universe, the other what he called a multiverse, or better perhaps a uni-multiverse. In a word, the concept of the world in the former case is that of a dialectical development of one Supreme Idea, such as Hegel essayed to delineate.

In the earlier part of these lectures I endeavoured to establish two points, first that the transition from such a purely ideal process to the historical world is inconceivable, as Hegel in spite of himself made clear ; and secondly, that from the point of view of the Idea or Absolute, such transition would be superfluous[1]. I must content myself by assuming that these points are established ; as also a third, reached in the present part, viz. that setting out from where we are, from the standpoint of the Many, we have no ground for assuming a Creator who does everything but only a Creator whose creatures create in turn. The real world must be the joint result of God and man (including under this term other finite intelligences both higher and lower in the scale), unless we are to deny the reality of that in us which leads us to the idea of God at all. The evolution of such a world then

---

[1] Cf. Lectt. II. VII.

plainly cannot be a case of evolution in the first sense. But if not, then where the Many have some initiative, —where development is epigenetic—contingency and conflict, fallibility and peccability seem inevitable; and these are at any rate relative evils, for they assuredly entail suffering.

Even so, it will be asked again, can anyone pretend that he sees no unnecessary suffering in a world like this, where storms devastate and plagues strike ; where ignorance consigns the noblest to exile, to torture and to death ; where vice lapped in luxury grinds down the poor and from its own crimes argues that there can be no God? In attempting to deal with the serious difficulty here raised it will be best to consider physical and moral evil apart[1]. Now if—to begin with the former— we were challenged to show directly that certain definite physical ills—fever germs or 'malignant' tumours, say— have somehow their requisite place in the world's eco- nomy, we certainly should be most presumptuous and unwise to take up the gage. But we may at least contend that on the other hand we are equally incom- petent to show conclusively that any assigned physical cause of suffering is really superfluous.

But then at once we find ourselves confronted with an old objection. The notion of any evil as unavoid- able, we shall be told, involves the contradiction of a non-omnipotent, or finite, God, and is, therefore, not theistic but atheistic. *Omnipotent*, I fear, is one of those question-begging epithets that everybody uses

---

[1] Intellectual evil, or error, may be practically regarded as belong- ing partly to the one partly to the other.

354 The Problem of Evil and Optimism

and nobody defines[1]. Thus it is not uncommonly taken
to imply not merely the power to do whatever it is
possible to do, but also the power arbitrarily to determine
what shall be possible; nay even that the impossible
shall be possible; in short that omnipotence absolutely
excludes impossibility. Thus we find Schopenhauer
saying:—"Even if Leibniz's demonstration, that among
the *possible* worlds this one is the best, were correct:
yet still it would not amount to a theodicy. For in
truth the Creator is the author not merely of the world
but of possibility too: he ought accordingly to have
devised this in such a way as to admit of a better
world[2]." Metaphysic of this sort is not to be met by
argument. It is sufficient to remark that at any rate
so long as there is no difference between possible and
impossible so long omnipotence can have no meaning:
two and two may be four or it may be five. Within
this mystical region, where 'naught is everything and
everything is naught,' determinate being or thought
or action there can be none. If there were an
omnipotent God he must emerge thence to act at
all and then could only do what is possible; though
what is possible would be determined, of course, by
what he is and only so. To proclaim creation restricted
by determinate possibilities to be an idea derogatory to
the sovereign majesty of God is but blind adulation;

---

[1] In a similar connexion it is interesting to find Mr Bradley
saying:—"I shall be told that the Governor of the Universe is
omnipotent. Perhaps; but as I never could find out what that
means, I can hardly be expected to admit it as true." *Mind*, O. S.
VIII. 259.

[2] *Parerga und Paralipomena*, II. § 157.

for it really amounts to denying that God is himself a definite being at all, is either intellectually or morally consistent. All determination is negation, Spinoza has truly said : to find in this an evil, a so-called metaphysical or logical evil, only shows what ambiguity the term may involve.

From such miscalled evils no world can be free. To take a simple illustration. Our decimal system of numeration has the inconvenience that its radix 10 has only two factors, while 12, the radix of the duodecimal system, has twice as many; and if we had had six fingers on each hand, we should doubtless have taken twelve as our radix and been so far, it is supposed, better off[1]. That in other respects we should not have been worse off is more than we know. Moreover the longer system still has defects—in fact, as many positive defects as the shorter[2]—whilst against its superiority in respect of divisibility may be set its greater complexity. But the point of our illustration is that no system of numeration is possible that shall be in all respects ideally perfect. Without being Pythagoreans and hailing number as 'omnipotent, the principle and guide of divine and human life,' we still cannot doubt, in these days when science calls itself measurement, that many of our so-called 'physical evils' depend ultimately on such miscalled 'metaphysical evil[3].' So far as *they* go at any rate there is no problem.

---

[1] Herbert Spencer regarded this 'evil' as so serious that he left, I understand, the bulk of his property to be expended in combating the decimal system and advocating the duodecimal.

[2] Cf. Herbert Spencer's *Autobiography*, vol. I. p. 531.

[3] Cf. A. Ott, *Le Problème du Mal*, 1888, pp. 153 f.

We come back then to the alleged superfluous physical evils. It is futile to attempt to imagine a world different in *type* from ours. This statement, we assume, cannot be gainsaid and from this we set out. Now the world, as we directly know it, consists as we have seen in a plurality of individuals, whom we may call plastic in so far as they are capable of experience. All of them, again, are intent on self-conservation or betterment. This, however, is not guaranteed to them altogether apart from their own efforts; but it is to be achieved in large measure through these. Even if there be a God he certainly has not made the world what it is to be, but rather endowed it with talents to enable it to work out its own perfection in conjunction with himself. This working out is what we call experience, and experience can never pre-suppose the knowledge or the skill that is only gained by means of it. Where several possibilities are open, a creature acting on its own initiative can only find out the right one by way of trial and often of error. Such error we may say is an evil; but we cannot straightway call it a superfluous, still less an absolute, evil, if it is an inevitable incident of experience as such, and if in general the experience is worth what it costs.

Can we, however, say that in general experience is worth what it costs? it will be urged. But can we say that it is not? we reply: *we* are not arraigning the constitution of the world and therefore it is for those who *are* to make their indictment good. Which way does the presumption lie? This for us is the final question. At this point there is one consideration that may help us. The more all things eventually work together for good the greater our assurance that Goodness is at the root of all. The attainment of such complete and enduring harmony, however, may well entail an exhaustive experience of possibilities as its indispensable condition. First thoughts are rarely the best, and the more haste we make often the worse we speed. The fittest to survive, we are told, appear only as the final outcome of innumerable continuous variations : *Natura non facit saltus.* Herein lies the significance for us of Leibniz's contention that whereas " a machine made by the skill of man is not a machine in each of its parts.... the machines of nature, our living bodies, are still machines in their smallest parts." Such thoroughness must imply slowness and much seemingly useless trouble if the process is to be that of experience and epigenesis. Like impatient children, we can hardly restrain the wish " to see the Supreme Good active in some other way than this which it has itself chosen,... or by some shorter path than the roundabout one " of creation through creatures, which it has itself entered upon[1].

But still there are those other physical evils, such as storms, droughts, earthquakes and the like, that can hardly be regarded as the direct consequence of incipient and imperfect experience. Can it be said that these are not absolute nor even superfluous evils ? In attempting to deal with them we must recall another characteristic of the world's evolution. At any stage in this process the world, we have seen, may be described as being in part comparatively fixed, in part still fluent, in part comparatively stable, in part still

---

[1] Cf. Lotze, *Microcosmus*, Eng. trans. II. p. 727.

developing: at once *natura naturata* and *natura naturans*. That the life and progress of society, all its spontaneity, initiative and individuality, would be ineffective without its conservative elements of stability— habit, custom, law and the like—is obvious. Yet these are not an unmixed good. Habit is ability indeed, but its blindness and fatal facility are proverbial. Custom, which according to Hume is the great guide of human life, Bagehot has called 'the most terrible tyranny ever known among men,' and yet, as again another has said,

> We draw
> Our right from custom: custom is a law
> As high as heaven, as wide as sea or land.

Summum jus, summa injuria is the maxim of equity; and yet injury means injustice.

The dubious character thus attaching to the conservative factors of the social world holds also of the more fundamental routine of what we often speak of apart as the physical world. Here, too, in what are called the conservations of mass and energy we have principles that are at once the indispensable conditions of stable construction, and yet tending always to destruction in so far as they count nothing stable that they can further level down—just as friction, again, renders locomotion possible and yet steadily retards it. All this perhaps may help to account for the world-wide association of matter with evil. How far down within this seemingly fixed mechanism the fluent processes of life extend we do not know; if there are such processes their *tempo*, so to say, is so different from ours that their significance escapes us. But in any case in their comparative fixity, not in their possible secular transformation, lie all their present advantages and disadvantages for us. That the advantages so far exceed the disadvantages is evident from the advances that the world has made, is making, and bids fair long to continue to make. Can we have the one without the other? If not, then the disadvantages are neither absolute evils nor in general superfluous evils: metaphysical or logical evils they may be called. But we may ask again if that means anything more beyond what all individuation seems necessarily to imply?

What we might perhaps call the temporary solidarity of physical good and evil is brought home to us in two ways: first, by the rash attempts that have been frequently made to show how things might have been better; and, secondly, by the ignorant prayers for favourable wind and weather or the like, that religion is supposed to countenance. The foolishness of the latter is obvious, inasmuch as the wind that was 'good' for the ship homeward bound would be bad for that bound outwards, and the weather that hastened the ripening of one farmer's corn might dry up the pasture of another. Such really impious petitions are as senseless as the belief in magic or the demand for perpetual miracles. If they were granted they would put an end to all order and render rational conduct impossible. As to the former—there are diseases indeed that seem to be unmixed evils, to be neither the collateral consequences of what once was good nor the indispensable conditions of any good

to come[1]. Leaving such cases aside it would be hard
to find a single instance in which suggestions for the
better remoulding of the physical world have not been
shown by men wiser than their authors to be only
specifications for a fool's paradise.

But there is yet another difficulty connected with
physical evil that is unquestionably serious, since it
weighs heavily on many earnest minds. The course of
evolution so far has conquered some evils and ame-
liorated others, they allow; but will this progress
continue unabated or will it not one day cease and
evil in its turn gain the ascendency? "The theory
of evolution," Huxley, for example, has said, "encourages no millennial anticipations. If, for millions of
years, our globe has taken the upward road, yet, some
time the summit will be reached and the downward
route will be commenced. The most daring imagination will hardly venture upon the suggestion that the
power and intelligence of man can ever arrest the
procession of the great year[2]." This is the language
of naturalism pure and simple, but if naturalism be
accepted as the ultimate truth of things, it is useless to
talk of a realm of ends at all: if the life of man and all
that it implies are but episodes in what Spencer called
the integration of matter and the dissipation of motion,
then indeed there is no more to be said. But if, as we
have seen reason for doing, we take a wider and deeper
view of evolution and regard this so-called realm of
nature as having itself all its reality and meaning

[1] But often they are the fruits of evil doing and often their
removal is within our power and is more than a negative gain.
[2] Evolution and Ethics, *Collected Essays*, IX. p. 85.

within the one world of living agents, why should we suppose the supreme end of this to be simply its own undoing, or take the meaning of the part to be the stultification of the whole? Only if nature is independent of spirit, and atheism, too, an established certainty, can we, as Huxley does, apply to evolution as a whole the words of Tennyson's *Ulysses* :—

> It may be that the gulfs will wash us down,
> It may be we shall touch the Happy Isles.

If Spirit is supreme, its end must be sure of realisation and the procession of its great year know no decline. Nor, happily, does the doctrine of the dissipation of energy, rightly understood, in any way justify the gloomy forebodings to which its misunderstanding has given rise.

But, while we have allowed that theism is essential before we can be confident that the world will not fail of the end that seems the only clue to its meaning, we have also had to allow that we have no theoretical proof of theism. On the other hand our discussion of the problem of evil has so far, we claim, brought to light nothing that disproves theism and removed much that at the outset appeared to make against it. We have still, however, to consider what is unquestionably the chief count in the whole indictment with which a theodicy has to deal—the fact of moral evil.

LECTURE XVII.

MORAL EVIL AND MORAL ORDER.

"THAT must needs have been glorious the decays of which are so admirable. He that is comely when old and decrepit surely was very beautiful when he was young. An Aristotle was but the rubbish of an Adam, and Athens but the rudiments of Paradise." These famous words of a seventeenth century orator and divine fairly represent the standpoint from which even to-day the question of moral evil is frequently discussed. That our world in its present state should be a hopeless ruin, which nothing short of the intervention of infinite wisdom and goodness could restore, is, it is held, conceivable; but that this world should be what it is as the result of a development on the whole steady and continuous is thought to be quite inconceivable. In short, God, it is said, created man in his own image and "he himself tempteth no man": to account for moral evil then we must, it is supposed, assume that man by his own wilful act has fallen from his high estate.

But why should *all* have sinned and come short of the glory of God? To answer this question the doctrine of original sin is added as a corollary to the doctrine of the fall. The whole human race, past, present, and future, is regarded as involved in one common perdition that is somehow the moral consequence of the action of the first and—as we must believe—the least experienced of its members. Is it not possible to account for the prevalence of moral evil in a way less shocking to ordinary morality than this? But first we may ask, does this account for it? Without still further supplement we find it does not. That a man wiser than the wisest should heed the voice of sense or sophistry is only credible if he is already infected with 'original sin.' Accordingly either a timeless or a prenatal fall has to be assumed; and, finally, the existence of a personal principle of evil in the shape of the devil with his maxim, Evil, be thou my good. In short, such speculations—all alike, be it noted, in ignoring the concept of evolution—fail altogether to explain the existence of moral evil, to say nothing of their inherent improbability : they leave it, as Kant had the candour to admit, an insoluble mystery. We have now then to inquire whether, when we do not ignore evolution, the problem of moral evil still remains equally insoluble.

First of all, if we are to stand by evolution, we shall have to invert Robert South's rhetoric, and rank primeval man a long way behind Aristotle, and his primitive resources a long way behind even the rudiments of Athenian civilisation. Hegel's saying, that Paradise without the so-called fall was—what indeed the word means—just *ein Park für Thiere*, a park for beasts, furnishes a better text for the evolutionist. For the human race, like the human individual, in the course of its development has certainly passed through the brute stage; and the transition from the ignorant 'innocence' of this level of life to 'the knowledge of good and evil' is surely as such a rise rather than a fall. Let us then endeavour to trace the course of this development and see if it is not really an advance.

Moral evil is doubtless essentially selfishness. Yet selfishness has its roots in that instinct of self-preservation, which is called the first law of nature and recognised by moralists of every school as a rational principle of action that arises as soon as self-consciousness is attained. When and how does what is thus, so to say, rooted in right nevertheless become wrong? To love himself a man must know himself, but he can know himself only through knowing other selves: neither self-love nor selfishness then is possible below the social level, as we have already had to remark more than once. With society moral order begins and in society moral evil may arise. Further, as society is based entirely on the mutual dependence and the mutual services of the persons who compose it, the cardinal principle of moral order is justice; and all immorality, whatever else it may be, is injustice. The very words themselves bear witness to this, in so far as *mores* or customs are the origin of law. But already in the gregarious habits of many of the higher animals and in the family life of others we find the unconscious germs of the altruism on which society rests are present along with the instinctive egoism that all life implies. Now at the outset it is obvious that the age of innocence is characterized by acts which have all the objective qualities of moral evil, though no guilt can be imputed to the agents.   When the moth flies into the candle-flame we might regard it as sacrificing its own future welfare for the sake of momentary gratification—behaviour which we should call imprudence, or injustice to self[1], if the moth were a reasonable person. The habits of the cuckoo in ejecting its foster-brothers from the nest and maltreating its foster-parents strike us as revolting instances of injustice and ingratitude; and would indeed be such, if only the cuckoo knew better.   To repeat: it seems, we say, in the first place indisputable that in the evolution of conduct acts objectively wrong are constantly committed before the individual has any consciousness of wrong-doing.   How then, we have to ask in the next place, does this consciousness of wrong-doing arise—or, more generally, under what circumstances does conscience appear ?

Before we can attempt to answer this question we ought, it may be thought, to make clear in what sense we understand such a very complex and ambiguous term as *conscience*.   But happily we are not concerned with all that conscience ever means but only with what it means always.   For one thing, it always means approval or disapproval : conscience always involves a judgment that 'accuses or else excuses.'   Such judgment again is always passed by the person himself upon his own conduct and motives.   It thus implies self-consciousness : without self-consciousness there is no conscience[2].

[1] Cf. Sidgwick, *Methods of Ethics*, 6th edn, p. 381.
[2] Hence the close relationship between the two terms, conscience and consciousness in its original sense of self-consciousness—as we find it say in Locke or Reid—a relationship so close that in French the one word *conscience* is still used for both.

Story of David & Nathan shews that we
are much quicker to realise other peoples
faults than our own : i.e. that we observe others
more easily than we observe ourselves.

366   *Moral Evil and Moral Order*

Finally conscience always implies a standard : only so
is it complete[1]. Our question then amounts to this :
How does the individual come by his standard?

A general answer is at once evident : he acquires
the knowledge of his standard as he acquires the
knowledge of himself—through social intercourse[2].
But we must try to be more specific. In the first
place then we may note that this advance from the
level of mere consciousness to that of self-consciousness is very gradual, so that with the child and the
savage the merely conscious or objective attitude
decidedly preponderates. Accordingly other selves, as
belonging to the objective world, are observed continually and directly, but the experiencing self only
occasionally and reflectively—more or less retrospec-
tively—in the exceptional circumstances that evoke
the subjective attitude. Two consequences follow
from all this : first, the one that we have just noted
—viz. that acts which are objectively selfish will be
constantly committed though there is as yet no consciousness of their selfishness; secondly, that this
objective selfishness will nevertheless be frequently
apparent to others, and will be disapproved. The
story of David and Nathan may serve as an illustration,
if we compare the swiftness of David's condemnation
of another's cupidity with his tardiness to realise his

[1] It is worth remarking that Locke in the first three editions of
his *Essay* defined conscience as "nothing else but our own opinion
of our own actions." In later editions he changed this to "our own
opinion or judgment of the moral rectitude or pravity of our own
actions"—thus explicitly recognising the possession of a standard as
essential.

[2] Cf. above, Lect. VI. pp. 122 ff.

own. To be sure we cannot exonerate David, impulsive though he was, as we exonerate a child or a savage. But that after all only lends point to the instance; for if, where conscience is developed, in the heat of passion such things are still possible, can we do else than suppose that they are indefinitely more possible where conscience has yet to be developed, and also that they are indefinitely more innocent? So then, while still unconscious of our own wrong-doing, we become judges of the wrong-doing of others; and these two positions we continually interchange till at length we find both combined in our own person. Adam Smith in his *Theory of Moral Sentiments* was the first modern writer[1] to deal with our question at all satisfactorily, and the answer may be recapitulated in his words :—" Our first moral criticisms are exercised upon the characters and conduct of other people.... But we soon learn, that other people are equally frank with regard to our own. We become anxious to know how far we deserve their censure or applause.... We begin, upon this account, to examine our own passions and conduct, and to consider how these must appear to them by considering how they would appear to us if in their situation....It is evident that in all such cases, I divide myself, as it were, into two persons : and that I, the examiner and judge, represent a different character from that other I, the person whose character is examined into and judged of[2]." But we may sum

[1] He seems to have been anticipated by Polybius. Cf. Dugald Stewart's Introduction in his edition of Adam Smith's *Theory*, p. xxxi.

[2] *Op. cit.* Part III. ch. I. pp. 163 f.

up our answer still more succinctly in the language of
a later writer, by saying that a man's conscience finds
its first moral standard in 'the voice of his tribal self[1].'

Though this first standard is woefully defective,
still it carries within it the knowledge of moral good
and evil : the knowledge of previously unknown evil
that was already there but is now condemned, though
it be not straightway abandoned ; the knowledge of
previously unknown good that is henceforth approved,
though it be not always pursued. The transition to
this stage from the stage of innocence we find has been
gradual ; and *pari passu* inevitable evil—*as such non-
moral*—has become avoidable evil, evil that is freely
and consciously chosen—and *as such bad.* Is this an
advance? we ask. If the evil, now known, were never
forsaken and the good, now seen to be possible, never
pursued : if the words of Ovid, *Video meliora proboque,
deteriora sequor*, were universally true of all human
deeds, there certainly would be no advance. But that
is not what we find. At any rate what we do not find,
it will be said, is the knowledge of evil without the
commission of it, or the knowledge of good without its
omission ; and it is this fact after all that is the
gravamen of the whole problem. It *is*, no doubt, and
we must presently turn to it. Meanwhile we have
gained something if we have found in the theory of
evolution the means of divesting the problem of two of
the mysteries that have hitherto enshrouded it—the
doctrine of a fall from a state of moral perfection and
the doctrine of original sin. And we may hail it as a

[1] W. K. Clifford, *Lectures and Essays*, 2nd edn, pp. 290—293.

hopeful sign of the times that there are now theologians who have the courage to admit this[1].

But this appeal to evolution, it may be replied, after all only throws the difficulty one step further back. For if the germs of moral evil are present from the first, what is this but to allow of a sort of original sin scarcely less repugnant to our moral ideas than the questionable theological dogma that has been discredited? On the contrary the difference is surely profound. Original sin is described in the Westminster Confession as an "original corruption, whereby we are utterly indisposed...to all good and wholly inclined to all evil." The theory of evolution furnishes no warrant for such innate depravity of disposition. To regard our primary and spontaneous impulses as if they were already the germs of moral evil is to ignore the

---

[1] I will quote one passage in evidence and I quote it the more readily because its author is a friend and former pupil of my own :— "There is thus every reason to believe that the awakening of man's moral sense or sentiment, his discovery of a law by which he came to know sin, was an advance accomplished by a long series of stages. Consequently the origin of sin, like other so-called origins, was also a gradual process rather than an abrupt and inexplicable plunge. The appearance of sin, from this point of view, would not consist in the performance of a deed such as man had never done before, and of whose wickedness, should he commit it, he was previously aware ; it would rather be the continuance in certain practices, or the satisfying of natural impulses, after that they were first discovered to be contrary to a recognised sanction of rank as low as that of tribal custom. The sinfulness of sin would gradually increase from a zero ; and the first sin, if the words have any meaning, instead of being the most heinous and the most momentous in the race's history, would rather be the least significant of all." F. R. Tennant, *The Origin and Propagation of Sin* : Hulsean Lectures, 1902, p. 91.

W. 24

true meaning of 'moral' altogether[1]. Those impulses
constitute the basis alike for moral order and for moral
evil, but they are actually the one as little as the
other.

To identify moral evil with sin defined as enmity to
God is a still graver mistake, and one which has
greatly aggravated the difficulty of reconciling the
existence of moral evil with theism.   But neither
psychology nor the moral and religious development of
humanity, so far as we can trace it, will support such a
doctrine.   According to that doctrine all particular evil
thoughts or deeds are but *indicia* of the breach of the
first and great commandment of love to God.   But love,
like morality, we have found to be possible only when
the stage of social intercourse and self-consciousness is
attained.   Prior to that, man cannot be said consciously
to love even himself ; and till he has learned to love his
" brother, whom he hath seen, how can he love God,
whom he hath not seen ? "   In recent years, since the
importance of the historical method has been recognised,
an enormous mass of facts concerning primitive religion
and morality has been collected, but we are still sadly
lacking in insight into their true meaning and connexion.   In the earlier phases of its development
religion doubtless powerfully reinforced the sanctions
of the existing morality, but on the other hand probably
morality at first did more to elevate religion than
religion did to elevate morality.   Under the influence
of the higher religions however morality has unquestionably gained in what we may call inwardness as well as

[1] Cf. Tennant, *op. cit.* on "The ambiguous usage of the term
'Sin' and its derivatives," pp. 160 ff.

in authority[1]. Hence the deep sense of sin that is characteristic of the *awakened* Christian conscience. Sin, in fact, as Mr Hobhouse has well said, " borrows something of the infinitude of the Being against whom it offends and [so] puts a measureless gulf between Him and the sinner." Consciousness of sin cannot then be the first stage of moral evil. On the contrary just as morality is an advance upon the animal level, which as such cannot be called immoral, so this sense of sin is an advance upon the level of mere immorality, which as such cannot be described as one of enmity or estrangement between man and God. On the merely moral level self-righteousness is possible, on the higher religious level it is not : hence " there is joy in heaven over one sinner that repenteth more than over ninety and nine righteous persons that need no repentance." For such repentance is a new birth into a higher life ; but it is not deliverance from innate depravity : it is truly an advance on all that existed before, not a restoration of pristine innocence.

Here however let us return to the main question just now mentioned. Granted, it is urged, that the attainment of a knowledge of good and evil is an advance, why need all further advance be interrupted by lapses? The lapses in question consist in what we ordinarily call yielding to temptation, as in the fall our first parents are said to have yielded. The average child or man does not yield to every temptation, but only to some, while others are resisted. We can, it is thought, imagine an individual never exposed to temptations too strong to be overcome, and yet liable

---

[1] Cf. Matt. v. 27, 33, 43 ; vi. 1, 2, 16.

to temptations of ever increasing strength as his own moral strength increased ; just as a pine may tower a hundred feet above the plain with its leading bud still intact, if the strains it has to bear, though growing —and growing, because of its growth—never reach the breaking point.   Why is the world such that moral characters don't grow in this manner?   A wise parent, it is said, can do much to protect his child from excessive temptation ; and God, if he would, could surely do much more, could in fact do all that is needed. But that parents in this respect can be over-wise is proverbial : for 'fugitive and cloistered virtue' proves but a feeble and imperfect thing compared with the virtue that 'sallies forth and sees her adversary.' Young Washington turned out a better man through being entrusted with that famous hatchet than he would have done if kept out of the mischief into which it led him.   The leading bud of the forest-giant is in the end no greater than it was when the tree started as a sapling, nor is moral strength to be increased by cockering, though habits objectively good may grow apace as long as the conditions are favourable.   In short, reflexion, I believe, will convince us that a world in which the possibility of wrong-doing was prevented by the exclusion of all temptations that were really such, could neither be nor become a moral world at all.

"Call it a non-moral world then, if you choose," some will say ; "at all events it would be a better world than this which presumably you call moral."   So Huxley : "I protest," he said, "that if some great Power would agree to make me think always what is

'posse non peccare' r 'non posse peccare.'

true and do what is right on condition of being turned
into a sort of clock...I should instantly close with the
bargain. The only freedom I care about is the freedom
to do right; the freedom to do wrong I am ready to
part with on the cheapest terms to any one who will
take it of me[1]." But freedom and clockwork, freedom
and yet no choice; clockwork and experience, absolute
routine and yet continuous progress in self-knowledge
and self-control, are not these flagrant contradictions?
That imaginary non-moral world would indeed be a
perfect world of its kind; but it would be only a world
of automata between which complete harmony had
been pre-established. This actual world of ours can
lay no claim to such perfection; it has still to work out
its own salvation. But it is certainly a moral world,
for it acknowledges the authority of conscience even
when it disobeys: conscience is ever a power in it
working for the righteousness, in which alone the world
finds its own meaning and its supreme ideal. A world
entirely in leading strings may realise *an* ideal, but it
can have *no* ideal that is truly its own, no moral ideal.

Which now is the better world? In asking this
question we are reminded of Lessing's fine saying,
though it relates only to the first of the two goods
that Huxley wanted ready-made. " Did the Al-
mighty," said Lessing, "holding in his right hand
Truth, and in his left *Search for Truth*, deign to offer
me the one I might prefer;—in all humility but without hesitation, I should request—*Search for Truth*[2]."

---

[1] *Methods and Results*, Collected Essays, I. p. 192.

[2] Quoted among a number of similar passages by Hamilton
Metaphysics, I. p. 13.

As to moral good however no such alternative seems possible. " Nothing takes place morally," said Rothe, "except what takes place *through one's own self-determination* : this it is that converts it from a mere taking place into an *action*[1]." This is the main fact,— 'main miracle' if you will—"this power on thine own act and on the world" which evolution and morality alike imply. A world of so-called creatures devoid of all initiative would not be an evolving world as we understand evolution. Such a world might embody its Creator's will perhaps, if we could say *that* is willed which we need only conceive as thought ; but even if it could be held to *express* his will it still could never either know it or do it. The possibility of moral evil, in a word, is implied in any moral order that is evolved at all : to make this impossible is to make that impossible too. Of course to one who should prefer to be an immaculate puppet rather than a man with all his shortcomings but also with all his capabilities, there is no more to be said. But is such an irrational person conceivable?[2]

The sort of ideal world that we have just discussed would cease to be non-moral if regarded, not as the result of a pre-established harmony, but as the achievement of virtuous struggle crowned eventually with victory. So regarded we may call it the upper limit of moral evolution, the world in the era beyond good and evil, when evil is no more. At the other extreme we

---

[1] Quoted by Martineau, *A Study of Religion*, 2nd edn, II. p. 103. Martineau's whole section on *Moral Evil* is admirable.

[2] I am well aware that Huxley of all men was not really one of this sort.

can imagine a limit at and below which moral evil is impossible, because moral good is impossible; where the impulses of sense are so exclusive and so strong that prudence and virtue are out of the question. It is useless here to talk of temptation: this then we may call the lower limit of moral evolution. Between these two extremes lies our world, where moral evil, at once possible and avoidable, is yet continuously present: is it a hopeless venture to believe in God where such a state of things obtains? A world in which it *could* not obtain, we have argued, would assuredly not be better, for such a world would not be moral at all[1]. On the other hand a world in which it *did* not, though it still might, obtain, would, we must admit, certainly be a better world. But, for all that, the actual existence of moral evil in our world is only incompatible with a theocracy, if God is the author of this evil; if, in other words, God is the sole free agent and his so-called creatures only so many impotent vessels of honour or dishonour. Then indeed God and the world would be bad together, but God only would be morally evil. And that surely is a supposition as absurd as it is monstrous. Before the presence of evil in the world can be cited as evidence that God is not present in it, it must be shewn that the evil is such as not merely to retard but absolutely to prevent the onward progress of moral order and render the attainment of the upper limit of moral evolution for ever impossible.

Again we ask—Which way does the presumption lie? We are wont to say that a struggle between good and evil is now constantly going on, and then our

---

[1] "The world with its faults is better than a kingdom of angels without wills at all." Haller quoted by Kant, *Religion u.s.w.*, Hart. VI. 159.

There is no 'principle' of evil.
cf. aug. Even the devil is not his own nature

376   *Moral Evil and Moral Order*

question takes the form :—Which side, so far as we can judge, bids fair to win?   But in fact the question in this form is not truly put.   There is no such dualism of good and evil : they are not two coordinate powers; in a word, there is no *principle* of evil[1].   There is a moral order, but evil is only disorder.   This is the grain of truth in the contention so persistently maintained, that evil is essentially negative.   However woefully men mistake what is their real good, it is this none the less that each one constantly strives for : evil as evil is no man's aim.   The devil's aim it is indeed said to be, but we are none of us pledged to believe in the devil.   The struggle with evil then is not a struggle for supremacy like the battle of the gods and the Titans; it is an advance against hindrances, which exist only as hindrances, not as beings having ends of their own as Manichaeism supposed.   The moment the true character of any form of evil is apparent that moment the struggle to overcome it begins : hence the world-wide association between evil and darkness

So far then there is truth again in the ancient Socratic paradox that virtue is knowledge and vice involuntary. We cannot, of course[2], identify virtue and truth, vice and error : conduct is more than cognition, though, in proportion as it is intelligent, it always implies cognition. In impulsive action, we act first and know after ; but sooner or later experience brings wisdom : otherwise in fact the plane of deliberative action would never have been attained.   On this level too, with its 'practical

---

[1] Cf. Lect. VI. pp. 131 ff.

[2] As Aristotle in his criticism of Socrates long ago pointed out. Cf. *Eth*. VI. 13; VII. 5.   Also Mackenzie, *Manual of Ethics*, VIII. 7.

syllogism,' there may be genuine error—either as
regards the major premise, the principle, or as regards
the minor, the particular 'case,' but error of this sort
too is corrigible and tends with growing experience to
disappear.   There may however be the self-sophistica-
tion and casuistry which have made the 'wiles of the
devil' proverbial, and to which the manifold euphemisms
for every form of vice bear striking testimony.   But
they bear striking testimony also to the fact that evil
can only flourish disguised *sub specie boni.* This doubtless was part at least of what Socrates meant, and led
him, as it has led so many since, strenuously to advocate
moral education.   When then we compare the unity
and solidarity of the good with the motley, many-
headed shapes of evil ever at cross-purposes with each
other, the conservation common to all forms of good
and to no forms of evil ; when too we consider the close
connexion between the good and the true, on the one
hand, between error and evil on the other—have we not
ground for believing in the eventual triumph of the
good, have we not ground for maintaining that such
moral evil as we find in the world, terrible though
it is, is after all not such as to justify the atheistic
position ?

But there is still an old difficulty to consider.   The
moral evil in the world, it is said, is not confined to
human misdeeds, innumerable and often heinous though
they be : over and above them there is the want of
justice in what are supposed to be God's ways with
men.   "All things come alike to all : there is one
event to the righteous and to the wicked... : this is an
evil in all things that are done under the sun."   Well,

if there is a God at all his ways are certainly not our ways. The writer of Ecclesiastes seems to rate them morally below our ways, the writer of Isaiah as much above them as the heavens are higher than the earth. What is the real difference? Earthly monarchs have been known directly to interfere in the affairs of their subjects in order to exalt the worst and humble the best, but can we possibly regard the prosperity of the wicked and the suffering of the righteous as due to divine intervention in this way? An immoral government of the world would indeed leave us no choice but atheism, and would so put an end to theodicies altogether.

But untrained minds none the less picture to themselves God's relation to the world as simply analogous to that of a sovereign to his subjects. And accordingly they find the solution of the difficulty raised, not in atheism, but in the view expounded by Job's comforters. In spite of appearances to the contrary, that is to say, there *is*, they maintain, strict moral government and the Judge of all the earth does right. Seeming misfortune is really punishment. So men thought when the tower of Siloam fell, and so the wide world through many think still. When then one man wilfully injures others he is the unwitting instrument of divine justice; and though society in punishing his crime performs a like office for him, what is to be said if, yielding to compassion, it proceeds to succour his victims? Deliberate attempts to frustrate the ends of justice would surely themselves call for punishment. Again on this view might not the man in pursuit of worthy ends rely on the words of the Psalmist, which the tempter misquoted, and be confident, if he were indeed truly doing right, that *no* evil could befall him[1]? In short, as Professor Royce, who has dealt excellently with this difficulty, sums it up, "the result is here indeed a moral fatalism, of an unexpected, but none the less inevitable sort[2]." Its logical outcome rigorously pursued would be to render moral evil impossible and moral good inevitable—and that, we have already seen, is contradictory. We may conclude then that the contingency. in the world, of which physical evil is a part, cannot be construed into a sign of moral imperfection in its constitution : such contingency is inseparable from any creation that is evolutionary in such wise as to leave free agents more or less initiative.

At this point it might be objected · But if God does not interfere either to reward or to punish, then the only moral government there is in the world is the work of his creatures : 'their initiative' is the whole, and the imperfection we find is no longer surprising. But what sort of God is one that only conserves the world on its physical side,—maketh his sun to rise on the evil and the good and sendeth rain on the just and the unjust—but leaves it morally to itself, to sink or swim as it may ? No moral government is better certainly than an immoral government, but is it the best possible ? But this objection is still coloured by the same crude anthropomorphism as the foregoing. Just as creation used to be conceived as accomplished only in the piecemeal fashion of a human artificer,

---

[1] Cf. Matt. iv. 6; Ps. xci.
[2] *The World and the Individual*, II. p. 404: cf. the whole section, pp. 399—405.

completing now this now that, so it was assumed that
divine government must take the form of special interferences, as in plagues and thunderbolts, sudden death
and other so-called 'judgments.' Special providences
like special creations, however, belong to a creed outworn; though the ideas of creation and providence may
be valid still. But from the standpoint of pluralism
they will be conceived as one continuous process of
evolution, not as two distinct series of acts, one of
which is an interference with the other[1].

Events that once impressed the untutored savage
as supernatural are now recognised as belonging to
nature's routine; yet such events were doubtless important factors in the early evolution of religion. Has
this glimmer of the Divine beyond nature characteristic
of primitive superstition utterly died out, or has it
grown clearer with advancing knowledge? Is the
evidence for theism greater or less? Less, unquestionably—in fact none at all—if we seek only for
miraculous signs, and maintain that apart from such
special interpositions the whole cosmic order is non-
moral. Then indeed, unless we are prepared to cast
science to the winds, we are left to picture the microcosm pitted against the macrocosm, as Huxley did,
and, having done its best, doomed perchance to failure[2].
But the evidence will be more, certainly—in principle

---

[1] On the other hand apart from pluralism, apart that is to say
from the co-operation of finite agents—from the standpoint of
absolute singularism—in other words, there would be no meaning in
process or evolution at all. Call time only appearance if you like;
still meanwhile this appearance is the universe of our discourse.

[2] Cf. preceding Lecture, p. 360.

all the external evidence that in an evolving world
seems possible—if, regarding rational agents and their
history as an integral part of the one cosmic order and
the part that gives meaning to the whole, we find no
hint of purpose or worth in it unless it be the realisation of the good ; if, further, we find this ideal consciously adopted as their end by the best part of mankind and unconsciously acknowledged by all inasmuch
as all seek the good ; and if, lastly, we find that even
physical evils are often ' trials ' that tend to strengthen
virtue, to enhance and ensure the good attained, but
never invincible obstacles presenting a solid front such
that all the powers of good cannot prevail against it.
All this, as I have said, we do find ; and it means that
moral order is *the* order of the world. No one ever
put this position so forcibly as Fichte : moral order—
the *ordo ordinans* he called it, as the parallel of the
Spinozistic *natura naturans*—was for him the Absolute,
a pantheistic moral principle but not a personal God.
But need we, nay can we, stop here ? So far certainly
we need not, and Fichte in the end did not. The
immanence of the good in the world as the informing
principle of its evolution, the standard of its worth at
any stage and the end towards which the whole
creation moves, is not in itself incompatible with the
transcendent reality of this principle as a Supreme
Being. To deny this reality may entail no formal
contradiction ; but it leaves us to face the difficulties of
absolute pluralism which theism removes and to forego
the confidence which theism inspires. For order in
the practical sphere, in the realm of ends, cannot be
merely a relation, but must imply *that which orders*, as

382 Moral Evil and Moral Order

Lotze used ever to maintain[1]. That which orders then, if it be not the One we have called God, can only be the Many who would then be miscalled his creatures. It must certainly be in part the latter, if morality is to have any meaning; but why can it not be both? For the existence of moral evil in an evolving world like ours would only debar us utterly from accepting this solution if such evil were radical and absolute. Still, it may be replied, even granting that we have no evidence of an essentially evil principle at work in the world so far as we know it, yet the part of it that we know is exceedingly small: elsewhere such a principle may exist. I can only reply by asking what conceivable reason could there be for the existence of absolute evil? Its existence would be the overthrow of reason altogether, and carry us back at once to the absurdities of the pessimism of Schopenhauer and von Hartmann.

It may be well to anticipate a possible but somewhat perverse objection for the sake of another topic to which it naturally leads. We have admitted that if theism is to be defensible this must be the best possible world, and yet have allowed that a world in which moral evil, though it might obtain, actually did not, would be a better world than this. Now these two positions, it may be said, are inconsistent. But are they, provided we carefully distinguish? *This* world we say is one in which, though moral evil actually obtains, it need not. Why does it? Not because of any necessitation on God's part but because of the free acts of us, who are joint-workers with him in the

[1] Cf. *Microcosmus*, Eng. trans. II. pp. 673 ff.

world's evolution. So far as God's part in the world is concerned, this world and the better world supposed are on a par : the inferiority in fact of this world is due to us. But can we conceive this world evolving orthogenetically, as a biologist would say, without its peccability passing over into sin just as its fallibility passes over into error ? Perhaps we cannot, but we need not therefore deny either that the straight course is ideally the better or that the fault is ours. But some who seek to vindicate the ways of God to men have implicitly denied one or both : the fall equally with the creation they refer to God's decree and justify as abounding to his glory : the history of the world, though a human tragedy, thus, as Martensen has said, becoming a divine comedy. It is strange that self-glorification should be attributed as a motive to God in a religion to which we owe the far higher and more appropriate conception of God as Love. But this is not the point to which I want now to refer, but rather the idea embodied in such words as *O felix culpa Adami quae meruit talem et tantum habere redemptorem !* referring to the *dénoûment* of the said drama. Whatever else we may think of Jesus of Nazareth called Christ and of the religion that he founded, at least we must recognise the soul of good, evoked by things evil, which they reveal. Nobody ever read Seeley's *Ecce Homo* without being profoundly impressed by this. No wonder then that Christian speculation, seeing in sin the occasion of this revelation, should have regarded the whole so-called ' plan of salvation ' and the evil which it presupposes as divinely foreordained. And yet surely this cannot be, for to make moral evil

essential to the perfection of the world would leave us
no choice, just as to make it impossible would leave us
none ; the inevitable can have no moral quality. Such
doctrine, in a word, overreaches itself. But the more
good comes even through evil the more reason have
we for believing the Good and it alone to be verily the
Supreme. It is in this way that the Christian ideal
promises to solve the problem of moral evil.

LECTURE XVIII.

THEORIES OF A FUTURE LIFE.

Of all the ills that flesh is heir to, death is commonly accounted the chief. And yet if we look only at life on this earth and the general economy of nature here, it seems hardly disputable that death in itself—apart from its possible circumstances—is no evil either for the individual or for the species to which he belongs; while it is good for the progress of development on the whole. For the individual animal, natural death means release after its end—the perpetuation of the species—has been accomplished. For the species, death in general means the survival of the better adapted, the more vigorous and the more enterprising; and therefore it means also increased opportunity for the advance to life of a higher form. As regards the mere animal we may say with Hegel, that "death shows the species to be the power that is superior to the immediate individual. For the animal, the process of the species is the highest point of its vitality. But it never gets so far as to have a being for itself within its species: on the contrary it is subservient to the supremacy of this[1]." And this is so, we may add,

---

[1] *Encyclopaedia*, § 221.

because the merely animal individual shows little or no trace of true personality : so we have natural histories of species, but biographies only of persons.   It is only in the case of self-conscious beings then that the fact of death, in removing them completely from out our bourne of time and place, gives rise to anxious questionings. We cannot say of *them* that they existed solely for the sake of the species biologically regarded.

Nor can we say, as Hume did, "that if any purpose of nature be clear, we may affirm that the whole scope and intention of man's creation, so far as we can judge by natural reason, is limited to the present life[1]."   If that were so, the universal belief in a future life and all man's moral and religious ideals would be unaccountable anomalies, a cruel and senseless mockery without a parallel : not in this wise do we interpret the swallow's migratory instincts or the squirrel's preparations for its winter sleep.   Within the whole range of the wide world's literature we find no more constant theme than just this disparity between man's possibilities and aspirations, on the one hand, and the narrow scope afforded them in the brief span of the present life, on the other.   It is true, as we have had to note more than once already, that these possibilities and aspirations belong to the individual man only through his organic connexion with the over-individual, Man or humanity as a whole.   But it does not follow that each person is but an instrument subservient to this—*le*

---

[1] "On the Immortality of the Soul." *Essays*, Green and Grose's edn, II. p. 400, one of the essays that Hume suppressed, and well he might, for its arguments rest on a cynical and ignoble estimate of humanity that has seldom been surpassed.

grand Être so called—is himself in no sense an end but just a means : it does not follow that his one function is *vivre pour autrui* and nothing more. As a complex machine is only an arrangement of simple machines, so —if the individual were only a means—humanity at best could only be a system of means, and like the machine, could only have an end beyond itself, an end in which it had itself no share. If however humanity— or to speak more generally, if spiritual society—is an end for itself, then the persons who constitute it must share in this end. We cannot bring the parts under one category and the whole under another. This in-consequence is one fatal defect of the Comtian 'enthusiasm of humanity,' from which the Christian is free[1]. But there is the other defect. The conditions of our present life are inadequate to our highest personal and therefore also to our highest social ideals. " My kingdom," the Christian spirit—nay, the religious spirit everywhere—says, " is not of this world." More-over evil is not overcome unless it is overcome in each individual.

But while this sense of the incompleteness of our personal life if death is to terminate it, has grown with our moral and religious progress and is most keenly felt by the best of men and by men at their best; yet, on the other hand, the difficulties besetting all our attempts to specify—even in the vaguest way—the natural conditions of such a life have grown still more

---

[1] There is the less need to dwell on this point since it has been already dealt with very fully by T. H. Green—cf. his *Prolegomena to Ethics*, §§ 184 ff. The fallacy involved is also clearly exposed by Dr McTaggart, *Studies in the Hegelian Cosmology*, §§ 12 ff.

remarkably; and they weigh most heavily on those whose knowledge is most profound and whose intelligence is most exacting. We approximate, in a word, to a sort of antinomy: what our practical reason says ought to be, science tends to say cannot be. The qualifications I have used are important. First the opposition is not definitely an antinomy: what the heart affirms the head does not explicitly deny. Physical difficulties in the way of a future life do not detract from the moral worth of such life: they may even add to it, if moral advance is the condition of their removal. The many arguments now in vogue against a future life seem never to be directly opposed[1] to its desirability: what they chiefly contest is its possibility. Again we say, difficulties do not make a thing either impossible or inconceivable; all therefore that science can do is to urge the want of antecedent probability, so long as we keep to what we at present know.

The dogmatic rationalists before Kant's day usually disposed in advance of such difficulties by metaphysical arguments demonstrating the soul's essential simplicity and imperishability. It is true that the subject of experience cannot be resolved into a complex of subjects, although all experience as interaction implies such complexity. Nor can the subject be analysed

[1] "An over-anxious desire to prove the immortality of the soul is not by any means an evidence of a religious temper of mind. Indeed, the belief in immortality may easily become an unhealthy occupation with a future salvation, which prevents us from seeking for salvation here." E. Caird, *The Evolution of Religion*, 1893, vol. II. p. 243. This sort of selfish 'other-worldliness' has no doubt called forth condemnation and thus has tended indirectly to discredit the morality of the belief in a future life.

into merely objective relations, as in presentationism, since objects always imply relation to a subject. So far we seem justified in regarding the subject of experience as ontal not phenomenal: it is certainly the source of all our categories concerning reality—substance, cause, end, and the like. But Kant revived a distinction which the rationalists' arguments for immortality too much overlooked; though Locke might have taught them better—the distinction, I mean, between substantial identity and personal identity. Such reasonings as those of the Leibniz-Wolffians can afford us no assurance of a personal future till personal identity is shown to be something more than a temporary form or property, any number of which in succession the same soul may acquire and lose. Of this sort is the immortality assumed in the ancient and widely-spread belief in the transmigration of souls. The soul is held to remain identically the same, the various lives it leads being in general determined by the bodies into which it enters. Kant however entertained a still stranger supposition, not the transmigration of the same soul to different bodies, but the complete transference of the same personality, that is to say the same self-consciousness, to different souls or substances, on the analogy of the complete transference of the motion of one elastic sphere to another with which it collides. Thus on either view all that we know as our self-conscious life would have to be regarded as a mere accident of the soul whose reality it was none the less supposed to reveal.

But what is preeminently of worth to us is not mere persistence of being but just this continuity of our personal life. This, which the theory of metempsychosis seems to sacrifice more or less completely, would on Kant's supposition be entirely retained. So that if his supposition were sound, we might be content with urging, as Lotze has already done, that it yields everything that we practically care about. " No one who wished the doctrine of immortality to be assured," said Lotze, "could concern himself with anything but that continuity of his consciousness which he desired not to lose; he would be heartily indifferent to the question whether the thing in itself which was to be the substratum of that continuance occupied in the series the position n or $(n+1)^1$." May be, but he would be but a very shallow thinker who *could* be assured in such a case. What guarantee should we have, if Kant's analogy were sound, that our personality, being only a bundle of accidents, would always or usually be passed on entire ? If our whole consciousness is separable from its substratum, how are we to know whether this is one or many : how can we tell what it is, or be sure that it is anything at all ? To all these questions save the last Kant's reply is *Ignoramus* : the last it never occurred to him independently to raise or seriously to entertain at all. A view of the soul, that could lead to such analogies, give rise to such questions, and yet furnish no answer to them, we surely may suspect.

Nor is it difficult to find the source of these defects : ultimately and in the main it was none other than the *Essay concerning Human Understanding* of our own John Locke. Here we find the same analogy, the

---

[1] *Metaphysic*, Eng. trans. § 244.

same phenomenal dualism of matter and mind, the one perceived by external, the other by internal sense, and above all the same category of substance and accident applied alike to both. Yet all the while both Locke and Kant were aware of facts incompatible with thus levelling down all the constituents of experience to one plane and handling all with the same categories. This Locke showed in his recognition of the knowledge of our own existence as intuitive and our knowledge of the existence of other finite beings as only sensible; and still more Kant in his recognition—in what he called the synthetic unity of apperception—of every subject of experience as, to use Lotze's words, 'an independent centre of action and reaction.' The very abstractness of the category of substance which led Kant to formulate the principle now known as the conservation of mass, and his description of substance as the name given to the *phenomenon* that is thus conserved, show clearly the inapplicability of this category of substance and accident to what Kant himself has over and over again emphatically declared is not phenomenal. His attempts to resolve it into some *tertium quid* between phenomenon and thing *per se* plainly indicate that he had taken more of Hume into his system than it could assimilate. His constant shuffling of transcendental Ego, logical Ego and empirical Ego forcibly reminds one of thimble-rigging.

Let us then make bold to regard our self-conscious life, not as a flux of accidents pertaining with we know not what all beside to some substratum or other, but as the actions and reactions of a thing *per se* or rather of a subject in a world of such, as the intercourse of such a subject with other subjects. Instead of regarding all souls as substances we have proceeded rather on the spiritualistic interpretation of all substances as souls. And it is worth remarking that a monadology of this sort still haunted Kant's speculation from his earlier days and was constantly cropping out in his later critical writings[1]. This is notably the case, for example, in his solution of the third antinomy; for the logical possibility of freedom, whereby the solution is effected, presupposes the actual existence of a plurality of things *per se* or substances, whose actions determine the so-called course of nature[2]. Between the abstract category of substance and what we may call the real category of things or substances, from which it is abstracted, there is a world of difference. The history of philosophy, I incline to think, shows this abstract concept of substance to be, as Schopenhauer maintained, either useless or mischievous. If the individuality of the concrete thing is dropped then substance becomes synonymous with matter or stuff—for which ' form ' is but an accident—this is indeed its popular meaning and the meaning too unquestionably the predominant one with Kant. The mischief, as respects our present problem, begins when mind too is regarded as substance, as it was by Descartes and Locke. But apart from the categories of individuality and activity that of substantiality is inadequate to define either the idea of God or that of a soul. It is also too indeterminate and empty

[1] Cf. B. Erdmann's *Kant's Kriticismus u. s. w.*, 1878, pp. 73—75: also a dissertation by a pupil of Erdmann's, O. Riedel, *Die monadologischen Bestimmungen in Kant's Lehre vom Ding an sich*, 1884.

[2] Cf. above, Lecture XIV. pp. 302 ff.

to admit of either individuality or causality being deduced or dialectically developed from it, though itself readily to be abstracted from the concrete 'things' with qualities which manifest their being by their activity[1].

But if we were to discard the category of substantiality and content ourselves with that of mere actuality, what reasons would remain for expecting our life to continue indefinitely? Well, at any rate the category of substance will not furnish a reason : it would at best only state the fact, or rather only subtly beg the question. So far perhaps we may agree with what Lotze intended in saying :—"The question of the immortality of the soul does not belong to Metaphysic. We have no other principle for deciding it," he continues, "beyond this general idealistic conviction :— every created thing will continue, if and so long as its continuance belongs to the meaning of the world ; every one will pass away, whose actuality had only in some transitory phase of the world's course a place (*Stelle*) that justified it[2]." But it would still remain an open question whether the evolution of the world's meaning would not be at least as well met, (and a more intimate unity and continuity secured,) by the mutual adaptations and adjustments of the same individuals, as by the annihilation of some and the creation of others. Anyhow it is meanwhile safe to say—strange as it may sound—that we have no positive evidence, either *a posteriori* or *a priori*, that the latter is the

---

[1] Cf. Sigwart, *Logik*, 2nd edn, § 77 (1) ; Lotze, *Metaphysik*, § 245; *Naturalism and Agnosticism*, earlier edns, II. pp. 192 f. ; 4th edn, pp. 484 f.

[2] *Metaphysik*, *loc. cit.*

method which in fact obtains. We say All men are mortal, but not one of us has experienced death ; not one of us knows anything therefore of what for the subject immediately concerned it really is. If we knew that the individual's existence began with that of the body, we might argue that it would also probably end with it : but here again the empirical basis for such an argument fails us. Finally, if the materialist's contention were established, if soul and body were shown to be identical, that certainly would leave no further room for doubt. But we may say with some confidence that science itself has once for all renounced materialism of this sort[1]. Altogether—so far as the mere persistence of the individual subject now actually existing goes—we may fairly maintain that the burden of proof after all rests with those who would dogmatically deny it.

But, as already said, the mere persistence of the individual subject will not content us : it is in the continuity of our personal life that we are supremely interested, and facts force us to admit that we cannot straightway infer the one from the other. It seems useless to say

> The eternal form will still divide
> The eternal soul from all beside,

unless we have some basis for conjecturing how much

---

[1] "If the belief in immortality is essential to morality, physical science has no more to say against the probability of that doctrine than the most ordinary experience has, and it effectually closes the mouths of those who pretend to refute it by objections deduced from merely physical data." Huxley, 'Science and Morals,' *Collected Essays*, vol. IX. p. 143.

or how little can be 'eternal form.' Whatever has been gradually acquired, may for all we know be lost again; and indeed much of it, so far as present experience goes, appears, at first sight, to be entirely lost. Some continuity of memory is indispensable to personal continuity, and is commonly held to require some continuity of organism. Continuity of environment again appears not only to be a necessary condition of organic continuity, but to be also essential to any further personal development. But how is such continuity conceivable beyond the grave?

As regards memory the difficulties so commonly felt are largely due to bad psychology. Memory, though common thought and language associate it so intimately with objective records, obviously cannot be really identified with these; for they presuppose it[1]. Of the subjective function, apart from which records are not records, no explanation, no definition or description even, that does not already imply it, has—so far as I know—ever been, or—as I believe—ever will be given. We are tempted perhaps sometimes to describe memory as the perception of what is distant in the past and to develop the many analogies there are between it and the perception of what is distant in space. But one difference at any rate there is and that difference is fundamental. Distance in space implies only objective order: two men walking together may both see the same landmark, say a mile in front of them; but though they may look back a year in time, the experiences they remember will strictly speaking never be in a like sense the same. Memory furnishes us with no

---

[1] Cf. *Naturalism and Agnosticism*, ii. pp. 156—159; 4th edn, pp. 448 ff.

such common range in time as vision yields us in space : there is at least this much justification for Kant's treatment of time as the form of internal perception. The subjective marks peculiar to memory proper cannot be identified with any merely objective order ; and so, we may question if all connexion between the subject and its past experience is permanently dissolved simply by the apparent obliteration of certain objective records. Hence the truth—so far—of Fries's contention[1] that the problem to explain is not memory but obliviscence : about that there is, however, no special difficulty[2].

Moreover, strictly speaking, the universe contains at this moment the potential record of every event that has ever happened ; and every subject, that has advanced beyond the ideal limit of the 'naked monad,' is able to some extent to read this record, and to read it to a greater extent and more distinctly the further its own experience has developed. And again, at the level of self-consciousness, over and above the merely passive memory or reminiscence, that has to wait till the record is clear, we have the active memory or recollection that can search its own archives; and we have also the intelligence that can seek out and interpret other records beyond any imaginable limit. The gradual achievement of such increased independence and

---

[1] *Neue Kritik der Vernunft*, 2te Auf. 1. (1828) pp. 138 f.

[2] Herein the analogy with space holds good. Distant objects in a landscape can in general only be clearly seen if they are of sufficient magnitude, and distant events in a lifetime can in general only be clearly remembered if they are of sufficient moment. Again as there may be positive obstructions in the way of our vision so there may be in the way of our memory, and the body—as in disease—is known to be a frequent source of such obstructions.

initiative is just that advance from sentient individual
to rational person, from soul to spirit, which philosophy
from Plato onwards has steadily recognised as a fact,
though it has seldom ventured to account for it as
a continuous development. If now—in addition to the
subjective factor implied in all memory—we take into
account this increased independence which the spiritual
level secures, and along with this the fact that in what
we may call the world order the new is continuous
with the old, we surely have some ground for thinking
it possible that the departed spirit may re-collect itself,
even without the body. Nay, it will not be absurd to
suppose with Kant that at this level "the separation
from the body would be the end of the sensuous
employment and the beginning of the intelligible employment of our faculty of knowledge. The body would
then have to be considered, not as the cause of our
thinking but only as a restrictive condition of it and
therefore...as an impediment of our pure and spiritual
life[1]." The spirit is often willing when the flesh is
weak ; but here we have a literal rising through its
death to higher things. At any rate we must hold
firmly to the position that it is function that determines
structure, not structure that determines function ; that
the soul is the entelechy of the body, not *vice versa*, to
use the phrase of Aristotle's which Leibniz adopted.
It then surely becomes reasonable to suppose that the
spirit that has so far transcended the body is not wholly
undone with its undoing, emphatically reasonable if we
find, when we come presently to inquire, that there are

---

[1] *Critique of the Pure Reason*, 1st edn, p. 778. Max Müller's
trans., p. 667.

teleological grounds of supreme moment, why this
should not be.

And yet, we must allow that we can hardly frame
more than the vaguest conjectures how—so far as it is
verily disembodied—the soul or spirit proceeds, if needs
be, to clothe itself anew ; albeit we have no reason to
regard it, let me remark again, as reduced in the
interim to the level of a naked monad.   But there is
at any rate a closely analogous case, where a like
renewal actually happens, though our ignorance of the
process is almost as complete.   If, however, we knew
nothing at all of embryology, and if it happened—as
Leibniz in fact supposed—that the process of dying
consisted in a reversal or 'involution' of the process
of growth and differentiation, so that the true corpse,
so to say, should be again nothing but a tiny and
apparently homogeneous speck of protoplasm—so small
that a few consecrated pill-boxes might almost suffice
for the *campi santi* of the world—we should, I fancy,
be quite as sure as we can now be that the renewal of
such a life was an idle dream.   And yet in the embryo,
a like speck, we have

> Although the print be little, the whole matter
> And copy of the father,—eyes, nose, lip,
> ....
> The very mould and frame of hand, nail, finger.

May we not then suppose that if the germinal soul can
accomplish so much the separated spirit can accomplish
more[1] ?   But it will be replied the germ is an organism,

[1] I have, since writing the above, chanced upon the following
interesting anticipation :—"Abstractly considered, that is considered
without relation to the difference which habit and merely habit

not a disembodied soul. That is true unquestionably
and it is important ; for any continuity of life with no
continuity of either organism or environment seems
quite inconceivable. But there is nothing in our
present knowledge to show that there cannot be any
other mode of embodiment than that with which we
are here familiar, and that we have not manifold other
relations with our environment besides those which the
organism as we know it is supposed to explain—or
rather perhaps that our environment has not such relations with us, of which we at present have no clear
consciousness. It is futile to attempt to specify these
possibilities by imagining an astral body, an ethereal
body or the like ; and to talk of a subliminal self seems
only to betray ignorance of the real problem, which
relates not to the self but to the continuance after
death of its *rapport* with the world.

But we may at least lay stress on the huge gap in
our present scientific knowledge concerning the connexion of body and mind—a gap which there seems little
prospect of our filling up, whether we work, so to say,
outwards from psychology or inwards from physiology
—if such inaccurate phraseology may be for brevity's

produces in our faculties and modes of apprehension, I do not see
anything more in the resurrection of a dead man than in the conception of a child ; except it be this that the one comes into his world
with a system of prior consciousness about him, while the other does
not : and no person will say that he knows enough of either subject
to perceive that this circumstance makes such a difference in the two
cases, that the one should be easy, and the other not so. To the
first man, the succession of the species would be as incomprehensible
as the resurrection of the dead is to us." Paley, *Evidences of Christianity*, Tegg's edn of his works, p. 114.

sake allowed.   Here there must be facts in plenty of which we are wholly ignorant, and here, *it may be*, that as an original but little known writer has supposed, " in the course of this life the nervous system by its ultimate habitudes should frame a finer organization, and that this in the moment and act of death should be disentangled from the coarser frame[1]."   Or more likely, *it may be*, as Bonnet and the younger Fichte supposed, that within the changeable 'external body' there is from the first an 'inner body' that shapes it and outlasts it[2].   Or again, with still more probability, *it may be*, as Thiele supposed, that this invisible body is not built up from without nor present from the first as 'form-principle' of the external and changing body, but that it will be gradually elaborated as the soul's development requires, just as the bodies which it has outworn were elaborated to subserve its needs during the lower stages of its development[3].   But all such hypotheses, and there are many, like the gap in our knowledge that leaves room for them, do not reach beyond the dualism of common thought ; fail in fact to get down to the bed-rock of experience that underlies all such problems.   More fundamental than any seeming dualism of body and soul is the duality of subject and object in experience, and this—for spiritualistic monism—means the interaction of subjects with other

[1] W. Cyples, *An Inquiry into the Process of Human Experience*, London, 1880, p. 431.

[2] C. Bonnet, *La palingénésie philosophique*, 1769.   J. H. Fichte, *Psychologie*, 1864, i. pp. 63 f.   A similar view, it is interesting to note, was entertained by the physicists, Balfour Stewart and Tait : cf. *The Unseen Universe*, 2nd edn, 1875, pp. 159 f.

[3] G. Thiele, *Die Philosophie des Selbstsbewusstseins*, 1895, pp. 506 f.

subjects, transcends the opposition of person and thing. It means too, that the organism is the result of such subjective interaction, not that this interaction is the result of it; more generally still, that subjects are the prime agents in maintaining the so-called physical world, not this the prime agent by which they are passively sustained. Till naturalism succeeds in converting this position the way to belief in a future life will always be open.

But again as regards the future environment we must admit, as in the case of the future organism, that in the complete absence of any experience we can do no more than conjecture. And obviously, if we are ignorant of the organism that is to be, we must be ignorant also of its specific environment; and *vice versa.* But after all, as just now said, there is for spiritualism no sharp line between the two, indeed even for materialism there is none: for the one as for the other, the organism is continuous with, and a part of, the objective world. All that we can reasonably assert is that between the old life and the new there must be some continuity of experience, if the new life is to be regarded as a future life and not as merely another life. There are two views to be considered: that of transmigration or reincarnation, accepted by the majority of the human race, and that of transfiguration, if we may so call it, prevalent among Christians. The one secures a continuity of environment that satisfies the imagination of survivors, but at the sacrifice more or less complete of that personal continuity which we must regard as essential. The other preserves this, but transfers it to an unseen world difficult to realise.

The objection to transmigration or metempsychosis[1] has been met by assuming that the personal discontinuity is only temporary, and that the successive lives of a given subject may be eventually connected through continuous but latent memories that are revived after death or when all the soul's *Wanderjahre* are over[2]. But even so, if this series is to have any real continuity or meaning, if it is to be not merely a series but a progression, then at every return to life, either Providence must determine, or the naturient soul must itself select, its appropriate reincarnation. Otherwise, if disembodied souls are to be blown about by the winds of circumstance like other seeds, we should only have a repetition of that outrageous fortune which the doctrine of transmigration was supposed to redress : the contingency that seems to pertain to the one birth we know of would only be manifolded, not removed.

This difficulty in turn has been met by the further and bolder assumption, that disembodied souls do in fact steer their own way back to a suitable re-birth. An atom liberated from its molecular bonds is described as manifesting an unwonted activity, technically known as 'the nascent state'; but still it does not recombine indifferently with the first free atom that it encounters, but only with one for which it has an 'affinity.' And "there seems to be nothing more strange or

[1] This term though commonly in use is obviously inaccurate. If we must needs have a Greek word, μετενσωμάτωσις used by Clem. Alex. is preferable.

[2] So, for example, Professor Campbell Fraser thinks. Cf. his *Theism*, vol. II. p. 249. And still more definitely Renouvier, *Le Personnalisme*, 1903, p. 220. A similar view was held by Max Drossbach, J. Reynaud and many others.

paradoxical," it has been said, "in the suggestion that each person enters into connexion with the body that is most fitted to be connected with him[1]." But the affinities of a given atom are, so far as we know, anything but select : not only will it combine with others of many kinds, but it seems to be absolutely indifferent to individuals within a kind. So far this analogy then, if it justified any inference at all, would, it may well be thought, hardly warrant us in expecting each person to find his next incarnation even within the species *Homo sapiens*. Still less would it lead us to expect that he could secure such parentage and surroundings as to admit of his turning the best of his past powers—as poet or patriot say—to full account, assuming that with the temporary lapse of definite memories these could be still retained.

But on the other hand it may be fairly urged that a liberated spirit ought to be credited with vastly more *savoir vivre* than a liberated atom. Further it must be allowed that this suggestion is quite in keeping with the conservation of values, which men like Lotze and Höffding regard as axiomatic—at any rate experience often verifies, and never certainly belies it[2]. Finally it minimises the objection to personal continuity that is often based on the facts of heredity[3]. And for my part

---

[1] McTaggart, *Some Dogmas of Religion*, 1906, p. 126.

[2] Cf. Lecture x. pp. 212 f., and Tennyson, *In Memoriam*, canto xlv :—

> This use may lie in blood and breath,
> Which else were fruitless of their due,
> Had man to learn himself anew
> Beyond the second birth of death.

[3] It is worth while to note that against this objection Kant proposed a similar reply, the "transcendental hypothesis, namely,

I must confess that this difficulty seems by far the most serious of any that beset the hypothesis of a plurality of lives. The traducian doctrine of the soul's origin is hard to reconcile with any true spiritualism, while the creationist doctrine is alien to the theory of evolution and open to other obvious difficulties besides. Indeed, if by difficulty we mean something that we fail to work in with, and adjust to, facts or ideas that we accept absolutely; then I make bold to deny, Dr Rashdall notwithstanding[1], that the theory of pre-existence 'creates new difficulties.' It involves 'a ramifying network' of assumptions unquestionably; but if it 'is certainly not capable of positive disproof,' the objector is bound to show that the result of the whole is worthless. Till then, summarily to reject it involves the still more extravagant assumption that we have exhausted all possibilities and that what may be only our lack of knowledge of its empirical conditions is tantamount to a proof of its impossibility[2]. As Kant, whose words I have adopted, has said, this arrogance of negation does

that all life is really intelligible only, not subject to the changes of time, and neither beginning in birth nor ending in death...that if we could intuite ourselves and other things *as they really are*, we should see ourselves in a world of spiritual natures, with which our only true community did neither begin at birth nor will end with the death of the body, both being merely phenomena" (*Critique of the Pure Reason*, M. Müller's trans. p. 668). It is also interesting to learn that shortly before the publication of the *Critique* Kant dogmatically taught both the pre-existence and the immortality of the soul. Cf. Max Heinze, *Vorlesungen Kant's über Metaphysik*, 1894, p. 547 of the reprint from the Transactions of the Royal Society of Saxony.

[1] *Theory of Good and Evil*, 1907, vol. II. pp. 346 f.
[2] Cf. Kant, *Critique*, 1st edn, p. 780, M.M. p. 681.

not eliminate in the least the practical value of such hypotheses. The appeal to ignorance no doubt cuts both ways : it does not allow us to treat hypotheses as knowledge, but on the other hand it does not destroy their working utility if, consistently with what we do know, they enable us even tentatively to reach a completer and more satisfactory *Weltanschauung*. As regards this particular hypothesis of pre-existence and a plurality of lives, its complexity is no advantage certainly ; but even so the disadvantage is reduced in proportion as the separate assumptions are analogous with actual experience and consilient with each other. After all it should give the scornful objector pause, to think how many of the vital processes, about which we have definite knowledge, involve an elaborate adjustment of multifarious details that would be utterly incredible but for its familiarity. Is it then unreasonable to expect still more marvellous conjunctions in the wider dimensions of the world beyond the grave ? And is it not also possible—just because of such wider dimensions— that what to us seems complicated or impossible is really as simple as say movement into a third dimension, which yet a being confined to two might fail to understand ? To the theist at any rate it is conceivable that, without any arbitrary interventions, subjective processes and objective influences may be there at work which are not merely retributive but remedial also. Such notions are of course more or less akin to the Christian doctrines of purgatory, angels, intercession and the like.

This brings us naturally to the theory of the future life characteristic of Christianity, *viz.* as a final and irrevocable state of existence in a so-called unseen and eternal world. The difficulty here is not so much our inability to imagine such a purely spiritual form of life ; but rather the utter gulf that according to this doctrine must lie between this life and ours. That a man should pass at once from earth to heaven or hell seems irrational and inequitable ; and the lapse of ages of suspended consciousness, if this were conceivable, would not diminish this discontinuity. But between one active life and another there may well be such an intermediate state of mental rumination, so to say, and reflexion, as many theologians have assumed. This state, it has been said, "is not a domain of deeds and works, for the external conditions for these are wanting …it is the domain of inwardness, of silent consideration and pondering, a domain of recollection (*Erinnerung*) in the full sense of the word[1]." We can perhaps suppose that this process may be a preparation for a new life, as just now hinted, provided—though with re-birth, the body, as Plotinus held, "be the true river of Lethe, and the soul plunged in it forgets all"—the change in character is notwithstanding still somehow retained. But it is hardly credible that any spiritual clarifying based on a single life—or series of lives—that is not more refined and matured than ours, could fit many, or indeed any, of the children of men for that final consummation which Christianity describes as eternal life. At length, however, and sooner for some than for

---

[1] Martensen, *Die christliche Dogmatik*, 1856, § 275. Such a self-purgatory of all souls seems a worthier idea than the one-sided expiatory purgatory of the Roman Church, which has so little moral efficacy that it may be curtailed by extraneous ceremonial.

others, a stage might be reached, when—so to say—
the 'disembodied' spirit would pass beyond the range
of attraction of the seen and temporal and enter the
confines of the eternal world ; at once tending towards,
and drawn on by, that outer constellation of the choir
invisible, to which it is best attuned.

But now in conclusion, again recognising to the
full the conjectural character of all these details, we
may nevertheless still maintain that they are of great use
in helping us to realise more definitely the possibility
of a future life.   On the main issue round which these
speculations turn, we must at least insist, *viz.* that if such
life is to have any worth or meaning, a certain personal
continuity and continuity of development is essential.
From this point of view death becomes indeed but
a longer sleep dividing life from life as sleep divides
day from day ; and as there is progress from day to
day so too there may be from life to life.   And we
may perhaps see another resemblance.   As we often
do things better for sleeping over them—though we
remember nothing of the subconscious processes through
which our plans have matured—so we may do better
in a future life, though the new awakening has crowded
out the memories of our sojourn in the other world.
In one important point indeed the analogy seems to
fail : our waking life is a continuous whole, the series
of repeated lives at first is not.   But even here on the
assumption that in the purely spiritual life of the other
world this continuity is resumed, the analogy again
holds good.   We have then however to equate our
earthly lives to dreams and death becomes not a sleeping but an awaking : *Mors janua vitae.*   And perhaps

it will seem less strange so to regard it, the more we think of the possibilities that the spiritual world may enfold.

It still remains, however, to consider what solid grounds we have for attaching any weight to these open possibilities.

LECTURE XIX.

FAITH AND KNOWLEDGE.

It was the hopelessness of the problem of evil, if this life is all, that brought us to the question of further life beyond the grave. Having now found reason for thinking that such a life can quite well be, we come to the moral arguments why it should be.

Of these at once the most ancient and the most universal is perhaps the juridical or retributive argument :—a man's lot in this life is 'a judgment' on his conduct in preceding lives ; and in the next he will be rewarded or punished for what he has done here. But the morality of our time has largely outgrown the paedagogic functions of such external sanctions and has found a truer and worthier interpretation of what they but crudely and imperfectly express. The concluding proposition of Spinoza's Ethics is the last word here : "Blessedness is not the reward of virtue but virtue itself." And so, of course, *mutatis mutandis*, of vice. The one fundamental argument for more life is not the need for adequate compensations—but for adequate opportunities, not the demand for fairer wages but for fuller work. A man is immortal till his work is done, we say ; and it is because we see that his work is not done, that his capacities are not worked out here, that we feel confident that death is not the end of him. For all things work together for good, we hold : indeed, to what other end and how else could they really or reasonably *work* together at all ? This is our fundamental postulate and the ultimate *ratio cognoscendi* of the theistic position. So then we may say with Professor Royce :—" If death is real at all it is real only in so far as it fulfils a purpose. But now, what purpose," he asks, " can be fulfilled by the ending of a life that is so far unfulfilled?"[1] In fine, the problem of evil seems insoluble, and any theodicy impossible, if this life be all. " Whoever believes in a *God*," said Rothe, "*must* also believe in the continuance of man after death. Without that there would not be a world that could be thought of as [realising] God's purpose[2]." Thus the one main argument, as I have called it, is entirely a moral argument : without it the 'open possibilities' we have just been considering would have no weight, and even with it they are not converted into scientific certainties. It may lead to faith but it cannot anticipate experience of what is 'behind the veil' of all we know.

This moral argument has been put several times with unusual power and eloquence in our recent literature, as for example by Martineau, Royce, Laurie and others ; for this reason I do not propose to enlarge upon it here, but only briefly to return to it presently, when dealing generally with Faith. There is however one earlier statement summing up the whole subject, part of which I will quote, as it leads on

[1] *The World and the Individual*, II. p. 440.
[2] *Stille Stunden*, p. 219, quoted by Martineau.

Kant "The realm of ends is at the same time the realm of nature."

The Moral Argument for Immortality 411

naturally to this topic, which I would now invite you to consider next. The passage occurs at the end of Kant's severe criticism of the supposed *theoretical* proofs of immortality prevalent in his time. Having there shown 'the impossibility of settling anything dogmatically with reference to an object of experience beyond the limits of experience' he concludes :—" Nothing is lost, however, by this with regard to the right, nay the necessity of admitting a future life.... The proofs which are useful for the world at large retain their value undiminished, nay, they gain in clearness, simplicity, and power when stripped of such dogmatic pretensions; for they bring reason back to its own peculiar domain, the realm of ends, which is, however, at the same time a realm of nature. But there too reason, as in itself a practical faculty, is entitled, without being confined to the conditions of nature, to extend the realm of ends and with it our own existence beyond the limits of our present experience and life. According to *analogy* with the *nature* of living beings in this world, concerning which reason must necessarily assume the principle that no organ, no faculty, no impulse, in short nothing superfluous or disproportionate to its use, and therefore aimless, is to be met with ; that on the contrary every being is precisely adapted to its vocation in life— according to this analogy, man, who yet alone can contain within himself the final end of all this, must needs be the only creature that is an exception to the principle. For not only his native capacities...but preeminently the moral law within him, go so far beyond all utility and advantage to be derived from them in this life, that the latter [the moral law] even instructs him, in the absence of *all* advantages, yes, even of the shadowy hope of posthumous fame, to esteem the mere consciousness of rectitude above all else and to feel an inner call, by his conduct in this world...to make himself worthy to be the citizen of a better, of which he possesses [only] the idea. This powerful proof, never to be controverted, accompanied by our constantly increasing acquaintance with the purposiveness pervading all that we see around us, by the prospect of the immensity of creation and therefore also by the consciousness of a certain illimitability in the possible extension of our knowledge along with an instinct commensurate to it, all this remains and always will remain, even though we must give up [the hope] from the merely theoretical knowledge of ourselves of understanding the necessary continuance of our existence[1]."

Here we have necessary continuance of existence asserted, though from the nature of the case all knowledge of it is denied, and asserted because of an incontrovertible proof of what theoretically we cannot understand! Surely this is a paradox if ever there was one. Yet underlying this paradox we shall find the basis on which the whole philosophy of theism rests. To Kant belongs the credit of having first made this clear, and that by his distinction, so often misunderstood, between the practical and the theoretical use of reason, and by his insistence on what he called the primacy of the former. Ignoring this distinction or assuming without question that the right to believe

---

[1] *Critique of the Pure Reason*, 2nd edn, pp. 424 ff. Max Müller's translation (amended), vol. II. pp. 504 ff.

in God and a future life is no better than the wish, the agnostic simply asks with Huxley: "Why trouble ourselves about matters of which, however important they may be, we do know nothing, and can know nothing?[1]" Or still more emphatically with Clifford he sums up his ethics of belief by declaring that "it is wrong always, everywhere and for any one, to believe anything upon insufficient evidence[2]." One tale is good till another is told: so all this agnosticism is true and trite so far as logic goes. But there is more in life than logic, and it is just its primary factor that our agnostics overlook. "The state of things is evidently far from simple: and pure insight and logic, whatever they might do ideally, are not the only things that really do produce our creeds[3]," as William James said in a classical essay that has made this theme one of the burning questions of our time. This, the connexion of faith and knowledge, is our present topic.

First of all we have only to recall facts that in the course of these lectures we have already had to deal with more than once. The whole process of the world, concretely regarded, we have found, so far as we have been able to trace it, is a process of evolution. Experience then means becoming expert by experiment. We do not begin by knowing but by learning. We gain knowledge by merely doing—and that whether we succeed or fail—and we gain it solely by doing: in the first instance at least, or by the race, it has been

[1] *Collected Essays*, vol. I. p. 162.
[2] *Lectures and Essays*, 2nd edn, 1886, 'The Ethics of Belief,' p. 346.
[3] *The Will to Believe*, p. 11.

gained only in this way. Hence that 'primitive
credulity' or trustfulness that characterizes our earliest
enterprises, when we do not wait till there are certain
and sufficient reasons for action: it is enough for
youthful energy if there are none such against action.
And happily it is so; for otherwise we might still
be what according to the zoologists our earliest known
forebears, the Social Ascidians, *were* in the long long
past and so in the clear green sea to this day *remain*.
Kant, it is worth remarking, was fully awake to this
point and refers to it teleologically in connexion with
this very question of the relation of the theoretical to
the practical reason. "If we were not designed," he
said, "to exert our powers till we were assured of our
ability to attain our object, those powers would remain
for the most part unused. For in general it is only by
trying that we first of all learn what they are[1]." Life
is made up of such attempts: self-betterment is its
main endeavour; knowledge is obtained only as fast
and as far as this paramount interest prompts us to
new efforts, and is valued primarily as a means to that
end. What is learnt takes at first the form not of
theoretical propositions, but of practical maxims, which
are thought of not as true but as useful. This difference is far deeper than it seems. In the first place,
such maxims are subjectively imposed imperatives
rather than objectively necessary affirmations; in the
next place, they imply always the concept of worth or
value, an axiological category to which there is no
purely objective counterpart; finally, maxims are true

[1] *Kritik der Urtheilskraft, Werke,* Hartenstein's edn, v. p. 184
note.   Power of Judgment

Connexion of Faith and Knowledge 415

—or, as we say, sound—or they are the contrary, solely in view of their practical consequences; deduction from objective premises is rarely thought of and would usually be impossible. Such is experience for the individual and in the concrete at all events. Conation is here the fundamental fact, at once the source of faith and the cause of knowledge. And there is here no dualism between the two : both merge in that primitive credulity which leads us to trust and to try before we know.

And now if we take a wider sweep and glance back at the history of the organic world, describing it, if you will, analogically, in terms of experience rather than in the language of biology—in which, however, such terms are more or less covertly implied—the parable will not be uninstructive. We shall find that almost every forward step in the progress of life could be formulated as an act of faith—an act not warranted by knowledge—on the part of the pioneer who first made it. There was little, for example, in all that the wisest fish could know, to justify the belief that there was more scope for existence on the earth than in the water, or to show that persistent endeavours to live on land would issue in the transformation of his swim-bladder into lungs[1]. And before a bird had cleaved the air there was surely little, in all that the most daring of saurian speculators could see or surmise concerning that untrodden element, to warrant him in risking his neck in order to satisfy his longing to soar; although, when he did try, his forelimbs were transformed to

[1] This being the process by which according to the teaching of biology reptiles first arose.

wings at length, and his dim prevision of a bird became incarnate in himself[1]. So put, these instances will seem largely fanciful, I am well aware—too Lamarckian even for Lamarck. Still they serve to bring out the one fact, *viz.* that when we regard the development of living forms as a continuous whole, we are forced to recognise, as immanent and operative throughout it, a sort of unscientific trustfulness, that from the very first seems to have been engrained in all living things. This trustfulness—might I say?—is comparable to the faith of Abraham, who, " when he was called to go out into a place which he should after receive for an inheritance, obeyed and went out, not knowing whither he went." No doubt with perfect knowledge all this would be otherwise ; but the point is that with limited knowledge such as ours there is always 'room for faith,' and always need for it : here the maxim holds, " Nothing venture nothing have." We trust and try first, not understanding till afterwards : our attitude in short is not unlike that of Anselm's famous *Credo ut intelligam.*

So far, then—psychologically and historically— there is nothing unique in the faith of theism at all ; it is only the full and final phase of an ascending series, beginning in an instinctive belief in the relatively better and ending in the rational belief in the absolutely Good, with its corollaries, the existence of God and the life hereafter. The gradual advance through impulse and desire to practical reason runs throughout on all fours with the advance through sensation and

[1] The first birds, we learn from certain fossil remains, were developed from a sort of lizard.

Logic can create nothing, but is entitled to criticise all

imagination to theoretical reason. At every stage the two form one experience, knowledge registering its progress and practical enterprise promoting it. Such enterprises imply faith, but we have this faith not solely '*on account of* the very limited amount of our knowledge and the possible errors in it.' In such enterprises our attitude is not cognitive but conative : we are not from 'want of knowledge on any subject coming to a particular conclusion on that subject.' But as active beings striving for betterment we see that the way is not closed against us and so we try to advance : we do so because such is our nature, and because our past experience justifies our faith.

But still, when we speak of reason *qua* practical having faith, we recognise that we have passed beyond the merely conative stage ; just as when we speak of reason *qua* theoretical leading to science, we imply that we have got beyond what Leibniz called *les consécutions des bêtes*. Further if these two aspects of reason are not two kinds of reason but one,—since even at this level experience is still one,—it follows that the supposed deliverances of reason in the one case as in the other are amenable to logic and open to challenge. Logic can create nothing, but it is entitled to criticise all. Science, it is commonly assumed, has *also* the right to call faith to account. But the verdict of logic so far has always been : No case. Faith contradicts nothing that science is in a position to affirm, and asserts nothing that science is in a position to deny. Science cannot disclaim it as error, nor can it appeal to science as truth. But what science can neither positively affirm nor positively deny may still count for something as being more or less probable; and 'probabilities are the guide of life.' In this sense the theist has been said to walk by faith not by sight: he is not sure, it is said, but he hopes for the best and acts accordingly. Religious apologists sometimes argue on these lines—Pascal, Butler and Paley, for example—but the prudence thus advocated is not faith; and assuredly it is not religion. Its effect on the individual's conduct, if he gets no further, will be proportional to his estimate of the probability of what still remains uncertain. We are then here still in the region of knowledge widely understood. Such prudence may be reasonable, but we must ascend to something more systematic before we are entitled to talk of practical reason and rational faith. This ascent philosophy should enable us to make and, if needs be, to criticise. Though the attempt to deal with theism from the standpoint of science is really an *ignoratio elenchi*, this charge cannot be brought against philosophy, at least not till positivism and agnosticism are triumphant. That, we may content ourselves meanwhile in saying, they are never likely to be[1].

Let us now briefly recall the main steps by which, starting from the pluralistic standpoint, we have advanced to the theistic position; and see whether, even admitting that it is not a theoretical but a practical position, it is none the less deserving of the title rational, neither transcending the domain of reason nor falling short of it. But a word first as to what in this connexion we are to understand by reason. Reason is concerned with the world in its totality either as being

[1] Cf. J. Seth, *A Study of Ethical Principles*, 1st edn, pp. 393 ff.

What is "Reason"? It is concerned with the world in its totality either as being a system or as having a meaning.

a system or as having a meaning : we may ask What is it? and also What is it for or Why is it? The two questions are intimately connected. From the *theoretical* standpoint we do not inquire about the 'why' till we know something of the 'what.' But, as I have had already to insist, the standpoint of theory is not the standpoint of life. Life is primarily active, not contemplative ; and thus it is only while striving for what is good that we learn what is true; only as interested in the 'what for' that we inquire about the 'what.' Even in common language to ask 'why' is to ask for 'the reason,'—that is not merely for the cause but chiefly for the end. It is with reason in this sense that we have now to deal.

There are those who say that to talk of the world as having a meaning or end at all is an unwarrantable assumption. This may be true as an abstract statement, that is so long as we separate structure and description from purpose and worth. And for science it is important to keep the two distinct : hence Bacon's depreciation of teleology, and hence too Kant's treatment of the category of End—unlike those of Substance and Cause—as only regulative and not constitutive. But can those who without reservation refuse to credit the world with a meaning give a reason for their position, and so justify themselves in stigmatizing as dogmatic or superstitious those who are not thus sceptical? If the world has no meaning, must we not say that it is an irrational world? But we are ourselves the highest beings in it of whom we have any direct objective knowledge. Unless then we are to stultify ourselves, all that we can mean in calling the world irrational is that it would be so apart from its relation to ourselves and other rational beings. It is but an awkward way of saying what Hamilton preferred to put more grandiloquently : " On earth, there is nothing great but man ; in man, there is nothing great but mind." We may call it faith, but we cannot call it irrational, to believe that the world has a meaning and a meaning for us.

But even granting that the world has a meaning, it is contended in the next place that since for us this meaning is not here and now realised, we do not certainly know what it is. We would fain, it may be, mould the world nearer to our heart's desire, but we cannot, it has been said, 'argue from the reality of desires to the truth of dogmas.' A good deal depends surely upon the rationality of the desires. This is the next point—have we ourselves any supremely rational aim ? Till we have, we cannot claim to have emerged from the tutelage of nature, to be ourselves rational and free.

In discussing this point it is enough to appeal to humanity at its present highest level. The best of men certainly recognise a moral ideal with which they identify their own highest good, and whose imperatives they therefore regard as absolutely binding and yet— because self-imposed—as also absolutely free. Now the moral ideal places the highest good of each in the highest good of all ; but for us it is only an ideal. But will any one say that it is irrational ? Happily, as it is, history furnishes us with many and striking instances of brotherly love and heroic devotion, and there is more zeal now than ever to promote goodwill among men :

does any one call these absurd or think the onward
course of philanthropy and self-consecration to the
public weal should be stayed? We will not pause to
remark how much more the moral ideal involves than
these ideas of themselves suggest; for already at this
stage we shall be met by the objection, that man being
what he is and the world what it is, the realisation of
even this much of our ideal is impossible. And if man
stands alone and if this life is all, the objection is hardly
to be gainsaid. But then we are confronted by a
serious dilemma. Either the world is not rational or
man does not stand alone and this life is not all. But
it cannot be rational to conclude that the world is not
rational, least of all when an alternative is open to us
that leaves room for its rationality—the alternative of
postulating God and a future life.

Without the idea of a Supreme and Ultimate
Being—least inadequately conceived as personal—transcending the world as the ground of its being, and yet
immanent in it as it is his idea, this world may well
for ever remain that *rerum concordia discors*, which at
present we find it. Ever since man attained to self-
consciousness and reason he has had ideals and will
always have them; and his ideals are the measure of
his worth and the sure marks of his true progress or
decline. But if we are to stop short with the pluralism
which is all that in fact we find—where all alike are
finite as well as interdependent—how do we know that
there will not always, as now, be incompatible ideals,
ideals therefore always imperfect? Perfectly to harmonize
egoism and altruism, for example, has always been the
great crux for moralists. A recent French moralist

who disclaims the theistic belief has argued with some force that a complete solution is in the nature of things impossible[1]; and a distinguished English moralist, as we know, without clearly committing himself as regards the theistic 'hypothesis,' concluded his work by saying: "If we reject this belief, the Cosmos of Duty is really reduced to a Chaos; and the prolonged effort of the human intellect to frame a perfect ideal of rational conduct is seen to have been foredoomed to inevitable failure[2]." We may accept his conclusion, though we can, I think, improve upon his reasons. It is not as providing adequate sanctions for the suppression of egoism—effectual it may be but scarcely moral—that theism provides the keystone to the structure of ethics. Over against other men a man may possibly be incorrigibly selfish, but with living faith in God selfishness towards him would not be possible. To any other being I may decline to say, Thy will not mine be done, but not to God, if I believe in him. The idea of this one divine Will necessarily implies the meaning of the world; for that is grounded entirely on it. It also implies the presence of a definite moral ideal as an eternal purpose, which finite wills alone might strain after for ever and never realise. With one creative Spirit over all we may well believe in a unity of the many created spirits, such that the highest good of all will prove to be the highest good of each. And in the light of this divine purpose we may well find the vocation and the meaning of our own individual life. The existence of this

---

[1] L. Bourdeau, *Le Problème de la Vie. Essai de Sociologie générale*, 1901.

[2] H. Sidgwick, *The Methods of Ethics*, 1st edn, 1874, p. 473.

The idea of God not only a postulate of the practical reason but also a 'regulative idea' for the theoretical reason 'acosmism': the doctrine that there is no world.

Necessity for Belief in God   423

Creative Spirit is matter of faith not of knowledge, to be sure; but may we not hold it to be a rational faith, since without it we are without assured hope in a world that is then without clear meaning?

But not only is the idea of God a postulate of reason as practical: it is also a 'regulative idea' for reason as theoretical. It has been the predominant tendency of theoretical speculation in fact to lay undue stress, if I may so say, on this idea; and so to render it completely indeterminate by denying not the existence of God but the reality of the world: not atheism, the doctrine that there is no God, but acosmism, the doctrine that there is no world, has been the usual outcome of so-called pure thought. Still we have found that mere pluralism, which begins with the world and proceeds in a more empirical fashion, has to content itself by accepting the undeniable unity, which the very idea of a world implies, as something ultimate which it can neither explain nor show to be self-explanatory. The theoretical demand for the ground of the world then, as well as the practical demand for the good of the world, is met by the idea of God. In this sense the words of Wundt are true: "Philosophy can prove the necessity of faith, but to convert it into knowledge, for that she has not the power[1]." Conviction here can come only by living, not by merely thinking: "If any man willeth to do his will he shall know of the doctrine whether it be of God."

It will be opportune at this point to notice a difficulty sometimes raised. If there verily is a God and a future life, surely facts of such moment would have been

[1] *System der Philosophie*, 1ste Auf. 4ter Abschnitt, *fin.* p. 444.

placed beyond question and not left where, if there is
room for faith, there must also be room for doubt as
well.   This is but a special form of the objection that
may be made to an evolving world as such, to a world
that temporarily is not, but only gradually becomes,
what its ideal implies, a world that, so to say, makes
itself instead of being posited ready-made.   Transcendent objections of this sort we cannot, I believe,
reasonably raise or profitably discuss.   If we could
intuite this world *sub specie aeternitatis* the objection
would lapse; so long and so far as we have to live in
it *sub specie temporis*, the objection is self-contradictory.
The most we can do is to find fault with the mode or
the pace of this world's actual evolution.   But even so,
the fact that knowledge has to grow from more to
more—that it cannot be passively imparted but must be
actively acquired—is so fundamental and universal a
characteristic of our evolution, as to make it very
doubtful if we can ever conceive of an experience which
develops at all developing on other lines.   In particular
the idea of God—like other 'ideas of reason'—obviously
could not be revealed to minds unfitted to assimilate
it; and yet could not fail to be acquired by those that
were.   The history of philosophy and religion shows
us accordingly the gradual emergence of this idea,
crude at first, but progressively elaborated, both for
theory and for life, as the mind of man grew in intelligence and insight, and his heart in purity and
singleness of aim.   If the slowness of this progress
depress us—as well it may—still we have to remember
that, inasmuch as we are free agents, this progress
must depend on our own lives and efforts.   But there

is one doctrine of the theology in vogue which gives special point to the objection we have considered[1]— the doctrine *viz.* that those who die outside the pale of Christianity are 'lost eternally.' This 'moral enormity,' as Mill called it, at any rate rational theism must disavow. Texts in support of such a doctrine may be cited no doubt—but Christianity is a bigger thing than texts, and happily the spirit of Christianity is clearly against it, as Christians themselves are coming more and more to see.

Our moral ideals lead not only to faith in God, but also, supported by this faith, to belief in a future life. The question of the rationality of this belief depends, we have allowed, on the value we are entitled to assign to man and to his work. The mere wish to live longer is no reason for believing that we shall live again; while a claim to live again based on personal merit seems more arrogant than rational. This is true but scarcely relevant. It is not a question of private wishes or of extraneous rewards : it is a question of the status of a rational free agent who has chosen or is capable of choosing the moral ideal as his end. The ideal is there and is meant to be realised : it is rational to believe this and all it implies, if it is rational to believe anything. One thing that it implies in an evolving world like ours is a gradual advance from the *status quo* of humanity, whereon the ideal has dawned, ever forwards unto the perfect day. Humanity already has yearnings and aspirations that the flesh-pots of Egypt—material and temporal well-being—can never content; is it, impelled by these longings for higher

---

[1] Cf. J. S. Mill, *Three Essays on Religion*, 1885, pp. 114 f.

things, destined to wander aimlessly in the wilderness for ever unsatisfied?

Well, at all events, it may be said, we see other creatures remaining apparently stationary at lower stages of development which man has already left behind; and is it not then likely that, in turn, other rationals, more highly endowed and better placed than we, may realise the ideals which but a few men among all mankind imperfectly surmise and fitfully long for? We can worship where we cannot emulate, just as a dog worships his master and is the better for it, though he will never become a man. It is better that we should 'pitch our behaviour low, our projects high,' and die outright as philosophers unsatisfied, rather than live while we live as brutes in whom the light of reason has never shone. Better assuredly, but still assuredly not good. Nor is the analogy on which this counsel of renunciation rests altogether a sound one. It is true that diversity of endowment is an ultimate characteristic of our world. As St Paul put it:—"All flesh is not the same flesh.... There is one glory of the sun, another glory of the moon, and another glory of the stars." What advance is possible within each kind we cannot tell. But at least advance seems possible so long as an ideal, more or less consciously recognised or felt, incites to efforts towards its attainment. This is life in the fullest sense, and this too is faith in the widest sense: *so lange man strebt, glaubt man, und so lange man glaubt, strebt man*[1]. The lower animals seem in general content with their lot: they struggle to exist rather than to advance, and so we

[1] Chalybäus, *Speculative Philosophie von Kant bis Hegel*, 1860, concl.

may describe theirs as a stationary state; they seem to
have attained to an equilibration with their present
conditions. This is emphatically not the case with
man—he always has ideals—and so far the analogy
just now appealed to as a ground for resignation, fails
in the essential point.

Yes, the positivists will say, we believe that humanity
in the distant future will realise our ideal; but what
we know of evolution leads us to suppose our relation
to this consummation to be that of forerunners and
harbingers of the good which posterity is to have and
to hold. As the extinct anthropoids stand to us, so
we stand to the over-men who are to succeed us ;

> For all we thought and loved and did,
> And hoped and suffer'd, is but seed
> Of what in them is flower and fruit.

We remain without the promised land, but we do not
wander aimlessly in the wilderness : we know what we
work for and we work unselfishly : when our work is
done, we should be content to depart in peace. In
evolution there is an order of generations as well as an
order of kinds, and it is as unreasonable to repine
because we are not angels, as to complain because a
better time is coming that we shall not see. After all
ours is better than those which went before; and so it
may always be ; for there is really no finality. Those
who realise one ideal will find another beckoning them
onwards, which they in turn will strive after but not
attain :

> Hope springs eternal in the human breast,
> Man never is, but always to be blest.

Forcible as such reasoning may seem from its own

standpoint of thorough-going relativity, it is essentially incoherent and irrational. It does not descend deep enough to see the full meaning of personality nor rise high enough to come in sight of what is meant by the Supreme Good. It moves entirely on the naturalistic plane, where there are no causes that are not in turn effects and no ends that are not in turn means—in a word no autonomous beings, who initiate their own actions and are ends in themselves. A realm of such ends, as ideally at least an absolute unity, implies one Supreme End for the whole and for each of its members, the precise opposite of what a system of means implies, where both the whole and the parts alike lack any end of their own at all[1]. The wearisome procession of generation after generation of mortals in pursuit of an *ignis fatuus*, all hoping, all working for what none attain, might divert a Mephistopheles but would certainly not be a realm of ends.

Again in appealing to evolution the naturalistic theory of progress overlooks the one point in which the moral differs from the natural. Natural evolution is concerned primarily with the type, moral with the single life. Neither heredity nor natural selection nor even tradition can take the place of personal election. Apart from this, though we follow the stream of tendency that makes for righteousness, we cannot claim to be 'unselfish or to know what we are striving for.' Further the realisation of the moral ideal is not a process, like the development of a language or an art, that can accomplish itself piecemeal through the instrumentality of successive generations, acting more or less

[1] Cf. Lecture XVIII. p. 387.

unconsciously and without set purpose. From first to last faith in this ideal is a personal thing ; in personal conviction and choice it must begin, whether the person is born early or born late. Is it then rational to suppose that in the one case he cannot achieve it at all, and in the other has it thrust upon him ? But it is certain, if this life is all, that complete attainment is impossible ; for as the dissolution of the organism will then extinguish the individual, so the dissolution of the solar system will extinguish the race. Hence the moral ideal, as it leads to faith in God, leads also to the belief that the spirit world has other dimensions than those of the time and space that encompass the world of phenomena. For what is the alternative ? When a man desiring to build a tower lays the foundation but is not able to finish he becomes a mockery and his work is called a 'folly.' And has not God been mocked and life called the vanity of vanities on the assumption that the present world is all ? But since faith in the unseen and eternal is open to us, is it not rational to embrace it, since there the essentially rational, the absolute Good is not merely a hope but reality ? And in the name of reason what else indeed can it be ?

Summary.

1. Disavowal of any attempt to solve completely the riddle of the universe.

2. But what standpoint towards it is most fundamental? Answer: that which recognises the duality of experience - viz. the subjective & objective element present in all experience.

3. But the attitude of the subject towards the object is . 2fold .. it is both cognitive (theoretical) & conative (practical)

LECTURE XX.

THE REALM OF ENDS.

It only remains now in bringing these lectures to a close to summarize briefly the main course of our inquiry, to state as positively as may be the results that we seem to have attained and finally to glance at some topics for further reflexion which they suggest.

At the outset we disavowed any attempt completely to solve the so-called riddle of the universe. This much modesty is common to all schools of philosophy alike in our day. The universe as a whole is but partially accessible to us at the best; but we make up for this defect to some extent by viewing it from different standpoints. It is therefore important first of all, if we can, to ascertain which of these is the most fundamental and to orientate the rest to this. One characteristic belongs to them all—that duality of subject and object that enters into all experience. But the subject's attitude towards the object is twofold: it is both cognitive and conative, or, as we often say, both theoretical and practical. Though these subjective attitudes are not strictly separable, yet the practical terminates in the theoretical so soon and so far as what we immediately want is *only* to know. And so it comes about that, ignoring the subject and its practical

4. objectively considered. Nature & the universe is regarded as something to be described. subjectively. it is regarded as a Realm of [?] - something to be understood.

relations, forgetting even what knowledge implies (as we forget the eye when intent only on what we see), we are led to conceive the universe as in itself *only* objective. From this standpoint we call it Nature, and we ask simply what is it: the one problem here is to find a precise and comprehensive description; and the result is what Newton called *Natural Philosophy*. No complementary abstraction is possible when we turn to the subjective factor of experience: we may here misinterpret the objective but we cannot leave it out of account. It pains or pleases, helps or hinders us: in interaction with it our life primarily consists, and we are forced therefore to try to understand it: so we ask what it means. From this standpoint Spinoza's *Ethics* may be regarded as the pendant to the work of his contemporary Newton. "All individual things" said Spinoza "are animated, albeit in divers degrees," and again "every thing has in itself a striving to preserve its own condition and to improve itself[1]." This is at all events the more primitive view: is it also the more fundamental? We conclude that it is, first, because it takes account of both the factors of experience; and secondly, because, while it is impossible from the standpoint of Nature to reach Spirit, it is only from the standpoint of Spirit that Nature can be understood: in a word we take the universe to be spiritual—a realm of ends.

But what is its constitution? For even from the standpoint of Spirit it is possible to regard the universe in two aspects: it is One and it is Many. The Many

[1] *Ethics*, II. xiii. Schol., *Short Treatise on God, Man and his Wellbeing*, bk I. ch. v. A. Wolf's edn, 1910, p. 47.

But is the universe one or many?

Answer: we must begin with Pluralism for that is what we first experience.

432   *The Realm of Ends*

Pluralism means "individuals animated in various degrees and striving towards self-preservation or betterment"

are relative to each other : the whole is absolute.   We
are of the Many : with them we interact.   It is with the
plurality then rather than with the unity that man is first
of all practically concerned.   The unity of the world,
as Kant has said, is an idea of our reason, not an
object of our experience ; and it was not till man had
lived long and thought deeply that this idea of the
One or the Absolute first dawned.   It is certain then
that the pluralist's standpoint is the more primitive : is
it also in itself the more fundamental ?   We cannot say
this, we can hardly even suppose it.   Why then begin
with it ?   But have we any choice ?   The attempt—to
a speculative mind so attractive—to begin with the
One has, we know, often been made, and surely we
may add, has as often failed.   Moreover when more
closely examined these essays in pure thought turn
out to be 'infected' with the empirical.   Like a rocket
they dazzle in the void, but the stick can always be
found which directed their course and betrays their
origin.   Nevertheless this tell-tale stick is not only
dropped but forgotten, and the pluralistic aspect of the
universe not explained but explained away.   If the
speculative enterprises of the past can be any guide
for the future, they show that we have no choice but
to begin where we are, and that we only deceive
ourselves when we try to start by transcending experience.   Accepting this teaching of history then, we
began our inquiry about the universe as a realm of
ends from the pluralistic standpoint.

We began, that is to say, with 'individuals animated
in various degrees and striving for self-preservation or
betterment.'   But with what do they strive ?   With

This "striving" when analysed shows
 Some ideas already realised — natura naturata.
 Other ideas still to be realised — natura naturans.
But in each case the idea is that of the good.

The Start from the Pluralistic Standpoint 433

others who either actively compete with them or at
least stand in their way.   And also, we should have to
add, with their physical environment; were it not that
pluralism, in regarding every 'thing' as in some degree
animated, does away with the distinction between
persons, widely understood, and inert things altogether. *Legitimacy*
In support of this bold assumption an appeal is made *of this.*
to the principle of continuity, confirmed as it is by the
fact that every advance of knowledge so far has only
disclosed simpler forms of life and further analogies
between the organic and what we call the inorganic.
It is also contended that there is no evidence that any
two beings in the world are exactly alike; which is
just what selfhood or personality implies, and the
physicist's concept of atoms denies.   Again the constants
and uniformities, with which his analysis ends, are
regarded as simply statistical results, such as frequently
hide the diversity and spontaneity of animated beings
when they and their actions are taken *en masse*.   This
diversity and spontaneity are held to be fundamental;
and the orderliness and regularity we now observe, to
be the *result* of behaviour, not its presupposition.   We
are supposed to be dealing, not with a system of
concepts which can be unfolded deductively, but with
concrete agents whose intercourse and development
can only be studied historically.   On the one side we
have what is done, ideals realised; on the other what
is still to do, ideals still to be realised: or adopting
scholastic terms, we have *natura naturata* and *natura
naturans*.   The idea of the good is the master clue;
for this is what all striving and all ideals imply.   The
process throughout is that of trial and error, which all

There is experiment & error in the process:
There is also contingency but not pure chance or utter chaos.
You may call this process Evolution but
The Pluralist believes in "epigenesis" rather than in "Evolution"

Epigenesis is really the Creation of new Values.

experience involves; but there is no pure chance and
no utter chaos. Contingency however is inevitable;
we find it accordingly on every hand, not only in
human affairs or in animated nature but in the so-called
physical world as well.

Still through all a steady tendency is apparent to
replace this mere contingency by a definite progression;
the further we advance the more we see of guidance
and direction. With this progression we are familiar
under the name of evolution, a term too firmly established to be lightly set aside. It is all the more
important therefore to bear in mind that—though he
continues to use the word—what the pluralist understands by it is something widely different from that
explicating of what is implicit from the first, which is
the literal meaning of evolution, and the meaning that
it still holds when the universe is primarily contemplated
from the standpoint of the One. But the pluralistic
meaning is more accurately expressed by the rival
term 'epigenesis'; that is to say, the origination by
integration of new properties in the whole, which its
constituents in their isolation did not possess. Such
integration has been called 'creative synthesis': a
melody compared with its component notes or a regiment with its soldiers as disbanded may serve as
instances. Such syntheses arise wherever there are
active individuals bent on working out a *modus vivendi*
with each other; as we see most conspicuously in the
development of society. What is thus created are not
new entities but new values; and these tend not only
to be conserved but to make higher unities and worthier
ideals possible; and that without assignable limits.

Epigenesis
D3

Moreover, when at length the level of human culture is attained, we reach a good that is not diminished by being shared, and one that yields more the more it has already yielded. And here—in form at any rate—the final goal of evolution comes into sight, not a pre-established harmony but the eventual consummation of a perfect commonwealth, wherein all cooperate and none conflict, wherein the many have become one, one realm of ends.

With the Many pluralism began, with the Many it ends. But did it really begin at the beginning and does it really reach the end? Is the pluralistic standpoint absolute? This is the question to which at this point we returned. But if we *had* to begin as we did, this question really converts itself into one concerning what I called the upper and the lower limits of pluralism. Does pluralism naturally suggest some end beyond itself, and presuppose something as the ground of itself? The problems of the universe would be fewer as well as simpler if all the life in it were confined to this planet; so much so that we find philosophers and theologians again and again attempting to prove that this is in truth the case, as mankind for ages had been wont to suppose. But the ignorance and special pleading common to all these attempts justify us nevertheless in ignoring them. If then we regard the universe as teeming with living orbs, how are we to imagine these as ever constituting the commonwealth of worlds: in view of our own utter isolation how is *this* higher unity ever to be achieved? Such questions lead the pluralist to apply the principle of continuity upwards as well as downwards. To connect these otherwise isolated

And The 'higher' & 'lower' limits of pluralism
neither of which are absolutely attainable
leads to consideration of 'Creation' & so of 'Theism' –
by their suggestion of the existence of a Prime Mover.

worlds he is driven to assume a hierarchy of intelligences
of a higher order, and so is led on to conceive a
Highest of all. But still, so long as we hold to the
principle of continuity, this Supreme Being will only
be *primus inter pares,* only one of the Many ; he will
also, like the rest, be confronted and conditioned by
others, so long at least as we hold to the historical
standpoint. Thus while pluralism suggests a transcendent upper limit, it is one to which knowledge
cannot actually attain. Again the principle of continuity
and the historical method, the standpoint that is to
say of evolution, suggest also a lower limit, and this
proves to be equally unattainable. In attempting to
regress to an absolute origin, we seem only to get
nearer to the utterly indeterminate that affords no
ground for distinct individuals at all ; where there is
no *natura naturata,* and where in order that the *nasci*
may begin, we seem to require a transcendent Prime
Mover standing apart from the nascent Many. May
not the two limits, then, which its cardinal principles
of continuity and evolution do not enable pluralism to
attain, be really related ? This question leads us to
the idea of creation, and so to the discussion of Theism.

Not content with the admission that pluralism on
examination points both theoretically and practically
beyond itself, many advocates of singularism have
attempted to show it up as radically absurd. These
attempts do not appear successful. That an absolute
totality of individuals is self-contradictory and that an
absolute individual is not, is more than anyone has yet
proved. That a plurality of individuals in isolation
should ever come into relation is inconceivable indeed,

Theism as completing pluralism, not abolishing it.
'creation' as meaning the 'creation' of 'creators'

but only because a plurality without unity is itself inconceivable. That individuals severally distinct as regards their existence could not interact is however a mere *dictum*. Pluralism takes the world as we find it, as a plurality of individuals unified in and through their mutual intercourse. 'Radically empirical' this certainly is, but if it be true, it cannot be radically absurd; and if it be not true, then we are entitled to ask the singularist how he ever got started on the *a priori* road. We approach theism then as promising to complete pluralism, not as threatening to abolish it, as providing theoretically more unity in the ground of the world, and practically a higher and fuller unity in its meaning and end.

Starting from the Many as real we can never reach an Absolute into which they are absorbed and vanish: they are our *ratio cognoscendi* of God as their *ratio essendi*. As related to them, God must be limited and determined by them: he cannot be as if they were not. If then he is not to be merely one of them, not merely *primus inter pares*, this limitation must be an internal limitation; God, we must say, is their Creator; and in creating them he has determined himself. And by this the pluralist means even more than at first it seems to mean. Theists in our day profess to accept the evolution hypothesis, but hardly as pluralism interprets it, not as epigenesis or creative synthesis but rather as the literal unfolding of a plan completely specified in every detail. "Unless creators are created, nothing is really created" the pluralist maintains, "and the idea of creation would never enter our minds at all."

At this point we have the remarkable conjunction

of naturalism and orthodox theology in opposition to pluralism—Hobbes and Jonathan Edwards in league against the 'personal idealist.' Careful analysis, we thought, enabled us to make good distinctions that the determinist either overlooks or denies—the distinction, for example, between self-determination, implying teleological categories, and determination according to fixed law, implying only mechanical categories; and again the Kantian distinction between the efficient causality of the thing *per se* and the schematized causation according to 'a rule of succession,' to which the thing *per se* may give rise but which never could give rise to it; the distinction, that is, between the pattern of filled time and the agents who do the filling. But if we could start, not from these agents, the Many, but from the One *conceived as absolute*, the necessitarian position would be unavoidable and the predestinarian right. But then, as we have all along maintained, the world, as we know it, would be impossible. The only way out of this *impasse*—not between pluralism and theism, mind, but between theism and atheism—appears to be the *via media*, that "*all* is not decreed, that the *total* possibilities, however far back we go, are fixed; but within these however far forward we go, contingencies are open[1]." This way alone seems to lead towards the solution of another problem, the gravest that theism has to face—the problem of evil.

From the standpoint of the Many, evils are hard to bear but easy enough to account for, but from the standpoint of the One, evil seems to be simply a contradiction, an impossibility. If theism be true, then

[1] Lecture XIV. p. 315.

evil can only be relative and must gradually disappear: if theism be not true, though evils remain relative, they may never disappear. In any case, evil as absolute, as a principle, is an absurdity—this the speculations of pessimists sufficiently show. " God can do no evil, it is agreed ; if then this world were verily his creation, there could not be any, even relative, evil in it." This conclusion forms the major premise of the prosecution in the great theodicy, as Leibniz called it. Once again we may say the main issue is between theism and atheism ; and since the fact of relative evils is indisputable, the verdict must be for atheism, if this conclusion is sound. For if the world as it is be as God decreed it, the moral evil in it *would be* his work. But if our contention will hold, that though God created us, he created us free and to be co-workers with himself, then this moral evil, which proximately at all events is our doing, will be really and ultimately ours. If however our contention is not sound, then the whole case, prosecution and defence alike, is either an illusion and a farce, or there is no God at all.

Still, granting this contention meanwhile, what of those physical evils which do not seem to be either proximately or remotely attributable to us? But first, there is one restriction that the idea of any determinate world, no matter what, imposes upon itself in being determinate—its parts must be compossible: nothing in it can do everything. The idea of a world the parts of which are in no way to limit each other is as unthinkable as the idea of an absolutely omnipotent God who is to create it. To object that God himself can only be finite, and must be limited from without, because he

440 *The Realm of Ends*

Physical evils act as incentives to evolution.

cannot override eternal truths, is the merest sophistry.
The demand for absoluteness of this sort is a demand
not for God but for the Indeterminate, a supreme
unity of opposites which is the same as nothing.
Leaving aside such so-called physical evils as are in
this sense metaphysical, the negations which all determination involves, we can fairly ask concerning the
physical ills that are admittedly contingent, whether we
have in general any reason to suppose that they are
superfluous and not rather the indispensable condition
of advance, and so as an incentive really good. The
world, ever pressing forward, entered on the stage of
conscious life as soon as it was possible, not waiting till
the fierce strife and turmoil of what we call the elements
had wholly abated, but rather driven by struggling
with these to new adaptations that tended to raise it
above them. At this stage such incentives were largely
of the nature of a *vis a tergo* : only as the advance has
proceeded, have these given place to motives which
partake more and more of the nature of a *vis a fronte*.
The pressure of physical evils having first led to the
solidarity of the social state, this has ushered in the
attraction of those ideals that Hegel called the objective
spirit.

It is characteristic of man that he stands at the
parting of the ways ; and under the influence of both
physical ills and spiritual ideals, is led eventually to
conclude that he has no abiding city here and to seek
a city yet to come. Meanwhile the dimensions that
circumscribe this spatial and temporal world afford us
no sure clue to the wider dimensions of that more spiritual world beyond ; nor do they enable us to conjecture

and The evidence of purpose that we already have (& have acted on) justifies us in thinking that this purpose holds for the future – Knowledge justifies faith.

how the two are connected or how the transition is to be made. But none the less our hold on those higher spiritual ideals leads us to believe in God and forces us to think we were not made to die. But anyhow, it is urged, all that we are sure of are the ills and the vanities of the present; and if we must infer from the known to the unknown, is it not more likely that death will end them than that it will mend them? That present evil should set us hoping for future good is natural, but to argue from evil now to good hereafter is surely not rational. No, it is replied, vanity and vexation of spirit are not all that we find. Thoughtful men have been driven to call life an enigma but few have been willing to curse it as a folly or a fraud; it has too much meaning, shows too much purpose for that, though its secret and its goal be not yet clear. Mists may envelope us, mountains seem to bar our way; but often we have heard when we could not see, and found a way by pressing forward, though, while we halted, there seemed no way at all. These are the two voices—faith and knowledge—how come they to put such different interpretations on the very same facts? Because knowledge is of things we see, and seeks to interpret the world as if they were the whole; while faith is aware that now we see but in part, and is convinced that only provided the unseen satisfies our spiritual yearnings is the part we see intelligible— what ought to be being the key to what is.

And now to state succinctly the positive results we seem to have attained. They may be gathered up under four heads relating to Method or standpoint, to

Summary of Results.

I. Method. Experience of the Many
Suggests (this it does not prove) the One.

442 *The Realm of Ends*

God or the One, to the World or the Many, and to Faith in the Unseen.

I.   As to method—we have started from what we are, cognitive and conative subjects; and from where we are—so to say *in mediis rebus*—in a world consisting to an indefinite extent of other like subjects. No speculation, no dialectic, no ontological deduction, is needed to reach this position ; and without it all these alike are impossible. But beginning thus, we are led both on theoretical and on practical grounds to conceive a more fundamental standpoint than this of the Many, namely that of the One that would furnish an ontological unity for their cosmological unity and ensure a teleological unity for their varied ends, in being—as it has been said—'the impersonated Ideal of every mind[1]'— the One, as ultimate source of their being and ultimate end of their ends. But though we can conceive this standpoint, we cannot here attain to it or see the world from it. It is there, like their centre of gravity for the inhabitants of a planetary ring, but the aspect of the world from thence is more than we can conceive. Attempts to delineate this have been really but projections of our own eccentric and discursive views : creative synthesis as human implies aspects, creative intuition as divine is beyond them. The result of all attempts to begin with the One is only to lower our idea of the world, not to raise our idea of God. His *modus operandi*, if even this phase is allowable, in creating, conserving, and ruling the world is beyond us.

II.   As to God from the point of view of man, then, we can only regard him as Spirit, as possessing

[1] Howison, *Limits of Evolution*, 2nd edn, p. xiv.

II God - "The one" is supreme & personal : but
man is, within limits - free.
The one is the ground of the many.

God   443

intelligence and will, and so as personal. But while we
must admit such attributes carried to their limit to be
beyond us, we cannot regard God as absolute in such
wise as to deprive ourselves of all personality or initiative. How God created the world, how the One is the
ground of the Many, we admit we cannot tell ; but since
it is from the Many as real that we start we are forced to
say that creation implies limitation; otherwise the world
could be nothing. Such theism would be acosmism.
But while we have to maintain that in determining the
world—his world—God also determines himself, it would
be absurd to suppose that in thus determining himself
he, so to say, diminishes himself. Such determination
may be negation, nay must be, to be real at all ; but it is
not abnegation. God does not transform, differentiate
or fractionate himself into the world, and so cease to
be God. Such theism would only be pantheism, which
is truly but atheism. But now, finally, if the world,
though God's world, the expression and revelation of
himself, is yet not God, if though he is immanent in
it, he is also as its creator transcendent to it, surely
the greater the world—the greater the freedom and
capacity of his creatures—the greater still is he who
created and sustains and somehow surely overrules it
all. Oriental servility and *a priori* speculation have
made God synonymous with an 'Infinite and Absolute'
that leaves room for no other and can brook none. To
express dissent from this view, the unfortunate term
'finite God,' devised by those who uphold the view, has
been accepted from them by its opponents. As used by
the former, it implies and was meant to imply imperfection and dependence, to place God in line with the Many

and to deny his transcendent supremacy. So understood a finite God is a contradiction, of course. But
the term 'finite God,' as accepted by the latter, means
for them all that God *can* mean, if God implies the
world and is not God without it: it means a living
God with a living world, not a potter God with a
world of illusory clay, not an inconceivable abstraction
that is only infinite and absolute, because it is beyond
everything and means nothing, an ἀπειρόθεος as
Thomas Davidson, I believe, called it.

　　III. And now as to this living world, of which
God is the ground, this realm of ends which he
respects because it is his end—it is, we say, a world of
self-determining, free, agents, severally intent on attaining more good or at least on retaining the good they
have. We note three main characteristics—contingency
in part, stability in part and progress in part—all
involved in experience as epigenetic. There is contingency, for a common *modus vivendi* is still to seek;
there is stability, for all effectual cooperation is conserved as good; and there is progress, so long as the
ills we have or the goods we know not of prompt to
further efforts. But goods we know not of are ideal;
and ideal ends are only possible on the plane of rational
life: the brutes at least leave well alone, and species as
soon as they are adjusted to their environment remain
stationary, so long at least as that remains unchanged.
Such a stationary state may be possible where progress
is due solely to the *vis a tergo* of actual physical ills; it
is impossible, even though these should cease, once the
Good as an ideal has loomed in sight, and begun as
a *vis a fronte* to draw spirits onwards. But it has taken

untold ages to accomplish that finite amount of progress which the pressure of material want promotes ; can we then expect the indefinite progress that spiritual possibilities open up will be easily or speedily achieved ? Compared with the interval between the lowest forms of merely animal life and the highest, the interval between civilised man and man in the infancy of the race, is vast ; and yet, so far as we can judge, the time it has occupied is correspondingly brief. The greater definiteness and steadiness of purpose that intelligence brings and the permanent tradition that social cooperation makes possible have then unquestionably accelerated the rate of progress on the whole.

But now struggles of a new order arise through this very progress itself. Moral evils spring up and grow apace in the rich soil of worldly prosperity ; for the intelligence and social continuity that make nobler ideals possible can also subserve the ends of selfishness, injustice and oppression. Thus the greatest enemy of mankind is man : so it has always been, so it may long continue to be. Yet here too there has been progress ; and the vision of a new era, when righteousness shall cover the earth as the waters cover the sea, evokes the lip-service of multitudes and the life-devotion of a few. But time, that tries all things, will assuredly bring more and more to take the lesson to heart that

Man must pass from old to new,
From vain to real, from mistake to fact,
From what once seemed good to what now proves best.

But why, we ask, must the lesson be so slowly learnt ? Because to be effectually learnt, it must be learnt by heart, every jot and tittle of it by actual living experience.

Advanced to the plane of social intercourse and rational discourse, man has sought out many inventions, preferring at first what looks easy to what seems arduous, what looks near to what seems remote, what looks tangible to what seems visionary. This we call worldly wisdom. The more all its schemes are found to fail, the more clearly will stand out the one straight and narrow way—at first so hard to find and still so hard to ascend—that verily leads to life. As from geology we learn of species after species that have disappeared in the process of adjusting organism to environment; so in history we learn from the rise and fall of empire after empire that only righteousness exalteth a nation and that those that pursue evil perish. It is thus in the light of evolution that the mystery of evil becomes clearest. God is the creator of the world, we say : his end can only be the Good— no other is even conceivable. But in a world created for the Good there can be no inherent, no ineradicable evil. The process of evolution must then in itself be good, the one way possible to actual good for creatures that are created to achieve it. And if again we ask why the way is so long and the progress so devious and so slow, we can but suppose it is so because only so can the progress be thorough and the way assuredly the best ; this we may well believe is why " the mills of God grind slowly and grind exceeding small." Only after proving all things can we hold fast to that which is good.

But now—and this leads on to our last head— does this not come near to saying, it may be asked, that the best of all possible worlds is a world without

God is the `ground` of the world as (a) living active Spirit.
Its realm of `ends` is this one? (P. 444)

God and the World   447

God? is it not practically atheism, in short? and if not
that, still, if the world is left severely alone to work out
its own salvation, what have we but the God-forsaken
world in which the so-called deists are said to have
believed?   Not atheism, certainly, for faith in God as
the ground of the world affords us an assurance, which
we could not otherwise have, that complete harmony
and unity, the good of all in the good of each, is really
attainable, nay, will verily be attained.   Whereas, if
we stop at a plurality of finite selves in interaction, we
have no guarantee, cannot even reasonably expect,
that such a totality will ever attain to perfect organic
unity.   Nor does the theism to which pluralism points
leave no place for God *in* the world; it is then not deism:
creation, if we think, we shall see can be conceived only
as continuous presence[1].   If God is the ground of the
world at all he is its ground always as an active, living,
interested, Spirit, not as a merely everlasting, changeless and indifferent centre, round which it simply whirls.
Still God's action in the world must be for us as inscrutable as his creation of it: indeed there is no
reason why we should attempt to discriminate between
them.   In calling God transcendent we seek only to
express that duality of subject and object which we
take as fundamental to all spiritual being, not to
suggest that his relation to the world must be thought
under the category of external causation, like the
interaction of object with object.   This is obviously
inadequate.   Nor is the relation of God to the world
comparable to the interaction of one finite subject
with another; for between them there is no such

[1] Cf. above, Lect. XII. pp. 260 f.

dependence as that which connects them both with
God. We trench upon the mystical when we attempt
to picture this divine immanence, 'closer to us than
breathing and nearer than hands and feet.' It is this
which stirs the 'cosmic emotion' of poets like Wordsworth, Goethe, Browning and Tennyson, to this that the
inward witness of the spirit refers which is the essence
of religious experience everywhere. In both there
opens out in varying degrees of clearness and certainty

> The true world within the world we see,
> Whereof our world is but the bounding shore.

This is the unseen world, the world not realised, in
which faith moves.

IV. In keeping with the great principle of continuity,
everywhere displayed in the working out of the world's
evolution, we have found this faith foreshadowed in the
upward striving that is the essence of life. Consider
for a moment the development of the senses. The
first clear response is to mechanical contact, and we
have as the first specific sense, the sense of touch.
From this is presently differentiated the sense of
hearing, when objects not yet present to actual touch
give premonitions of their proximity by the vibrations
they set up: hearing is thus the faith of touch. As
hearing to touch so smell stands to taste: it is a
foretaste that further extends the objective range.
A freckle or pigment-spot is all that light at first
produces; but when its hints are *heeded* and the pig-
mented retina that first arose is furnished by the
organism's own prophetic efforts with directing muscles,
it exchanges its passive sight for active vision, and
opens out a vastly wider objective world. In keeping

Faith is striving or striving is faith.

with all this is the place of faith on the higher plane
where it contrasts with intellectual sight : it is like a
new sense that brings us face to face with an unseen
world. What does this mean ? Let us go back a step.
Here as everywhere—in its highest as in its lowest
form—faith is striving and striving is faith. The whole
conscious being is concerned : there is not merely the
cognition of what is, there is also an appreciation of
what it is worth, a sense of the promise and potency of
further good that it may enfold ; there is a yearning to
realise this ; and there is finally the active endeavour
that such feeling prompts. It is through this faith that
man is where he is to-day, through it that mountains
have been removed and the unattainable verily attained.
More life and fuller achieved by much toil and struggle,
an ascent to higher levels not movement along the line
of least resistance—this is the one increasing purpose
that we can so far discern, when we regard the world
historically as a realm of ends in place of summarising
it scientifically under a system of concepts.

And how do we stand now ? That the present
world and progress on the plane of the present world
do not and never will meet our highest needs—about
this there is little question. But where in what is, in
what we have so far attained, can we discern those
eternal values that point upwards and beyond this
present world ? Surely in all that we find of the
beautiful and sublime in this earth on which we dwell
and the starry heavens above it ; in all that led men
long ago to regard nature as a cosmos ; in all that is
best and noblest in the annals of human life ; in these
very needs themselves that the seen and temporal fail

to meet; and above all, in that nascent sense of the
divine presence which constitutes the truly religious
life, and converts faith into the *substance* of things
hoped for, the *evidence* of things not seen.   But now
a third question at once suggests itself.   Faith on the
lower levels was justified by its results: can we here
too apply this test of success or failure?   The founder
of Christianity at any rate did not hesitate to appeal to
it :—" Beware of false prophets.   Ye shall know them
by their fruits : do men gather grapes of thorns or figs
of thistles ? "   And, in fact, this is the test that is and
will be applied ; for, as I have already said, however
much in theory men consider premisses, in practice they
consider only results.

A powerful practical argument in favour of religious faith might be worked out on the following
lines :—first we might point to its *universality* : no
race of mankind is wholly without that feeling of
dependence on the supernatural and mysterious, which,
as Schleiermacher thought, is the common characteristic
of religious emotion.   Next we might point to its
survival : no race has yet outgrown it.   There have
been periods of religious decline, no doubt ; but they
have sooner or later involved moral and intellectual de-
cadence as well.   And in these days when faith is said
to be waning, we find that "things are in the saddle
and ride mankind," and whither that tends history has
made only too clear.   Hitherto—in keeping with the
judgment by results—such times have been followed
by periods of revival and awakening ; and there are
happily signs of such in our own day.   Lastly we
might point to the *advance* of religion that has usually

accompanied the increase of morality and intelligence ; nay we might show that religion has largely furthered such advance. And here by way of contrast I may refer briefly to a strange prophet, whose writings are at this moment exciting the keenest attention—I refer to Nietzsche. As the struggle for existence and the survival of the fittest have brought man to the highest place as the paragon of animals, so in time they will lead, he teaches, to a yet higher being, the *Uebermensch* or Over-man. But this higher man, he foretells, will reject the existing morality of liberty, equality and fraternity, founded on the golden rule of benevolence and brotherly love—the morality of slaves as he contemptuously names it. The new morality will be the morality of heroes, that is egoists : might will be right. As man now subjugates the lower animals to his own ends, so the Over-man will exploit feebler men and —as it has been sarcastically put—rise on stepping stones of *their* dead selves to higher things. In short a race is to appear, so Nietzsche and others would have us believe, that is to try the experiment of life wholly on the lines of what is called 'modern thought' and wholly without faith in God or a world to come. I do not think the growing Nietzsche cult will last long or in the end do harm. If the terrible experiment must be tried[1] we may safely anticipate the result : it will be Hobbes's state of nature over again ; till the world retraces its steps.

It will be said, perhaps :—'The regenerate Christian is already an *Uebermensch*, no longer "natural man," but "spiritual" in the Pauline sense ; nor is his experience fairly described as subjective belief in God ;

[1] When writing this sentence (in 1902) I feared, like many, that the experiment *would* be tried, and it has been !

it is actual love of God and conscious communion with him.' We have no right to question this ; though we must admit that such inward conviction of the reality of religious experience is, for *the purposes of our discussion*, to be classed as faith, not as knowledge, in so far as it is—epistemologically, though not psychologically—subjective, incommunicable, and objectively unverifiable. In so far, however, as he lets his light shine and men see his good works, the religious man affords practical evidence of the worth of his faith. With enough of such light, the justification of faith would be sure.

One final question, among the many that suggest themselves, I must not wholly omit. We have been contemplating the universe as a realm of ends. If we were asked what is the end of this realm of ends we might answer rightly enough that its end can only be itself; for there is nothing beyond it, and no longer any meaning in beyond. It is the absolutely absolute. Still within it we have distinguished the One and the Many, and we have approached it from the standpoint of the latter. In so doing we are liable to a bias, so to say, in favour of the Many : led to the idea of God as ontologically and teleologically essential to their completion, we are apt to speak as if he were a means for them. Those who attempt to start from the standpoint of the One betray a bias towards the opposite extreme. The world, on their view, is for the glory of God : its ultimate *raison d'être* is to be the means to this divine end. Can we not transcend these one-sided extremes and find some sublimer idea which shall unify them both ? We can indeed ; and that idea is Love. But here again we trench on the mystical, the ineffable, and can only speak in parables. Turning to Christianity as exhibiting this truth in the purest form we know, we find it has one great secret—dying to live, and one great mystery—the incarnation. The love of God in creating the world implies both. *Leiblichkeit ist das Ende aller Wege Gottes,* said an old German theologian. The world is God's self-limitation, self-renunciation might we venture to say? And so God is love. And what must that world be that is worthy of such love? The only worthy object of love is just love: it must then be a world that can love God. But love is free: in a ready-made world then it could have no place. Only as we learn to know God do we learn to love him: hence the long and painful discipline of evolution, with *its* dying to live—the converse process to incarnation—the putting off the earthly for the likeness of God. In such a realm of ends we trust "that God is love indeed, and love creation's final law." We cannot live or move without faith, that is clear. Is it not then rational to believe in the best, we ask; and can there be a better?

6 . 9. 30 .

*Distinction between
the contingency of Chance
and
the Contingency of freedom*

SUPPLEMENTARY NOTES.

I. THE MEANING OF CONTINGENCY. (Lect. IV. p. 76.)

While preparing these lectures for the press I have been asked by a friendly critic for a definition of contingency. Possibly the request was prompted by the conviction, commonly enough entertained, that there is really no contingency in the world at all; and this, it is supposed, any serious attempt to define contingency would sooner or later disclose. Absolute chance is certainly nonsense; and relative chance, it may be said, is after all not really chance, and implies nothing but ignorance or—it may be—irrelevance to the matter in hand. The truth of this I have already fully admitted in the text; but I have also distinguished between the contingency of chance and the contingency of freedom[1]. It is the latter contingency that is here in question, and, whatever may be said of its validity, its meaning at least seems clear. If the future of the world is partly determined by the conduct of free agents there will continually be new beginnings that were not foreseen; and new possibilities will become imminent, that no knowledge of the past can surely forecast. All these possibilities will find a place within a certain 'domain' (to adopt a mathematical term), inasmuch as the world was never a chaos, but definite from the first[2]; and so we say there is no absolute contingency, no utter caprice.

[1] This has been stigmatized as a 'very scholastic distinction,' and one implying 'a system of pluralism,' as if that would suffice to dispose of it! With this objection I have already attempted to deal elsewhere. Cf. *Naturalism and Agnosticism*, 3rd edn, ii. pp. 293 f.; 4th edn, pp. 614 f.

[2] Cf. Lect. IV. pp. 70 f.

Though contingent for others, a man's acts are not contingent for him : if they were, we should have to admit absolute contingency or chance. But if not contingent for him, then must they not for him be necessary? So it has been argued as if 'conditioned by' were the same as 'conditioned for.' This further problem, however, is dealt with later. Cf. Lectures XIII. and XIV.

But the contingency in the so-called 'physical world,' referred to at the close of this Lecture, cannot, it may be thought, be the contingency of freedom : here then to deny immutable law is, it would seem, to assert absolute chance. We cannot, of course, affirm that a star or a meteor or a cluster of particles is an individual. But neither can we be confident that they are always and necessarily the merely inanimate aggregates we commonly take them to be. All that pluralism contends for, however, is simply that the real beings these phenomena imply have some spontaneity and some initiative[1]; and to these essential characteristics of all real individuals the uniformity, as well as the diversity, of the physical world is due—the former as *Natura naturata*, the latter as *Natura naturans*.

II. DR HOWISON ON CREATION. (Lect. XI. p. 245.)

" Not to know how a thing can be is no disproof that the thing must be and is," Mr Bradley has said, as Fries indeed had said before him. To this truth we have appealed while admitting that creation is to us inexplicable. But Dr Howison seeks to cut us off from this appeal by asserting vehemently and repeatedly that the idea of creation is self-contradictory— if the creatures, that is to say, are to be free agents and not merely machines. We must, he contends, either accept the logical consequences of Jonathan Edwards or deny their premise : he prefers to do the latter. " Better the atheism of a lost First Cause...than the atheism of deified Injustice with

[1] Cf. Lect. III. pp. 65 ff.

its election and reprobation by sheer sovereign prerogative[1]."
Very true, but the one vital question to settle first of all
is whether or no we are really shut up to these alternatives—
forced to relinquish any idea of creation or give up freedom
altogether.

Despite his impressive earnestness, however, Dr Howison
seems not to have troubled himself about this wider question
at all. As a pluralist he, of course, disallows the absolutist's
version of the world—that the Many are but 'modes or
expressions of the sole self-activity of the One.' This granted,
he begins by simply assuming that there is nothing left but
"the Oriental, Augustinian, monarcho-theistic idea of creation
at a certain date by sheer fiat and out of fathomless nothing."
From this assumption he next advances to his main position
"that creationism must logically exclude the possibility of
freedom. *For the Creator cannot, of course, create except by
exactly and precisely conceiving, otherwise his product would not
differ from non-entity.* The created nature must therefore
inevitably register the will and the plan of the Creator[2]."
This is true, but it is at all events not to the point: on the
contrary the sentence I have put into italics covertly assumes
that this 'plan' cannot be the existence of a world of free
agents. An exact and precise conception of a machine is
possible, but an exact and precise conception of such a world
is, it is taken for granted, logically impossible. How then do
we come to have it?

Dr Howison plays unawares with a double-edged weapon
here. For that exact and precise definition of a free agent,
which he declares to be a contradiction from the standpoint of
the Creator, he regards as essential from the standpoint of
the free agents themselves. They subsist only by 'defining or
positing' themselves, at once "in terms of their own inerasible
and unrepeatable *particularity* and of the supplemental indi-
vidualities of a whole world of others"—in other words they

---

[1] *The Limits of Evolution*, 2nd edn, 1905, p. 341 *fin.* Cf. also above
Lect. XX. p. 438.   [2] *Op. cit.* p. 397.

assign themselves a place in a series " that must run through
every *real* difference from the lowest increment over non-
existence to the absolute realisation of the ideal type[1]." If
exact and precise conception leave no room for freedom, what
room can be left by unambiguous definition and position in
a continuous series ? If Spinoza was right in denying freedom,
as we understand it, in the one case, was not Schopenhauer
equally right in denying it in the other? Whether my *essentia*
is really ' posited ' by God or by myself can make no difference
to its logical character. If I must either be a non-entity or
'utterly pre-determined,' like a machine, by exact and eternal
specification, it is all one as regards the question of freedom
how my *essentia* is raised to *existentia*. But if I verily am
a free being, ' rational and untrammelled, with will to choose
unpredestined,' there can be no contradiction in this my
essence ; and there is then certainly none in postulating God
as the ground of its existence. And such postulation removes
a serious difficulty in Dr Howison's own theory, precisely the
difficulty in fact that has led us to advance from pluralism to
theism. That the world of the Many should verily be a realm
of ends if it have in the One its rational ground seems
altogether credible. But that the Many should freely posit
themselves so as to form a ' spontaneous harmony providing
for *all* individual differences compatible with the mutual
reality of all' seems infinitely improbable. In such a vast
election how is the precedence settled? After all Dr Howison,
try as he may, does not escape ' the sheer sovereign prerogative' that creation implies. The One and the Many, he
admits, " are *different* and *unchangeably* different ; they are
even different *in species*"; for there is in every finite soul
'a derivative life absolutely foreign to God,' on account of
which, for lack of a better name, it has been called a
' creature[2].'

Dr Howison's initial assumption will strike most people as
out of date. The creationism ' of the old theology and of the

---

[1] *Op. cit.* pp. 351–4 f.   [2] *Op. cit.* pp. 429, 363 f.

plodding realist alike'—as he styles it—so far from being the only one in vogue, has long been superseded. There are but few thoughtful people nowadays who regard the world as somehow made at a certain point of time by the transeunt activity of a so-called First Cause. Such a view I have already attempted to deal with. And now after all, what does Dr Howison himself tell us? "*Real creation*," he says, "*means such an eternal dependence of other souls upon God that the non-existence of God would involve the non-existence of all souls, while his existence is the essential supplementing Reality that raises them to reality; without him they would be but void names and bare possibilities[1].*" 'Void names and bare possibilities' in such a context may fairly be taken as a rhetorical periphrasis for 'nothing,' and 'supplementary' as therefore superfluous: in short God is here unequivocally declared to be the ground of the existence of the Many. Again, in a later passage he says: "The self-existent perfection of deity itself freely demands for its own fulfilment the possession of a world that is in God's own image and such a control of it as is alone consistent with its being so: a *divine* creation must completely reflect the divine nature, and must therefore be a world of moral freedom[2]." Surely here it is unmistakably recognised that though—or rather that because—God is the one ground of the world, the Many are free.

What then are we to make of the contention that "creationism must logically exclude the possibility of freedom"? At first we might naturally suppose that creationism must here be used not with 'the real meaning' just defined, but in the inappropriate sense of 'the old theology and the plodding realist' that is now discarded by Dr Howison in common with the rest of us. A free agent 'utterly predetermined' as well as a machine not 'exactly and precisely' specified is, we agree, a contradiction and a non-entity. Plainly then the souls that God 'raises to reality in fulfilment of his

---

[1] *The Limits of Evolution*, 2nd edn, 1905, p. xvii. Italics Dr Howison's.
[2] *Op. cit.* p. 75.

own perfection and reflecting his own nature' cannot be either : for all that, the real meaning of creation may remain. But no, it is the real meaning of creation, as we understand it, that Dr Howison declares to be impossible. But how can it be both real and impossible? Obviously one or other of Dr Howison's positions must be surrendered, and, in point of fact, we find him explaining away the first, keeping it to the ear and breaking it to the hope. "Creation has a most real meaning, though indeed *not a literal but only a metaphorical one*[1]!"

The only ground of the world, Dr Howison maintains, is 'a principle of connexion between all minds, God included,' and this principle is not ontological but logical and teleological. "As Final Cause, God is at once (1) the Logical Ground apart from which, as Defining Standard, no consciousness can define itself as *I*, nor consequently can exist at all ; and (2) the Ideal Goal toward which each consciousness in its eternal freedom moves[2]." Now a logical ground cannot be the ground of the existence of anything ; that much surely is certain. Again, to affirm that I am in virtue of my own self-definition or self-position seems only a Hegelian way of saying that I exist of myself and know of no other ground for my being. So far (1) is just the position of the mere pluralist. And so in like manner is (2) : the Ideal there, is only the pluralistic goal, not a reality but an end. We may say indeed that ideals are always final causes ; but to talk of final causes as real is, I fear, but philosophical barbarism. Up to this point, then, it seems clear that Dr Howison has not got beyond 'uncompromising pluralism.' We have seen, however, that it is not only open to the pluralist to postulate the reality of God, but reasonable, theoretically and practically, to do so. But Dr Howison thinks, Kant notwithstanding, that his ' concrete logic' enables him to supersede postulation by proof,

[1] *Op. cit.* p. 392. Italics mine. There is here, I fear, some confusion between symbol and meaning, means and end. Meaning is never metaphorical though often conveyed by metaphor.

[2] *Op. cit.* p. 391.

and to resuscitate 'the thrice-slain ontological argument.' This in its amended form he has himself thus concisely summarized : " The idea of every self and the idea of God are inseparably connected, so that if *any* self exists, then God also must exist ; but any and every self demonstrably exists, for (as *apud Cartesium*) the very doubt of its existence implies its existence ; and therefore God really exists[1]."   But is not the first premise here utterly dogmatic and flagrantly untrue, at least in the form which the present argument requires ? That we cannot have the idea of God without the idea of self is true ; but the converse, that we cannot have the idea of self without the idea of God, Dr Howison, though he is continually asserting it, has nowhere shown to be true.   On the contrary, in one interesting passage, he rightly urges that—as regards knowledge of his existence—God " only takes the common lot of every soul, the fact of whose being must be gathered by all the rest from the testimony of their own interior thought[2]."

Dr Howison then, we may conclude, while rightly disallowing the creationism of Augustine and Edwards, along with that of Spinoza, as alike incompatible with the freedom of the created, has not succeeded in providing another in their place.   Nor has he shown that the idea of creation advocated in the text involves any contradiction : indeed it would hardly be going too far to say that all that is intelligible on the subject in his own valuable book is really reconcilable with this.

[1] *The Limits of Evolution*, 2nd edn, 1905, p. 359.   To *demonstrate* the intuitive certainty of one's own existence, by the way, is a feat of which Descartes was not really guilty.   Further, Dr Howison's version is much nearer the old cosmological argument than it is to the ontological; and it is perhaps needless to add that the cosmological argument, if sound, would be very damaging to him.

[2] *Op. cit.* p. 258.

III. Relation of Body and Mind.

(Lect. xii. pp. 254, 258.)

The difference we have noted between the 'functional' relation of subordinate monads to their own dominant and their 'foreign' relation to other dominants, is the prime source of the difficulties that beset dualism, when—assuming two distinct and disparate substances—it attempts to explain the connexion of mind and brain. When, on the other hand, this connexion is regarded from the standpoint of monadism these difficulties seem to vanish, so soon as this difference is clearly recognised. There are two cardinal facts that together give rise to this so-called 'psychophysical problem,' both name and thing. First, there is the psychological fact that neither in perception nor in action is there any immediate experience of brain processes, intervening prior to the one and subsequent to the other. Most human beings live out their lives without knowing that the brain has any connexion with mind at all. Secondly, there is the fact that the physiologist, who traces the centripetal processes, that stimuli set up, till they reach the brain, and then traces the centrifugal processes that next ensue, till they reach the muscles, thereby learns nothing either of the perceptions that follow upon the former, or of the volitions that precede the latter, of these processes. Thus Aristotle—to take but one instance out of many—who knew a good deal about both psychology and physiology, was quite unaware of any connexion between mind and the brain ; which he regarded "simply as a cold, moist and senseless organ destined to countervail the excessive heat of the heart." But the conferences of psychologists and physiologists have at length placed the intimate correspondence between *psychosis* and *neurosis* beyond doubt. The living being, that the psychologist regards ejectively as mind, the physiologist regards objectively as mechanism ; and together they find that the more complex the mind the more complex the mechanism; and *vice versa*. The problem is rightly to interpret this correspondence, so certainly, yet so indirectly, ascertained.

At the outset there are two points on which we shall have to insist: one that we may fairly call an established truth, and another that is fundamental for monadism. First, whereas the mechanism that is the one object of the physiologist's study is altogether phenomenal, the mind that the psychologist studies is not—as the naturalist vainly strives to maintain—merely phenomenal or epiphenomenal; since it implies the subject, or dominant monad, to whom such phenomenal experiences belong. Secondly, the real agents, whose appearances alone constitute the physiologists' phenomena, are here regarded as monads that minister as subordinates to this subject, or dominant monad. We have then to account for the fact that these monads, which to the physiologist appear as extended matter, Leibniz's *materia secunda*, are for their dominant monad not in this wise phenomenal at all. In other words, we have—if we can— to explain how, corresponding to the brain that for the physiologist is but a *small part* of the external world and continuous with it, there is for the psychologist the presentation to an active subject, distinct from it, of *the whole* of this external world—except, of course, that small part, the brain, presented only to the physiologist.

To begin: we note first that the complexity and distinctness of the world, as object for a given subject, vary with its point of view. But the standpoint, or, as we might also say, the rank of a monad depends on its retinue of subordinate or ministering monads. For it, these are not objective, *i.e.* constituents of its objective world. To become such they must lose their functional relation as ministering subjects and take on that other, the foreign relation, which they have only for an outside observer, like the physiologist; and at the same time their dominant monad—unless they are replaced—must be impoverished to a corresponding extent. The two relations are in this respect incompatible. And now it is this incompatibility that gives rise to the psychophysical problem, so hopeless for the Cartesian dualism with its disparate substances, and so simple for the personal idealist.

We observe next that functionality is the main category of life : it suffices to mark off the organic and individual from the inorganic and its divers aggregations. But, though there is a real analogy between the relation of a subordinate monad and its dominant and the relation of an ὄργανον or instrument to the worker who uses it, there is yet an important difference between the two. To the tyro, his instrument is at first a foreign object and nothing more ; but as he masters it, he becomes less conscious of what it is and attends only to what it does. The surgeon, for example, while operating, feels not his sound, but what it is probing ; when he lays it down however, it becomes for him but an object once more. The function of the subordinate monad, then, is more intimate than that of an organ or instrument, literally understood ; for the relation here is not that of subject to object, but rather that of subject to subject. It means all that can be meant by immediate *rapport* or, as some in these days would prefer to say—psychopathy.

But we get no light on this from our individual experience : that it is and what it is, first dawn upon us at the higher level where, over-individual or social ends being present, social 'organization' becomes an object of reflexion[1]. Here, as already pointed out, we observe cases innumerable of behaviour consequent solely on 'sympathetic rapport'— between private citizens and public officials, for example[2]. These officials are persons too, no doubt ; but so far forth

---

[1] We have in this one more instance of our knowledge of the higher enabling us to interpret the lower. Cf. Lect. VII. pp. 145 f.

[2] Cf. Lect. X. pp. 218 f. It is true, as Lotze has remarked, that "there may be many intermediating processes producing the conditions on which this *rapport* depends"; but if we look closer we find no mediation so far as the *rapport* itself is concerned.

as their social functions are concerned, their position is analogous to that of subordinate monads; and here all interest in them for 'the man in the street' comes to an end. They are like Mr Wemmick in Jaggers' office, so different from Mr Wemmick with his aged P. at the Fort. Nor has the average man any interest in the technical details on which the effective working of, say the post office or the police, actually turns: he only knows what they mean and confidently relies on their services. Now our social organization secures to its individual members wider acquaintance with their environment as well as fuller control over it than are possible in a more primitive society, and this again more than is possible to the naked and isolated savage. And the like holds good within organisms. Again, in organisms as in societies the cooperation of their members, so far as it is effective, is due to consentience and mutual adaptation rather than to external constraint Once more, in organisms 'the technical details,' as we have called them—here the neural processes that come before perception and those that follow upon volition—are beyond the individual's interest or ken, till the reflective study of other organisms brings them to light as objective facts. It is in this way indeed that the ideas of organ and function first arise.

But these extra-cortical and subsidiary processes, that have no concomitants in the immediate experience of the dominant monad, have still for all that their psychical side; just as truly as the internal arrangements of the post-office, though unknown to people at large, have their own social *rapport*. Indeed the facts of what we may call comparative neurology, normal and abnormal, though they admit perhaps of objective description, can, we may fairly say, be interpreted only subjectively. And this biologists and even physiologists are coming to recognise more and more. As the Ptolemaic astronomy was overwhelmed by the complex machinery of cycles and epicycles which new facts led it to assume, so our modern physiology has been encumbered by the reflex mechanisms that have accumulated as the science has advanced—a sign to many that a Copernican era for physiology also is at hand[1]. We may attempt, by parity of reasoning, either to advance from simple reflexes to more and more complex reflexes, keeping that is to the mechanical standpoint throughout; or to regress from our own level of self-conscious experience to ever lower levels, without for-saking the subjective standpoint. Both attempts have been made; and the first has proved definitely a failure. Therefore some have supposed that possibly, as the complexity advances, the physical gradually becomes psychical; but this is to take refuge in what at Oxford they call μετάβασις εἰς ἄλλο γένος; it is not reasoning at all but legerdemain[2]. The physiologists on the other hand who adopt the second alternative replace the system of reflex mechanisms increasing in complexity, by a hierarchy of zooids or psychoids comparable to inde-pendent organisms of varying rank, in a word, by a system of subordinate monads controlled by a dominant monad[3].

[1] "The impetus given to biology by the doctrine of adaptation under natural selection...seems hardly as yet to have begun its course as a motive force in physiology. But signs begin to be numerous that such an era is at hand. The infinite fertility of the organism as a field for adapted reactions has become more apparent. The purpose of a reflex seems as legitimate and urgent an object for natural inquiry as the purpose of the colouring of an insect or a blossom." Professor C. S. Sherrington, *The Integrative Action of the Nervous System*, 1905, p. 236. "If we examine a reflex, such as that of assuming a normal position or removing an irritant, it soon appears that the process is by no means the blind mechanical response which it may at first sight be taken to be.... Indeed the physical response varies endlessly according to circumstances. It is the end attained, and not the physical response, which is simple and definite. A mechanism which attains ends in this way is inconceivable." J. S. Haldane, "Life and Mechanism," *Guy's Hospital Gazette*, 1906. Cf. also H. Driesch, *Science and Philosophy of the Organism*, vol. II. 1908, pt iii.; O. Langendorff, Nagel's *Handbuch der Physiologie*, Bd IV. 1909, pp. 293–297.

[2] *Naturalism and Agnosticism*, 3rd edn, I. pp. 265 ff.; 4th edn, pp. 259 ff.

[3] Chief among these physiologists was E. Pflüger, who already in 1853 talked of 'spinal-cord souls' (*Rückenmarkseelen*). For the lower centres of the nervous system, he maintained, display the same kind

And this interpretation has the support of numerous biologists, who trace back the genesis of the *Metazoa* or multicellular organisms to 'loose colonies' of unicellular organisms or *Protozoa*. The new cells, resulting from the division of an old one, in these cases remain associated instead of scattering; whereupon some differentiation and division of labour ensues as the natural result of their varied relation to each other and to the environment. In consequence they are no longer a law to themselves; without ceasing to be individuals they become subordinate to an 'over-individual[1].'

The complete intimacy of the *rapport* between the dominant monad and its subordinates, which is here assumed, will suffice, we have argued, to account for the fact that the organism has 'windows,'—is, so to say, diaphanous for its own subject and yet opaque to all subjects besides. To the latter it has solely an objective relation, to the former it has primarily what we seem driven to call a subjective or intersubjective relation. But, it will be objected, what right have we to call that anything, of which we have confessedly no direct knowledge? Whereas in social organization we are aware of our fellow-men as persons who communicate and cooperate with us, we cannot by any amount of introspection or reflexion attain to any such acquaintance with these so-called subordinate monads. Is it not plain then, that in the essential point this far-fetched analogy completely breaks down? On the contrary; for—as already noted—in the social organism there are public functionaries innumerable to whose existence we pay no heed till the social organism is deranged, as in a strike, for example. Similarly, it is often only through

of adaptation of action to situation, as the supreme centre displays : the difference between them, though striking, being still only a difference of degree. If we are to regard these lower centres as purely mechanisms, then we ought, in consistency, he argued, to follow Descartes and hold that all animals are but mechanisms.

[1] Cf. above, Lect. III. pp. 58 f., and Lect. VI. pp. 121 f. An elaborate exposition of the whole subject will be found in E. Perrier's *Les Colonies animales et la Formation des Organismes*, 2me edn, 1898.

organic pain that we are first made aware of the *rapport* that
has failed in the working of our organs. This fact is all too
familiar to impress us as it ought. Oddly enough—in spite of
his dualism—to Descartes belongs the merit of first insisting on
this fact, that, as he put it, mind and body compose a single
substantial unity. Accordingly he rejected Plato's view of
the body as merely the vehicle and instrument of the soul;
for if this were true, he urged, " I should not feel pain when
my body is hurt, seeing I am merely a thinking thing, but
should perceive the wound by the understanding alone, just
as a pilot perceives by sight when any part of his vessel is
damaged[1]." It is this 'intimacy,' by Descartes miscalled
substantial unity, that leads us to call the relation of the
subject to its organism an internal or functional relation or
rapport; and though it is too immediate to be called knowledge, yet, when we reach the level of self-conscious reflexion,
this may fairly be appealed to as furnishing evidence of the
reality of such a relation.

F. A. Lange in his *History of Materialism* concludes the
long chapter on Brain and Soul by saying: " The manner in
which the external physical process (*Naturvorgang*) is at the
same time *an inner something* for the conscious subject—this
is just the point that lies beyond the limits of natural knowledge altogether." At all events, so far the monadistic
position seems to be nearest to these limits; and, in view
of the altogether elementary character of presentation and
feeling, it is hard to imagine any further advance. The only
alternative left seems to be that adopted by the occasionalist;
and perhaps to some this may seem preferable.

---

[1] Meditation VI. Veitch's edn, p. 160.

IV.   The Temporal and the Eternal.

(Lect. x. p. 194, xiv. pp. 305, 315.)

Notwithstanding these passages in the text, I am told that "the whole question as to the kind of reality that belongs to time seems to be evaded in these lectures," and thus my "lack of appreciation for the Hegelian view—that God is the eternal reality of which the world is the temporal expression" —is explained.   Accordingly I am asked to give some "clearer indication of the way in which time is related to eternity." The difficulty is that the meaning of these terms themselves is not clear.   But that they have some relation to each other is obvious from the fact that eternity is always described by reference to time.   Setting out from such description I must then attempt, as far as a brief note will allow, to meet these candid criticisms.

Eternity has been defined as infinite duration without succession, as an absolute *nunc stans*, or as a *totum simul.* But duration, succession, and simultaneity, 'the three modes of time,' as Kant called them, are mutually implicated; so far then these definitions are either incomplete or contradictory. Duration is length of time regarded as uniformly flowing; apart from such succession it would have no measure, and to speak of an infinite duration would in that case be meaningless.   "The now," said Hegel, "is nothing but the single now: duration is the universal of this now and that now."   How then can the instant 'now' endure, or stand, absolutely?   Also 'now' as a position in time is always relative to other positions, so that an absolute 'now' is unmeaning.   Finally though an indefinite number of events may be strictly simultaneous, yet simultaneity—as distinct from contemporaneity—does not involve duration.   But 'infinite duration' is usually regarded, not as excluding succession, but as involving endless succession.   As we do not say that the whole of 'immensity,' to use Locke's word, is spaceless, so here we should not say that eternity as a whole is timeless; but simply that it is infinite *a parte post* and also *a parte ante*. And this is its ordinary or lexical meaning: that is eternal which exists 'from ever-lasting to everlasting.'

At this point we may be reminded of Hegel's definition of eternity as 'absolute timelessness.' But this is an admission of the futility of all attempts, by reference to time, to determine what is here meant; for a negative definition, as such, is plainly no determination. But since we know of nothing but 'the truths of reason,' which we can speak of as absolutely timeless, we should be led at once to suppose that this, the Spinozistic meaning of eternal, was Hegel's meaning too. And it was: "only the natural is subject to time," he said: "the true, the idea, the spirit is eternal[1]." But if God is only eternal in the sense in which the laws of thought are sometimes called eternal, he cannot be real at all; he may be an Idea, he cannot be a Spirit. To be sure an idea has reality as the mental image or thought of a conscious being, but it is only *used* as a symbol or meaning, and as such may have validity but not existence[2]. So far Hegel is in the same boat with Spinoza, a craft built essentially on the lines of the Cartesian rationalism, and 'written off' by Kant as shipwrecked through just this fallacious confusion of idea and reality.

But we have set out from time as formal and abstract, it will be said: in the concrete, for perception, the temporal is the transient, the phenomenal, the natural; and the eternal is the immutable, the noumenal, the spiritual. Time, said Hegel, is Chronos begetting and devouring his children. But if this tragic spectacle is verily the expression of 'God's eternal reality,' eternal cannot mean 'out of all relation to time and change.' The stress is now, not on absolute timelessness, but

[1] *Naturphilosophie*, § 258.

[2] This position has, in my judgment, been established beyond cavil by Lotze (*Logic*, § 416) and again by Bradley (*The Principles of Logic*, §§ 6 ff.).

on a certain functional relation to the temporal process of the world's evolution[1]. We have passed, in fact, to the contrast between the noumenal and the phenomenal, the spiritual and the natural. The question then arises : How is change related respectively to these opposites ? In dealing with this question we have, of course, to set out from our own experience, and so doing we come at once on Kant's paradox—change pertains only to the permanent and substantial, not to the transitory and accidental[2]. From our standpoint, that of spiritual monism, a succession of events is a *change* only for an experient : from the standpoint of scientific description it is but a case of *alteration*. Strictly speaking, then, change for a spiritualistic philosophy implies in general some voluntary action on the part of one or more subjects and some non-voluntary perception on the part of others ; in other words it implies that intercourse which we call life. These subjects, however, are not phenomenal but noumenal. To their efficient activity we refer the phenomenal or natural world, that we perceive as 'filled time' or the course of events. The attempt to represent our experience as but a part of this course was the mistake of the sensationalist psychology of Hume and his successors : they failed to distinguish between alteration and change, between a succession of presentations and the presentation of succession. The content of filled time is doubtless phenomenal, but the reality which is the source of this content cannot be so : the efficient cannot be its own effect. So far,

[1] Cf. A. O. Lovejoy, 'The Obsolescence of the Eternal,' *Phil. Rev.* 1909, p. 490.

[2] "To arise and to pass away are not changes of that which arises and passes away. Change is a way of existing that follows on another way of existing of the very same object. Hence whatever changes is *permanent* and only *its state alters*. As this alteration or alternation (*Wechsel*) then concerns only determinations that can cease as well as begin [to be], we may say—using an expression seemingly somewhat paradoxical—that only the enduring (the substance) is changed, the variable undergoes no change but only an *alteration*, in so far as certain determinations cease and others begin." (*Critique of the Pure Reason*, First Analogy, Max Müller's trans. (amended), pp. 164 f.)

time alone, as the abstract form of alteration or succession, is not adequate to represent change as concretely experienced and involving both efficient and effect. So far too, experients are out of time, though functionally related to it—as said already in the second passage of the text.

The Hegelian distinction between eternal reality and temporal process then applies not only to God but also to us. But if so, the natural and temporal cannot be exclusively the expression of God's reality; and, in fact, only the experience that it is—at least in part—the expression of our own, could ever have led us to the idea of God, as spiritual and eternal, at all. But it is proverbial that extremes meet. So here : it is all one to assert with the sensationalist that our life is but a flux of presentations, and to deny with the absolutist that in the world's evolution our purposes are expressed. On either view experience becomes utterly inexplicable. If we avoid these extremes, then just as our life cannot be resolved into a temporal flux of phenomena, so the life of God cannot be resolved into the timeless content of an Absolute Idea. Both the living God and his living creatures, we are led to say, have alike a functional relation to the world's process.

There will be important differences between the two, of course, and the main difference is obvious at once. Our life is one of development, God's life is always perfect. So far unchangeableness may be attributed to God, as it can be to none beside. We come thus upon a third, what in technical language would be called the axiological, meaning of eternal; and this raises many difficulties, both as regards the divine life and our own. In contrast to God, who is blessed for evermore, "Man never is but always to be, blessed" the satirist has said. If on this ground eternal and perfect are fitting designations only of the one unchanging life, are not temporal and imperfect alone appropriate to the life that only is life so long as it is change? But on the other hand, as this life of continuous development is the only life that we know or can understand, can what is eternally or absolutely the same, though we call it perfect, be called a life? Nay, if reality implies activity, or in other words 'functional relation to the world's process,' can purely static being be called real at all in any sense that we can understand? Thus in equating perfect and eternal we seem after all to be back at the Spinozistic or Absolutist standpoint, where the Many are absorbed and the whole world vanishes. And yet can we be content to say, not only that we are never to attain perfection, but to suppose that—after all—God, if he be veritably a living God, can never attain it either? Thus we are confronted by two problems: in the case of man to connect progress and perfection, in the case of God to connect perfection and life.

Beginning with the latter—it is plain that the absolutely perfect could not change, if by changing it became imperfect; for were this possible it could never have been perfect. Moreover, if change in the sense of development is the only possible form of life, then absolute perfection must mean a sort of Nirvana or utter quiescence. But unless all activity is essentially an imperfection, there is no contradiction in Aristotle's doctrine of pure or perfect activity (ἐνέργεια ἀκινησίας). But it will have to be more than a 'beatific vision,' if it is to be the ground of the world or to have the faintest interest for us. "An ἐνέργεια that ever generates the supreme pleasure of self-contemplation (νόησις νοήσεως)[1]" will not suffice; rather we must have that 'intellective intuition' which I have already endeavoured to describe[2]. Such pure activity limited by no alien 'matter,' such constancy of purpose 'without variableness or shadow of turning,' implies not change, either in the sense of alteration or of development, but unchangeableness in the sense of continuous perfect life. It is true that such life passes our understanding, but we can at least regard it as the limit towards which our own life points. And this leads naturally to our second problem.

But first the attempt to represent the Divine perfection as

---

[1] Cf. the essay on Activity and Substance in Dr Schiller's *Humanism*, 1903, pp. 211 ff.

[2] Cf. Lect. XI. pp. 234 ff.

involving 'eternal knowledge,' in such wise that—as my critic maintains—" for the divine intuition past, present and future, are all equally real and in that sense all equally present," calls for some notice. I have indeed already tried to deal with this in the last of the three passages to which this note refers; still for completeness sake it may be well to recur to it again and add one or two remarks. "The three times, past, present and future," said Augustine, "are three affections of the soul; I find them there and nowhere else. There is the *present* memory of past events, the *present* perception of present ones, and the *present* expectation of future ones[1]." The filled time of experience involves all three more or less. Such is the psychical present as distinct from the 'clock present'; and its 'span,' it is assumed, may range from zero where the two agree, up to infinity where "*der Augenblick ist Ewigkeit.*" But this span may be infinite and yet not all-inclusive; just as the series of odd numbers is infinite, though all the even numbers are left out. Moreover where the span is finite, as in our own experience, it never embraces more than a fraction of the events that lie within its limits. But then we are all confined to a definite 'centre,' while God we regard as omnipresent. Can we then still suppose that *his* span is not all-inclusive? If the relation of the future to the present is identical, save for difference of sign—as a mathematician would say—with that of the past to the present, we should certainly have no ground for such a supposition. There is no contradiction in a complete knowledge of all that has been ; for what has been is as fact equally real with what is. Why then should there be anything contradictory in a complete knowledge of the future? Well, if there were not, we should have to say with Augustine, *futura jam facta sunt*[2]. But this is just what we cannot say ; for it is an obvious contradiction.

Yes, to us it may be, some will still contend, inasmuch as we live in time and experience things successively. The

---

[1] Quoted by Baron F. von Hügel, *The Mystical Element of Religion*, 1908, vol. II. p. 248.

[2] *De Trinitate*, v. 16. Quoted by Hamilton, *Reid's Works*, p. 976.

whole point is that the divine experience is timeless, is eternal. "Time is the moving image of eternity," but the movement is illusory, like that of the landscape to the railway traveller. Yes, but there is real movement at the back of this illusion; and the question at once arises what is the real at the back of 'the time illusion'? The restlessness and change begotten of want and imperfection, it will be replied. But this is too much at once: both change and defect are real and not illusory, we admit; for the moment, however, it is only the former that concerns us. And the admission of the reality of change is enough to dispose of this spectacular theory of time in relation to eternity, and to justify our contention that expectation is not on a par with memory. The only basis for anticipation is past experience; but though the past is one factor in determining the future, it is only one. There is beside, the initiative of personal agents, to whom the whole filling of time is due; and who, therefore, are not in time, as phenomena; though, as noumena they are functionally related to it. Unless then God has preordained all that is to be done, it is surely a contradiction to say even of him that he has such a knowledge of the future as we have of the past.

The mention just now of defect and restlessness brings us back once more to the second of the problems to which the conjunction of eternal and perfect gave rise. Granted that perfection and changeless activity are not incompatible, anyhow, it is urged, creatures can never be perfect, for development implies not only activity but change, progress towards perfection, it may be, but never actual attainment. What is perfect is perfect always; and what is imperfect, how-ever long it last, must be imperfect still. "To exist in time is the same thing as to exist imperfectly," Plotinus is reported to have said, and conversely to exist imperfectly is the same thing as to exist in time. But though perfection does not, strictly speaking, admit of degree; it is still, we may reply, not absurd to speak of a perfection that is relative to kind. The hyssop and the fir-tree are not necessarily imperfect because they are not cedars. Unless it were possible for God's creatures to have a perfection of their own, how could perfection be attributed to God himself? Yet in an evolving world none could have it, if all progress as such implied imperfection. But, yet again, what else could we say, if all progress were but a succession of means to an end that ceaselessly recedes and never is actually realised? This dualism of means and end, 'the most mischievous of all dualisms' as Höffding calls it, is here however out of place. Evolution is not means to an end, it is itself end. "Single moments in a man's life," as Höffding truly says, "ought not to be merely means for other moments; past and present merely means for the future. Nor will they be, if work and development themselves retain immediate value and can thus themselves be ends....The child is then not simply a man in the making; childhood becomes an independent age with its special tasks and its own appropriate value. In this wise every period of life, every part of the course of time, is to be understood. Then will it be possible in the midst of time to live in eternity....'Eternity' appears then not as the prolongation of time...but as an expression for the permanence of value during the alteration (*Wechsel*) of the times[1]." Finally—it is hardly needful to repeat—the active agents in weaving this variegated texture of time are not themselves part of its stuff, do not themselves exist in time.

But if what does exist in time is imperfect those who have wrought it must be and must remain imperfect, it will be rejoined. To say this is to judge the future by the past and the whole by the part. Our development, it must be confessed, is not strictly 'orthogenetic'; it does not take the ideally straightest path. But it will do so more as it advances; and there may be creatures in whom it has always done so or at any rate does so now. And as with God so here perfection will not imply inaction. There may be progress in perfection as well as progress towards it; thus St Luke

---

[1] *Philosophy of Religion*, Eng. trans. 1906, pp. 56 f. (amended).

tells us that "Jesus increased in wisdom and stature and in favour with God and man."

Such a life of perfect development, that is, of entire accord with the Divine ideal, Christianity describes as 'eternal': "to know God, this is life eternal." It is a life that endures and yet is not temporal. Is there any sense in which we can understand this contrast of temporal and eternal, and if so what? "The world passeth away and the lust thereof, but he that doeth the will of God abideth for ever." We have here imperfect unsatisfying life, on the one side, as perishing; and on the other, perfect life as all-satisfying and finally conserved. The one is empty, the other has eternal value: the one is always wearing away, the other abideth for ever. For the 'time-seeking,' 'self-serving' man, it is said, dooms himself to endless disappointment, whereas the man who loses himself in steadfast devotion to God can never fail. The lapse of time, though quantitatively it should be alike for both, is qualitatively wholly different. Even now, whenever we are satisfied, there is an absorption in the fulness of the present, such that *dem Glücklichen schlägt keine Stunde*, as Schiller said. Then there is rest, not in the sense of lifeless inaction, for effective energy may at such times be maximal; but rather in the sense of that ἠρεμία which Aristotle associates with the Divine ἐνέργεια ἀκινησίας[1]. It is perhaps this oneness with the Divine will and this likeness to the Divine constancy that have led to the mystical interpretation of such eternal life as a sort of re-absorption of the creature in the Creator—when time shall be no more. There may be some truth beneath this mysticism perhaps; but, if so, all *our* attempts to conceive it end, as here, in contradictions.

To resume then: we have briefly considered three senses in which time and eternity are contrasted, the formal, the ontological and the axiological—if such technical language may be allowed; but in none can we find any justification

[1] Cf. F. C. S. Schiller, *op. cit.* p. 211 n.

for the Hegelian view, that "God is the eternal reality of which the world is the temporal expression"; unless indeed this is interpreted in such wise as to leave the world genuinely a realm of ends in the pluralistic sense. That, it cannot be, if the temporal is reduced from the phenomenal to the illusory (from *Erscheinung* to *Schein*, as a German would say); nor if the eternal is raised from the noumenal to the logical, cut off from living activity by apotheosis in the firmament of ideas.

V. THE DIVINE EXPERIENCE.

(Lectt. XI.—XX.)

This too is an important topic, which—like the last—has been, I am told, in these lectures unduly neglected. In the first plan of them, there was, I may say, to be one lecture bearing this very title. But at one time, the lack of definite knowledge gave me pause, and at another, the mass of speculation and controversy there was to handle; and so the lecture was never written. Still, under provocation, I now append a few remarks—and more or less under protest too—since they only bring together what has been already said more or less incidentally in the text.

To have experience is to be a person among persons. But we are persons in a world of others who *exist* independently of us. God is not in this wise a person: and though it be true that he is confronted by the world and active in it, still other persons are not for him merely objective (known through sense and intellection) or merely ejective (known through instinct or interpretation). Again, the world for God is the world in its unity and entirety: his is not a perspective view, such as 'standpoint' implies; nor is it a discursive view, such as our limited attention entails. God is ubiquitous and omnicontuitive, to coin a term. Finally, self-consciousness and reason in God are

not as with us incomplete and intermittent. There are no
'broken lights' in him: he alone can say I am that I am.
We may then either describe God as super-personal; or,
following Lotze, say "Perfect Personality is in God only: to
all finite minds only a pale copy of it is allotted[1]."

Yet the divine creative intuition and the divine knowledge
are to be distinguished; for the knowledge presupposes the
creation, and the relation of creator and created involves just
that dependence which the relation of knower and known
excludes. For knowledge does not posit or constitute its
objects, which for spiritualism are the manifestations or
utterances of free agents or subjects. Now, if we regard
the divine knowledge as knowledge in this sense, and if we
can understand it in no other, it seems to follow, as already
said[2], that what God merely knows is the world as there
and as a whole, all that it has been, all that it is, and—
being what it is, all that it tends further to become. His
purpose or creative ideal is perfectly definite, unchangeable
and assured. But the world's future history, the course
by which that purpose is to be attained, depends not on
him alone but also on the free agents, whom he sustains
but never constrains. This course then is not part of
his creation; nor is it, we seem entitled to conclude also,
part of his knowledge. Then God, it will be triumphantly
objected, does not know what will happen to-morrow, may
not even know, if I hesitate between bacon and fish for
breakfast, which I shall choose. Yet this retort should not
disconcert us: the issue is too serious to make it likely
that it can be thus summarily decided. Fore-knowledge of
the future is, we may contend, something of a misnomer.
It is either not strictly *fore*-knowledge or it is not strictly
knowledge. The astronomer we say calculates or predicts a
future eclipse: but what he calculates is not fore-knowledge
and what he predicts is only a probability. If the world

[1] *Microcosmus*, E. t. ii. p. 688.
[2] Cf. Lect. XI. p. 236 above.

were all routine or mechanical, to forecast the future would be possible; but pure mechanism is an abstraction and is incompatible with the novelty that the real world contains. But even we are not in a state of blank ignorance concerning the morrow, and God, who knows both tendencies and possibilities completely, is beyond surprise and his purpose beyond frustration. If that purpose is verily to allow his creatures some initiative, to associate them as co-workers with himself, it surely must needs imply some self-limitation and some contingency.

And now what of the divine activity in view of such limitation and contingency, what of the divine office in the realisation of God's world and ours? It is that Providence "that shapes our ends rough-hew them how we will." That it consists of special interferences we have every reason to doubt[1]; but if we call it 'general,' this must be in the sense, as Kant said, "that no single thing is left out." But the *modus operandi*, so to say, here as in creation, is to us inscrutable. We may well believe, however, that, for example, —over and above the natural advance or decline that they entail—all our good deeds render us more, and all our evil deeds render us less, amenable to divine influence or inspiration: the former thus tending, as Christianity teaches, towards life and light, the latter towards degeneration and darkness. But how God works with us or against us in the government of the world, we must again admit we do not know.

But now if this divine experience is to be really experience, living experience, in any sense that we can at all understand —and to talk of it in any other would be nonsense—the world's history, in which God is present, must surely be more than a mere show or *Darstellung*, as Hegel called it, of what in every detail is eternally decreed. Providence, Jacobi has said, is "what, in opposition to Fate, constitutes the ruling

---

[1] Cf. Lect. XII. pp. 249-51, above. What is there said *a propos* of Occasionalism applies, *mutatis mutandis*, to Providence.

principle of the universe into a real God." The doctrine of prescience and preordination may imply for us only the Christian idea of fate, as Leibniz called it, not the Mohammedan, since we have to act in ignorance of the divine decrees. But that doctrine robs the divine experience itself of all seriousness and assigns to the Highest a rôle that thousands of earnest and thoughtful men have regarded as altogether unworthy. Even if we rejected the eternal reprobation that is part of it and supposed all to end happily, the whole would still be devoid of any moral value : the actions would be the acting of puppets not the deeds of free persons. And as to the dramaturge himself, we might credit him with a singular hobby, but we could not possibly regard him as the God of the living, the God who is Love.

SOME REPLIES TO CRITICISMS.

As pointed out in the text (p. 24, *n.* 2), the use of monism sometimes in a qualitative, sometimes in a quantitative sense is apt to mislead. It has in fact misled an *Athenaeum* reviewer, who twits me with "the enormous changes the lapse of a dozen years has wrought" in my philosophical outlook; inasmuch as my earlier Gifford Lectures concluded with Spiritualistic *Monism* and these—with no hint of the change— begin with Spiritualistic *Pluralism*. This silent conversion is attributed to 'the mighty effect' William James has had 'on the most deeply-rooted prejudices of philosophers.' Both the change and the cause of it are alike imaginary and have their source only in the carelessness of a brilliant but rather slap-dash writer. A reviewer of the former series with far more discrimination—though even he is confused by the ambiguity of the term Monism—was led to say that they "prepare us to expect a system of pluralism like that which Professor W. James seems to favour[1]." As to my lamented friend, William James, that we differed widely is shewn by his book *A Pluralistic Universe,* and our differences were the occasion of some correspondence, which I might quote but that his letters to me are now in the hands of his biographer. The moral of all this is to emphasize the desirability of adopting, as I have done, Professor Külpe's term Singularism to signify what I have called quantitative monism in dis- tinction from monism in the qualitative sense, the meaning given to it by Wolff, who introduced the word.

[1] D. G. Ritchie, *Phil. Rev.* 1900, p. 263.

Two distinguished critics who have spoken of this book on the whole appreciatively object that the treatment of pampsychism is 'the least adequately argued' and 'the least convincing part' of my work.   But one of them adds: "I do not find any necessary connexion between Dr Ward's Theism and his pampsychism[1]."   In a sense this is true, and that a sense which is to me important.   Thus in concluding the earlier lectures I had said: "How far below, how far above, the historical [implying the psychical] extends, we cannot tell.   But above it there can be only God as the living unity of all, and below it no longer things, but only the connecting, conserving acts of the One Supreme[2]."   Again, in these later lectures I have said: "Since we cannot actually verify the indefinite regress which the existence of bare monads implies, and since we cannot shew that the indirect mediation of our finite intercourse is not a fact, we have no means of deciding between the two alternatives" of pampsychism and the occasionalism maintained by Berkeley and Lotze[3]. Further, I have been so far impressed by the philosophical competence of the second of these alternatives as to argue at length against Leibniz's depreciation of it.   Finally, I have allowed that "the most we can say is that the pluralist alternative is the *prior* as well as the simpler and...seems adequate."   In a word, much as Kant held it to be the business of science to *describe* the world in terms of mechanism, so I have endeavoured 'to *interpret* the world strictly in terms of Mind.'   But now my two critics contend, not for limiting pampsychism by occasionalism, to which procedure I see no fundamental objection, but for displacing spiritualistic monism by dualism.   Once theism is accepted it may seem comparatively unimportant whether we regard the realm of nature as something existing *per se* as truly as the realm of mind, or as nothing more than the orderly and continuous

---

[1] Prof. I. A. Leighton, *Phil. Rev.* May 1912, pp. 360 ff.
[2] *Naturalism and Agnosticism*, 3rd edn, II. p. 280; 4th edn, p. 570.
[3] Lect. XII. p. 260.

intervention of God. But the point on which I feel impelled to insist is this: We cannot begin with theism, nor unless dualism is refuted can we ever attain to it. Naturalism, which regards matter as wholly independent of mind and mind as wholly dependent on matter, is the inevitable outcome of dualism and has ever barred the way to theism[1].

The same critics contend that I have put an undue strain on the principle of continuity. It leaves us, Professor Leighton urges, "in the dark as to how a momentary consciousness [that is a bare monad] without memory developes into a unitary and continuous mind." I have already admitted this difficulty (cf. pp. 195–7, 265), and suggested such explanation as seems possible to us who are unable to regress even in thought to any absolute beginning (cf. pp. 259, 266, and 68). A monad permanently without memory could, we may well suppose, never develope into what Leibniz called a conscious monad. But even so, as sensory and conative, its momentary experiences would have a meaning or value as pleasurable or painful. Again, we may fairly suppose that, as I have said, many such monads would fall into relations which, as mutually helpful, they would tend to retain. On the lines of such primitive affinities advance seems clearly possible to that organization and consentient unity which the perceptual and all higher levels of finite experience imply. For in this way one monad might attain to a dominance which it might indefinitely increase. However, Professor Leighton thinks it "simpler...to suppose that non-mental objects interact with minds," prefers, that is to say, Cartesian dualism to spiritualistic monism. But surely we are entitled to ask him to clear up the difficulties besetting such 'interaction,'—both in regard to external perception and in regard to the relation of body and mind—that neither Descartes nor his successors have so far overcome. But "is not our very concept of mind dependent on its contrast with body?" he asks. To propose

[1] Cf. *Naturalism and Agnosticism*, parts iv. and v. and Lect. I. above.

such a question is to outvie even Descartes. Anyhow "is not the fact that pan-psychism is a recrudescence of primitive animism a pretty serious objection?" he continues. But surely it is notorious that nothing is farther from the fact! One might as well identify pampsychism and fetichism at once.

The other[1] is of opinion that if Leibniz's pre-established harmony is abandoned any thorough-going continuity must go with it. In that case, he seems to argue, "the qualitative characteristics of what we apprehend as material are in no sense...deducible from the activity of mind": we must, in fact, take them to be 'as ultimate as reality itself.' Briefly I am supposed to be confronted with the dilemma: Either pre-established harmony and windowless monads or dualism with its discontinuity between matter and mind. Let us examine the argument. "If we insist 'that material phenomena are only the manifestation of minds' still even phenomenal manifestations need accounting for," says Professor Dawes Hicks. But surely to say that "they are as ultimate as reality itself is ultimate" can only mean that as soon and as long as there are determinate realities there are determinate appearances also. Now Dr Hicks agrees with me in holding that matter, as understood by Descartes and the mechanical theory, will not account for such appearances. But he contends that, mere 'qualities' or 'properties' though they are, they are such as the interaction of monads will not account for either. But here we must distinguish between simple sensory qualities and such as are complex. If, to take yellow for example, we regard it as simple, we cannot indeed find any specific reason why there is such a quality. We can say however that were the realities concerned different, then yellow would be replaced by some other quality, x: but with this the same question would recur again and only the same answer could be given. As Dr Hicks himself has said: "It is puerile to ask how reality came to be." The monads then being such as they are, their simple appearances, as already

---

[1] Professor G. Dawes Hicks, *Hibbert Journal*, July 1912, pp. 941 ff.

said, appear as they do. Both are alike ultimate; but what warrant does this fact afford to dualism? But when we turn to complex qualities the case is altered. Here the distinction, which Dr Hicks allows to be important, between "mechanical conjunction [mere summation] and 'creative synthesis'" comes in[1]. Such synthesis implies subjective activity: subjects cannot, of course, synthesize arbitrarily, but apart from purpose or interest will not synthesize at all. The result, if they do, will, as I have said, "entail new properties which the component factors in their isolation did not possess" (p. 102). True, we can never tell how this process began, can never, as I have repeatedly urged, regress to the monads or to simple properties; though the principle of continuity implies both these limiting concepts. But we can still say that even at the limit sensible qualities depend on active beings, but are not ontologically on a par with them; in other words, that qualities imply substances and that the phenomenal *per se* is a contradiction.

But Dr Hicks maintains that synthesis is often entirely mechanical, "in the sense that it takes place wholly below the level of conscious or purposive activity." In saying this he altogether forgets that when the term 'mechanical' is applied in such a case, as it is by Lotze whom he quotes, it is only figuratively applied and is applicable at all simply on account of the many analogies there are between the *working* of mechanism and the effects of habit. To sustain his position he must shew that there are any habits that are not the result of creative processes of trial and eventual success: this, I venture to think, he would find it very hard to do. "If spatial perception," he continues, "be a conspicuous example of creative synthesis (p. 105), so also is the fluidity of water that ensues when oxygen and hydrogen...are chemically combined. The synthesis is as little the result of *purposive* activity on the part of the apprehending subject in the one case as in the other." There is, I fear, a grievous confusion

[1] Cf. above, Lect. v. p. 104.

here. Can it be said that spatial perception is psychologically on a par with the simple apprehension of fluidity ; or that this has anything whatever to do with the chemical synthesis, H_2O ? The sensation involved is practically the same whether the fluid be water or wine or turpentine. Again, can it be said that the creative synthesis involved in the perception of space, which we cannot decompose, is at all comparable to the chemical process of combining hydrogen and oxygen to form water, that can be decomposed again with ease? And yet there may be purposive activity in both cases ; but it will be different in the two. In spatial perception we have the activity of a single subject who acquires thereby a more definite acquaintance with its environment. In chemical synthesis, so called, the activity of several subjects is concerned, who gain by the co-operation of which their affinity is the sign—supposing, of course, that there are monads answering to the chemical elements at all, which is however a question for the present at any rate beyond our ken[1].

I am in no way surprised by these objections to pampsychism : indeed, I rather expected a general outcry against it as a patent absurdity. It is at first blush so alien to our ordinary common-sense view of the world that, I confess, it was long before I could bring myself to entertain it. But common-sense was equally prejudiced in favour of dualism, and that has lost ground enormously since Berkeley's day. The same may quite well happen with present prejudices against monadism. And indeed I seem to see a considerable resemblance between the contemporary replies to Berkeley and the replies of some of my own critics. Thus the *Times* reviewer writes : " On the ordinary view, nature provides the theatre, the scenery and properties for the spiritual drama.... It is impossible, however, to construct the world out of pure internalities; a body is needed for every soul." Berkeley did not deny ' the ordinary view ' that it is harmful to run one's head against a post : " the only thing whose existence I deny," he

[1] Cf. Lect. III. p. 63.

said, " is that which philosophers call Matter or corporeal substance." And the pluralist or personal idealist does not deny
the soul's need either for its environment or its body : what
he denies is—what Berkeley too denied—that these essentials
of developing experience imply the existence of independent
and disparate substances, the things as distinct from the
persons of the ordinary view. To speak of souls as ' pure
internalities ' is to recognise this dualism between matter
and mind. Leibniz thought to avoid the *impasse* to which
Cartesian dualism led by joining in Berkeley's rejection of
matter while retaining with him Descartes' ' concept' of mind.
The logical consequence for Berkeley and Leibniz alike, as
Reid clearly saw, was a solipsism which barred the way
to theism and pre-established harmony as effectually as
materialism did. In fact, the theory that presentations are
but 'subjective modifications'—as in this respect the counterpart of materialism—is well called 'mentalism.' But the
pluralism of our day emphatically rejects both dualism and
mentalism, as I have tried to shew at length. For it the
actual intercourse and increasing integration of monads is as
much a basal fact as their pre-established harmony and mutual
isolation was for Leibniz. Its critics, therefore, cannot and
must not assume that a soul for it is a ' pure internality.' If
they are to criticize pluralism effectively they should temporarily at all events divest themselves of assumptions that it
does not accept.

A reviewer in *The Nation* (Feb. 10, 1912) after noting that
" in the concluding lectures there is an appeal to what are
called ' moral arguments,' in virtue of which it is contended
that, if belief in God and a future life is not theoretically
impossible, our moral ideals justify us in accepting it," next
remarks: " It is perhaps regrettable that the fundamental
principles upon which the argument rests are scarcely mentioned, and nowhere defended in the course of the book.
It is assumed...that we cannot refuse to decide whether
the world is rational or not, even though the evidence is

admittedly inadequate." This is hardly a fair and is certainly an incomplete statement of the facts. In the first place it ignores the distinction between the theoretical and the practical standpoints, between the standpoint of knowledge and the standpoint of life. Yet on this distinction the whole argument turns; and the argument, so far from being 'scarcely mentioned,' is both expounded and defended at length[1]. In the next place, so far from arguing that "we cannot [theoretically] refuse to decide...even though the evidence is admittedly inadequate," the whole of the discussion arises just because the questions raised avowedly lie, so far as theory is concerned, 'beyond the utmost extent of its tether.' In short Kant's position as to the "impossibility of settling anything dogmatically with reference to an object of experience beyond the limits of experience" was the starting point (p. 411). In the third place, the whole process of the world's evolution is recalled to shew "that almost every forward step in the progress of life could be formulated as an act of faith—an act not warranted by knowledge" (p. 415)—and yet the means of its extension. The faith of theism is described as 'only the full and final phase of such an ascending series': it is and can be only a practical decision; it is not and cannot be a theoretical one; for this to be valid must be necessitated just as that to be an act must be free. Whether it is also rational only philosophy can decide, for philosophy alone includes both the theoretical and the practical within its ken. It only remains briefly to restate the issue. The world has progressed so far that the best of men are dominated by moral ideals, and the question arises : Can these ideals be realised? if they cannot, the world, in spite of this advance, is not rational : if they can, it is. But we know nothing that compels us to say that they cannot. At the same time theism and its corollary, a future life, would meet all our practical needs and give besides a theoretical completeness

[1] Cf. Lect. XIX. especially pp. 413-419 and pp. 419-423.

to our *Weltanschauung* that it must otherwise lack. There are many who say then, in the words of a writer, with whom I have reason to think this reviewer may sympathize: " Let us learn, then, that energy of faith which enables us to live constantly in the vision of the good ; and let us descend, in action, into the world of fact, with that vision always before us[1]." Is such a practical decision to be called irrational or be stigmatized as pragmatism ? My reviewer, however, continues : " To one who regards experience as incomplete, unsystematic and not in any sense a vital unity, the arguments contained in these lectures will make little appeal." Of course in such a case this must be so, and till such objectors are met it is useless to talk to them of theism. I have tried to deal with this ' previous question' in the three lectures on the Problem of Evil, but many of my dearest friends, and doubtless many beside, remain unconvinced. But happily I can say also that those personal friends and doubtless many beside, notwithstanding their scepticism, are among those animated by that adherence to moral ideals, which enables them 'to live constantly in the vision of the good.' And assuredly the lives of all such men strengthen the ground for 'believing in the eventual triumph of the good' and help to undermine 'the atheistic position' (p. 377). Such men are meliorists, as George Eliot called them, not pessimists. With them, as with John Stuart Mill, devotion to the welfare of our fellow-creatures surely will often awaken "the feeling that in making this the rule of our life we may be co-operating with the unseen Being to whom we owe all that is enjoyable in life." "The conditions of human existence," said Mill, "are highly favourable to the growth of such a feeling inasmuch as a battle is constantly going on...between the powers of good and those of evil[2], and in which every even the smallest help to the right side has its value in promoting the very slow and often almost insensible

[1] B. Russell, *Phil. Essays*, 1910, p. 64. The reviewer being, as I was credibly informed, Mr Russell himself.

[2] But cf. p. 375 *fin.* above.

progress by which good is gradually gaining ground from evil, *yet gaining it so visibly at considerable intervals as to promise the very distant but not uncertain final victory of Good*[1]." Reflexions of this kind, to which the doctrine of epigenetic evolution, as I have tried to shew, gives greatly enhanced value, render the problem of evil, appalling though it be, far less formidable than it is if we accept any theory of pre-established harmony, lightly as Leibniz's jubilant optimism affected to regard it. And 'the religion of the Future,' which Mill believed such reflexions will inspire, must, I think, diminish the number of such objectors as this reviewer mentions and must at the same time decrease the force of their objections.

Another reviewer[2] also comments on my 'vindication of faith.' But his complaint is, not that in calling it 'rational faith' I have gone too far, but that in failing to recognise in it as 'loving faith' a 'Higher Immediacy' which implies 'a quite specific factor in our personality,' I have not gone far enough, have been content with "only a pale copy of the vehemently active and enthusiastic Faith which Religion demands, and as history shews, has so often found." I have said so little about religious experience that I can hardly blame this critic for overlooking it; but I have said enough, I think, to shew that he is none the less mistaken in saying that I have deliberately set its claims aside[3]. I have given reasons for regarding this topic as beyond the purview of lectures like the present, and anyone who has—I will not say a knowledge of James's *Varieties of Religious Experience*, but—merely a nodding acquaintance with the so-called psychology of religion, will agree. 'Vehemently active and enthusiastic faith,' as history shews, has often been the scourge of mankind: to appeal to it without very careful preliminary investigation is either special pleading or it is

---

[1] *Three Essays on Theism*, 3rd ed. p. 256. Italics mine.
[2] *The Church Quarterly Review*, April 1912.
[3] Cf. *e.g.* p. 186 and note ; also pp. 450, 451 f., 479.

courting disaster. My critic ought to have seen this instead of complaining that this book is not likely "to lead an inquirer to...the tranquillity and the joy of final religious faith[1]!"

Professor A. E. Taylor in his only too laudatory notice of this book[2], which nevertheless has greatly encouraged me, does not think "that it follows from the admission of freedom and contingency that there are future facts outside God's knowledge." "We expect," he says, "intimate friends to know how we shall choose to behave in danger or temptation, and we should be hurt if they did not....If we may pass to the limit, then there is no logical difficulty in believing that much in the same way, God knows...how we shall comport ourselves in all. If a choice of mine could take God by surprise, how could He still be 'God who knoweth our necessities before we ask'?" I have already anticipated this objection[3]. Its fatal defect, as it seems to me, lies in regarding divine predestination as equivalent to what our confident expectation would be if carried to the limit of absolute certainty. No, not 'predestination' but 'prescience' it may be replied. But I should rejoin in the words of Priestley's colleague, Belsham, also a pronounced necessitarian: "It is always to be remembered that the prescience of an *agent* necessarily includes predestination, though that of a *spectator* may not. It is nonsense to say that a Being does not mean to bring an event to pass which he foresees to be the certain and inevitable consequence of his own previous voluntary action[4]." Besides, a man's formed character or habits are never the whole of the man: the more original and creative he is the less what he may yet do will be disclosed by what

---

[1] I would offer the same reply to Dr A. Crespi who in an interesting account of this book in the Italian magazine, *Cænobium* (Nov. 1911), has also regretted that I have left religious experience out of my argument.

[2] *Mind*, 1912, pp. 427–37.

[3] Lect. XIV. p. 310 f.

[4] T. Belsham, *Elements of the Philosophy of the Human Mind*, 1901, p. 307, quoted by Dugald Stewart.

he has already done. Friendship would be a vastly tiresome
—in fact, an impossible—thing were this not so ; and equally
a divine creative love that could be satisfied with creatures
'exactly and precisely specified' as machines must be and as
only machines can be[1]. It is just the power to do and to
initiate without being ready-made that constitutes a free
agent, a person who can never be reduplicated, as a machine
can always be. But it does not follow that with a world of
such free agents God will always or ever be liable to surprises.
It implies that he will always be interested : indeed he could
not be a God of love if he were not. Yet the continuity
between the actual and the possible and his complete
knowledge of both make his main purpose secure: to use
Martineau's words, "we cannot defeat his aim, but can only
vary the track." But even this variation is not beside his
purpose; rather it is essential to it that there should be such
variations. If a world of free agents is better than 'a block
universe,' then we must, I think, agree with Martineau that
"foreknowledge of the contingent is not a perfection," that
God could not "but render some knowledge conditional for
the sake of making any righteousness attainable." But if
creation necessarily involves absolute prescience then I can
see no alternative but to deny creation, as Dr Howison has
actually done ; for there is no denying freedom[2]. Substitute
providence for prescience, continuous control for eternal
decree, and the whole difficulty vanishes and nothing of value
is lost. I do not believe that if St Augustine were living in
these days he would call 'impious' this solution of a question
that pressed heavily on his mind.

Another vexed question concerning which Professor Taylor
dissents from me is that as to the pre-existence of souls. But
I think he is under some misapprehension. He seems to
think that in rejecting the 'creationist theory' of the soul's
origin, as I have done (pp. 205, 404), I am denying its

[1] Cf. above, pp. 458, 480.
[2] Cf. above, p. 455 ff.

creation altogether. But all that I understand by 'creationism' in this connexion is the doctrine upheld by Augustine, Aquinas, Calvin and many others, that each soul is specially created and made to vitalise the embryo at the moment of its conception. This doctrine, Leibniz—with whom Professor Taylor supposes himself to agree—certainly did not accept. On the contrary, Leibniz set out a doctrine of pre-existence substantially identical with that I have here sought to defend.

Finally, in two or three cases Professor Taylor thinks that I have misrepresented Christian theology at its best. First of all he tells me that if I had heeded 'the much better authority of St Thomas' instead of quoting the Westminster Confession I should have dealt more gently with the doctrine of original sin. Well, I am willing to believe that "in this respect," as Dr Tennant says, "the Roman theology is more philosophical than that of the symbols of Protestant Christendom[1]." But I feel sure that any one who will consult the quotations from the XXXIX Articles, the decree of the Council of Trent and other confessions, given by Dr Tennant[2], will see that I have nothing of substantial importance to retract. Again, in quoting Mill's denunciation of 'the moral enormity' of the dogma *nulla salus extra ecclesiam* Mr Taylor thinks that I have been unjust to 'the great Christian Churches.' I wish I could think so; but at all events it is hardly fair to suppose that I have laid this 'charge upon Christianity,' for I have expressly said: "Happily the spirit of Christianity is clearly against it, as Christians themselves are coming more and more to see." Even Mill had said: "It is nowhere represented that Christ himself made this statement." But I am amazed that Professor Taylor should have appealed to Dante in support of his position. In the twentieth canto of the *Del Paradiso*, to

---

[1] *The Origin and Propagation of Sin*, 1902, p. 153.

[2] *Op. cit.* pp. 151-159. Dr Tennant however omits the Xth of the Anglican articles.

which he refers, Dante tells how he learnt that both Trajan and Ripheus miraculously "quitted not their bodies as Gentiles but as Christians," and in the tenth canto of the *Del Purgatorio* represents Trajan as actually delivered from hell by the prayers of St Gregory. Surely this is in keeping only with a belief that 'virtuous heathen could be lost eternally.' "Another theological matter upon which" Mr Taylor thinks I am "imperfectly informed is the Roman doctrine of purgatory." But why he should say this—though I will not deny it—I do not know; for I have only found fault with that miscalled purgatory for being merely 'ex-piatory,' and this he himself admits and condemns.

REPLIES TO FURTHER CRITICISMS

Since the second edition of this book was published an article by Professor J. H. Muirhead entitled "The Last Phase of Professor Ward's Philosophy" has appeared in *Mind*[1]. This perhaps, it may be thought, calls for some notice.

I note then, in the first place, that I am credited with being a pluralist and an inconsistent one into that. Albeit, had my critic read with a little care either the introductory chapter or the final one summarising the whole; had he even read the first two paragraphs of the preface; nay, had he but heeded the secondary title of the book—*Pluralism and Theism*—which he never mentions, he might have learned better. As a matter of fact, I am not and never have been a pluralist; though I hold, and have always held, that experience, from which speculation must and therefore always does start, is for us primarily an interaction of the Many. I have tried to explain and to defend this position at length; and no one who thinks fit to criticize my 'philosophy' has the right to ignore it: for me that position is fundamental. Mr Muirhead, however, having an insight into my mind that I do not myself possess, professes to know and to have shewn (!) that I have been actuated only by an ignorant 'fear of Absolutism' which a better knowledge of 'idealist writers' would have shewn to be groundless[2]. So convinced is he of this, that, instead of examining my method, he dismisses it as 'obscure,' and proceeds to 'extricate' my argument from this obscurity as a preliminary to his own criticism. This clarifying process is accomplished in a single

---

[1] N. S. vol. XXII. 1913, pp. 321–330.

[2] Perhaps if Mr Muirhead had deigned to examine the two chapters I have devoted to Hegel he might have been less confident about either my fear or my ignorance.

page of small print, though some irrelevant references to my supposed relations to Hobbes and to Hegel—about which I have said nothing—are thrown in. To the book itself there are but three references; the first and last concern quite subsidiary points and the second does not justify a misleading statement which it is cited to support.

As a result Professor Muirhead finds the problem of my 'philosophy' resolve into two : "How are we to conceive of the process of history in its beginning? What guarantee have we of its continuance and completion?"—two questions '*roughly corresponding* to the two parts of the book.' In his opinion, however, the division falls not where I have made it, but at the end of Lecture VI; for (omitting Lectures VII and VIII, which I have allowed are a digression) Lecture IX is said to begin with 'an intricate argument' for the possible existence of intelligences of a higher order, perhaps of a supreme intelligence. This betokens the search for the guarantee on which the second part is supposed to turn. Between the two I am charged with having 'exchanged my pluralistic starting point for that of the philosophy I set out to oppose.' No statement could well be more untrue. I have never attempted to cross 'the ugly broad ditch' between the Absolute Idea and the Many: on the contrary I have done my best to expose the futility of all such attempts. I neither start outside nor end outside the world of minds. All that at the outset I proposed to myself was simply "to ascertain what we can know or seriously believe concerning the constitution of a world *interpreted throughout and strictly in terms of Mind*[1]." But 'the assumption of the ultimateness of the plurality,' which Mr Muirhead imputes to me, is, as he truly says, "impossible to harmonize with the idea of an enclosing unity," a Supreme One. This is so obvious that most people would think twice before attributing such an attempt—even as a possible 'inadvertence'!—to any writer worth notice. William James, a professed pluralist who recognised no such transcendent unity therefore described himself as a 'radical empiricist.'

[1] Preface, *init.*

I too in Professor Muirhead's eyes am such a radical empiricist, and according to his analysis, I start from 'the lower limit' of pluralism which is 'merely given.' Yet I have expressly said, "Of course, we cannot start from the beginning; for that is not where we are. How far towards a hypothetical beginning the principle of continuity will reasonably carry us is just one of the questions we have to decide. But we must start where alone reflexion on experience can arise, at the level of self-consciousness.... It is assumed [on the principle of continuity] that there exists an indefinite variety of selves, some indefinitely higher, some indefinitely lower than ourselves[1]." Obviously, neither the upper nor the lower limits of such an indefinite series can fall *within* any definite experience of ours: neither can be 'merely given.' Still as experience advances we get ever more insight, whether the question we ask be Whence, Whither or Why[2]. To such immanent reflexion on the course of history and the progress of knowledge I have exclusively appealed. To start with the Many is from this standpoint unavoidable : to assume such plurality to be ultimate, or to be given as it began, would be unwarrantable. If we refrain from reflecting on experience, there is nothing for us but radical empiricisms: pluralism, as such, I have confessed, "can never furnish anything deserving to be called a philosophical justification of itself." Experience can neither by regressing reach its lower limit or origin nor its upper limit or final end[3]. But by reflexion from within concerning these limits, "we are led," I have said, "both on theoretical and on practical grounds, to conceive a more fundamental standpoint than this of the Many, namely that of the One. This would furnish an ontological unity for their cosmological unity and ensure a teleological unity for their varied ends[4]." Only if this One, to which reflexion from the pluralistic standpoint leads us, were the Absolute One of Mr Muirhead's idealist writers, would his charge of a transition to their standpoint be sustained.

[1] p. 51 f.   [2] Cf. pp. 22 f.
[3] p. 200 f.   [4] p. 442.

W.   32

Schellings 'ugly broad ditch' separates both. There is no getting from Hegel's Absolute Idea to the real Many. Even Mr Bradley has allowed that their connexion is 'inexplicable[1].' And I too have fully admitted, nay insisted, on this; and the whole history of philosophy, as I have hinted, bears it out. Both sides, it seems to me, must give up something if the perennial problem of the One and the Many is to be solved. In other words, God *and* the Many are the only Absolute, if the Many whence we derive our idea of reality, are to stand. For philosophy as 'the thinking consideration of *things*'—to use Hegel's description of it, which implies the start from the Many[2]—there is a way forward thus far ; but there is no way back, if forsaking the *terra firma* of experience altogether, it attempts to soar beyond. This is the answer to the question, from which, as stated in the preface, I set out. Mr Muirhead in brushing aside my method, has ignored this altogether.

In view of this perversity, as I am tempted to call it, I hardly feel it needful to notice his many detailed criticisms springing as they largely do from this misunderstanding. But in part perhaps they may be traced to the fact that Mr Muirhead fancies himself so much as a clairvoyant critic. Of this peculiar trait I have already given one instance. He has also found out that I was 'embarrassed by a necessity' of which I was myself wholly unconscious ; that in one extremity, I was 'fain to borrow' from writers of his way of thinking whom I only happened to quote among many others ; that in another, I was 'fain to supplement' one principle by another—'without apparently being conscious of the *petitio principii*'—which, as I had said, it virtually implies ; that I 'only evaded a difficulty' which I never felt, by a distinction that, so far as I understand, I never made ; that I raised another—to me imaginary difficulty —by emphasizing as against Hobbes that there is no 'without.' As a matter of fact I have never referred to Hobbes in this connexion and therefore am not surprised to learn that my reply was merely verbiage. To one criticism it may be worth while

[1] Cf. p. 201.   [2] Cf. p. 137.

briefly to refer. On p. 79 I have quoted a passage from the article on 'Psychology' in the *Ency. Brit.* in illustration of 'the heterogony of ends' and this I have described as 'the objective realisation of an adaptation that was never subjectively intended.' It implies therefore no seeking of, no conscious impulse towards, betterment. Quite the contrary. Accordingly in the passages quoted a creature is spoken of as *getting* a better skin to fill while intent only on filling the skin it has. And as I had said still earlier: "Any advantage gained, though merely the result of good fortune would not be passively surrendered.... Thus a new standard of the self to be conserved would be reached[1]." The whole point of the quotation here is missed and missed because Mr Muirhead has brushed aside the main clue to the context—the historical method. His strictures on the faulty psychology of the illustration it would not only be tedious but out of place to consider here.

Professor A. Seth Pringle-Pattison in his able Gifford Lectures entitled *The Idea of God in the light of recent philosophy*, 1917, has severely criticized the theory of monadism which I have tried to make defensible in this book. I have allowed, it should be remembered, 'that we cannot actually verify the indefinite regress' which the Leibnizian monadology implies. "The most we can say is that...it is simpler [than the occasionalist theory, which is the other monistic alternative] and seems adequate[2]." The main positions taken up, *viz.* the start from the historical aspect of the world interpreted in conformity with the principle of continuity and the facts of evolution, the disclosure of the limits and the difficulties of pluralism, which the theistic ideal alone promises to transcend or to resolve, and the justification of faith in this ideal as theoretically and practically reasonable—these should still appeal even to thinkers like Professor Pringle-Pattison, to whom the occasionalist hypothesis at first sight 'may seem preferable,' as indeed it long seemed to me. So, while allowing

[1] p. 53.   [2] p. 260.

32—2

that pluralism on Leibnizian lines does not admit of empirical verification, I have tried to show that " evidence...of what was originally spontaneous and tentative becoming eventually automatic and regular, is forthcoming up to the *very verge* of our knowledge of whatever can be regarded as individual and unique at all[1]." Further, I still maintain that the more we trust Leibniz's cardinal presupposition, *Natura non facit saltus*, and concur in his rejection of the Cartesian dualism, the more assured the pluralistic standpoint will appear.

But my esteemed colleague disapproves of this attempt to advance ' beyond the usual psychological and biological limits' as 'difficult to reconcile with our common sense.' At the same time he acknowledges the ' genuine difficulty' there is in conceiving things as common sense does, and he also finds subjective idealism or 'mentalism' unsatisfactory. Yet further he warns us against being misled 'into thinking that the external ever existed as a mere external...as if the body of the universe existed, so to speak, like an empty case waiting for a soul[2].' On all this I would remark, that we cannot shut our eyes to 'genuine' difficulties out of deference to common sense, which never worries itself with the philosophical ' consideration of things.' Between common sense and the philosophy of it there is all the difference that lies between a fragmentary What and a systematic Why. But, of course, Professor Pringle-Pattison has his own solution of the difficulty, viz. that ' mind is organic to nature and nature organic to mind.' This statement is somewhat vague; but so far perhaps we are on common ground; and even further, if he saw his way to interpret the mutual implication of 'internal and external' as I do. That, however, I fear is not the case. Precisely how from his standpoint or that of S. S. Laurie—to

---

[1] p. 74. It was in this connexion that I quoted a single passage from the article by the late C. S. Peirce which has shocked my critic so much. A very similar expression was used by Schelling as well as by Hegel (cf. p. 143).

[2] *Op. cit.* p. 177.

whom in this connexion he constantly appeals—any cosmology could be worked out in detail is to me not clear. To the standpoint as such I see no objection. Where we differ will presently appear. But I will first endeavour to meet the strictures brought against my position as a whole.

Such 'animism' as he calls it, is, Professor Pringle-Pattison thinks, 'a too crudely simple[1] expedient' and one only devised to obviate certain epistemological and moral difficulties. I will say for myself that my critic is quite mistaken in supposing that the 'laudable desire to save spontaneity and freedom' led me to monadism as 'a way of escape from the complete determinism with which the mechanistic scheme seems to threaten human life[2].' My earlier Gifford Lectures would, I should have thought, have made this clear. Anyhow, my personal conviction of the cogency of the main arguments of those lectures would, in fact, have dispelled any haunting fear of the sort ascribed to me, if I had ever felt any.

Passing now to detailed criticism, Professor Pringle-Pattison begins:—"In the attempt to derive all laws from previous actions, this ultra-pragmatism[3] appears to overleap itself; for surely the very consolidation of actions into habits depends upon the pre-existence of a stable system of conditions. What meaning can we attach to actions *in abstracto* apart from any environment[4]." Obviously none : the very notion is plainly absurd and I am not aware that I have ever even remotely suggested anything of the sort. And not a word is cited by my critic to shew that in fact I have. Had I supposed that the cosmos began in chaos I should have well deserved Professor Pringle-Pattison's

---

[1] I have already claimed that it is comparatively simple (cf. pp. 248–60, p. 482) and that is surely not a disadvantage. How far it is crudely so remains to be seen.

[2] *Op. cit.* p. 183.

[3] I do not regard 'pragmatism' as a term of abuse, but I should like to know—apart from the motives mistakenly attributed to me—on what grounds I am ranked on the left or the right of the pragmatist centre, though I have never even whispered the pragmatist shibboleth at all.

[4] *Op. cit.* p. 184.

reprobation. But while recognising that I have expressly repudiated Peirce's 'tychism' he 'finds it difficult to see how I can logically escape its consequences,' and accordingly thinks it relevant to quote from Peirce's article at some length, as if he persisted in associating my position with Peirce's. *Inter alia* is the passage : " In the beginning...there was *a chaos* of unpersonalised feeling...without connexion or regularity." Now my Lecture IV dealing with this topic opens with a quotation from Lotze's *Microcosmos* which concludes thus : " Any attempt to set distinctly before ourselves the origin of natural forms must start from some *definite primitive state*, which—because it was this and no other—from the very first excluded from actuality much in itself possible, while of much else on the other hand it contained not merely the bare possibility but a more or less immediate and urgent positive ground for its realisation." Surely beginnings so different can hardly lead logically to the same consequences.

A definite primitive state of a totality of monads or entelechies, as Leibniz called them, all of them subject to the one supreme law of self-conservation obviously implies the complete absence of *habits* so far ; for it would not otherwise be a primitive state. But—unless it were such as to furnish nowhere and to none motives for action—*actions* could still take place ; and "anyhow, as a matter of fact, things did happen" (p. 266). Such actions on the part of individuals 'plastic and capable of development' would, *caeteris paribus*, lead on the more surely to habits the more frequently like situations recurred. So far as any particular individual was concerned the one indispensable condition of repeated experiences would be such a restriction of his 'effective environment' so to call it, as would permit him to exercise some selection within it and so to acquire gradually some control over it (p. 76 f.). As I have said in the text 'a narrow field' *i.e.* a very restricted 'system of conditions' would suffice for an *amoeba*, and one simpler still for the monads corresponding to atoms, if there are any. It is true, *cum grano salis magno*, as my critic contends, that "a system of unvarying natural order is demanded in the service of the higher conscious life as the condition of reasonable action[1]." But the higher conscious life is a very recent stage in the evolution of this planet ; and what is demanded for it was not a necessary condition for the lower forms of life which it presupposes and which prepared the way for it. And, doubtless, there are planets in plenty where creatures far below the rational level are the highest they can shew, as was once the case with our own. Nay more—going yet further back—in no star is there any trace of the molecular complexities with which we are familiar on this earth, and there are many stars in which most of the so-called chemical elements cannot be detected, and where the few that can be have simpler spectra than they ever present here. What then are we to say about stable systems of conditions ? From the historical standpoint the simplest thing to say is surely that stability is '*organic to*' development and development to stability, structure to function and function to structure, a given state, *natura naturata*, resulting from a prior process of *natura naturans*, and providing for further progress the needful που στω̂. This is what I understand by organic connexion.

The phrase 'conditions of action' in this context is more or less ambiguous. In the wider sense one condition of actions, and seemingly the first, is independent agents—so much first and independent indeed, that what are strictly and literally called conditions are regarded as consequent solely on this pre-existence and cooperation of agents. It was in this way, I take it, that custom, law and social order first arose; and to such a situation we have to go back if we are not to lose sight of what these terms imply. I have dwelt at length on this vital point elsewhere and though there are few more grievously overlooked I cannot return to it here[2]. But when conditions themselves are called pre-existent, yet other agents—or might

---

[1] p. 187.

[2] Cf. *Naturalism and Agnosticism*, 4th ed. pp. 542 ff., earlier edd. II. pp. 252 ff. Cf. also, Lotze, *Metaphysik*, §§ 36, 62, 68 *fin.*

we say patients—are implied whose states are subsequent to or dependent on such conditions. The sole realities concerned then are these agents or patients. But there is also a metaphorical use of terms such as condition, law, order, which directly implies neither, and that is their use by positive science to designate its empirically verified generalisations. I make bold to say: No law in this sense is either necessary or universal, and to speak of physical laws as 'unvarying' or 'inviolable' is in a philosophical discussion an unwarrantable hyperbole. What constancy we find in the world can only be attributed to the beings that compose it; and here it is not nature in the abstract but their individual natures that we want to get at. Our inability to do so at all, or at best only imperfectly, is one chief barrier to the progress of knowledge. It is these 'natures' which constitute the only real and ultimate laws and all our scientific generalisations are based on them[1]. When then Professor Pringle-Pattison talks of nature as a '*system* of order...conditioning action' he is guilty of the metaphysician's fallacy, he is hypostatizing abstractions; and I cannot follow. When, however, he talks of 'nature as a *realm* of law[2],' if that means 'a realm of ends' we are more nearly on common ground. But that only makes me more sensitive to differences. Perhaps—in keeping with an accepted maxim in polemics, I can best defend my own views by 'examining' his.

Professor Pringle-Pattison distinguishes external nature from the world of social relations, which he holds to be 'founded on it, to which it is essential' and from which it is evolved. It would seem then that external nature is prior to and largely independent of, rather than itself included in, the realm of ends. This looks like what most of us call naturalism and indeed Professor Pringle-Pattison himself speaks of it as 'the higher naturalism.' The resemblance lies in admitting to the full 'the mechanical aspects of the cosmos' on which its highest life is said to repose: the difference lies in 'repudiating

[1] Cf. Lotze, *Metaphysik*, §§ 32–4.   [2] *Op. cit.* p. 178 *fin.*

the mechanistic scheme as a self-existent underlying reality, of which everything else is the inexplicable outcome[1].' The difference is meant to be vital, but *pro tanto* the resemblance ceases to be clear. What precisely are we to understand by 'the mechanical aspects of the cosmos'? Philosophical expositions in which the term 'aspect' figures, are, I find, apt to be cloudy. Assuming the reference to be to a standpoint, then I very much question if the *real* world can from any standpoint be described as mechanical. The whole mechanical theory from top to toe is conceptual, and nowhere presents reality[2]. Taken for what it is, nobody is any more 'tempted either to deny or to minimise it' than Professor Pringle-Pattison claims to be. Who pleases may call the scheme an aspect, but the phrase is anything but a happy one. What we are all after are the 'real existences' of the cosmos; and as to these Professor Pringle-Pattison says—most truly, as I believe :—"Every individual is a unique nature, a little world of content...which constitutes an expression or focalisation of the universe that is nowhere else repeated[3]." This is Leibnizian enough, but how far does it hold, or—more definitely—is there anything real of which it does not hold? This question may be replaced by another, to which we may now turn.

What does Professor Pringle-Pattison understand by matter? I have searched his book in vain for a precise answer to this question, and can only refer to three or four relevant passages. (1) Quoting from an earlier work he says, that, conceived apart from "their consequents...the antecedents (matter and energy, for example) have no real existence— they are mere *entia nationis*, abstract aspects of the one concrete fact we call the universe[4]." But this still does not tell us what they are along with their consequents; it only states that abstract aspects as such can have no real consequents at all. (2) Later on he says :—" Ultimately I believe it is true that

[1] *Ibid.*
[2] Cf. *Naturalism and Agnosticism*, Lecture V.
[3] *Op. cit.* p. 267.   [4] *Op. cit.* p. 107.

506 *Replies to further Criticisms*

we cannot take nature as existing *per se*.... We find it impossible to conceive anything devoid of value (such as an unconscious material system would be) as ultimately real or self-subsistent, in other words, as a whole, a *res completa*[1]." But *res completa* is here ambiguous : as real it is incompatible with *res rationis*, which is not real : that however is the point already made. It is also the contrary of *res incompleta*, which does not imply unreality but only some lack. In this sense anything as yet only partially developed, though real is still not a *res completa*. And this seems to be the meaning here. Familiar with the adult form we do not regard an embryo as completed, 'viable' or self-subsistent : so ultimately—from the rational standpoint—we come to regard external nature. But even then we still want to know what this *external* nature really is. In the following passage we get a partial answer. (3) "The creation of a world of individual spirits...means 'eliciting'...out of the common fund of externality a *new* world of appreciation, of mutual recognition and of spiritual communion, to which the former *now* assumes a merely instrumental function, *a circuit made by the Absolute towards the formation* of beings capable of spiritual response[2]." Though still leaving it vague just what external nature or 'the common fund of externality' really means, this language seems to imply a sort of matrix or nidus out of which beings capable of mutual apprehension and appreciation are, willy nilly, 'elicited' or generated and which afterwards serves as their habitat and the medium of their life. At any rate it suggests a twofold process more or less 'equivocal' or 'circuitous'! In any case how such beings come to be we none of us know : as to this we are all agreed. But that the Absolute should deem a 'common fund' and 'a circuitous formation' needful to this end is a gratuitous, bewildering, nay a contradictory assumption. Nobody surely will prefer to suppose that Professor Pringle-Pattison deliberately meant this.

Returning now to the context of the second passage we

[1] *Op. cit.* p. 200.   [2] *Op. cit.* p. 295. Italics mine.

shall find intimations of what is more likely to have been his meaning. He there says:—" Spirit, we believe, therefore, is the *terminus ad quem* of nature. As it has been finely expressed by an Eastern thinker, 'all external things were formed that the soul might know itself and be free.' Unconscious nature thus assumes the character of a means or [qy. and] intermediary towards an end.... The instrumental or mediating function of the material world was the larger idealistic truth which underlay the mentalistic form of Berkeley's argument. But that may, I think, be held along with a frankly realistic attitude towards external nature[1]." The first sentence of this passage seems to refer to the generating or 'eliciting' stage of the seemingly twofold process of creation. But you can only elicit what is potentially, *i.e.* in some sense actually, there. We are thus reminded of Hegel's saying, Nature is the introduction to Spirit (*die Vorstufe des Geistes*). Does this mean that nature is mind—more exactly, is minds—in embryo, minds in process of evolving? That, of course, is the view of present-day monadism and there is ample evidence that it was Hegel's view too (*cf.* pp. 144 f.). And, recalling Professor Pringle-Pattison's insistence on the mistake of separating 'external' from 'internal,' one might surely attribute the same view to him. But when he goes on to refer to 'the instrumental or mediating function' of unconscious nature—the second of the supposed stages of the creative process—as 'indicating a real distinction within the world of facts as known,' and so as justifying 'a frankly realistic attitude towards external nature,' one is sadly puzzled. After all—his idealism notwithstanding—it is no wonder that Professor Pringle-Pattison should be suspected of dualism, of holding that what comes *between* mind and mind is really something disparate, just the inert particles of the physicist, in short. Are these, then, what he understands by matter[2].

[1] *Op. cit.* pp. 200 f.
[2] But if it is matter in this sense that is concerned in the second process it is this same matter that is concerned in the first, and comes presently to assume a new rôle.

Well, I trust that is not his meaning, and on the whole I cannot think it is. The reference to Berkeley confirms me in this. It seems to point rather to an occasionalism such as Lotze advocated (*cf.* p. 249) ; and then we should have two processes in the Absolute, but no Cartesian dualism. As already said, I have allowed that this is a position perfectly compatible with pluralism, and, in discussing the cosmology of theism (Lect. XII), it is to this theory that consideration is invited first of all. But I have pointed out at length the difficulties that seem to me to beset the assumption of a two-fold divine activity, and have tried to shew that dualism in this form is a needless complication (pp. 252–65). Professor Pringle-Pattison, however, has not thought it necessary to follow this discussion, contenting himself with direct objections to my own position. Here then, at any rate—however the dubious reference to a 'substructure of the spiritual' may be interpreted—is one dividing line between us.

The chief fault I have to find with Professor Pringle-Pattison's criticism, and a very serious one, is that he does not 'temporarily at all events divest himself of assumptions that I do not accept'—to repeat an objection already made to other critics (p. 487). To assume, for example, that 'a *speck*, as it were of consciousness is *put* behind (*sic*) each of the minutest atoms or ions' as 'an easy way out of a difficulty[1],' is a bad start in an attempt to refute a theory which, as Leibniz had already said, destroys atoms altogether (p. 65). In this book I have regarded dualism as refuted and done with. A writer who has not rejected it, root and branch, does not appeal to me. How far Professor Pringle-Pattison has broken with it we have found, I think, not as clear as might be wished. But I at least have hoped for the best. Of course all monads save 'bare monads,' the unattainable lower limit of the series, have their own bodies: these, however, consist not simply of 'material appearances' with a mental counterpart but of other, subordinate monads in functional relation with them.

[1] *Op. cit.* p. 203. Italics mine.

The mention of 'bare monads' brings us to another failure of my critic to face squarely the position he is seeking to controvert. Referring, I take it, to these, he describes them as "*admittedly no more* than the supposed inward aspect of purely mechanical reactions—the dynamics of a particle in psychological terms[1]." I should like him to make good this statement. If there are two things in the world entitled to exist separated by the whole diameter of being they are the so-called reactions of matter and the actions of mind. Inertia is not only the contrary of activity, it is the contrary of passivity : it is as Young defined it, just 'incapability.' Matter does nothing, suffers nothing, and knows nothing, that is about all we can say about it in psychological terms. What wonder then that starting like Berkeley from experience, Leibniz should say, *quod non agit, non existit.* So oblivious of this disparity is my critic, however, that in another passage, referring to the said bare monads, he asks :—"How does their behaviour to one another differ from a case of mechanical action as ordinarily understood ? And if the two are indistinguishable, what is the use of the monadistic construction ?[2]" I reply: their behaviour differs just by being behaviour and therefore something that we can understand, whereas 'mechanical action' as ordinarily understood is inconceivable— a conviction that dawned on physicists long ago and that the growth of science has only confirmed. As Professor Pringle-Pattison has himself said, "action cannot be intelligibly considered apart from the ideas of stimulus and response[3]." Can he so define these ideas as to make them applicable to 'mechanical actions,' while still discarding monadism?

The context of the passage in which the sentence just quoted occurs also calls for some reply. I have said that "behaviour implies always some situation as the *occasion* for every manifestation of activity" and added "but there is never any absolute or unconditional activity" (p. 51). I have also said—

---

[1] *Op. cit.* p. 204. Italics mine.
[2] *Op. cit.* p. 188.   [3] *Op. cit.* p. 187.

referring to the 'contrast between spontaneity or individual activity as *prima facie* a *fact* on the one side and the scientific *concept* of inert matter as a constant quantity on the other— "individualtiy is inseparable from mind and altogether foreign to matter" (pp. 279 f.). Professor Pringle-Pattison now asks:— " What is gained *for the cause of spiritual freedom* by endowing particles with a spontaneity of this kind? He further observes: The idea of spontaneity *in the abstract*...must reduce itself to sheer wilfulness[1]." In answer to his question I have first to say again that the motive he imputes to me was never any motive of mine at all. Next, I have again to ask him not to forget that I do not recognise what he calls 'particles' at all. As to his observation—the references I have just given should suffice to shew that the absurdity of entertaining the idea of 'spontaneity in the abstract' can no more be attributed to me than that of assuming 'actions *in abstracto* apart from any environment.'

In the latter part of Lecture III I have attempted to face the difficulties of extending the 'personalistic' interpretation of things beyond 'the usual psychological and biological limits' recognised by Professor Pringle-Pattison and common sense. In so doing I had to reckon with the 'tendency of physical science to diminish the seeming variety' even of the inanimate world by substituting quantitative constants in the place of its qualities. If the claim of this procedure to bring us nearer to the ultimate reality of things can be sustained there can be no talk of monadism. Solely on this ground I recurred to physical statistics, a topic with which I had already dealt for the same purpose elsewhere. The facts to which I appealed are not disputed and have done much to refute what I have called 'physical realism[2].' Natural constants correspond not to concrete individuals but to class concepts: how much diversity

---

[1] *Op. cit.* p. 157. Italics mine.
[2] Cf. *Naturalism and Agnosticism*, earlier edd. I. pp. 109 ff., 4th ed. pp. 105 ff. Cf. also Maxwell, *Theory of Heat*, 1894, pp. 315 f., and Sir J. Larmor, art. "Aether," *Ency. Brit.* I. p. 294a.

there is among the individuals to which they refer—if indeed
they refer to concrete individuals at all—we do not know. But
we do know that wherever we can ear-mark individuals,
diversity appears[1]. My reference to such facts Professor
Pringle-Pattison has construed as ' an argument [which] *seems
intended to prove...,*' and conjectures that the intention was to
'countenance the idea of contingency' and *pro tanto* to
discredit the idea of law. Nevertheless this is a mistake and
one for which I can see little or no justification.

It was *after* this discussion of ' the facts that seem *prima
facie* to make against the monadistic theory' (pp. 63–7) and
not *before* that I began this inquiry, how in a world of evolving
monads—regarded as nearly as may be to its beginning—law
and order might arise. I have there (p. 87) and throughout
recognised two possibilities—the theistic and the pluralistic.
But in accordance with the historical method, which I have
deliberately followed, the first question was to ascertain how
far on the analogy of our actual experience the pluralistic
alternative will suffice, how far law and order may be reasonably
accounted for in conformity with the principle of continuity
and the facts of evolution. In this further inquiry I made no
use of statistics. But I did assume what Professor Pringle-
Pattison regards as anomalous, *viz.* : that spontaneity implies
' the power of reacting differently in the same circumstances[2],'
and surely this is what learning by experience involves. I also
assume that experience leads at length to acting identically in
the same circumstances. Such is what is called secondarily
automatic action or habit, and with these I have identified
custom and routine, the 'dead selves' of Longfellow, the
'effete mind ' of Peirce and others. As to equating law with
' relevancy[3] '—this so far from teaching me better, is precisely
the teleological meaning of law that I have consistently maintained. Historically regarded, actions are always relevant in

---

[1] Cf. *Naturalism and Agnosticism*, earlier edd. II. pp. 89 ff., 4th ed.
pp. 383 ff.

[2] *Op. cit.* p. 186.   [3] *Ibid. fin.*

intention, always more or less 'appropriate reactions'; but at the outset they involve trial and error and 'practice alone makes perfect.' Here then contingency is inevitable by the way, but order and harmony—though not the starting-point— are none the less the goal. To recognise these historical facts can surely not be described as exalting contingency and depreciating law.

But the really vital difference between us concerns what Professor Pringle-Pattison calls 'externality.' The mutual implication of internality and externality, if these terms refer to what I have called the duality of subject and object, has always been to me fundamental. If they refer to the dualism of mind and matter, that is for me *ein überwundener Standpunkt*, which I do not intend to re-consider. The functional relation of a subject to its organism is, it has seemed to me, something *sui generis* and not to be identified with the relation of the subject to external things, which depends upon the organism. Whether my attempts, on monadistic lines, to interpret 'this interaction by means of physical organization' (pp. 254, 258, 461-7) will find any acceptance remains to be seen. Professor Pringle-Pattison anyhow has not referred to it, but I do not complain of that. Though perhaps if he had, the idea of a subject acquiring its 'organic vesture' by externalizing itself might have appeared more in keeping with idealism than his own idea of the external internalizing itself and so becoming a conscious centre or focus of the universe. According to the monadism of to-day the "objective world becomes the appearance of monads to one another[1]." As Professor Pringle-Pattison evidently regards this as a transparent impossibility, one naturally wonders how he understands it. Now he rightly recognises appearances as manifesting reality, not as veiling the thing *per se*; but he maintains that "finite beings know one another from the outside, as it were, the knower being *ipso*

[1] *Op. cit.* p. 179. And this by the way marks a 'great departure' from the 'windowless' monadism of Leibniz with its pre-established harmony, Professor Pringle-Pattison notwithstanding.

facto excluded from the immediate experience of any other centre[1]." Apparently then, he assumes that a thoroughgoing monadist denies the latter position. But that is not the case. Though the monadist now rejects Leibniz's denial of 'windows' so far as seeing *out* goes, he still admits that monads have no windows by which other monads can see *in*. Objects for him are still appearances ; but they are appearances due to other monads, not to external matter. In other respects the problem of presentation is the same for monadist and dualist alike. With this problem—if problem it may be called—I have dealt elsewhere, so far as it is the same problem for all[2]. In the present volume I have tried to treat of the so-called 'psycho-physical aspects' of it. Here one interesting fact presents itself at once, which may carry important consequences. Among the objects commonly recognised as animated, only a very few—our fellow men and the higher vertebrates—are sufficiently akin to ourselves to admit of some mutual understanding. The more intimate this *rapport* is, the more conduct is directly determined by it, and rises superior to physical constraint. We find creatures much lower in the scale understand each other and behave together in similar fashion. Where does this sort of *rapport* stop? How we answer this question will depend upon the value we set on the principle of continuity and the interpretation of evolution, *i.e.* on our preference for levelling down or levelling up. Perhaps, as Professor Pringle-Pattison suggests, it is only ' under the unconscious influence of the long dualistic tradition that we continue to think of the body in merely physical terms[3].'

We noted just now his query as to ' the *use* of the monad-istic construction.' He presently continues:—"Is it not obvious that our relation to these things [food, clothes, our bodies, etc.] is essential to finite being, and that if they are...'psychical'

---

[1] *Op. cit.* p. 293.
[2] *Naturalism and Agnosticism*, earlier edd. II. pp. 113 ff., 4th ed. pp. 405 ff.
[3] *Op. cit.* p. 126.

w.   33

centres...[this], so far as realized, would destroy their function and character for us?¹" Obvious, yes to the man in the street: plenty of people are squeamish about eating ripe Stilton, raw oysters or high venison; but probably they know nothing about vitamines or biochemistry.   Anyhow this difficulty was long since disposed of by Giordano Bruno, whose answer Leibniz developed in his theory of *materia secunda*².

No doubt it is as '*things*' that monads below our ejective level 'function in our life, not as other *selves*.'   Nobody ever pretended that they have any use for us as consumers ; but have we no other interests ? The only utility that monadology claims lies in the speculative difficulties that it avoids and the simplicity that it brings.   One of these difficulties Professor Pringle-Pattison has allowed to be a genuine difficulty ; but he has never faced it in grim earnest, never for a moment striven to divest himself—even while posing as a critic—of the preconceptions 'of the long dualistic tradition³.'

¹ *Op. cit.* p. 188.

² I have already dealt with this point. Cf. the article " Mechanism and Morals," *Hibbert Journal*, 1905, pp. 93 ff.

³ It is a pleasure to me to mention here an article, "On Certain Criticisms of Pluralism" in *Mind*, Jan. 7, 1919, by a young fellow-student of mine, C. A. Richardson.

INDEX

Absolute, The, ideals of reached by abstraction, 39–41 ; the world for these superfluous or illusory, 32–6 ; God-and-the-World as the concrete, 241 f.; objection to this, 242 ; reply, 243
Absolutism (*see also* Singularism), 52, 267
Action, springs of, the contrast of 'extra-regarding' and 'self-regarding' too extreme, 342–5
Activity, 7 f.; purposive, as presupposing order, 67 f. ; as producing it, 71 f., 75 f., 78
Adamson, R., 48
Agnosticism, its so-called Monism, 10; what it overlooks, 413
Argyll, late Duke of, on the Argus pheasant, 188
Aristotle, on Creation, 31 ; his Absolute, 38 ; his practical syllogism, 68 ; on the discontinuity between man and brute, 91 ; on *disjecta membra*, 120; on efficient cause, 274; on action, 330 ; soul as entelechy of the body, 397 ; on the brain, 461 ; on perfect activity, 472, 476
Aspects of the world, 1 f., 430; the natural and the spiritual as contrasted, 2 f., 431 ; the latter as the more fundamental, 10–3, 431 f.
Augustine, on predestination, 310 ; on time, 472 f.

Bacon, F., on the generating of new natures, 73; on final causes, 275
Bagehot, on custom, 358
Bahnsen, on Hartmann, 334 *n.*
Bain, denied the reality of self, 289 f.
Behaviour, 50, 62, 433 ; continuity between the natural and rational planes of, 342–5
Beneke quoted, 29
Bergson, Prof. H., his *élan vital*, 238 *n.*; referred to, 298 *n.*, 305; on 'concrete time,' 306 *n.*

Berkeley, his sense-symbolism, 216 f., as divine revelation, 261 f. ; his occasionalism, 248, 249, 482
Bionomics, as illustrating pluralism, 56–8
Birth, the problem of, 204 f.
Boehm, Jacob, and Hegel, 166, 182
Bosanquet, Prof. B., quoted, 136
Boscovich, his centres of force, 255 f.
Bradley, Mr F. H., quoted, 1, 24 ; on pluralism, 23 f., 201 ; on God and the Absolute, 43 f. ; on the idea of potentiality, 108 *n.*; on the ideal voluptuary as impossible, 345 *n.*
Buffon quoted on Nature's 'ill-assorted designs,' 86

Caird, E., on monotheism, 30 ; on Aristotle's theology, 32 f. ; on that of Plotinus, 33 ; on the social character of self-consciousness, 128 f.; on selfish interest in immortality, 388 *n.*
Categories, source of, 11 f.; Kant's table of, 228
Causa sui, the Absolute as, 32, 199 ; the Many as severally, 199
Causality, principle of, 275; as a postulate, 277
Cause, as category, 11 ; efficient and occasional distinguished, 75; its meanings, 273–5 ; the noumenal as cause of the phenomenal, 303 f., 438
Chance, 68, 75, 76, 267, 454 f.
Change, 305, 469 ; and alteration distinguished, 470 ; God as unchanging and yet living, 472 ; and imperfection, 473–5
Chaos, inconceivable, 70
Character, transmission of acquired, 210; a man's character and his nature, 286–8, and his objects, 289
Clifford, W. K., on conscience, 368 ; his ethics of belief, 413
Collier, A., as anticipating Berkeley, 249

33—2

524

Index

CAMBRIDGE: PRINTED BY J. B. PEACE, M.A., AT THE UNIVERSITY PRESS

BY THE SAME AUTHOR

NATURALISM AND AGNOSTICISM

The Gifford Lectures delivered in the University of
Aberdeen in the years 1896–1898.

4th edition, 1906.

London: A. AND C. BLACK.

New York: THE MACMILLAN COMPANY.

DATE DUE